JAPAN
A Documentary History

Volume I

The Dawn of History
to the Late Tokugawa Period

David J. Lu

An East Gate Book

M.E. Sharpe

Armonk, New York
London, England

An East Gate Book

Copyright © 2005 by David J. Lu

Library of Congress Cataloging-in-Publication Data

Japan : a documentary history / Vol. 1: The Dawn of History to the
Late Tokugawa Period / edited by David J. Lu.
p. cm.
"An East Gate book."
Includes bibliographical references and index.
ISBN 1-56324-907-3 (pbk. : alk paper)
1. Japan—History. I. Lu, David John, 1928–.
DS835.J37 1996
952–dc20
96-24433
CIP

Printed in the United States of America

The paper used in this publication meets the minimum requirements of the
American National Standard for Information Sciences—
Permanence of Paper for Printed Library Materials,
ANSI Z 39.48-1984.

∞

BM (p)   15   14   13

To

Kevin, Brian, Annamaria, Olivia, Naomi, and another little one on her way

Contents

Japan: A Documentary History is being published simultaneously in one clothbound edition, which includes the complete text, and two paperback editions: Vol. I: *The Dawn of History to the Late Tokugawa Period*, and Vol. II: *The Late Tokugawa Period to the Present*. The complete table of contents and the complete index appear in all three, and the pagination of the paperbacks is sequential.

Preface

The history of mankind is full of joy and vicissitude, and the history of Japan is no exception. "Man," to paraphrase Leopold von Ranke, "is a creature so good and at the same time so evil, so noble and at the same time so animal-like, so polished and at the same time so uncouth who, while seeking eternity, is bound by the fleeting moment." This book is a narrative of Japanese history as rendered by the Japanese people themselves at the time they lived. It shows their foibles and triumphs with their tears and laughter. There is a thread of common experience that they share with the rest of the world. As such, a documentary history has the power of immediacy not enjoyed by an interpretive history. It speaks directly to its readers beyond the constraints of time and space.

This book is intended not just for college students but has a broader audience in mind, including businessmen, diplomats, policymakers, and anyone interested in Japan. With that supposition, the following criteria are used in selecting the documents: (1) a given document must adequately reflect the spirit of the times and the lifestyle of the people of that age; (2) the emphasis must be placed on the development of social, economic, and political institutions, without neglecting important cultural attainments; and (3) some key documents must be studied in depth from different perspectives. Among the key documents so identified are Prince Shōtuku's seventeen-article constitution (604), Goseibai Shikimoku (1232), laws for military households (1615), Charter Oath (1868), Meiji constitution (1889), Shōwa constitution (1946) and the U.S.–Japan security pact (1960). In each case, the text is accompanied by commentaries. In the case of the Charter Oath, three different versions are reproduced, thus allowing us to study its drafting process. In the case of the Shōwa constitution, committee deliberations as well as comments by Japanese and American participants are reproduced. Many of these documents are not available in English elsewhere. As much as possible, duplication with existing sources in English is avoided. Close to three-quarters of the documents contained in this volume are original translations by this writer.

Some alert readers will find that this book is a successor to my two-volume *Sources of Japanese History* published in 1974. The first part of the present volume retains much of the 1974 edition, but a number of documents are added to show business practices in the Tokugawa period. The second part has extensive revisions and totally new chapters. Again serious consideration is given to Japan's economic might, which has resulted in a new chapter on Japan's emergence as an economic superpower.

I have been fortunate in being able to visit and observe the workings of more than 120 Japanese companies since the early 1980s. That experience is reflected in this new chapter. The debates extended by contemporary Japanese writers contained in Chapters 17 and 18 of this volume are refreshingly relevant to contemporary America, as these writers cope with many of the same problems facing us today. For close to a quarter of a century, I have been a contributor to the Japanese weekly *Sekai to Nippon* (The World and Japan). Through the pages of this paper, I too have been a participant in these ongoing debates.

In preparing the 1974 edition, I benefited greatly from the massive compilation of historical documents that the Japanese undertook to commemorate the centennial of the Meiji Restoration. In preparing the current edition, I benefited from disclosure of official documents made in commemoration of the fiftieth anniversary of the end of World War II. For example, Japan's right to self-defense and obligation to engage in peacekeeping operations under the U.N. Charter can now be definitely established. Documents made public in the fall of 1995 and winter of 1996 show clearly how the provisions of Article 9 are to be interpreted. These are contained in the documents added to Chapter 15, "Japan under Occupation."

There is no right or wrong way of using this book, but I would like to make one suggestion: Please read a chapter in one sitting instead of reading only one document. In this way you will not only be able to get the sense of the *zeitgeist* that governed the era but also discern the meaning of each individual document more clearly. Please do not hesitate to question statements and assumptions made by the writers. From whatever eras they come, treat them as if they were your contemporaries and engage them in a lively conversation.

Do not be discouraged if some of the *shōen* documents in Chapter 4 seem to recite various rights (*shiki*) endlessly like a litany. They are documents that defined the functions and entitlements for each inhabitant of a *shōen*. Not satisfied with merely reading and translating *shōen* documents, I diligently sought original documents. One day, I came upon a number of them on exhibit in the Osaka Municipal Museum. One of the documents had three lines drawn after the name of a peasant. The three lines represented the lengths between his fingertip to the first joint and to the knuckle of his right pointing finger. In an age when there was no way of identifying fingerprints and no other means of identification, this was a clever way to let an illiterate person "sign" his name. With this document, the peasant could claim his rightful share. Once identified in that fashion, the document assumed the quality of a living document. There is a phrase in Japan called "*seikatsu no chie,*" the wisdom that is gained from the experience of living. The documents contained in this book represent the sum total of Japan's *seikatsu no chie* over the ages.

Today we often hear of the excellence of Japanese management. One of its most frequently discussed features is their ability to reach a consensus. That ability can be traced back to the Goseibai Shikimoku of 1232. History is a continuing process. What is past is also prologue. This volume allows us to probe deeply into the roots of contemporary Japanese civilization.

Many Japanese friends have kept me informed of events in Japan and have supplied me with books and articles that have been of interest to them. They have filled the gap between my visits to Japan. These friends include Hirose Hideo, Kiyomiya Ryū, Shibata Yūzō, Shiina Takeo, Sumitomo Yoshiteru, and Takayama Michio. I thank them for giving me a chance to be in constant touch with Japan, which is an indispensable ingredient in preparing this new volume. Professors Ardath Burks, Marius Jansen, John Hall, Harry Harootunian, and Bernard Susser read part or all of the 1974 edition before it was published. I wish to thank them again for their encouragement and friendship.

I have had the privilege of meeting a number of contributors to this volume in person. It was good to renew acquaintance with some of them and make new friends in the summer of 1996 as this volume was readied for press. Conversations with them were akin to an old CBS program "You Were There." I hope that sense of participation in history is recaptured in the pages of this book. My gratitude for Japanese authors extends to Japanese publishers who have gone to an extraordinary length to make my contacts with the authors possible. Matsui Kaoru of the Edo Tokyo Museum was most gracious in helping select the illustrations from the Museum collection which now grace this volume.

I also wish to thank my former students at Bucknell University and at the Associated Kyoto Program. Their approving smiles, disapproving frowns, and intelligent questions have helped to shape and reshape the book. Because of them, this volume, in fact, is a far better book than the 1974 edition. This book, however, would have never taken its present shape without the gentle prodding of Douglas Merwin of M. E. Sharpe. Born in China and trained at Columbia in East Asian studies, he is a partaker of the true wisdom of the East. Angela Piliouras, the project editor, has been a delightful, cheerful, and enthusiastic co-worker. The staff of the Bertrand Library at Bucknell as always has been courteous and helpful. Finally, with love and affection, I wish to thank my wife, Annabelle, my constant companion for more than forty years, for her *naijo-no-kō* (help from within). We have jointly decided to dedicate this book to our grandchildren, and with it symbolically to express our hope for the coming century and for the new generation of scholars of Japan.

David J. Lu

Note on Japanese and
Chinese Names and Terms

Japanese names are given in this book in the Japanese order, that is, the surname precedes the given name. In the case of Americans of Japanese descent, however, the conventional order is maintained, that is, the given name precedes the surname. Macrons are employed to distinguish long vowels from short vowels. The Hepburn-Reischauer system of romanization is used, but the preference of the individual cited is observed, thus Konoye and not Konoe.

Chinese names are also given in the traditional order, that is, the surname precedes the given name. The *pinyin* Romanization system, with a few exceptions, is utilized throughout this volume.

JAPAN
A Documentary History

The Dawn of Japanese History

In 1947, an unknown amateur archaeologist, Aizawa Tadahiro, stumbled onto some tools of flaked stone in Iwajuku, Gumma prefecture. It was one of those unusual breakthroughs in our understanding of prehistoric Japan. The implements belonged to the third interglacial period, which meant that *homo sapiens* existed in Japan at that time. This was contrary to the accepted theories of the day, but soon afterwards other discoveries across the country—including hand axes, blades, points and microblades—confirmed that pre-modern hominids indeed lived in Japan between 150,000 and 200,000 years ago. Other discoveries, notably those at Niu, Kyushu in 1959, showed the trace of *homo sapiens* even earlier than the second interglacial period, or the period inhabited by the Neanderthal man in paleolithic Europe. In 1969 the complete skeletal remains of an elephant were found in Hokkaido, and in 1986, traces of elephant fat were detected in stone implements found in Miyagi prefecture. It meant the Japanese islands were once contiguous to the continent, fueling speculation about where the Japanese people originated.

These discoveries provided an unusual impetus for the study of Japan's past and its mythological accounts. These myths at certain periods in Japan's history were utilized by the ruling imperial clan to justify its claim to supremacy, by the Shintō revivalists as an article of faith, and yet at another time by the militarists to provide a doctrinal basis for Japan's imperial expansion.

The archaeological discoveries made it virtually impossible for any of the above claims to resurface. However, even if these myths were rejected as historical facts, they must still be reassigned a significant place in our understanding of the ancient Japanese people. From their sun worship, the coming of age ceremonies to marriage after servitude, these myths relate to us the life-style of an ancient people, and support the archaeological discoveries in verifying the existence of agriculture in their ancient past.

These myths are found in the *Kojiki* (*Records of Ancient Matters*) and the

3

Nihon Shoki (also rendered as the *Nihongi*, Chronicles of Japan) which are the oldest extant records of Japan compiled in 712 and 720 respectively. Even though the dates of compilation are relatively recent, compared to the records existing in other ancient civilizations, these two works refer back to much earlier ages. (As to how their oral tradition was preserved, how the *Kojiki* was written, and the philological explanation for the work, see Chapter II, Document 4.)

Documents 1, 2, 3, and 5 are taken from either the *Kojiki* or the *Nihon Shoki* which show the Japanese people's early attempt to explain the conflicts between the Sun line (the Yamato people) and the Izumo clans, the creation of the Izumo clans, and the supremacy of the heirs of the Sun Goddess.

While the Japanese people still lacked their own writing systems, scattered reports of Japan appeared in some Chinese historical works. The earliest contemporary account of Japan is found in the *Han shu* (History of the Earlier Han) compiled during the first century A.D. in China. It consisted of a 20–word sentence saying that "The Japanese people live beyond the Sea of Lolang [the present-day Korea], and are divided into more than one hundred counties, and from time to time send their tributes." Other accounts also appeared from time to time, but by far the most important one is found in the *Wei zhi* (History of Wei), *compiled around 297* A.D., which contains a section on Japan in its tales of peripheral peoples. Document 4 is a translation of this tale of the Japanese people, which is unrivaled in its description of Japanese customs and beliefs. The Wei history account also gives directions on how to reach the ancient kingdom of Yamatai, which poses an intriguing historiographical question.[1]

The final document comes from the *Engishiki*, an early tenth century compilation of laws and regulations which also contains Shintō rituals. Note Shintō's emphasis on the ritual cleanliness and its categories of major and minor offenses. Most major offenses one could commit against the community were those related to the disruption of its agricultural endeavors.

POWER CONTEST BETWEEN SUN GODDESS AND SUSANO-O

The following selection, taken from the Kojiki, *describes a power contest between Amaterasu, progenitor of the Yamato line, and Susano-o, progenitor of the*

---

[1]Was Yamatai located in Kyushu or Yamato? The Wei history discusses a civil war which took place in the third century A.D. If Yamatai were located in Kyushu, it would mean that the civil war so described and the resulting unification were of mere regional significance. On the other hand, if Yamatai were located in Yamato, it would mean that the civil war referred to was a "nationwide" uprising, and the emergence of Yamatai meant that a court strong enough to unify central and western Japan was in existence in the third century A.D. For this and other questions consult John Young, *The Location of Yamatai: A Case Study of Japanese Historiography* (Baltimore: Johns Hopkins University Press, 1958).

Izumo line. The culturally advanced Izumo was the strongest rival force to the Yamato line, and thus the myth takes special note of its subjugation.[2]

Sun worship was one of the key motifs in this myth. The central figure, Amaterasu, could be the Sun itself, or possibly a shaman who officiated in sun worship rituals.

Amaterasu's act of shutting herself inside a heavenly rock-cave and her eventual rescue have been variously interpreted as (1) an observance of the eclipse of the sun, (2) a rite of winter solstice, or (3) a requiem for the departed. The elaborate ritual that the deities performed to have Amaterasu reappear was intended to renew the waning power of the Sun. Since the Sun and the imperial line were inseparable, rejuvenation of the Sun would also have a propitious effect on the person of the reigning emperor. This rite of winter solstice combined with a requiem became one of the major court observances in the late seventh century.

Susano-o's offenses were the types of offense which were described in the Engishiki *(Document 6b).*

1 Amaterasu and Susano-o[3]

[Susano-o-no-Mikoto came to the heavenly abode of Amaterasu Ōmikami, his sister, to take leave of her, which was interpreted as a move to usurp her land. To prove his sincerity Susano-o engaged Amaterasu in a contest of bearing offspring, and Susano-o won.]

. . . Susano-o-no-Mikoto, drunk with victory, broke down the ridges between the rice paddies of Amaterasu Ōmikami and covered up the ditches. Also he defecated and strewed the feces about in the hall where the first fruits were tasted. Even though he did this, Amaterasu Ōmikami did not reprove him, but said: "That which appears to be feces must be what my brother has vomited and strewn about while drunk. Also his breaking down the ridges of the paddies and covering up their ditches—my brother must have done this because he thought it was wasteful to use the land thus."

Even though she thus spoke with good intention, his misdeeds did not cease,

---

[2]According to the myth, Ōkuninushi, son-in-law and heir to Susano-o, would later commend his land to the Yamato court, thus ending the rivalry. During the Nara period, each successive governor of Izumo, at the time of his installation, travelled to the imperial court to perform a special ceremony of obeisance, repeating the pledge Ōkuninushi presumably made at the time of commendation of Izumo. Thus there is a special link between myth and historical fact, attesting to the existence of their former rivalry. This ceremony was unique, and governors of other provinces were not required to perform it. Dōtaku (large bronze bells with geometric designs) and large tombs, distinct in pattern from those of Yamato, are found in Izumo, attesting to the distinct cultural attainment of the region. Izumo is located in the present-day Shimane Prefecture, on the Japan-Sea side of Southern Honshu; Yamato is located in the present-day Nara Prefecture.

[3]Adapted from Donald L. Philippi, tr., *Kojiki* (Tokyo: Tokyo University Press, 1969), pp. 79–86.

but became even more flagrant. When Amaterasu Ōmikami was inside the sacred weaving hall seeing to the weaving of the divine garments, he opened a hole in the roof of the sacred weaving hall and dropped down into it the heavenly dappled pony which he had skinned with a backwards skinning. The heavenly weaving maiden, seeing this, was alarmed and struck her genitals against the shuttle and died.

At this time, Amaterasu Ōmikami, seeing this, was afraid, and opening the heavenly rock-cave door, went in and shut herself inside. Then Takamano-hara (the abode of the heavenly deities) was completely dark, and the Central Land of the Reed Plains was entirely dark. Because of this, constant night reigned, and the cries of the myriad deities were everywhere abundant, like summer flies; and all manner of calamities arose.

Then the eight hundred myriad deities assembled in a divine assembly.... They gathered together the long-crying birds of the eternal world and caused them to cry. They took the heavenly hard rock from the upper stream of the river Amenoyasunokawa; they took iron from [the mountain] Amenokanayama. They sought the smith Amatsumara and commissioned Ishikori-dome-no-Mikoto to make a mirror. They commissioned Tamanoya-no-Mikoto to make long strings of myriad *magatama* beads.

They summoned Amenokoyane-no-Mikoto and Futotama-no-Mikoto to remove the whole shoulder-bone of a male deer of the mountain Amenokaguyama, and take *hahaka* wood from the mountain Amenokaguyama, and [with these] perform a divination. They uprooted by the very roots the flourishing *masakaki* trees of the mountain Amenokaguyama; to the upper branches they affixed long strings of myriad *magatama* beads; in the middle branches they hung a large-dimensioned mirror; in the lower branches they suspended white *nikite* cloth and blue *nikite* cloth. These various objects were held in his hands by Futotama-no-Mikoto as solemn offerings, and Amenokoyane-no-Mikoto intoned a solemn liturgy.

Amenotajikarao-no-Kami stood concealed beside the door, while Amenouzume-no-Mikoto bound up her sleeves with a cord of heavenly *hikage* vine, tied around her head a head-band of the heavenly *masaki* vine, bound together bundles of *sasa* leaves to hold in her hands, and overturning a bucket before the heavenly rock-cave door, stamped resoundingly upon it. Then she became divinely possessed, exposed her breasts, and pushed her shirt-band down to her genitals. The Takamanohara shook as the eight-hundred myriad deities laughed at once.

Then Amaterasu Ōmikami, thinking this strange, opened a crack in the heavenly rock-cave door, and said from within: "Because I have shut myself in, I thought that Takamanohara would be dark, and that the Central Land of the Reed Plains would be completely dark. But why is it that Amenouzume sings and dances, and all the eight-hundred myriad deities laugh?" Then Amenouzume said: "We rejoice and dance because there is here a deity superior to you." While she was saying this, Amenokoyane-no-Mikoto and Futotama-no-Mikoto brought out the mirror and showed it to Amaterasu Ōmikami. Then Amaterasu Ōmikami, thinking this more and more strange, gradually came out of the door and approached [the mirror].

Then the hidden Amenotajikarao-no-Kami took her hand and pulled her out. Immediately Futotama-no-Mikoto extended a *sirikume* rope behind her, and said, "You may go back no further than this!" When Amaterasu Ōmikami came forth, Takamanohara and the Central Land of the Reed Plains of themselves became light.

At this time the eight-hundred myriad deities deliberated together, imposed upon Susano-o-no-Mikoto a fine of a thousand tables of restitutive gifts, and also, cutting off his beard and the nails of his hands and feet, had him exorcised and expelled with a divine expulsion.

COMING OF AGE IN ANCIENT JAPAN

Aside from Susano-o, his father-in-law, Ōkuninushi was the most colorful hero of the Izumo myths. Unlike the deities of the imperial line, the gods of the Izumo clans were more man-like and partook of the joys and travails of mankind. Ōkuninushi's trials had traces of the practice of marriage after servitude and of the coming-of-age ceremony. According to the myth, Ōkuninushi died many deaths but at each turn he miraculously revived. This was akin to the ritualistic deaths performed at some coming-of-age ceremonies in the South Pacific. A young man had to prove his manhood through a ritualistic death, and in Ōkuninushi's case, the deaths were visited on him to prove his worthiness to become the future ruler of Izumo.

2 **Ōkuninushi-no-Mikoto and Izumo[4]** On Ōkuninushi's arrival in Izumo, Suseribime, daughter of Susano-o, came forth and saw him; they looked at each other lovingly and became man and wife. She went back inside and told her father: "A most beautiful deity has come." Then the great deity went out . . . and invited him in and made him sleep in a chamber of snakes. Then his spouse Suseribime-no-Mikoto gave her husband a snake-repelling scarf, saying: "When the snakes are about to bite, drive them away by waving this scarf three times." He did as he was told, and the snakes became calm of their own accord. Thus, he slept peacefully and came forth unharmed.

Once more the next night, Susano-no-Mikoto put him in a chamber of centipedes and bees. Again Suseribime gave him a scarf to repel the centipedes and bees, and told him to do as before. Then he came forth unharmed.

Again, Susano-no-Mikoto shot a humming arrow into a large plain and made

---

[4]*Ibid.*, pp. 98–103.

him go and fetch the arrow. When Ōkuninushi-no-Mikoto had gone into the plain, Susano-no-Mikoto set fire all around the edges of the plain. When Ōkuninushi-no-Mikoto could not find a way out, a mouse came and said: "The inside is hollow-hollow: the outside is narrow-narrow." Because the mouse had said this, he stamped his feet at that place and fell into a hole in the ground; while he was hidden there, the fire passed over. Then the mouse came out bearing the humming arrow in its mouth and presented it to him. . . .

At this time, his spouse Suseribime came along in tears, carrying funeral implements. Her father, the great deity, thinking that Ōkuninushi-no-Mikoto had died, went out on the plain. Then when Ōkuninushi brought the arrow and presented it to him, he led him inside the house, summoned him into a spacious hall, and had him pick the lice from his head. At this time his spouse gave to her husband nuts of the *muku* tree and red clay. He bit open the nuts, and put the red clay in his mouth, and spat out the mixture. Then the great deity, thinking that Ōkuninushi was biting open and spitting out the centipedes, thought lovingly in his heart of him and went to sleep.

Thereupon, Ōkuninushi took the hair of the great deity and tied strands of it to each of the rafters of the chamber. He took a huge boulder and blocked the door of the chamber. Carrying his spouse Suseribime on his back, he took away the great deity's sword of life and bow-and-arrow of life, as well as his heavenly speaking cither.

As he fled, the heavenly speaking cither brushed against a tree, and its sound reverberated along the ground. Then the sleeping deity, hearing this, was alarmed and pulled down the hall. However, while he was disentangling his hair which had been tied to the rafters, they had escaped far away. Then Susano-o pursued them as far as the pass Yomotsuhirasaka and looking far into the distance, called after Ōkuninushi, saying: "Using the sword of life and the bow-and-arrow of life which you are holding, pursue and subdue your half-brothers on the side of the hill; and pursue and sweep them down at the rapids of the river. Then, becoming Ōkuninushi-no-Kami and becoming Utsusikunitama-no-Kami[5] make my daughter Suseribime your chief wife. Dwell at the foot of Mount Uka,[6] root the posts of your palace firmly in the bedrock below, and raise high the crossbeam unto Takamanohara itself, you scoundrel!"

When he pursued the eighty deities using the sword and bow, he pursued and subdued them on the side of each hill, and pursued and swept them down at the rapids of each river.

Then he began the creation of the land.

---

[5]I.e., becoming the ruler of the land, the divine spirit of the land of mortals.

[6]This is where the Great Shrine of Izumo is located today. It was evidently an early social and political center of the Izumo region.

EMPEROR JIMMU'S CONQUEST OF THE EAST

*Again, a conspicuous effort is made by the myth-tellers to link the imperial line
with the Sun Goddess in this story of Emperor Jimmu. There is also assertion of
the superiority of the imperial line, and the emperor was presumed to rule all
"under heaven under one roof (Hakkō Ichiu)," which gave later nationalists
justification for Japan's imperialistic expansion.*

*In reading this selection, pay special attention to the year "kanototori." The
yin-yang and five element doctrines and the art of calendar-making were probably introduced to Japan from China between the sixth and seventh centuries.
According to these theories, the year kanototori is supposed to bring forth great
changes, and the most significant change is to occur every twenty-first time
kanototori takes place (each calendar operated on a sixty-year cycle, thus the
twenty-first time makes it every 1,260 years). The year 601 A.D. was a kanototori,
and was a year of great innovation and reform under Empress Suiko and Prince
Shōtoku (see Chapter II). Having this in mind the writers of the Nihon Shoki
probably decided to push back the legendary beginning of Japan 1,260 years, or
to 660 B.C.*

*Even though the founding of the empire in 660 B.C. had no historical founda-
tion, it was so accepted officially until 1945. The Founding Day of the Nation
was celebrated on February 11 every year. (The first day of the lunar calendar
in the year 660 B.C. would have fallen on February 11 in the Gregorian calendar.) In 1967, February 11 again became a national holiday in spite of strong
protests by many noted historians.*

3 **The Eastern Expedition of Emperor Jimmu**[7] Emperor Jimmu was
forty-five years of age when he addressed the assemblage of his brothers and
children: "Long ago, this central land of the Reed Plains was bequeathed to our
imperial ancestors by the heavenly deities, Takamimusubi-no-Kami and
Amaterasu Ōmikami. . . . However, the remote regions still do not enjoy the
benefit of our imperial rule, with each town having its own master and each
village its own chief. Each of them sets up his own boundaries and contends for
supremacy against other masters and chiefs."

"I have heard from an old deity knowledgeable in the affairs of the land and
sea that in the east there is a beautiful land encircled by blue mountains. . . . This

---

[7]From *Nihon Shoki (Chronicles of Japan)*, vol. 1, in *Kokushi Taikei (Major Compilation of National History)*, new and enlarged ed., vol. 1, no. 1 (Tokyo: Yoshikawa Kō
bunkan, pp. 111–115, 117, 126. A full English translation of the *Nihon Shoki* can be found
in William G. Aston, *Nihongi, Chronicles of Japan from the Earliest Times to A.D. 697*
(London: Allen & Unwin, 1956).

must be the land from which our great task of spreading our benevolent rule can begin, for it is indeed the center of the universe[8]. . . . Let us go there, and make it our capital. . . ."

In the winter of that year, on the day of *kanototori*, the Emperor personally led imperial princes and a naval force to embark on his eastern expedition. . . .

When Nagasunehiko heard of the expedition, he said: "The children of the heavenly deities are coming to rob me of my country." He immediately mobilized his troops and intercepted Jimmu's troops at the hill of Kusaka and engaged in a battle. . . . The imperial forces were unable to advance. Concerned with the reversal, the Emperor formulated a new divine plan and said to himself: "I am the descendant of the Sun Goddess, and it is against the way of heaven to face the sun in attacking my enemy. Therefore our forces must retreat to make a show of weakness. After making sacrifice to the deities of heaven and earth, we shall march with the sun on our backs. We shall trample down our enemies with the might of the sun. In this way, without staining our swords with blood, our enemies can be conquered." . . . So, he ordered the troops to retreat to the port of Kusaka and regroup there. . . .

[After withdrawing to Kusaka, the imperial forces sailed southward, landed at a port in the present-day Kii peninsula, and again advanced north toward Yamato.]

The precipitous mountains provided such effective barriers that the imperial forces were not able to advance into the interior, and there was no path they could tread. Then one night Amaterasu Ōmikami appeared to the Emperor in a dream: "I will send you the Yatagarasu,[9] let it guide you through the land." The following day, indeed the Yatagarasu appeared flying down from the great expanse of the sky. The Emperor said: "The coming of this bird signifies the fulfillment of my auspicious dream. How wonderful it is! Our imperial ancestor, Amaterasu Ōmikami, desires to help us in the founding of our empire. . . ."

At long last, the imperial forces caught up with Nagasunehiko and fought with him repeatedly, but could not gain victory. Then suddenly, the sky became darkened and hail fell. There appeared a mysterious hawk of a golden color which flew toward the Emperor and perched on the end of his bow. The brilliant luster of this hawk was almost like that of lightning. Bedazzled and confused the soldiers of Nagasunehiko were unable to fight with all their might. . . .

[Subsequently Nagasunehiko was killed by his overlord, and the Emperor continued to make his successful conquest.]

On new year's day, in the year of *kanototori*, the Emperor formally proclaimed his ascension to the position of the ruler of the universe by virtue of

---

[8]The universe was divided into six quarters: Heaven, earth, east, west, north and south.

[9]Yatagarasu was reported to be an incarnation of a deity. The term also referred to a bird in the Chinese mythology with three claws and of red color, residing in the sun.

being a descendant of Amaterasu Ōmikami.[10] This took place in the palace of
Kashihabara, and the year was counted as the first year of his reign. . . .

JAPAN IN THE WEI DYNASTIC HISTORY

*Japan was recorded in Chinese dynastic histories on a number of occasions. The
first contact Japan had with China occurred in 57 A.D. when a mission was sent
to the court of the Later Han dynasty. A tribute mission was again sent in 107
A.D. Dynastic histories give 13 entries for "five Japanese kings" between 413 and
502 A.D.*

Of all the Chinese records, the description appearing in the Wei zhi *(History
of Wei) is most thorough, giving a contemporary account of history, geography,
and the beliefs and customs of the Japanese people. The Kingdom of Wei existed
between 220 and 265 A.D. and its history was compiled about 297 A.D. The
existence of wet-rice cultivation and of sericulture is clearly indicated in the
excerpts reproduced below. The use of iron as described—important both for
cultivation and for warfare—is consistent with archaeological evidence available for the later Yayoi period.*

*As to the political structure of the country of Wa, rejection of men rulers in
favor of a female seems to indicate a widespread practice of shamanism. The
queen, Pimiko, obviously served as a medium as did her successor Iyo. Only
through a form of witchcraft was the country able to maintain a semblance of
unity. Note also that there was an attempt to gain assistance from Wei officials.
The use of animal bones for divination is supported by archaeological evidence.
The purification rites described in the Wei history are probably not confined to
the period after funeral services. Misogi, or water purification, is one of the
important Shintō rituals which survives today in a different form—the Japanese
love for bathing, especially in hot springs.*

4 **From the History of Wei**[11]   The people of Wa make their abode in the
mountainous islands located in the middle of the ocean to the southeast of the
Taifang prefecture.[12] Formerly there were more than one hundred communities.
During the Han dynasty their envoys appeared in the court. Today, thirty of their
communities maintain communication with us through their envoys. . . .

---

[10]The Japanese term for this cumbersome description is *amatsuhitsuki shiroshimesu.*

[11]From the *Wei zhi,* as reproduced in the original Chinese in Inoue Mitsutada, *Shinwa
kara Rekishi e (From Myths to History):* Chūō Kōronsha, *Nihon no Rekishi (A History of
Japan),* vol. 1 (Tokyo: Chūō Kōronsha, 1965), pp. 214–220.

[12]Established near the end of the Later Han dynasty. Its administrative center was
located near the present-day Seoul.

All men, old or young, are covered by tattoos. Japanese fishers revel in diving to catch fish and shell-fish. Tattoos are said to drive away large fish and water predators. They are considered an ornament. Tattoos differ from community to community. Some place tattoos on the left, and others on the right, some place large ones and others small ones. Tattoos also differ in accordance with the social positions. . . . Men allow their hair to cover both of their ears and wear head-bands. They wear a loin cloth wrapped around their bodies and seldom use stitches. Women gather their hair at the ends and tie in a knot and then pin it to the top of their heads. They make their clothes in one piece, and cut an opening in the center for their heads. They plant wet-field rice, China-grass (*ramie*), and mulberry trees. They raise cocoons and reel the silk off the cocoons. They produce clothing made of China-grass, of coarse silk, and of cotton. In their land, there are no cows, horses, tigers, leopards, sheep or swan. They fight with halberds, shields and wooden bows. The lower inflection of their bows is shorter, and the upper inflection longer. Their arrows are made of bamboo and iron and bone points make up the arrowhead. . . .

The land of Wa is warm and mild. The people eat raw vegetables and go about barefoot in winter as in summer. They live in houses. Father and mother, older and younger sleep separately. They paint their bodies with vermilion and scarlet, just as the Chinese apply powder. They serve food on bowl-shaped stemware (*takatsuki*), and eat with their fingers. When a person dies, he is placed in a coffin (which is buried directly in the grave) without an outer protective layer. The grave is then covered with earth to make a mound. When death occurs, the family observes mourning for more than ten days, during which period no meat is eaten. The head mourner wails and cries, while others sing, dance and drink liquor (probably *sake*, the Japanese rice wine). When the funeral is over, the entire family goes into the water to cleanse themselves in a manner similar to Chinese in their rites of purification.

When they travel across the sea to come to China, they always select a man who does not comb his hair, does not rid himself of fleas, keeps his clothes soiled with dirt, does not eat meat, and does not lie with women. He behaves like a mourner, and is called a "keeper of taboos."[13] If the voyage is concluded with good fortune, every one lavishes on him slaves and treasures. If someone gets ill, or if there is a mishap, they kill him immediately, saying that he was not conscientious in observing the taboos. . . .

When they undertake an activity or a journey and cannot reach a consensus, they bake animal bones to divine and tell good or bad fortunes. They first announce the object of their divination, and in their manner or speech, they are similar to Chinese tortoise shell divination. They examine the cracks on the bone made by the fire to tell the fortune.

In their meetings and daily living, there is no distinction between father and

---

[13]Literally, man with mourning death.

son, or between men and women. People enjoy liquor. In their worship, the high-echelon men simply clap their hands instead of bowing in the kneeled position. They live long, some reaching one hundred years of age, and others to eighty or ninety years. Normally, men of high echelon have four or five wives, and the plebians may have two or three. Women are chaste and not given to jealousy. They do not engage in thievery, and there is very little litigation. When the law is violated, the light offender loses his wife and children by confiscation, and the grave offender has his household and kinsmen exterminated. There are class distinctions within the nobility and the base, and some are vassals of others. There are mansions and granaries erected for the purpose of collecting taxes. Each community has a market place where commodities are exchanged under the supervision of an official of Wa. . . .

When plebians meet the high-echelon men on the road, they withdraw to the grassy area (side of the road) hesitantly. When they speak or are spoken to, they either crouch or kneel with both hands on the ground to show their respect. When responding they say "aye," which corresponds to our affirmative "yes."

Formerly the country had men as rulers. However, for seventy or eighty years after that, the country had disturbances and warfare. Finally people agreed to make a woman their ruler, and called her Pimiko (Himiko). She was adept in the ways of shamanism, and could bewitch people. In her mature years, she was yet unmarried and had her younger brother help her rule the country. After she became the ruler, there were only a few who ever saw her. She had one thousand maidservants, but there was only one manservant attending her. His functions were to serve her food and drinks, to communicate messages, and to enter and leave her quarters. The queen resided in a palace surrounded by towers and barricades, with guards maintaining a constant watch. . . .

In the sixth month of the third year of Zhengzhi (239 A.D.)[14] the queen of Wa sent her grand steward Nashomi to the prefecture [of Taifang], requesting that he be allowed to have audience with the Emperor to pay tribute. To governor, Liu Xia, assigned an official as a guide to escort the party to the capital. . . . An edict of the [Wei] Emperor said as follows: ". . . You reside in a distant place, but have sent an embassy to pay tribute. This is manifestation of your loyalty and filial piety which we appreciate exceedingly. We therefore confer upon you the title 'Ruler of Wa, Friendly to Wei.' . . . We beseech you to rule your people in peace and compassion, and continue to show your filial piety and devotion. . . ."

In the sixth year [of Zhengzhi, 242 A.D.], the Emperor sent his edict and a yellow banner bearing the imperial insignia to Wa . . . in care of the prefecture. In the eighth year [244 A.D.], a new governor, Wang Qi, arrived at his post. At

---

[14]The original gives the date of the second year of Zhengzhi, which from internal and historical evidence was in error.

that time the Queen of Wa had difficulties with Himikoko, king of Kuna [located to the south of Wa], and sent her envoys to the prefecture to explain the conditions of their warfare. The governor sent an official by the name of Zhang Zheng as his envoy to transmit the imperial edict and yellow banner, and to give instructions to Wa through the latter's official Nashomi. But at that time Pimiko died, and a great mound—more than one hundred paces in diameter—was erected. More than a hundred men and maidservants followed her to the grave. A king ascended the throne, but the country would not obey him. Murders and assassinations were practiced on one another, and more than one thousand were killed in this fashion.

Finally a relative of Pimiko, named Iyo, a girl aged thirteen, was made queen and order was restored to the country. Zhang and others representing Wei gave instructions to Iyo [thus showing Wei's support of her]. Iyo sent her delegation consisting of twenty members under her grand steward Isako, to accompany Zhang Zheng and others [returning to Wei]. On the occasion of their visit to the capital, the Japanese envoys presented thirty men and maidservants, and also offered the court five thousand white gems and two pieces of curved jade and twenty pieces of brocade with different designs.

THE LEGEND OF PRINCE YAMATOTAKERU

In a memorial submitted to the Emperor of Southern Song in 467, a Japanese king boasted of his might in the following terms. "My ancestors donned armor themselves, traversed the mountains and rivers, and spared no time for rest. They conquered fifty-five communities of the hairy people in the east, subdued sixty-six communities after crossing the sea to the north. . . ." The last phrase probably refers to Japan's engagement in Korea which took place in the latter part of the fourth century. The term "hairy people" was often used synonymously with the Emishi (later called Ezo) people who inhabited the northeastern region of Japan. Thus the memorial gives collaborative evidence to the continued effort on the part of the Yamato court to conquer Japan's eastern regions, the subject also of Yamatotakeru's conquest. Subjugation of the Emishi was completed in the seventh century. As to the legend itself, it was probably composed sometime between the middle of the fourth century and the middle of the sixth century, giving a composite picture of many heroes who perished in this endeavor. However, the story was cast in the form of an individual who incurred the displeasure of his father, the Emperor, and as an alienated youth, set out on his conquest virtually alone. Incidentally, the Kumaso, referred to in the earlier part of this legend, may be the name of a tribe, or of the two regions, Kuma and So. The two regions are in the southern part of Kyushu. The exact dates of the Yamato court's conquest of these regions are not established.

5   **Conquest of the Eastern Frontier by Prince Yamatotakeru**[15]   In the summer of the 40th year of Emperor Keikō's reign [12th emperor], there was a rebellion by eastern barbarians, and the frontier was in a state of siege. . . . The Emperor addressed his ministers. "The eastern country is not secure, and numerous rebellious chieftains have sprung up. In the case of the Emishi, the revolt is total, and they frequently steal from our loyal subjects. Whom can I send to suppress this rebellion?" To this inquiry, none of the ministers knew how to answer.

[After another prince had refused to bear arms, concealing himself in the thicket,] Yamatotakeru-no-Mikoto manly proclaimed. "It has not been many years since I subdued the Kumaso. Now the Emishi in the east are rebelling against us. If we allow it to continue, there can be no universal peace. Your subject is aware of the difficulties and begs of you to be sent to quell the rebellion." The Emperor gave a battleaxe to Yamatotakeru-no-Mikoto and gave him the following charge: "We hear that the eastern barbarians are men of violent disposition, making crime as their credo. Their villages have no chiefs, and towns have no masters. Each one of them covets a territory and plunders one another. Their mountains and fields are inhabited by malicious deities and demented demons, who stop traffic and bar the roads to cause difficulties. Amongst those eastern barbarians, the Emishi are the most powerful. Their men and women live together in promiscuity, and they make no differentiation between father and son. In winter they dwell in holes, and in summer they live in nests. They use furs as their clothing, and drink blood. Brothers are suspicious of one another. . . . When they receive a favor, they forget it, but if an injury is done them, they repay it with vengeance. . . . They plunder our frontier, and steal from our people the hard-earned products in agriculture and sericulture. When attacked, they hide in the grasses and if pursued, they enter into the mountains. From the olden days, they have not been able to receive the influence of our benevolent civilization. . . . Heaven has taken pity on my want of intelligence and on the unmanageable conditions of the country, and has sent you to execute the work of heaven so as to perpetuate the existence of our imperial institution. My empire is your empire, and this position I hold is your position. Use your profound judgment and wisdom to guard against iniquity and rebellious movement. Exercise your authority with majesty and pacify people with virtue. Whenever possible subjugate people without recourse to arms. Use carefully chosen words to teach moderation to rebellious chiefs. If it fails, eradicate those malicious demons by displaying your armed might. . . ."[16]

When Yamatotakeru-no-Mikoto first reached Suruga, the brigands falsely

---

[15]*Nihon Shoki*, op. cit., pp. 212–215, 218–220.

[16]These moralizing passages are clearly an imitation of Confucian precepts as found in Chinese historical writings.

pledged allegiance. They urged the prince to hunt, claiming that their field was rich in large deer, whose breath was like the morning mist and legs like dense woods. Yamatotakeru-no-Mikoto believed their words, and went into the middle of the field to hunt. The brigands, intending to kill the prince, set the field ablaze. Realizing that he had been deceived, the prince brought out his flint and steel (*hiuchi*) and kindled a counter-fire. [One version of the *Nihon Shoki* says: "The prince wore the sword Murakumo which wielded itself and mowed away the grasses near him, enabling him to escape. Hereafter, his sword became known as Kusanagi.[17]] The prince cried out: "I am almost betrayed," and burnt all the brigands and exterminated them . . .

[Having completed his conquest of the eastern frontier,] Yamatotakeru-no-Mikoto turned to Owari, and married a daughter of the lord of Owari by the name of Miyazuhime, and remained there for a month. While there he heard that there was a ferocious deity on Mount Ibuki in Ōmi. He took off his sword and left it in the house of Miyazuhime, and then set out on foot to investigate. When he reached Mount Ibuki, his way was blocked by a great serpent which was the incarnation of the mountain god. Without knowing that the main deity took the shape of a serpent, Yamatotakeru-no-Mikoto reasoned: "This great serpent must be a messenger of that ferocious deity. Unless I can kill the main deity, there is no use being bothered by its messenger." So he strode over and went on. The mountain god raised up clouds and made freezing rain to fall. The hills were covered with mist, and the valleys were darkened. The prince could no longer find his way. . . . All he could do was to brave the mist and force his way onward. Finally when he succeeded in escaping from the mountain, he was not quite himself, looking like a drunken man. . . .

It was at that time Yamatotakeru-no-Mikoto first became ill. With great difficulty, he made his way to Owari and entered the house of Miyazuhime, and then moved on to Ise and to Ōtsu. . . . When he reached the field of Nobo, the pain became almost insufferable. He made arrangements to have the prisoners he obtained in wars against the Emishi sent to the Ise Shrine as part of his thanks offering, and dispatched Kibi-no Takehiko to the Emperor to report [on his impending death]. . . . The prince died on the field of Nobo at the age of thirty. . . . The Emperor ordered his ministers and functionaries to bury the body of the prince in a *misasagi* (tomb) of the Nobo field in the land of Ise.

Now Yamatotakeru-no-Mikoto, taking the shape of a white bird, left his *misasagi* and flew towards the direction of Yamato. The ministers opened the coffin, only to discover the empty clothing remaining, and there was no corpse. Messengers were sent to follow the trace of the white bird. It stopped on the plain of Kotohiki[18] in Yamato, so another *misasagi* was erected. The white bird

---

[17]The term *kusanagi* means to mow away grasses. The sword became one of the three imperial regalia held to symbolize succession to the imperial throne.

[18]Here the place name conveys some poetic imagination. It means the plain of *koto* (a Japanese music instrument) playing.

flew on again until it reached Kawachi, and remained in the village of Furuichi. Accordingly a third *misasagi* was erected. Men of those days called these three *misasagi*, "the white bird *misasagi*." Finally, the white bird soared high above in heaven, and nothing is buried in the *misasagi* except his clothing and official cap. . . .

EARLY SHINTŌ RITUALS FROM THE *ENGISHIKI*

The Engishiki *was compiled between 905 and 927 under the command of Emperor Daigo. It is one of the greatest compilations of laws and precedents (kyaku and* shiki*) and invaluable in the study of the court system in the Heian period.*

Volume eight of the Engishiki *contains Shintō rituals called* Norito*. These rituals are obviously of much earlier origin than the date of its compilation in the tenth century, and show Shintō practices in their pristine form. The* Norito *calls upon the spirits of gods or of things to answer men's supplications. It is simplistic and practically devoid of metaphysical speculation. The first selection, the grain-petitioning festival, is self-explanatory. The second selection, the purification ritual, is of special significance in that it gives a list of heavenly offenses and earthly offenses. The heavenly offenses were essentially those interfering with agriculture and mischievous acts against community functions (compare Document 1). Earthly offenses included suffering from leprosy, a blight, and calamities by thunderstorms. These were considered offenses, because they could be caused by a curse cast upon the people suffering from them. That curse could hover over the entire community, and thus the rite of purification became an important part of the community functions. The ritual was performed regularly in the imperial court in the sixth month of the year to purge the country of all offenses and curses.*

6 From the *Engishiki*[19]

(a) The Grain-petitioning Festival
I humbly speak before you,
   The Sovereign Deities whose praises are fulfilled as
      Heavenly Shrines and Earthly Shrines
   By the command of the Sovereign Ancestral Gods and Goddesses
      Who divinely remain in the High Heavenly Plain:
This year, in the second month,
   Just as grain cultivation is about to begin

---

[19]Adapted from Donald L. Philippi, tr., *Norito: A New Translation of the Ancient Japanese Ritual Prayers* (Tokyo: Kokugakuin, 1959), pp. 17–18.

I present the noble offerings of the Sovereign Grandchild[20]
And, as the morning sun rises in effulgent glory.
Fulfill your praises. Thus I speak.

I humbly speak before you,
   The Sovereign Deities of the Grain:
The latter grain[21] to be vouchsafed by you [to the Sovereign Grandchild],
   The latter grain to be harvested
      With foam dripping from the elbows,
   To be pulled hither
      With mud adhering to both thighs—
If this grain be vouchsafed by you
   In ears many hands long,
   In luxuriant ears;
Then the first fruits will be presented
   In a thousand stalks, eight hundred stalks:
Raising high the soaring necks
   Of the countless wine vessels, filled to the brim;

Both of liquor and in stalks I will fulfill praises.
From that which grows in the vast fields and plains—

   The sweet herbs and the bitter herbs—
To that which lives in the blue ocean—
   The wide-finned and the narrow-finned fishes,
   The sea-weeds of the deep and the sea-weeds of the shore—
As well as garments
   Of colored cloth, radiant cloth,
   Plain cloth, and coarse cloth—
In these I will fulfill your praises.
Before the Sovereign Deities of the Grain
   I will provide a white horse, a white boar, a white cock,
   And various types of offerings.
And will present the noble offerings of the Sovereign Grandchild
   And fulfill your praises. Thus I speak.

(b) The Purification Ritual

[The ritual opens by calling upon all the assembled princes of the Emperor's family, the Ministers of State, and all other officials, to listen. The nature of the

---

[20]Sovereign Grandchild is a common title for each Emperor as being a descendant of the Sun Goddess.

[21]Rice is the favorite cereal of the Japanese, and the strange phraseology employed to depict the labor of the peasant represents rather forcibly the process of churning the muddy soil of the swampy fields in which it is grown.

Emperor's title to rule over the land is then stated, after which we have a list of the offenses of which the nation is to be purged.]
    The various offenses perpetrated and committed
        By the heavenly ever-increasing people to come into existence
        In this land which he is to rule tranquilly as a peaceful land:
First, the heavenly offenses:
        Breaking down the ridges,
        Covering up the ditches,
        Releasing the irrigation sluices,
        Double planting,
        Setting up stakes,
        Skinning alive, skinning backwards,
        Defecation—
        Many offenses [such as these] are distinguished and called the heavenly
            offenses.
The earthly offenses:
        Cutting living flesh, cutting dead flesh,
        White leprosy, skin excrescences,
        The offense of violating one's own mother,
        The offense of violating one's own child,
        The offense of violating a mother and her child,
        The offense of violating a child and her mother,
        The offense of transgression with animals,
        Woes from creeping insects,
        Woes from the deities on high,
        Woes from the birds on high,
        Killing animals, the offense of witchcraft,
        Many offenses [such as these] shall appear.
    When they thus appear,
    By the heavenly shrine usage,
        Let the Great Nakatomi[22] cut off the bottom and off the top
            Of heavenly narrow pieces of wood,
        And place them in abundance on a thousand tables;
        Let him cut off the bottom and cut off the top
            Of heavenly sedge reeds
        And cut them up into myriad strips;
        And let him pronounce the heavenly ritual, the solemn ritual words.
    When he thus pronounces them,
        The heavenly deities will push open the heavenly rock door,
        And pushing with an awesome pushing
            Through the myriad layers of heavenly clouds,

---

[22]An ancient family which served the Yamato Court in a priestly capacity.

Will hear and receive [these words].
Then the earthly deities will climb up
   To the summits of the high mountains and to the summits of the low
      mountains,
   And pushing aside the mists of the high mountains and the mists of the low
      mountains,
   Will hear and receive [these words].

When they thus hear and receive,
Then, beginning with the court of the Sovereign Grandchild,
   In the lands of the four quarters under the heavens,
   Each and every offense will be gone.
As the gusty wind blows apart the myriad layers of heavenly clouds;
   As the morning mist, the evening mist is blown away by the morning wind,
      the evening wind;
   As the large ship anchored in the spacious port is untied at the prow and untied
      at the stern
      And pushed out into the great ocean;
   As the luxuriant clump of trees on yonder [hill]
      Is cut away at the base with a tempered sickle, a sharp sickle—
   As a result of the exorcism and the purification,
      There will be no offenses left. . . .
Hear me, all of you:

Know that [all the offenses] have been exorcised and purified
   In the great exorcism performed in the waning of the evening sun
   On the last day of the sixth month of this year. Thus I speak.
   Oh diviners[23] of the four lands,
      Carry them out to the great river
      And cast them away. Thus I speak.

---

[23]In the purification ritual, it is the diviners (*urabe*) who carry away the offense-bearing articles and cast them into the river.

CHAPTER II

The Impact of Chinese Civilization

Japan's cultural borrowing from China began in earnest with the introduction of Buddhism in 552 A.D. (or 538 A.D.) and continued uninterrupted until the end of the Nara period in 784.

If any single term can characterize these two and a half centuries, they may be called a period of "Chinese fixation."[1] When Prince Shōtoku wanted to curtail the powers of the great clans and enhance the prestige of the imperial institution, it was to China that he looked for inspiration. When the Taika reforms were initiated, the systems of land tenure and taxation then in force in Tang provided the necessary models. So was the case with the enactment of the Taihō-Yōrō codes which set the administrative and criminal codes to be used for generations to come (Documents 1–3). The Chinese language was employed in early historical writings, along with an attempt to write history in the indigenous tongue which used Chinese characters phonetically. Just as the Chinese people utilized history to create a new self-image, "the holistic ideal, the belief in moral dynamics and a pronounced Sino-centrism,"[2] so did the Japanese people create an image of a "divine land." History was also used to claim legitimacy for the reigning imperial line (Document 4). In the imperial court, news from China brought by returned students was eagerly received. Men and women consulted the *yin-yang* philosophy, the five elements and the twelve horary signs to look

---

[1]Compare the term "American fixation," used by Professor E. O. Reischauer in his *Japan, Past and Present* (New York, Knopf, 1964), p. 256.

[2]Arthur F. Wright, "On the Uses of Generalization in the Study of Chinese History," in Louis Gottschalk, ed., *Generalization in the Writing of History* (Chicago: University of Chicago Press, 1963), p. 43.

into the future and to find answers to perplexing day-to-day problems. Exchanging poems written in Chinese was considered the highest accomplishment in polite society, and the Chinese poems were also employed to impress upon foreign visitors Japan's cultural advancement at diplomatic receptions. The *Kaifūsō*, the first compilation of Chinese poems, completed in 751 and thus ahead of the *Manyōshū*, typified Japan's adulation of China. The first permanent capital of Nara, with its broad-patterned avenues, temples and pagodas, was a replica of the imperial city of Changan. Even in selecting the location of this new capital, the Chinese geomancy was carefully consulted.

However, indigenous elements did not completely submerge when Japan imported Chinese thought and institutions. From the very beginning there was an attempt for adaptation, not mere imitation. This trend was most clearly discernible in the Taihō-Yōrō codes (Document 3). As long as the Chinese institutions provided a means for enhancing the power of the imperial court, they were eagerly adopted. In the case of propagation of Buddhism, the same attitude held true. It was less for spiritual pursuit, and more for political gains that Buddhism was encouraged (Documents 6, 7, and 8). This pragmatic approach and the coalescence of indigenous and alien elements were in large measure responsible for the success of Japan's cultural importation.

In their cultural borrowing, the Japanese were selective. They chose only those features of Chinese civilization most advantageous to Japan. For example, Japanese Buddhism was deeply influenced by the Buddhism of northern dynasties, which maintained a strong belief in the ability of Buddhism to protect the state. This was, of course, attractive to Japanese rulers. On the other hand, in literature, a far stronger influence came from southern China, independently of Buddhism in that region.

The relatively long period of time that Japan was subjected to Chinese cultural influence also helped facilitate successful assimilation of this alien civilization. What was once foreign became familiar through a process of education and continuous exposure. Generation after generation of Japanese elite who were educated in Chinese classics shared a certain set of common values with their Chinese counterpart. Meanwhile, the difficulty of sea passage prevented the two groups from becoming homogeneous in their life-styles and world views. The Japanese elite retained their perspectives distinct from the Chinese ones. Yet to the Japanese elite the Chinese values and Japanese perspectives were both part of their heritage. Gradually they created a culture distinctly their own, naturalizing Chinese elements to suit the requirements of the new age in Japan. Then in later years, the culture thus nurtured by the elite would seep downward to become the heritage of the common man.

THE REGENCY OF PRINCE SHŌTOKU

The flowering of civilization and new confidence in the fate of the imperial institution characterized the regency of Prince Shōtoku which lasted from 593 to

622. In 604, the Prince promulgated the so-called Seventeen Article Constitution.[3] *It was not a basic law in the sense that we understand the term today, but was more of a series of moral precepts and injunctions. In this stylistically correct Chinese writing, the "constitution" quotes freely from Confucian, Legalist, Taoist and Buddhist works. There were unabashed claims for the right of the sovereign (Articles 3 and 12), and attempts to create a "bureaucracy" to replace the domination of the great clans (Articles 7, 8, 11, 13, and 15).*

Some of these professed aims remained mere pious wishes, and there is no evidence indicating that the Constitution was ever shown to the great clans whose powers it intended to curtail. However, it could have remained within the imperial household and set the standards which were to be pursued. In this sense, Prince Shōtoku paved the way for the eventual success of the Taika reforms. The era of Prince Shōtoku coincided with the period when the term Tennō *was first used to denote the reigning sovereign. The word* ten *corresponds to the Chinese* tian *or heaven, and* nō *to* huang *or ruler. Thus the term* Tennō was endowed with new sacerdotal and political significance. He was not a mere emperor who ruled by the mandate of heaven, but one who was coeval with heaven.

1 **The Seventeen Article Constitution, 604 A.D.**[4]   Summer, 4th month, 3rd day [12th year of Empress Suiko, 604 A.D.]. The Crown Prince personally drafted and promulgated a constitution consisting of seventeen articles, which are as follows:

I. Harmony is to be cherished,[5] and opposition for opposition's sake must be avoided as a matter of principle. Men are often influenced by partisan feelings, except a few sagacious ones. Hence there are some who disobey their lords and fathers, or who dispute with their neighboring villages. If those above are harmonious and those below are cordial, their discussion will be guided by a spirit of conciliation, and reason shall naturally prevail. There will be nothing that cannot be accomplished.

II. With all our heart, revere the three treasures.[6] The three treasures, consisting of Buddha, the Doctrine, and the Monastic Order, are the final refuge of the

---

[3]There is a controversy over the authorship of the Constitution, with some evidence pointing to the fact that Prince Shōtoku was not its real author. However, the document does reflect the *zeitgeist* which governed the reign of Prince Shōtoku, and it can be read in that context.

[4]*Nihon Shoki (Chronicles of Japan)* in *Kokushi Taikei (Major Compilation of National History)*, new and enlarged ed., vol. 1, no. 2 (Tokyo: Yoshikawa Kōbunkan, 1967), pp. 142–146.

[5]From the *Analects* of Confucius, I, 12.

[6]*Ratna-traya* in Sanskrit, referring to Buddha, *Dharma,* and *Sangha.* The *sangha* stands for the community of seekers united by their knowledge and right conduct.

four generated beings,[7] and are the supreme objects of worship in all countries. Can any man in any age ever fail to respect these teachings? Few men are utterly devoid of goodness, and men can be taught to follow the teachings. Unless they take refuge in the three treasures, there is no way of rectifying their misdeeds.

III. When an imperial command is given, obey it with reverence. The sovereign is likened to heaven, and his subjects (*yatsuko*) are likened to earth. With heaven providing the cover and earth supporting it, the four seasons proceed in orderly fashion, giving sustenance to all that which is in nature. If earth attempts to overtake the functions of heaven, it destroys everything. Therefore when the sovereign speaks, his subjects must listen; when the superior acts, the inferior must follow his examples. When an imperial command is given, carry it out with diligence. If there is no reverence shown to the imperial command, ruin will automatically result.

IV. The ministers (*machikimitachi*) and functionaries (*tsukasa tsukasa*) must act on the basis of decorum,[8] for the basis of governing the people consists of decorum. If the superiors do not behave with decorum, offenses will ensue. If the ministers behave with decorum, there will be no confusion about ranks. If the people behave with decorum, the nation will be governed well of its own.

V. Cast away your ravenous desire for food and abandon your covetousness for material possessions. If a suit is brought before you, render a clear-cut judgment. . . . Nowadays, those who are in the position of pronouncing judgment are motivated by making private gains, and as a rule, receive bribes. Thus the plaints of the rich are like a stone flung into water, while those of the poor are like water poured over a stone.[9] Under these circumstances, the poor will be denied recourses to justice, which constitutes a dereliction of duty of the ministers (*yatsuko*).

VI. Punish that which is evil and encourage that which is good. This is an excellent rule from antiquity. Do not conceal the good qualities of others, and always correct that which is evil which comes to your attention. Consider those flatterers and tricksters as constituting a superb weapon for the overthrow of the state, and a sharp sword for the destruction of people. Smooth-tongued adulators love to report to their superiors the errors of their inferiors; and to their inferiors, castigate the errors of their superiors. Men of this type lack loyalty to the sovereign and have no compassion for the people. They are the ones who can cause great civil disorders.

---

[7]*Catastro yonayah* is Sanskrit. The four processes of being born from eggs, from a womb, moisture-bred, or formed by metamorphosis (e.g., butterflies from caterpillars), hence, all creatures.

[8]The Chinese word *li* is variously translated decorum, courtesy, proper behavior ceremony, and gentlemanly conduct.

[9]The plaints of the rich meet with no resistance, while those of the poor have no efficacy.

VII. Every man must be given his clearly delineated responsibility. If a wise man is entrusted with office, the sound of praise arises. If a wicked man holds office, disturbances become frequent. . . . In all things, great or small, find the right man, and the country will be well governed. On all occasions, in an emergency or otherwise, seek out a wise man, which in itself is an enriching experience. In this manner, the state will be lasting and its sacerdotal functions will be free from danger. Therefore did the sage kings of old seek the man to fill the office, not the office for the sake of the man.

VIII. The ministers and functionaries must attend the court early in the morning and retire late. The business of the state must not be taken lightly. A full day is hardly enough to complete work, and if the attendance is late, emergencies cannot be met. If the officials retire early, the work cannot be completed.

IX. Good faith is the foundation of righteousness, and everything must be guided by good faith. The key to the success of the good and the failure of the bad can also be found in good faith. If the officials observe good faith with one another, everything can be accomplished. If they do not observe good faith, everything is bound to fail.

X. Discard wrath and anger from your heart and from your looks. Do not be offended when others differ with you. Everyone has his own mind, and each mind has its own leanings. Thus what is right with him is wrong with us, and what is right with us is wrong with him. We are not necessarily sages, and he is not necessarily a fool. We are all simply ordinary men, and none of us can set up a rule to determine the right from wrong. . . . Therefore, instead of giving way to anger as others do, let us fear our own mistakes. Even though we may have a point, let us follow the multitude and act like them.

XI. Observe clearly merit and demerit and assign reward and punishment accordingly. Nowadays, rewards are given in the absence of meritorious work, punishments without corresponding crimes. The ministers, who are in charge of public affairs, must therefore take upon themselves the task of administering a clear-cut system of rewards and punishments.[10]

XII. Provincial authorities (*mikotomochi*)[11] or local nobles (*kuni no miyatsuko*) are not permitted to levy exactions on the people. A country cannot have two sovereigns, nor the people two masters. The people of the whole country must have the sovereign as their only master. The officials who are given certain functions are all his subjects. Being the subjects of the sovereign, these officials have no more right than others to levy exactions on the people.

XIII. All persons entrusted with office must attend equally to their functions.

---

[10]Here is an indication of the influence of the Chinese legalist, Han Fei Zi.

[11]Other renditions for the term *mikotomochi* are *kuni no tsukasa* and *kokushi* (provincial governors). However, the system of provincial governors was not established during the time of Prince Shōtoku's regency. Thus, Article XII gives some credence to the theory that Prince Shōtoku was not the author of the "Constitution."

If absent from work due to illness or being sent on missions, and work for that period is neglected, on their return, they must perform their duties conscientiously by taking into account that which transpired before and during their absence. Do not permit lack of knowledge of the intervening period as an excuse to hinder effective performance of public affairs.

XIV. Ministers and functionaries are asked not to be envious of others. If we envy others, they in turn will envy us, and there is no limit to the evil that envy can cause us. We resent others when their intelligence is superior to ours, and we envy those who surpass us in talent. This is the reason why it takes five hundred years before we can meet a wise man, and in a thousand years it is still difficult to find one sage. If we cannot find wise men and sages, how can the country by governed?

XV. The way of a minister is to turn away from private motives and to uphold public good. Private motives breed resentment, and resentful feelings cause a man to act discordantly. If he fails to act in accord with others, he sacrifices public interests for the sake of his private feelings. When resentment arises, it goes counter to the existing order and breaks the law. Therefore it is said in the first article that superiors and inferiors must act in harmony. The purport is the same.

XVI. The people may be employed in forced labor only at seasonable times.[12] This is an excellent rule from antiquity. Employ the people in the winter months when they are at leisure. However, from spring to autumn, when they are engaged in agriculture or sericulture, do not employ them. Without their agricultural endeavor, there is no food, and without their sericulture, there is no clothing.

XVII. Major decisions must not be made by one person alone, but must be deliberated with many. On the other hand, it is not necessary to consult many people on minor questions. If important matters are not discussed fully there may always be fear of committing mistakes. A thorough discussion with many can prevent it and bring about a reasonable solution.

THE TAIKA REFORMS

After the death of Prince Shōtoku in 622, Japanese politics was dominated by the Soga clan. It was a period of inertia. The traditional uji *system and its attendant hereditary privileges were no longer suitable to the requirements of the new era. In 645, a palace coup was successfully executed by Prince Naka-no-ōe (who later reigned as Emperor Tenchi, 661–671) and Nakatomi-no Kamatari. The two then jointly embarked on the Taika reforms.*

The basic aims of the reforms were to bring about greater centralization and to enhance the power of the imperial court. To do so, the Japanese government

---

[12]From the *Analects* of Confucius, I, 5.

was to be reorganized on the model of the Tang, and the system of land tenure and taxation (in Japanese so, yō, chō) *then in force in China was to be adopted.*

It was a gigantic step forward in an attempt to nationalize land and to create a network of institutions subordinate to the central government. However, in practice, the provisions of the edict remained pious wishes, for the government lacked power to enforce them. Even if the edict had been implemented, it would not have meant demise of the strong clans. While their lands were nationalized, they were assigned official positions and given stipends which continued to sustain them economically. And based on this economic power, they would in later years once again erode the power of the central government.

2 **The Reform Edict of Taika, 646** A.D.[13] As soon as the New Year's ceremonies were over, the Emperor promulgated the following edict of reforms:

I. Let the following be abolished: the titles held by imperial princes to serfs granted by imperial decrees (*koshiro*); the titles to lands held directly by the imperial court (*miyake*); and private titles to lands and workers held by ministers and functionaries (*omi, muraji* and *tomo no miyatsuko*) of the court, by local nobles (*kuni no miyatsuko*), and by village chiefs (*mura no obito*). In lieu thereof, sustenance households[14] shall be granted to those of the rank of Daibu (Chief of a bureau or of a ward) and upwards on a scale corresponding to their positions. Cloth and silk stuffs shall be given to the lower officials and people, varying in value.

It is said that the duty of the Daibu is to govern the people. If they discharge their task diligently, the people will have trust in them. Therefore it is for the benefit of the people that the revenue of the Daibu shall be increased.[15]

II. For the first time, the capital shall be placed under an administrative system. In the metropolitan (or capital) region, governors (*kuni no tsukasa*) and prefects (*kōri no tsukasa*) shall be appointed. Barriers and outposts shall be erected, and guards and post horses for transportation and communication purposes shall be provided. Furthermore bell-tokens shall be made and mountains and rivers shall be regulated.[16]

One alderman (*osa*) shall be appointed for each ward (*bō* or *machi*) in the

---

[13]*Nihon Shoki, op. cit.*, pp. 224–226.

[14]The term "sustenance households" is a loose translation of the Japanese term *hehito* or *fuko*. It refers to a certain number of households which were assigned to the officials in place of the serfs taken from them. Generally taxes remitted by these households became personal income of the officials. The rights to these sustenance households were hereditary.

[15]The phrase is a verbatim quotation of a passage in the "Chronicle of Hui Di", *History of the Former Han Dynasty (Han Shu)*.

[16]Bell-tokens entitled their bearers to use post-horses which were kept for official use only. By the regulation of mountains and rivers is meant the posting of guards at ferries and mountain passes, thus delimiting the boundaries between provinces.

capital, and one chief alderman (*unakashi*) for four wards. The latter shall be responsible for maintaining the household registers and investigating criminal matters. The chief alderman shall be chosen from those men belonging to the wards, of unblemished character, strong and upright, who can discharge the duties of the time effectively. In principle, aldermen of rural villages (*ri*) or of city wards, shall be selected from ordinary subjects belonging to the villages or city wards, who are sincere, incorrupt and of strong disposition. If a right man cannot be found in a village or ward in question, a man from the adjoining village or ward may be appointed.

The metropolitan region shall include the area from the Yokogawa (river) in Nahari on the east, from (mount) Senoyama in Kii on the south, from Kushibuchi in Akashi on the west, and from (mount) Afusakayama in Sasanami in Ōmi on the north.

Districts are classified as greater, middle and lesser districts, with districts of forty villages constituting greater districts; of from four to thirty villages constituting middle districts; and of three or fewer villages constituting lesser districts. The prefects for these districts shall be chosen from local nobles (*kuni no miyatsuko*), of unblemished character, strong and upright, who can discharge the duties of the time effectively. They shall be appointed as prefects (*tairei*) and vice prefects (*shōrei*). Men of ability and intelligence, who are skilled in writing and arithmetic shall be appointed to assist them in the tasks of governance and book-keeping. . . .

III. It is hereby decreed that household registers, tax registers, and rules for allocation and redistribution of land shall be established.[17]

Each fifty households shall be constituted into a village (*ri*), and in each village there shall be appointed an alderman. He shall be responsible for the maintenance of the household registers, the assigning of sowing of crops and cultivation of mulberry trees, prevention of offenses, and requisitioning of taxes and forced labor. . . .

All rice-fields shall be measured by a unit called a *tan* which is thirty paces in length by twelve paces in breadth.[18] Ten *tan* make one *chō*. For each *tan*, the tax (*so* or *denso*) shall be two sheaves and two bundles of rice; for each *chō*, the tax shall be twenty-two sheaves of rice.

IV. Old taxes and forced labor shall be replaced by a system of commuted taxes based on [the size of] rice fields (*denchō*). These taxes shall consist of fine silk, coarse silk, raw silk, and floss silk, which are to be collected in accordance with what is produced in the locality. For each *chō* of rice field, the rate shall be one rod (i.e., 10 feet) of fine silk. For four *chō* of rice field, the rate shall be one piece of fine silk which is forty feet in length by two and a half feet in width. If

---

[17]The *denryō* (land regulations) says: "In distributing land, two *tan* shall be given to a man as his allotment land (*kubunden*), and two-thirds of that amount to a woman. . . ." See Chapter IV, Document I, for further information.
[18]One *tan* as existed then represented 0.294 acre.

coarse silk is substituted, the rate shall be two rods per *chō*, and one piece of the same length and width as the fine silk for every two *chō*. . . .

A separate household tax (*kochō*) shall also be levied, under which each household shall pay one rod and two feet of cloth, and a surtax consisting of salt and offerings. The latter may vary in accordance with what is produced in the locality. With regard to horses for public service, one horse of medium quality shall be contributed by every one hundred households, or one horse of superior quality by every two hundred households. If the horses have to be purchased, each household shall contribute one rod and two feet of cloth toward the purchase price. With regard to weapons, each person shall contribute a sword, armor, bow and arrows, a flag, and a drum.

Under the old system, one servant was supplied by every thirty households. This system shall be altered to allow every fifty households to furnish one servant to work for various officials. These fifty households shall be responsible for providing rations for one servant, by each household contributing two rods and two feet of cloth and five *masu*[19] of rice in lieu of service (*yō* or *chikara shiro*).

Waiting women in the palace shall be selected from among goodlooking sisters or daughters of officials of the rank of vice prefect or above. Every one hundred households shall be responsible for providing rations for one waiting woman. The cloth and rice supplied in lieu of service (*yō*) shall, in every respect, follow the same rule as for servants.

LAW AND ADMINISTRATION UNDER THE TAIHŌ-YŌRŌ CODE

In the first year of Taihō (701), a new ryō *(administrative code) and* ritsu *(penal code) were issued and became effective the following year. These are known as the Taihō laws, but they are not extant. A revision of these laws was made in the second year of Yōrō (718). This revised code is extant and is usually but incorrectly referred to as the Taihō code. In any event, the administrative system first laid down in the Taihō code in 701 became the theoretical basis of government until the mid-nineteenth century. During the years of civil and military dictators, administrative methods experienced certain changes, but all of them paid formal respect to this hierarchical system established in 701.*[20]

---

[19]Or *shō*. One *shō* equals 1.638 quarts.

[20]The editor is indebted to George B. Sansom, "Early Japanese Law and Administration, Parts I and II" in *TASJ*, 2d ser., vol. 9 (1932) and vol. 11 (1934) [Note: The letters *TASJ* stand for *Transactions of the Asiatic Society of Japan*. A number of translations rendered by members of the Asiatic Society of Japan are reproduced in this volume. They represent their pioneering labor of love for which this writer wishes to pay his special tribute.]; James I. Crump, Jr., " 'Borrowed' T'ang Titles and Officers in the Yōrō Code" in *Occasional Papers*, Center for Japanese Studies, University of Michigan, II (1952); and James I. Crump, Jr., "T'ang Penal Law in Early Japan," ibid., IV (1953).

Some observers contend that the promulgation of the Taihō or Yōrō code marked the climax of Japan's cultural borrowing from China. There was no doubt that the adoption of the administrative and penal codes was inspired by the example of Tang. Indeed some sections of the Yōrō code were taken verbatim from the Tang codes. However, these facts should not obscure us from realizing the Japanese ability for adapting alien institutions to meet Japanese requirements.

It seems clear that the framers of the Taihō-Yōrō codes knew that the Japanese problem lay in establishing an all-powerful imperial house. They were undoubtedly aware that there were many features of the Tang code and government which could be inimical to such a goal. Thus the Taihō-Yōrō codes rejected the "incorrigibly democratic" aspects of the Chinese bureaucracy which would have opened administrative positions to scholars irrespective of their lineage. In the end, the codes served to perpetuate the hereditary aristocracy and the imperial household in Japan.

There was greater incidence of emulation of the Tang code in ritsu, or the penal code. However, a penal code is the product of a given society which cannot be readily transplanted into another society. In many instances, the ritsu provisions were simply not enforced. On other occasions, the Japanese eliminated concepts which were not consistent with Japanese tradition. For example, the Tang concept of the illegality of marriage within the extended family or clan (persons of the same surname) was nowhere to be found in the Taihō-Yōrō codes.

Two basic questions emerge in the study of the Taihō-Yōrō codes. As stated by Sir George Sansom, "The first is the question of their origins. To what extend are they based on Chinese codes, to what extent are they adapted to meet Japanese requirements? The second is the question of their enforcement. To what extent were the codes in practice actually operative?"[21]

3a   The Administrative System, 718 A.D.   [Under the Yōrō code, all administration centered around the imperial family and the court. The central government consisted of two main divisions—the Department of Religion and the Department of Administration, with the former taking precedence over the latter. The following is an abridged translation of relevant portions of the Ryō no Gige, a commentary on the ryō undertaken in 833 to provide an authoritative version of the existing codes.[22] The passages enclosed in parentheses ( ) are original Japanese terms, and those enclosed in brackets [ ] are explanations provided by the translator, Sir George Sansom.]

[21]Sansom, op. cit., vol. 9, p. 118.
[22]Sansom, op. cit., vol. 11, pp. 94–77.

The Department of Religion (Jingi Kan)

The Minister (*Haku*) shall be responsible for the proper performance of [Shintō] religious ceremonies and keeping registers of all [Shintō] priests and corporations of attendants of shrines.[23] He thus has charge of all the traditional religious ceremonies connected with the accession and enthronement of the Sovereign; the festivals of First Fruits, Harvest, etc.; the placating of Spirits; oracles and divination [by priestesses and by means of the tortoise].

The Council of State (Daijō Kan)

The Chancellor (*Daijō diajin* or *Dajō daijin*) shall be a leader and pattern, setting an example to the Four Seas [i.e., to all people, including the barbarians]. He must order the State and deliberate upon the Way [the Confucian principles of virtue in a ruler]. He must harmonize *yin* and *yang*. If there is no suitable person, there shall be no appointment made.[24]

The Minister of the Left (*Sa daijin*) shall supervise all State business. [He is in effect the Prime Minister, responsible for the execution of policy and the proper discharge of the functions of the whole administrative body, since the Chancellor himself is the Supreme Counsellor, and personally transacts no official business. The *Sa daijin* was sometimes styled *Ichi no Kami*, which is equivalent to Prime Minister.]

The Minister of the Right (*U daijin*) is the counterpart of the Minister of the Left [but ranks after him].

The Great Counsellors (*Dainagon*) shall be four in number. They are to take part in deliberations upon all matters, to tender advice to the Sovereign and to convey his pronouncements. [In commentaries they are described as the "mouthpiece" of the Sovereign, but they were supposed not merely to transmit his words but to ensure that he spoke wise words and refrained from speaking unwise ones. They therefore sifted the Imperial utterances as well as examined memorials which were addressed to the Throne.]

The Minor Counsellors (*Shōnagon*) shall be three in number. They shall deal with minor matters concerning memorials and edicts, shall have charge of seals and tokens and the despatch of official correspondence. [The *Shōnagon* were trusted officials, generally of the 5th rank, and were at the same time Chamberlains. They kept the great Imperial Seal and the seal of the Council of State, and being responsible for the despatch of official communications to the provincial

---

[23]The important posts in this department were as a rule hereditary in such families as the Nakatomi and the Imbe. The *Haku* was at first a member of one of these clans, but later the office became hereditary in the Shirakawa family.

[24]In practice the post often remained unfilled, and the office tended to lose its importance as the custom of appointing regents grew.

governments, they also had custody of the seals and tokens by which the commands of the Sovereign or the orders of the Government were authenticated and transmitted by post-horse to their destinations. The staff of their office was as follows:]

Two Secretaries (*Dai geki*) to scrutinize the drafts of Imperial pronouncements and to draft memorials from the Council of State. [These were responsible permanent officials of the 7th, later the 6th rank, men skilled in composition and calligraphy. Their posts soon became hereditary in such families of Confucian scholars as the Kiyowara and Nakahara.]

Two Junior Secretaries (*Shō geki*).

Ten Scribes (*Shisho*) to copy documents and keep them in order.

The Controller of the Left (*Sadaiben*) controls the four Ministries (*shō*) of State:

Nakatsukasa (Ministry of Central Affairs). The Minister (*Kami*) is in constant attendance upon the Sovereign and advises him on matters of ceremonial and precedent. He scrutinizes the drafts of Imperial rescripts and edicts and transmits memorials to the Throne after examining them. He supervises the compilation of official chronicles; the keeping of lists of Court Ladies and palace women and the records of their services, promotions and ranks; the registers of population, land-tax (*so*) and labor-tax (*chō*) of all provinces; the registers of monks and nuns.

Shikibu (Ministry of Ceremonial). The Minister is to keep registers of officials, central and provincial; to review their services and recommend promotions, transfers, appointments and dismissals; to supervise their behavior at Court and to regulate their precedence at Court Ceremonies; to keep a record of their Court ranks and to recommend rewards for merit; to deal with the appointments and reception at Court of provincial officers; and to have charge of education and examination for government service.

Jibu (Ministry of Civil Administration). [It dealt with the ceremonial in its broader aspects, not as it affected officials alone. It was largely concerned with matters of ritual, genealogies and religious observances, and its functions were similar to the "Ministry of Rites" in China.] The Minister is to regulate family names [i.e., to scrutinize genealogies], succession [of persons holding the 5th rank and upward], marriages [of the same persons], auspicious omens [in their relation to funeral ceremonies, etc.], funeral rites, posthumous awards [of rank or gifts], national mourning, and the reception of foreign envoys.

Minbu (Ministry of Popular Affairs). [Its chief business was to supervise the people who were neither officials nor nobles, but plain producers.] The Minister is to be responsible for the registers of population; the labor tax; family obligations [i.e., exemptions from labor tax in deserving cases]; rewards for meritorious conduct; servants and slaves; bridges and roads, harbors, fences, bays, lakes, mountains, rivers, woods, and swamps, etc.; rice lands in all provinces. [The Ministry kept plans and records of these topographical features because the information was needed as a check upon tax returns and the transport of produce paid as tax. It was not directly responsible for the upkeep of roads, bridges, etc.]

The Controller of the Right (*U daiben*) controls the four Ministries of State:

Ryōbu (Ministry of War). The Minister is in charge of registers of military officers, both metropolitan and provincial; records of their services; transfers and promotions; records of their court ranks; registers of *hyōshi* [equivalent to non-commissioned officers]; court assemblies [annual assemblies at the capital of official delegates despatched by Provincial Governors to report on affairs in their provinces and to recommend promotions, rewards, etc., of civil and military officers serving under them]; rewards and emoluments; the allocation of troops, arms and equipment for war service and ceremonial; fortifications; beacons.

Gyōbu (Ministry of Justice). The Minister is to be responsible for the investigation and judgment of offenses; registers of free (*ryōmin*) and unfree (*senmin*) people [i.e., of the civil status of suitors and defendants]; imprisonment; claims for debt.

Ōkura (Ministry of the Treasury). The Minister is in charge of the receipt and issue of tax-goods (*chō*) from the provinces [usually textiles], coins, gold, silver, jewels, copper, iron, bones, horns and leather, furs and feathers, lacquer, hangings and curtains, weights and measures; the assessment of prices for sale and purchase; miscellaneous tribute goods.

Kunai (Ministry of the Imperial Household). The Minister is in charge of receipts and issues [by the bureaus and offices under him]; tax-goods (*chō*) from all provinces and miscellaneous tax-goods; tax-rice; official lands (*kanden*) [crown rice lands situated in the metropolitan region]; reports and orders regarding Imperial food-produce; delicacies from all quarters [i.e., tribute other than the prescribed taxes, and gifts of special foods from different localities].

3b The Law of Households (koryō)[25]

[Under the Yōrō code, the whole country was divided into provinces (*kuni*). Each of these provinces was placed under the jurisdiction of a provincial governor (*Kami*). In theory, he represented the throne, and combined all religions, civil, military, and judicial functions. The governor in turn was to be assisted by district officials. However, in practice, the provincial and district governments were regarded mainly as tax collecting agencies.

One of the means of collecting taxes was to maintain registers of people. The following excerpts are from the Law of Households which shows how these registers were kept. In reading the following passages, note the incidence of absconding by "free" people and measures adopted to prevent it, as well as frequent references to the family system].

1. A village (*ri*) is composed of fifty households, and over each village shall be placed a headman (*richō* or *mura no osa*). In mountainous, remote and sparsely populated regions the number may be fixed according to convenience.

---

[25]Sansom, *ibid.*, pp. 134–149.

5. The head of a household (*ko*) shall be the person who is head of the family. Households shall be divided into (1) taxable households and (2) exempt households, according as they comprise taxable or exempt members. The exempt categories, as stated in the *Ryō no gige*, are: (1) members of the Imperial Family; (2) persons of the 8th rank and upwards: (3) males of sixteen years and under; (4) certain persons "covered" by their relationship; (5) old people; (6) deformed and crippled people; (7) diseased people; (8) all female members of a household; and (9) servants and slaves.

6. The following classification of members of a household must be used:

Males and females up to the age of 3	infants
Males and females from 3 to 16	children
Males and females from 16 to 20	youth and girls
Males of 21 and upwards	able-bodied
Males of 61 and upwards	elders
Males of 66 and upwards	aged men

9. Households shall be formed into groups of five families, under the headship of one person who is responsible for the good conduct of the group. Members of the group must keep one another informed of the arrival and departure of guests from distant places and of their own journeys.[26]

10. When a household absconds, the group shall be responsible for its pursuit. If it cannot be brought back, it must be retained on the register for three years, during which period the group and the relatives of the absconders in the village are to be responsible for the cultivation of its allotment and for the payment of its tax [in kind and in labor]. After three years its allotment returns to the State. When a member of a household absconds, the household is responsible for his tax for six years, after which he may be removed from the register and his allotment reverts to the State.

18. The tax registers (*keichō*) must be compiled annually. Before the 30th day of the 6th month each year the metropolitan and provincial officers must demand returns from the head of each household, giving the year, the name of the household and a list of its members. The registers must be transmitted under joint seal to the Chancellor's Office (*daijōkan*) by the 30th of the 8th month.

19. The registers of population (*koseki*) must be compiled every six years, starting from the beginning of the 11th month and following the prescribed forms. There shall be one volume (i.e., a separate roll) for each village, and three copies of each volume, all marked with the name of the province, district, village, and the year. The work shall be completed by the last day of the 5th month. Two copies shall be sent to the Chancellor's Office and one copy retained in the province.

20. The registers of population and tax registers must contain particulars of

---

[26]The object of this article is to prevent taxable persons from absconding.

the age and capacity of the members of a household, viz. whether able-bodied, old, infirm, whether liable or exempt in respect of labor tax, whether entitled to servants, etc., and the provincial authorities must satisfy themselves by personal inspection that these particulars are correctly stated.

22. The registers of population must be kept for five periods (of six years).

23. In the sharing of inheritance (upon the decease of the head of a house) all property must be added together, namely servants, slaves, land, houses and other property, and shared out as follows:

The mother (being wife of the householder)	2 shares
The stepmother	2 shares
Children of the wife	2 shares
Children of concubines	1 share

A wife's property brought with her from her own family is not subject to sharing. If the brothers of the heir are dead, their shares go to their sons—i.e., the sons of a child by the wife receive 2 shares, the sons of a child by a concubine 1 share, divided up equally.[27]

24. Males may marry at the age of fifteen, females at the age of thirteen.

25. A woman before marriage must obtain the consent of her family, viz. paternal grandfather and grandmother, father and mother, uncles and aunts, cousins, etc.

26. When a marriage contract has been made it may be annulled if without proper reason the marriage does not take place within three months, or if one of the parties is detained in a foreign country and does not return for one year, or if one of the parties is convicted of a crime.

Even after a marriage has been completed, the wife may be permitted to marry again if the husband is detained abroad for five years when there is issue of the marriage or for three years when there is no issue, or if the husband has absconded and does not return for three years when there is issue or for two years when there is no issue.

28. The seven grounds for divorce of a wife by her husband are: (1) if she is childless (e.g., without a male child); (2) if she commits adultery; (3) if she disobeys her parents-in-law; (4) if she talks too much; (5) if she steals; (6) if she is jealous; and (7) if she has a bad disease. In all cases the husband must write a notice of divorce which must be signed jointly by the parents and near relatives. Those who cannot write must make their mark.

Even when there are grounds for divorce a wife will not be sent away in any one of the following three cases: (1) if she has maintained (the household) during the period of mourning for her parents-in-law during which time the husband

---

[27]It is not clear whether "children" here means only sons. From the text and the commentaries it would appear that daughters and concubines receive only a half share.

could not work; or (2) if since marriage the household has risen in status; or (3) if there is nobody to receive her (i.e., if there is no member of her family or other sponsor of the marriage to whom she can return). But these exceptions shall not apply if she has been guilty of a grave offense against piety or of adultery or has a bad disease.

33. The governor of a province shall once a year make a tour of his territory, when he shall take note of local customs; enquire after the health of persons of one hundred years of age; examine the cases of persons detained in prison, and put right any injustices; carefully inspect the work of administration and law, deal with the complaints of the people; warmly encourage the five teachings and promote agriculture.[28]

If he learns of the existence in a district of persons of great learning or of especially good character (e.g., models of filial piety, loyalty, integrity, generosity, etc.) he shall recommend them for reward. If there are persons of evil or disorderly conduct he shall examine and correct them.

The governor must carefully examine the conditions in each district, and judge the merit of the district officials by the state of the fields, the number of criminal cases, etc. He must report on their suitability to the Central Government, but in cases of urgency, he should dismiss an offending district officer forthwith.

45. When owing to flood, drought or pests there threatens to be a failure of the harvest, the provincial or district authorities shall, if there is a shortage of supplies and relief is to be given, upon examinations of the facts, act upon their own discretion and report to the Council of State.

HISTORY AS A MEANS OF SOLIDIFYING THE IMPERIAL POWER

The Jinshin rebellion occurred in 672, one year after the death of Emperor Tenchi, and pitted Prince Ōama, Tenchi's brother, and Prince Ōtomo, Tenchi's son, against each other. (For a triangular love affair between Tenchi, Prince Ōama, and Princess Nukada, see Document 5.) The rebellion ended in the triumph of Prince Ōama who then became Emperor Temmu (r. 673–686). One of the measures that Temmu adopted was to order the compilation of a historical work to remedy errors "handed down by the various houses." Indirectly it was intended to bolster Temmu's claim to "legitimacy" after the bloody rebellion. The work was not completed during his reign but had to await the reign of Empress Gemmei in 712 in what was to become known as the Kojiki *(Records of Ancient Matters).*

---

[28]The five teachings are the five rules of pious duty, viz., the duty of a father—justice; of a mother—affection; of an elder brother—friendship; of a younger brother—respect; of a child—obedience.

The Kojiki *is divided into three volumes, with the first volume recording the age of gods, or Japan's mythological past, and the second and third volumes providing accounts of the reigns of legendary Emperor Jimmu through Empress Suiko (r. 592–628). Unlike the* Nihon Shoki, *which was compiled as an official history in the Chinese style and completed in 720, the* Kojiki *was essentially a narrative history based on many old tales preserved through oral transmission. As a historical record it may be less reliable than the* Nihon Shoki, *but is a valuable gold mine for the study of Japanese folklore.*

The preface reproduced below takes the form of a memorial to the throne and explains the reasons for the compilation of the work and of the difficulties encountered by the compiler. By 712, Japan had yet to develop her own writing system, and every indigenous tale had to be transcribed in Chinese characters, either ideographically or phonetically.

While the text of the Kojiki *itself does not cover the reign of Emperor Temmu, the preface freely refers to his reign with adulatory terms. The* Kojiki *as a work was an attempt to glorify the imperial line by asserting its divine descent. At the same time, the preface endowed in Temmu all the virtues of a sage-king of Confucian China. Thus by combining indigenous Japanese myths with Confucian virtues, the imperial line could make a newer and bolder claim to its supremacy. History was made a handmaiden of the imperial power, and there was no historian of the calibre and independence of Sima Qian[29] to emerge in Japan.*

4 Preface to Kojiki, 712 A.D.[30] I, Yasumaro, do say:

When the primeval matter had congealed but breath and form had not yet appeared, there were no names and no action. Who can know its form? However, when heaven and earth were first divided, the three deities became the first of all creation. The Male and Female here began, and the two spirits (Izanagi and Izanami) were the ancestors of all creation. . . .

Thus, though the primeval beginnings be distant and dim, yet by the ancient teachings do we know the time when the lands were conceived and the islands born; though the origins be vague and indistinct, yet by relying upon the sages of antiquity do we perceive the age when the deities were born and men were made to stand. . . .

The borders were determined and the lands were developed during the reign of Emperor Seimu, and the titles were corrected and the clan names selected during the rule of Emperor Ingyō. Although each reign differed in the degree of swiftness or slowness, and each was not the same in refinement and simplicity;

---

[29]Author of the *Shi ji,* or *Historical Records,* died about 85 B.C., during the former Han dynasty.

[30]Adapted from Donald L. Philippi, *Kojiki* (Tokyo: Tokyo University Press, 1969), pp. 37–44.

yet there was not one [ruler] who did not by meditating upon antiquity straighten manners which had collapsed, and who did not by comparing the present with antiquity strengthen morals and teachings verging on extinction.

Coming now to the reign of Emperor Temmu: Already as latent dragon he embodied the royal qualities, and the repeated thunderpeals responded to the times.[31] Hearing the song in a dream, he knew that he was to receive the Dignity. But the time of Heaven had not yet come, and cicada-like he shed his wrappings in the southern mountains. As popular support grew for his cause, he walked tiger-like in the eastern lands.[32] The imperial chariot proceeded with quick willingness, crossing over the mountains and rivers. The six regiments shook like thunder, and the three armies moved like lightning. The spears and javelins revealed their might, and the fierce warriors rose up like smoke. The crimson banners gleamed upon the weapons, and the treacherous band collapsed like tiles. Before a fortnight had elapsed, the foul vapors had been purified. Thus they released the cattle and rested the steeds, and returned peacefully to the capital. Furling the banners and putting away the halberds, they remained singing and dancing in the city.

As the star rested in the region of the Cock [673 A.D.], in the second month, in the great palace of Kiyomihara he ascended the throne and assumed the Heavenly Dignity. In the Way he excelled the Yellow Emperor; in Virtue he surpassed the King of Zhou.[33] Grasping the regalia, he ruled the six directions; gaining the Heavenly Lineage, he embraced the eight corners. Adhering to the Two Essences, he put the five elements in right order.[34] He set forth profound principles to implant good practices, and he proposed noble manners to issue throughout the land. Not only this, his wisdom was vast as the sea, searching out antiquity; his mind was bright as a mirror, clearly beholding former ages.

Whereupon, the Emperor said:

"I hear that the Imperial Chronicles (*Teiki*) and Fundamental Dicta (*Honji*) handed down by the various houses have come to differ from the truth and that many falsehoods have been added to them. If these errors are not remedied at this time, their meaning will be lost before many years have passed. This is the

---

[31] Emperor Temmu reigned from 673–686 after his victory in the Jinshin rebellion of 672 against Prince Ōtomo. "Latent dragon" is a Chinese expression for the "crown prince," and the "repeated thunderpeals" are signals calling him to the throne. The following paragraphs show an elaborate attempt to justify Temmu's accession and to glorify his reign.

[32] The future Emperor Temmu, shortly before the death of the preceding Emperor Tenchi, renounced the world (i.e., shed cicada-like his worldly adornments) and retired to Mount Yoshino for purely tactical reasons. He went to the eastern part of the kingdom and rebelled against Prince Ōtomo, Tenchi's son and chosen successor, in 672.

[33] The Yellow Emperor was a legendary Chinese ruler. The king of Zhou may refer either to King Wen or Wu, Confucius' idealized rulers of Zhou.

[34] The Two Essences here refer to the *yin* and *yang*. The five elements are water, fire, wood, metal, and earth.

framework of the state, the great foundation of the imperial influence. Therefore, recording the Imperial Chronicles and examining the Ancient Dicta (*Kuji*), discarding the mistaken and establishing the true, I desire to hand them on to later generations."

At that time there was a court attendant whose surname was Hieda and his given name Are. He was twenty-eight years old. He possessed such great native intelligence that he could repeat orally whatever met his eye, and whatever struck his ears was indelibly impressed in his heart. Then an imperial command was given to Are to learn the Imperial Sun-Lineage and Ancient Dicta of Former Ages. However, the times went on and the reign changed before this project was accomplished.

Prostrate, I consider how Her Imperial Majesty [Empress Gemmei, r. 707–715], gaining the One [i.e., the throne], illumines the Universe; being in communion with the Three [i.e., heaven, earth, and man], nurtures the populace. . . .

Hereupon, appalled at the mistakes in the Ancient Dicta, she determined to correct the corruptions in the Imperial Chronicles. On the eighteenth day of the ninth month of the fourth year of Wadō [711 A.D.], an imperial command was given to me, Yasumaro, to record and present the Ancient Dicta learned by imperial command by Hieda no Are. Reverently, in accordance with the imperial will, I chose and took them up in great detail. However, during the times of antiquity, both words and meanings were unsophisticated, and it was difficult to reduce the sentences and phrases to writing. If expressed completely in ideographic writings, the words will not correspond exactly with the meaning, and if written entirely phonetically, the account will be much longer.[35] For this reason, at times ideographic and phonetic writings have been used in combination in the same phrase, and at times the whole matter has been recorded ideographically. Thus, when the purport is difficult to gather, a note has been added to make it clear; but when the meaning is easy to understand, no note is given. . . .

In general, the account begins with the beginning of heaven and earth and ends with the reign of Empress Suiko. . . .

SONGS OF MYRIAD LEAVES

The Manyōshū *is the oldest anthology of Japanese poetry, and was compiled in the mid-eighth century. It contains about 4,500 poems including the typical thirty-one syllable* waka, *or* tanka *(short poems),* chōka *(long poems),* sedōka *(5, 7, 7; 5, 7, 7 syllables) and other seldom-used poetical forms. Its poems are less stylized than those in the later anthologies. Unlike the melancholy air of the*

---

[35]If translated entirely into literary Chinese, there will be discrepancies between the ideographic text and the original traditions; if written entirely phonetically, a much greater number of ideographs will be required to express the same meaning.

poems of later periods, the Manyō *poems are known for their directness and unaffected air. The freedom of expression in the* Manyōshū *is seldom matched, and human passions are often depicted spontaneously and even impulsively. Thus the human pathos, emotions and travails which greeted the princes and common men alike during the period of great political changes, witnessed in this chapter, are recaptured in the poems of the* Manyōshū. *The following selections must be read with this in mind. (The explanatory notes between the poems are supplied by the editor.)*

5   From the Manyōshū[36]   *Adulation for the Emperor:* During her reign, Empress Jitō (r. 686–697) made thirty-one imperial visits (*kunimi*) to different parts of the land. They were conducted to survey the general state of affairs, agricultural production, or matters relating to the subjugation of alien or local chieftains. The spirit of one of such trips was captured by Kakimoto no Hitomaro.

> Our great Sovereign, a goddess,
> Of her sacred will
> Has reared a towering palace
> On Yoshinu's shore,
> Encircled by its rapids;
> And, climbing, she surveys the land.
> The overlapping mountains,
> Rising like green walls,
> Offer the blossoms in spring,
> And with autumn, show their tinted leaves,
> As godly tributes to the Throne.
> The god of the Yū River, to provide the royal table,
> Holds the cormorant-fishing
> In its upper shallows,
> And sinks the fishing-nets
> In the lower stream.
>
> Thus the mountains and the river
> Serve our Sovereign, one in will;
> It is truly the reign of a divinity.
>
> Envoy
>
> The mountains and the waters
> Serve our Sovereign, one in will;

---

[36]Except as noted, poems are selected from Nippon Gakujutsu Shinkōkai, *The Manyōshū* (Tokyo: Iwanami Shoten, 1940), pp. 5, 11, 19, 21–22, 29, 47, 172–174, 200, 205–207.

> And she, a goddess, is out on her pleasure-barge
> Upon the foaming rapids.

On the occasion of the Empress climbing the Thunder Hill, Hitomaro also composed the following song of adulation:

> Lo, our great Sovereign, a goddess,
> Tarries on the Thunder
> In the clouds of heaven!

Political Intrigues: Empress Jitō ascended the throne after the death of her husband, Emperor Temmu, to insure succession by her grandson. This was necessitated by the untimely death in 689 of her son, Prince Kusakabe. Prior to that, in order to make her own son the Crown Prince, the Empress placed a false charge of rebellion against Prince Ōtsu, forcing him to commit suicide. The popular, urbane and gifted prince was a son of Emperor Temmu by another consort, and was a leading contender for the throne. The following poems composed by his sister, Princess Ōku, Priestess of the Shrine of Ise, poignantly mirror the sorrow of parting for the one who embarked on a journey toward a certain death.

> To speed my brother
> Parting for Yamato,
> In the deep of night I stood
> Till wet with the dew of dawn.

> The lonely autumn mountains
> Are hard to pass over
> Even when two go together—
> How does my brother cross them all alone!

And when she arrived in the capital, after his death:

> Would that I had stayed
> In the land of Ise
> Of the Divine Wind.
> Why have I come
> Now that he is dead!

> Now that he is no more—
> My dear brother—
> Whom I so longed to see,
> Why have I come,
> Despite the tired horses!

To the aggrieved sister, Prince Ōtsu's last song:

> Today, taking my last sight of the mallards
> Crying on the pond of Iware,
> Must I vanish into the clouds!

must have served as a reminder of the tender moments in the tragic life of the Prince, including the love he felt toward one Lady Ishikawa:

> Waiting for you,
> In the dripping dew of the hill
> I stood, —weary and wet
> With the dripping dew of the hill.—
>
> > By the Prince.

> Would I have been, beloved,
> The dripping dew of the hill,
> That wetted you
> While for me you waited.—
>
> > By the Lady.

Love Songs: The plain of Yamato with its capitals of Asuka, Fujiwara, and Nara, and with Mt. Kagu, Mt. Unebi, and Mt. Miminashi surrounding it, provided the ground for many passionate love affairs and intrigues. Emperor Tenchi (r. 661–672) likened his love for one Princess Nukada, his brother's consort, to the triangular love affairs of the three hills of Yamato:

> Mount Kagu strove with Mount Miminashi
> For the love of Mount Unebi.
> Such is love since the age of the gods;
> As it was thus in the early days,
> So people strive for spouses even now.

Eventually Princess Nukada became a consort of Emperor Tenchi. One day when she was on an imperial excursion for collecting wild flowers, a man approached waving his sleeves to gain recognition. It was her former beau, Prince Ōama (Emperor Temmu, r. 673–686):

> Going through the fields of wild flowers,
> The field reserved for the party of His Majesty.
> Has not the field ranger seen it?
> The waving of the sleeves of my Prince![37]

---

[37]This and the following poems are translated by the editor.

The gazing eyes of the two met and he sang in response:

> My love, resplendent in color and scent,
> Must I refrain from loving thee,
> Because thou art no longer mine?

No longer could she return to Prince Ōama; she sadly discovered that the Emperor's affection was showered upon other consorts:

> While waiting for you,
> My heart is filled with longing
> The autumn wind blows—
> As if it were you—
> Swaying the bamboo blinds of my door.

Poverty: The *Manyōshū* is rich in the works of common men and reflects the conditions of those suffering people. The following "song of poverty" is by Yamanoue no Okura:

> On the night when the rain beats,
> Driven by the wind,
> On the night when the snowflakes mingle
> With the sleety rain,
> I feel so helplessly cold.
> I nibble at a lump of salt,
> Sip the hot, oft-diluted dregs of *sake:*
> And coughing, sniffing,
> And stroking my scanty beard,
> I say in my pride,
> "There's none worthy, save I!"
> But I shiver still with cold.
> I pull up my hempen bedclothes,
> Wear what few sleeveless clothes I have,
> But cold and bitter is the night!
> As for those poorer than myself,
> Their parents must be cold and hungry,
> Their wives and children beg and cry.
> Then, how do you struggle through life?
> Wide as they call the heaven and earth,
> For me they have shrunk quite small;
> Bright though they call the sun and moon,
> They never shine for me.
> Is it the same with all men,

Or for me alone?
By rare chance I was born a man
And no meaner than my fellows,
But, wearing unwadded sleeveless clothes
In tatters, like weeds waving in the sea,
Hanging from my shoulders,
And under the sunken roofs,
Within the leaning walls.
Here I lie on straw
Spread on bare earth,
With my parents at my pillow,
My wife and children at my feet,
All huddled in grief and tears.
No fire sends up smoke
At the cooking-place,
And in the cauldron
A spider spins its web.
With not a grain to cook,
We moan like the "night-thrush."
Then, "to cut," as the saying is,
"The ends of what is already too short,"
The village headman comes,
With rod in hand, to our sleeping-place.

Envoy

Nothing but pain and shame in this world of men,
But I cannot fly away,
Wanting the wings of a bird.

Songs of Frontier Guards: As a means of solidifying its power over the distant areas, the Yamato Court sent frontier guards (*sakimori*) to these areas.[38]

The frontier guards of various provinces
Having assembled, went on board ships
When I see their parting
There is no way of my escaping.

Whose husbands are they
Going away as frontier guards?
I gaze at the one who asks with envy
My heart is filled with sorrowful thoughts.

---

[38]These four poems are translated by the editor.

Receiving the awe-inspiring imperial command
When the morrow comes
We'll have to sleep with the reeds
Our wives not being there.

Gentle breezes drifting from my hometown
But no one brings news of my wife
Alas I am alone!

The frontier guards' commander, Ōtomo no Yakamochi (d. 785), was generally credited with compiling the *Manyōshū*. He was at his best when he exhorted
his men to acquire the values of loyalty and dedication, showing at the same time
his sympathetic understanding of their sacrifices. The following representative
poem of his symbolizes the end of the glorious *Manyō* era.

Our Sovereign's far-off court
Is Tsukushi, the isle of unknown fires;[39]
It is the citadel defending
Her empire against the foreign enemy.

Therefore, though all the provinces she rules
Are full of men without number,
Those of the Eastland, as fierce fighters
Who, going forth to battle, never turn back,
Are for their valour rewarded;
To them the imperial word is given.—

Upon which you go, counting the weary days,
Away from the sight of your mother,
Away from your young wife's embrace.
From Port Naniwa of wind-blown reeds
Your stately ship, many-oared,
With her crew ranged in the morning calm
And with her oars bent against the evening tide,
Sail column-wise with others.

"May you, ploughing your way through the waves,
Arrive safely in good time;

[39]The surface of the sea off the coast of the province of Chikugo sometimes appears as
though illuminated at night—a phenomenon which remains still unexplained. Hence,
shiranuhi (unknown fires) is used as a pillow word for Tsukushi, of which the province
forms a part.

And in obedience to the imperial command
Serve with a manly heart,
Passing from garrison to garrison;[40]
And when your duty is done, may you return
In happiness and health!"

So she prays,

Putting the sacred wine-jar at her bedside.
Pining and waiting for you these long days,
And her black hair spread out—[41]
Your sweet young wife!

Envoys

When the soldier-husband went forth
Carrying a quiver on his shoulder,
How bitterly she must have wailed—
His wife so loath to part!

How sad was the parting
Of the Eastlander from his wife—
He brooding on the long years
Of separation!

BUDDHISM AS PROTECTOR OF THE NATION

Buddhism came to Japan in 552 A.D. (or 538), and contributed to the establishment of new national institutions and to the development of a new set of values. Its images, paintings and psalmody were beautiful and overpowering, bridging the distance between this world and the other world. They seemed to contain magical powers far more potent than those found in the liturgies of the indigenous Shintō cult.

The power of Buddhism was not overlooked by the ruling sovereigns. For example, after the Jinshin rebellion, Emperor Temmu periodically decreed observance of Buddhist practices and payment of stipends to Buddhist monasteries (Document 6), obviously in an attempt to acquire merits and to achieve peace and harmony in his realm.

The most popular Buddhist sutra in Japan through the Nara period was the

---

[40]The frontier guards posted at one garrison were shifted to another at the end of each season.

[41]A form of magic to ensure the safe return of an absent person.

Sutra of the Golden Light *(Document 7). It claimed that if the sutra were studied diligently, the Four Deva Kings would come to defend the country from calamities and from pestilence. The scripture was presumed to have the power of protecting the state, and could provide rules for administration. In 741 Emperor Shōmu ordered that provincial monasteries and nunneries be established throughout the country, and provided sustenance households for them (Document 8). He was the same emperor who erected the statue of Roshana Buddha and built the Tōdaiji (temple). The new faith was well provided for, and in return "protected" the nation.*

The idea that Buddhism could protect the nation was not created in Japan, but its origin can be traced to the Buddhism of the northern dynasties in China. Its application in Japan was both an act of faith and a shrewd political move. The monasteries and nunneries became the outposts for the influence of the imperial power. The imperial court, which lacked physical power to gain allegiance from remote provinces, was able to bring the remote provinces securely under its fold through the moral suasion provided by the newly found faith.

There is no doubt that the acceptance of Buddhism before and during the Nara period was motivated mainly by a desire for greater material and political benefits and there was very little spiritual quest. However, at the same time, Buddhism was also able to serve as a "magic garden" to stir Japanese imagination for greater creativity, in architecture, sculpture, and literature.

6 **Temmu's Propagation of Buddhism, 676–685** A.D.[42]   On this day [Autumn, eighth month, 17th day, fifth year of the reign of Temmu, or 676], the Emperor ordered all the provinces to release living things.

Winter, eleventh month, 20th day. Messengers were sent to all parts of the country to expound the *Sutra of the Golden Light* and the *Ninnō Sutra.*[43]

Summer, fifth month, 1st day [680]. By the imperial command, a gift of varying amount consisting of coarse silk, floss silk, raw silk, and cloth was made to each of the twenty-four temples located within the capital.

The expounding of the *Sutra of the Golden Light* was begun this day in the imperial palace and in the temples.

Winter, eleventh month, 12th day. The Empress was taken ill. The Emperor in praying for her recovery made a vow on her behalf, and began the erection of the

---

[42]*Nihon Shoki*, op. cit., pp. 342, 343, 353, 355.

[43]*Karunikaraja-prajnaparamita Sutra* (or *Sutra of the Benevolent Kings*). In this sutra the Buddha explained to King Prasenajit and fifteen other benevolent kings how they could protect their countries against all kinds of calamities by means of the divine power of the Great Bodhisattvas of the Five Quarters. (See M. W. de Visser, *Ancient Buddhism in Japan*, vol. 1 (Leiden: E. J. Brill, 1935), pp. 12–13.

Yakushiji.[44] He ordered the ordination of one hundred persons to enter the Buddhist priesthood. As a result the Empress recovered and an amnesty was proclaimed.

Spring, third month, 27th day [685]. The Emperor decreed that every household in every province should erect a family Buddhist shrine in which to place an image of Buddha along with Buddhist sutras. These shrines were to be worshipped and offerings of food were to be made to them.

7   Sutra of the Golden Light of the Most Excellent Kings[46]   At this time,

the Four Deva Kings[47] and others in unison replied to the most Gracious Lord: "Fitting indeed! If there are kings who propagate and study this precious *Sutra of the Golden Light*, we the Four Deva Kings shall come to protect them always, and be with them at all times. Whatever calamities may befall or curses cast upon them, we the Four Deva Kings shall extinguish them. Eradicating all fears and pestilence from among them, we shall increase their longevity, and let them share in the propitious happiness of heaven. Their hearts' desires shall be fulfilled and there shall be an outpouring of joy. We shall also make all soldiers in their countries to become strong. . . ."

Buddha replied and said: "If a king studies this *Sutra of the Golden Light* and lets its knowledge spread throughout his country, there will be four kinds of benefits for his ministers and functionaries. The four are as follows: First, the ministers and functionaries will become friendly, respectful and loving toward each other. Second, they will become cherished ones in the heart of the king and will be revered by priests, brahmans, large countries and small countries alike. Third, they will respect the law, pay less attention to material wealth, and seek no worldly gains. And their good names shall be known everywhere and venerated by the people. Fourth, their lives shall be prolonged and become peaceful and joyful. These are then called the four benefits. If there is a country where this sutra is preached, priests and brahmans shall gain four kinds of victories. The four are as follows: First, they will not be in want of clothing, food, sleeping quarters, and medicine. Second, they will all gain peace of mind, and meditate and study the sutra. Third, they will find a good place of abode by the mountains and trees. Fourth, they will all become content according to their hearts' desires.

---

[44]Dedicated to Yakushi Nyorai (Sansk. Bhechadjyaguru), the teacher of medicine. This temple was completed in 697 but later moved to a site near Nara. Today it still serves as the main temple for the Hossō sect.

[45]*Bussha* or *miyaraka*. It is probably similar to the present-day *butsudan* (household Buddhist shrine).

[46]In Sanskrit, *Suvarna-prabha-sottama-raja Sutra*. From *Shōwa Shinsan Kokuyaku Daizokyō (Compendium of Major Buddhist Sutras Translated into Japanese)*, vol. 4 of Sutras (Tokyo: Tōhōshoin, 1928), pp. 368–369.

[47]The Four Deva Kings are Vaisravana, Dhartarastra, Virudhaka and Virupaksa. All of them are given the task of protecting Buddhist nations.

These are then, called the four victories. If there is a country where this sutra is taught, all the people will become happy and prosperous. There will be no more pestilence, and all the business houses will gain many riches in their business transactions, and realize the dream of happiness and prosperity. These are called various merits and benefits."

At this point, the Four Deva Kings and a host of others asked Buddha: "Most Gracious Lord! These deep meanings contained in the sutra, if they exist, we must all know. There are thirty-seven types of laws to aid us in attaining wisdom given by the Tathāgata (he who has thus come to lead the path, another name for Buddha) which have been in existence and have not been extinguished. If this sutra is extinguished or destroyed, then the Sacred Law may also be extinguished."

Buddha answered, saying: "Well spoken, well spoken, I therefore beseech all of you good men to have diligence in studying, upholding, meditating, and mastering every phrase, every sentence, every paragraph and every volume of this *Sutra of the Golden Light*. And for the sake of all sentient beings, preach and spread its teachings. If you do so, you shall have peace and joy in long nights, and acquire unlimited merits."

8   Erection of Provincial Temples[48]   In the thirteenth year of Tempyō [741], 24th day of the third month, the Emperor [Shōmu] decreed, saying: "We, even though lacking in virtue, have been entrusted with the responsibilities of governing the country. We have not been able to spread our beneficent rule, and day and night We are besieged with the feeling of inadequacies. Of old, enlightened kings carried on the work of former sovereigns, and brought peace to the nation and joy to the people. They eradicated calamities and brought about happiness. What was the secret behind their beneficent rule which enabled them to attain these goals? Lately, annual grain crops have not been abundant, and we have been visited by pestilence frequently. Remorse and trepidation are mixed in Our mind, and We work diligently to atone for Our sins.

"Seeking widely to benefit all sentient beings, and to gain happiness for all uniformly, We sent messengers in past years on fast horses to shrines everywhere in our country and increased their stipends. Last year We ordered that every province should erect one golden image of Buddha Skakamuni, sixteen feet in height, and write out one copy of the *Daihannyakyō*.[49]

---

[48]From vol. 14 of the *Shoku Nihongi*, in *Kokushi Taikei, op. cit.*, vol. 2, pp. 163–164.

[49]*Mahaprajnaparamita Sutra* (or *Sutra of Great Wisdom*), translated into Chinese in six hundred volumes by the famed Tang monk, Xuan Zang between 600 and 663. The sutra teaches that all objects, differing in nature one from the other, are homogeneous with the absolute reality, and vice versa. The distinction between the phenomenal and noumenal worlds is but subjective; they are in fact of our own making, the product of our own mind. The sutra is believed to have the power of setting men free from all evils. (See Harper H. Coats and Ryugaku Ishizuka, *Hōnen, the Buddhist Saint: His Life and Teaching* (Kyoto: Chionin, 1925), pp. 269–270.)

"From the past spring until the harvest time in the fall, the wind and rain were orderly and the five crops grew abundantly. It happened in this manner, as if the spirit, the seer, has answered Our supplications, recognizing Our sincerity. With fear and trembling, and without engaging in Our own speculations. We have consulted the scriptures. It is said that in the countries where the *Sutra of the Golden Light* was explained, read and propagated devoutly, the Four Deva Kings would always come to protect them. Thus all calamities would be eradicated and fear and pestilence would be extinguished. The hearts' desires would be fulfilled, and there would be continuous joy.

"Thus We command that each of the provinces shall with reverence erect a seven-storied pagoda, and write out a copy each of the *Sutra of the Golden Light* and the *Sutra of the Lotus of the Wonderful Law*.[50] We also plan to make special copies of the *Sutra of the Golden Light* in golden characters, and deposit a copy in each of the pagodas. It is Our desire that the Sacred Law prosper, and be transmitted eternally, coeval with heaven and earth. The benefit of the protection of the Sacred Law encompasses both this world and the world on the other shore. It must be made known to all. The building of a temple is, at the same time, the finest decoration for the state. Thus a good location must be found, which must be made permanent. If the location is too near a population center, unwittingly it may acquire the undesirable stench. If it is too far away from a population center, unwittingly it may make the gathering of the people a burdensome chore.

"Ye provincial governors (*kuni no tsukasa*) must perform your duties diligently, and make yourselves pure. Let the heaven know of your sincerity that it may abide by you and protect you. Let the people near and afar know Our august wishes."

---

[50]See Chapter III, Document 1.

The Early Heian Period

Near the end of the Nara period, the monk Dōkyō made an abortive attempt to usurp the throne. It was symptomatic of the corruption of Buddhism and of its political power, and the lesson was not lost to the later rulers of Japan. Emperor Kammu moved the capital from Nara first to Nagaoka (784) and then to Heian (the present-day Kyoto) in 794. He did so, at least in part, to escape the corrosive influence of the six Buddhist sects of Nara. In addition, he closely scrutinized commendation to or purchase of lands by the temples. On a more positive side, he permitted and even encouraged monks to study in mountains and forests, away from established Buddhist centers.

These measures created a climate for the growth of a new type of Buddhism, and two new faces responded to the challenge. The first was Saichō, who was born in 767. He was ordained in 785 at the Tōdaiji in Nara, but instead of remaining in that Buddhist center, he withdrew to Mt. Hiei. In 804, he accompanied the Japanese embassy to Tang China and remained there for eight months. He studied the scriptures, organization of monasteries, methods of instruction and Buddhism's relations to the secular power. On his return he received the imperial assent to establish a new Tendai sect in Japan which was based on the teachings of the *Lotus Sutra* (Document 1).

One of the crowning achievements of Saichō was to have the Imperial Court grant Mt. Hiei the right to ordain its own priests, which came shortly after Saichō's death in 822. As a young man, Saichō questioned the wisdom of ordaining only those people who were "not prisoners, debtors or slaves," which seemed to imply inequality of men before Buddha as well as the over-pervasive power of the state. By obtaining the power to ordain its own priests, Mt. Hiei was able to challenge the authority of the six Nara sects and to ascertain a certain measure of independence from the temporal power of the state.

Kūkai (774–835) was another of the most notable Buddhist masters of this age. In the year 804, he was selected to accompany the Embassy to Tang, the same Embassy to which Saichō was also attached. He remained in China for three years. While in China, he met Huiguo (746–805), the seventh patriarch of the True Words (*Shingon* in Japanese, or *Mantrayana* in Sanskrit) sect, who treated him as his chosen disciple. After his return, he began the Shingon sect which prospered under the patronage of Emperors Heizei and Saga.

According to Kūkai, man can attain enlightenment and Buddhahood in his earthly form, in the body received from the parents (*sokushin jōbutsu*), and the surest way for such enlightenment is through the esoteric teachings of Shingon. In 830, he completed a treatise entitled *Ten Stages of the Religious Consciousness of the Esoteric Mandara*, in which he expounded the essence of the Shingon teachings.

By stressing that all sentient beings can attain Buddhahood, and that man can attain Buddhahood in his earthly form, the two new sects paved the way for the later rise of popular Buddhist sects in which universal enlightenment was assured. However, by insisting on the transmission of secret doctrines only to the initiated, they severely limited the application of their universalistic tendencies. While claiming independence from the temporal power, the two new sects did not hesitate to assert their role of "protecting" the state, and in return received patronage from the court. Thus, the two sects still remained essentially the religion of the aristocratic society.

Eclectic tendencies could be detected in both of these new sects, and in the case of Tendai, the teachings of Shingon always constituted part of its doctrine. The attraction of Shingon came from its aesthetic quality, as shown in its elaborate rituals of the transmission of the law, and from its ability to import the Tang culture, including the scriptures and artifacts. The headquarters of the two sects—Mt. Hiei and Mt. Koya—became centers of great learning. Another important contribution of the monasteries of these days was their invention of the *kana*, the Japanese syllabary, without which the development of Japanese literature is almost inconceivable.

Importation of new doctrines from China remained one of the greatest aspirations of Japanese monks. One of such monks was Ennin (794–864). His eagerness to seek the Law is recorded in his diary (Document 3), which is considered one of the finest examples of Chinese writing. The practice of sending embassies to China was suspended in 894 when the power of Tang was at its nadir. This incidentally also marked the beginning of a period of looking within, enabling the Japanese to naturalize Chinese civilization and create a new Japanese civilization.

The continued prosperity of Buddhism did not go unchallenged. In 914, a distinguished Confucian scholar, Miyoshi Kiyotsura submitted to the throne a Statement of Opinion on Twelve Matters to the throne (Document 4). In it, he deplored the growth of luxury, deterioration of public finances, and the decline of morality among the aristocratic class. These in his view were caused by the excessive trust the nation placed in Buddhism. Obviously there was a Confucian contempt for luxury and for the lazy Buddhist monks, but it remains one of the most significant documents which came to grips with the ills of society.

To maintain their elegant life style, the aristocratic class vied against one another for imported goods from China (Document 5). It was *de rigueur* for their men to be trained in Chinese classics, but they used the language only inelegantly. Women were denied opportunities for education (Document 7), but some learned to write elegantly in the vernacular. When men's fixation with things Chinese waned, it was women who created a new indigenous tradition in literature. They recaptured the evanescent beauty of times past, a civilization that was gone with the wind.

By the tenth century, the capital city of Heian showed many signs of urban decay (Document 8), and the nobility who inhabited the city had fallen no less, exhibiting their proclivity toward trivia and superstition (Document 9). The common people's disdain for arrogant priests (Document 10) and for the court life (Document 11) are found in some *setsuwa bungaku* (tale literature), which show that the daily lives of the poor were poles apart from the court's privileged existence (compare Document 12).

THE LOTUS OF THE WONDERFUL LAW

The Sutra on the Lotus of the Wonderful Law *(Sk.* Saddharma-Pundarika Sutra*) was rendered into Chinese by numerous Tripitaka translators. The most important and most widely used version is the one translated by Kumarajiva in 406, which became known in Japan by the name of* Myōhōrengekyō. *The founder of the Tiankai (in Japanese Tendai) sect in China, Zhikai (538–597) made this the basis of his doctrine and wrote three large commentaries—the* Myōhōrengekyō Gengi *(Mystic Meanings of the Lotus Sutra),* Mongu *(the Text), and* Makashikan *(Great Meditation and Knowledge)—to expound his views, and give guidance to religious practices. These constituted the basic texts of the Tendai sect both in China and Japan.*

The sect claims that the teachings of the Buddha can be divided into five periods. The first four, while containing an element of truth, are still transitory, whereas the teaching found in the Lotus Sutra *is the final one. The sutra itself is sometimes called the* Sutra of the Only Vehicle. *According to the second chapter of the sutra, Buddha appeared in this world to teach all creatures Tathagata knowledge, "by means of one sole vehicle, to wit, the Buddha-vehicle (*Buddhayana*). . . . There is no second vehicle, nor a third." This is an attempt to replace the three vehicles, which included hearing Buddha's teaching (the vehicle of the pratyeka-buddhas), attaining enlightenment through one's own effort (the vehicle of the shrayakas), and helping others toward enlightenment (the vehicle of the bodhisattvas). Implicit in this teaching is the superiority of the Lotus, and the doctrine of universal enlightenment for all sentient beings comes through very clearly.*

The following selection, taken from Kern's translation from the original Sanskrit rendered in 1884, contains a parable of the burning house in which the superiority of the one vehicle over the three vehicles is shown. The use of parables in Buddhist sutras inspired the rise of morality tales, which often captured the life-style and sentiment of the common man. Two of the most representative compilations of such tales were the Konjaku Monogatarishū (Tales of the Old and New), *and* Uji Shūi Monogatari (Tales from Uji) *(Documents 7–9). And through these morality tales, Buddhist teachings found greater popular acceptance.*

1   **A Parable of the Burning House**[1]   Let us suppose the following case, Sariputra. . . . There was a certain housekeeper, old, aged, decrepit, very advanced in years, rich, wealthy, opulent; he had a great house, high, spacious, built a long time ago and old, inhabited by some two, three, four, or five hundred living beings. The house had but one door, and a thatch; its terraces were tottering, the bases of its pillars rotten, the coverings and plaster of the walls loose. On a sudden the whole house was from every side put in conflagration by a mass of fire. Let us suppose that the man had many little boys, say five, or ten, or even twenty, and that he himself had come out of the house.

Now, Sariputra, that man, on seeing the house from every side wrapt in a blaze by a great mass of fire, got afraid, and . . . calls to the boys: "Come, my children; the house is burning with a mass of fire; come, lest you be burnt in the mass fire, and come to grief and disaster," But the ignorant boys do not heed the words of him who is their well-wisher; they are not afraid . . . nor know the purport of the word "burning"; they run hither and thither, walk about, and repeatedly look at their father; all, because they are so ignorant.

. . . The man has a clear perception of their inclinations. Now these boys happen to have many and manifold toys to play with, pretty, nice, pleasant, dear, amusing, and precious. The man, knowing the disposition of the boys, says to them: "My children, your toys, which you are so loath to miss, which are so various and multifarious, [such as] bullock-carts, goat-carts, deer-carts, which are so pretty, nice, dear, and precious to you, have all been put by me outside the house-door for you to play with. Come, run out, leave the house; to each of you I shall give what he wants. Come soon, come for the sake of these toys." And the boys, on hearing the names mentioned of such playthings as they like and desire, quickly rush out from the burning house, with eager effort and great alacrity, one having no time to wait for the other, and pushing each other on with the cry of "Who shall arrive first, the very first?"

The man, seeing that his children have safely and happily escaped, goes and

---

[1]Adapted from H. Kern, *Saddharma-Pundarika or The Lotus of the True Law* (New York: Dover Publications, reissue, 1963), pp. 72–79.

sits down in the open air on the square of the village, his heart is filled with joy and delight. The boys go up to the place where their father is sitting, and say, "Father, give us those toys to play with, those bullock-carts, and deer-carts." Then, Sariputra, the man gives to his sons, who run swift as the wind, bullock-carts only, made of seven precious substances, provided with benches, hung with a multitude of small bells, lofty, adorned with rare and wonderful jewels, embellished with jewel wreaths, decorated with garlands of flowers, carpeted with cotton mattresses and woolen coverlets, covered with white cloth and silk, having on both sides rosy cushions, yoked with white, very fair and fleet bullocks, led by a multitude of men. To each of his children he gives several bullock-carts of one appearance and one kind, provided with flags, and swift as wind. That man does so, Sariputra, because being rich, ... he rightly thinks: "Why should I give these boys inferior carts, all these boys being my own children, dear and precious? I have such great vehicles and ought to treat all the boys equally and without partiality. As I won many treasures and granaries, I could give such great vehicles to all beings, how much more then to my own children." Meanwhile the boys are mounting the vehicles with feelings of astonishment and wonder. Now, Sariputra, what is thy opinion? Has that man made himself guilty of a falsehood by first holding out to his children the prospect of three vehicles and afterwards giving to each of them the greatest vehicles only, the most magnificent vehicle?

Sariputra answered: By no means, Lord. That is not sufficient to qualify the man as a speaker of falsehood, since it only was a skillful device to persuade his children to go out of the burning house and save their lives. Nay, besides recovering their very bodies, O Lord, they have received all those toys. If that man, O Lord, had given no single cart, even then he would not have been a speaker of falsehood, for he had previously been meditating on saving the little boys from a great mass of pain by some able device. ...

The venerable Sariputra having thus spoken, the Lord said to him: Very well, Sariputra, quite so; it is even as you say. So too, Sariputra, the Tathagata is free from all dangers, wholly exempt from all misfortune, despondency, calamity, pain, grief, the thick enveloping dark mists of ignorance. He, the Tathagata, endowed with Buddha-knowledge, forces, absence of hesitation, uncommon properties, and mighty by magical power, is the father of the world,[2] who has reached the highest perfection in the knowledge of skillful means, who is most merciful, long-suffering, benevolent, compassionate. He appears in this triple world, which is like a house the roof and shelter whereof are decayed, [a house] burning by a mass of misery. ... Once born, he sees how the creatures are burnt, tormented, vexed, distressed by birth, old age, disease, death, grief, wailing, pain, melancholy, despondency; how for the sake of enjoyment, and prompted

---

[2]Here the Buddha is represented as a wise and benevolent father, he is the heavenly father, Brahma. As such he was represented as sitting on a "lotus seat."

by sensual desires, they severally suffer various pains. In consequence both of what in this world they are seeking and what they have acquired, they will in a future state suffer various pains, in hell, in the brute creation, in the realm of Yamaraja (king of the dead); suffer such pains as poverty in the world of gods or men, union with hateful persons or things, and separation from the beloved ones. And while incessantly whirling in that mass of evils they are sporting, playing, diverting themselves; they do not fear, nor dread, nor are they seized with terror; they do not know, nor mind; they are not startled, do not try to escape, but are enjoying themselves in that triple world which is like unto a burning house, and run hither and thither. Though overwhelmed by that mass of evil, they do not conceive the idea that they must beware of it.

Under such circumstances, Sariputra, the Tathagata reflects thus: "Verify, I am the father of these beings; I must save them from this mass of evil, and bestow on them the immense, inconceivable bliss of Buddha-knowledge, where-with they shall sport, play, and divert themselves, wherein they shall find their rest. If, in the conviction of my possessing the power of knowledge and magical faculties. I manifest to these beings the knowledge, forces, and absence of hesitation of the Tathagata, without availing myself of some device, these beings will not escape. For they are attached to the pleasures of the five senses, to worldly pleasures; they will not be freed from birth, old age, disease, death, grief, wailing, pain, melan-choly, despondency, by which they are burnt, tormented, vexed, distressed. Unless they are forced to leave the triple world which is like a house the shelter and roof whereof is in a blaze, how are they to get acquainted with Buddha-knowledge?"

Now, Sariputra, even as that man with powerful arms, without using the strength of his arms, attracts his children out of the burning house by an able device, and afterwards gives them magnificent, great carts, so Sariputra, the Tathagata possessed of knowledge and freedom from all hesitation, without using them, in order to attract the creatures out of the triple world which is like a burning house with decayed roof and shelter, shows, by his knowledge of able devices, three vehicles, viz. the vehicle of the disciples, the vehicle of the pratyeka-buddhas, and the vehicle of the bodhisattvas. By means of these three vehicles he attracts the creatures and speaks to them thus: "Do not delight in this triple world, which is like a burning house, in these miserable forms, sounds, odors, flavors, and contacts. For in delighting in this triple world you are burnt, heated, inflamed with the thirst inseparable from the pleasures of the five senses. Fly from this triple world; betake yourselves to the three vehicles. . . . I give you my pledge for it, that I shall give you these three vehicles, make an effort to run out of this triple world. And to attract them I say: "These vehicles are grand, praised by the Aryas, and provided with most pleasant things; with such you are to sport, play, and divert yourselves in a noble manner. You will feel the great delight of the faculties, powers, constituents of Bodhi, meditations, the eight degrees of emancipation, self-concentration, and the results of self-concentration, and you will become greatly happy and cheerful."

KŪKAI'S VIEW OF THE SUPERIORITY OF BUDDHISM

According to the preface to the Directions to the Teachings of Three Doctrines, *Kūkai (774–835) entered the governmental university at the age of eighteen, and studied the* Book of Poetry, Spring and Autumn Annals, Book of History, *and other Confucian classics. Sometime later, by chance, he received a book from a Buddhist monk, and to test its validity he withdrew to the mountains and forests of Shikoku. When the efficacy of its teachings was manifested, he decided to renounce the world. This move was criticized by his relatives and teachers as a step directly counter to the teachings of Confucianism which valued loyalty and filial piety. In response to this criticism, Kūkai stated that because of diversity of human nature, sages of old taught different doctrines. The three doctrines of Buddhism, Taoism and Confucianism were all sacred. In any event, Kūkai reasoned, if a person pursued one of the three doctrines, "how could he be charged as deviating from the ways of loyalty and filial piety?" In this spirit he wrote the book, which is at once a defense of the Buddhist faith as well as an autobiographical account of his spiritual quest.*

The book is divided into three volumes. It takes the form of a stage play with five principal actors. Prince Tokaku, a believer in Confucianism, was worried about the behavior of his beloved nephew, Shitsuga, and engaged Professor Kibō, the Confucian scholar, Master Kyobō, the Taoist monk, and the Monk Kamei, the Buddhist priest, to teach the nephew. As the dialogue between the five progresses, Kūkai skillfully conveys the theme that no doctrine is superior to Buddhism. In the first book, Professor Kibō teaches the doctrines of good and evil, loyalty and filial piety, and of upward mobility in society. With this teaching Shitsuga shows his repentance. However, in the second book, Master Kyobō describes the way of departing from the secular concern and the art of longevity as taught by Taoism, and asserts the latter's superiority. Then in the third book, the Monk Kamei takes his turn and points out that full understanding of the karmic conditions is indispensable in effectuating good work toward all sentient beings, which is the true act of loyalty and filial piety. The final climactic scene shows all participants paying obeisance to the Monk Kamei, praising the teachings of Buddha.

In writing this work, Kūkai freely emulated the style of the Wenxuan *or* Literary Selections, *China's most important anthology of literature compiled by Prince Xiang Ming (501–591), heir apparent to the Liang throne in South China. This in itself is testimony to the breadth and depth of his Chinese education.*

2 **Directions to the Teachings of Three Doctrines, 797[3]**   Thereafter, Professor Kibō, the Confucian scholar, and Master Kyobō, the Taoism priest, pros-

---

[3]From *Sangō shiiki* in *Nihon Koten Bungaku Taikei* (*Major Compilation of Japanese Classics*) Vol. 71 (Tokyo: Inwanami Shoten, 1965), pp. 136–145.

trated, bowed deeply in their kneeling position, and said: "We have in the past placed our trust in the unworthy pebble-like substance, and indulged in the joys of this world. . . . Having heard the gracious teaching of yours, we know the shallowness of our own ways. We deeply repent of our mistakes of yesteryears and wish to work diligently to gain righteousness for tomorrow. We beg of you, our gracious monk, to give us directions to know the ultimate."

Kamei answered, saying: "Indeed, well said. You have regained [your senses] without deviating [from truth] any further. I shall again discuss the causes of suffering in life, and impart to you the joyous knowledge of nirvana. This is not discussed by the King and Duke of Zhou or by Confucius. Nor is it revealed by Laozi and Zhuangzi. . . ."

Thus saying he unlocked men's [hardness of] minds and in flawless eloquence recited "the Stanzas on the Sea of Life and Death,"[4] and revealed the "merits of great enlightenment." Poling up the river with the raft of noble eightfold path,[5] raising the mast of diligence and sail of concentration, defending against bandits with armors of patience, and browbeating enemies with swords of wisdom, whipping the horse of seven senses to cross over the depths, and going through this world of illusion by the chariot with four forms of prayers, then one can attain the covered jewel hidden in the topknot of the King, and be given dominion over his estate.[6]

The long passageway to the ten stages of comprehension of ultimate truth can be completed in but one instance. The three *kalpas*[7] required for the attainment of enlightenment are not beyond reach. Thereafter one can discard heavy burdens encountered at each of the ten stages to witness the truth, and mount the platform of two changes (where desire is changed to wisdom, and birth and death are changed to nirvana) to proclaim the Sacred Law over the Buddhist nations. Having attained harmony and equality, the mind is consistent with reason and without prejudice, and the four mirrors of wisdom are afar from the scorn of honor of the world.

This indeed is the essence of Buddha. He remains unchanging and is above life and death. Beyond the myriads of *kalpas* he is in nirvana. Over the three

---

[4]Men's misery is likened to a great sea.

[5]It consists of right view or understanding, right aspiration, thought or purpose, right speech, right action, right mode of livelihood, right endeavor, right mindfulness and right concentration.

[6]A metaphor for Buddha's promise to his disciples that they can attain Buddhahood.

[7]*Kalpa* is a term used to denote a long period of time. The three *kalpas* are the past *kalpa* (Sk. *Atita-vyuha-kalpa*), the period of those whom the world glorifies; the present *kalpa* (Sk. *Pratyutpanna-bhadra-kalpa*), the period in which the wise are born; and future *kalpa* (Sk. *Angata-naksatratara kalpa*), the period of the stars. These *kalpas* are each divided into four periods, namely, (1) growth or formation, (2) perfection, making fit for habitation, (3) destruction, and (4) voidness or nothingness. See Harper H. Coates and Ryugaku Ishizuka, *Hōnen, the Buddhist Satin: His Life and Teaching* (Kyoto: Chionin, 1925), p. 308.

great *kalpas*, he can remain in the state of non-action.[8] Great and powerful indeed is he! The Yellow Emperor, Emperor Yao, and Fu Xi[9] are unworthy of holding his sandals. Sakradevendra, and Brahma cannot even support his wheels adequately. . . .[10]

Even before the four comprehensive vows[11] of Bodhisattvas were attained, Buddha showed compassion and kindness to all sentient beings who were estranged from reality.[12] Desirous of having myriad beings to attain buddhahood in myriad places, the Buddha permitted his countenance to appear in myriad towns (even though in his true form he was invisible). The way of perfection through the ages began with the eight stages of life,[13] and ended with the attainment of the body of Buddha ruling over pain, punishment, extinction, and the way. Buddha's illustrious teachings were spread by his disciples to the eight corners of the country, and his compassion and love were partaken by sentient beings spread in ten different directions. . . .

This indeed is the teaching transmitted to us by Buddha, but comprises only a small part of his Law. Neither the inconsequential crafts of the hermits[14] nor the picayune teachings of this world[15] are worthy of our consideration.

Upon hearing this, Kibō and others trembled with the thought of the bad karma they accumulated in the past, became ashamed of the erroneous teachings of Confucianism and Taoism to which they were formerly attached, and became sorrowful that they did not know the compassionate teachings of Buddha before. However, they were joyful that they came into contact with the true Law . . . saying: "How thankful are we to have been able to meet this

---

[8]The Chinese term *Wuwei*, or non-action, describes one of the most important theories of Taoism. "*Dao* does nothing and yet there is nothing that is not done." Here the word is used interchangeably with the Buddhist concept of nirvana.

[9]Yao was China's legendary sage king, and both the Yellow Emperor and Fu Xi were China's culture heroes. The latter was credited with the invention of writings, fishing and trapping.

[10]Brahma is the first person of Hindu Brahmanical Trimurti, and Sakradevendra means the mighty Lord Indra of the Devas. They were adopted by Buddhism as guardian deities but placed in inferior positions.

[11]To attain enlightenment, all bodhisattvas have to take these vows: (1) even though sentient beings are innumerable, I will save them all; (2) though the number of evil passions is countless, I will cut them all off, (3) though the doctrines of the Buddhas are inexhaustible in number and extent, I will know them all, and (4) I will surely attain the highest perfect enlightenment. . . .

[12]Literally fell into ditches, hence unable to perceive anything but shadows.

[13]The typical life for those aspiring toward Buddhahood: (1) ascent to heaven, (2) coming down from heaven and abiding in his mother's womb, (3) coming forth from his mother's womb, (4) leaving his father's palace and becoming a monk, (5) conquering all evil spirits, (6) attainment of enlightenment, (7) turning the wheel of the Law, and (8) entering nirvana.

[14]Referring to Taoism.

[15]Referring to Confucianism.

most unusual great teacher, who gives us the most precious of Buddhist teachings. . . . If we had not been able to meet you in this manner, we could have been condemned to the three evil births of hell, hungry ghosts, and creatures that walk on all fours. This is so, because our base desires for sensuality, sound, scent, taste and touch would have placed us there. Now receiving your kind teachings for the less enlightened, we are happy and secure. . . . How shallow are the teachings of Confucius and of Taoism. Henceforward, we shall make our skin into paper, our bones into brushes, use our blood as ink and our body as an inkslab[16] to write indelibly your teachings as our guide. Thus we can embark on our voyage through the sea of birth and death to the other shore."

ENNIN'S SEARCH FOR THE LAW

Early Heian Buddhism continued to seek inspiration from religious teachings and practices of China, and many worthies went to China to seek the Law. One of such notables was Ennin (794–864), who went to China with the Japanese embassy in 838. The following year, his plan to return to Japan was thwarted when the ship he boarded at Dengzhou Shandong, drifted back to the same port. He remained in China for nine additional years, and made pilgrimages to Wutai and the capital city of Changan where he met learned priests who instructed him in the doctrines of Tendai, Shingon and Zen. On his return to Japan in 847, he brought back more than five hundred volumes of Sutras and Shastras and many other sacred objects. In 854, he was appointed the chief abbot of Enryakuji in Mt. Hiei. He made the administration of the sacrament of kanjō, or sprinkling of water upon the head, part of the established rituals for the state (849), which was previously privately administered by Saichō. Through Ennin's influence, the Tendai teachings became increasingly eclectic in nature, combining the practices of the Shingon sect. Esoteric Shingon practices, such as praying for rain or clear sky, for quick recovery or health, or for suppression of enemies became in vogue in Heian Buddhism, at least due in part to Mt. Hiei's and Ennin's acquiescence to such practices. The prevalence of esoteric practices eventually would lead Heian Buddhism to the path of corruption and to the nadir of its influence, and Buddhism would have to await its revival through Genshin (942–1017) and other reformers (see Chapter 5).

In the following selections, observe closely the difficulties that Ennin had to face in China, and the joy he experienced when he discovered that he was treading the same path that his master Saichō trod once before. That in essence was the spirit of those who sought the Law.

---

[16]From the *Kegon Sutra* (*Flower Wreath Sutra*).

3   **Ennin's Diary of His Pilgrimage to China**[17]   *The Japanese monks in search of the Law inform this monastery:* A document in which the monk Ennin, his attendant monks Ishō and Igyō, and his servant Tei Yūman request the monastery to write the prefecture and subprefecture to give them official credentials to wander and beg as their destiny permits.

We monks, having in mind merely our longing for the Buddhist teachings, have come from afar to this benevolent land with our hearts set on sacred places and our spirits rejoicing in the pilgrimage. It is said that Mt. Wutai and some other places are the source of the teaching and the places where the great saints have manifested themselves. Eminent monks from India have visited them, crossing their precipitous slopes, and famous patriarchs of China have there attained enlightenment. We monks have admired these glorious places and, having chanced to meet with this happy destiny, have by good fortunes come to this holy land. Now we wish to go to these places to fulfill our long-cherished hopes, but we fear that on the road others will not honor our reasons for traveling. We have heard that the Learned Doctor Prajna petitioned for official credentials on behalf of some mendicant monks, and that they were allowed by Imperial edict to practice their mendicancy. Thus, this started of old and has continued until recent times.

We humbly hope that this monastery, in accordance with the laws and precedents of the land, will address the prefecture and the subprefecture, asking for official credentials. If it does so, the ... glorious fame of the Monastery Administrators will stir foreign lands afar, their encouraging magnanimity will gloriously manifest the sunlike Buddha, and we shall be more indebted to you.

The full statement is as above. The statement of the matter is as given above. Respectfully written.

The twenty-sixth day of the ninth moon of the fourth year of Kaicheng [839].

The Japanese monks in search of the Law from the Enryakuji.

Third moon, twenty-fifth day, [840]. . . . From Wencheng xian in Dengzhou to Chingzhon there have been plagues of locusts for the past three or four years which have eaten up the five grains so that the officials and commoners alike have gone hungry. In the Dengzhou region they have been using only acorns for food. It is difficult for traveling monks passing through this rugged area to obtain provisions. Millet costs eighty cash per *dou* and non-glutinous rice one hundred cash per *dou*. We are without provisions to eat, and so I prepared a statement and sent it to the Assistant Regional Commander, the auxiliary official Zhang, asking for provisions.

The Japanese monk in search of the Law, Ennin, asks to be given provisions for his meals.

---

[17]Edwin O. Reischauer, *Ennin's Diary: The Record of a Pilgrimage to China in Search of the Law*, pp. 148–49, 196, 222–25. Copyright © 1955, E. O. Reischauer. Reprinted by permission of John Wiley & Sons, Inc.

The said Ennin and others left their homeland far away in order to search for Buddhist teachings, but, because he is asking for official credentials, he has not yet moved on. He makes his home anywhere and finds his hunger beyond endurance, but, because he speaks a different tongue, he is unable to beg for food himself. He humbly hopes that in your compassion you will give the surplus of your food to the poor monk from abroad. You have already given him a certain amount, and he is extremely embarrassed to be troubling you now again. He humbly sends his disciple Ishō to inform you. Respectfully stated. . . .

The auxiliary official gave us three *dou* of non-glutinous rice, three *dou* of flour, and three *dou* of millet, so I prepared a letter to thank him.

Fifth moon, Sixteenth day, [840]. Early in the morning we left the Chulinssu and, following a valley, went ten *li* east and ten *li* toward the northeast to the Tahuayenssu and entered the Living Quarters Cloister and lodged there. After the forenoon meal we were sent to the Nirvana Cloister and saw Abbot Fa-chien lecturing on the *Makashikan*[18] in a fairly high two-storied hall. More than forty monks seated in rows were listening to him lecture. We then saw the Tendai Abbot Chih-yüan Ho-shang in the lecture congregation listening to the *Shikan*. It was impressive and beautiful in the hall beyond description.

When the Abbot said, "I have completed lecturing on the fourth scroll," we waited until he had come down from the lecture seat and then went to the room of Zhiyuan Heshang to pay him reverence. The Priest inquired after us and was courteous. Abbot Fajian, who has recently come from the Western Capital (Changan), and Abbot Wenjian, who has long been at this mountain, and the more than forty auditors at the lecture are all of the Tendai Sect. Meeting together, we inquired after one another and rejoiced over meeting at the place of lecture.

Zhiyuan Heshang of his own accord said, "The Learned Doctor Saichō of Japan went to Tiantai in the twentieth year of Zhonyien [804] in search of the Law. Lord Lu, the Prefect of Taizhou, himself provided him with paper and scribes, and they copied several hundred scrolls which he gave to the Learned Doctor Saichō. The Learned Doctor, on obtaining the commentaries, returned to his native land." They asked him about the prosperity of the Tendai Sect in Japan, and I related in brief how Nanyou Vashi[19] was reborn in Japan. The congregation rejoiced greatly, and the Abbot Zhiyuan, on hearing me tell of the rebirth of Nanyou Dashi in Japan and the spread of Buddhism there, was extremely happy.

---

[18]One of the basic works of the Tendai Sect dictated by the founder Zhikoi. They are collectively known as *The Three Great Lotus Works*.

[19]The monk Huisi (515–557) who was considered to be the second patriarch of the Tiantoi Sect in China. He was the teacher of the third patriarch, Zhiyi, the real founder of the sect.

CONFUCIAN VIEW OF BUDDHISM

*In 794, the year of the founding of the capital city of Heian, Emperor Kammu
adopted two measures to encourage study at universities. One was to modify the
hereditary privilege (*on *in Japanese and* yin *in Chinese) which permitted without examination the entrance of sons of high-ranking officials into officialdom,
by stipulating that higher positions would be granted to those who took examinations. The other was to institute scholarship fields (*kangakuden*) for sustenance
of students at the universities.*

*Students in the universities majored either in Chinese classics or history. And
the official encouragement of learning created a climate in which the knowledge
of Confucian classics, the* Historical Records (Shiji), *the* History of the Former
Han Dynasty (Han shu) *and the* Literary Selections (Wenxuan) *became a sign of
educated men. Confucian ideals became part of the official thinking. The reign
periods of Engi (901–923, Emperor Daigo) and Tenryaku (947–967, Emperor
Murakami) are often considered the best periods in the Heian history, at least in
part due to the observance of Confucian ideals and to the equitable manner in
which officials were presumed to have been selected.*

*Miyoshi Kiyotsura (or Kiyoyuki, 848–919) was the product of this Japanese
Confucian tradition. His career included Professor of Literature, Provincial Governor, Rector of the University, and State Councilor.*

*The following "Opinion on Twelve Matters" was submitted to Emperor
Daigo in 914, through which Miyoshi was, in a sense, asking the imperial court
to rethink Japan's "national priorities," by discarding many time-worn Buddhist
practices. And true to his Confucian training, he advocated reinvigoration of
university education through which the country could gain new national leaders
who could bring honor and glory to the nation. Only the section dealing with
university education is fully translated. In addition, a substantial portion of the
opening remarks and a portion of the section urging proscription of luxurious
living are translated. The remainder is given in an outline form.*

4 **Statement of Opinion on Twelve Matters, 914[20]** Your subject submits
this statement with trepidation, realizing that his offenses in speaking out in this
manner may merit a death penalty. In examining the ancient records, it is found
that our Imperial Household was known for its tradition of enlightenment . . . the
tax assessed was light, and people were seldom impressed into corvée duties.

---

[20]From the *Honchō Monzui*, Book 2 in *Kokushi Taikei (Major Compilations of National History)* new and expanded ed., Vol. 29B (Tokyo: Yoshikawa Kōbunkan, 1965), p.
41–53. For a complete translation in a Western language, see Inge-Lore Kluge, "Miyoshi
Kiyoyuki, sein Leben und seine Zeit," in *Deutsche Akademie der Wissenshaften zu Berlin
Institut fur Orientforschung,* Veroffenlichung #35 (Berlin: Akademie-Verlag, 1958).

Those who were above showed their kindness and nurtured those who were below. Those who were below with sincerity sustained those who were above. In the governance of the country, it was like regulating one's personal behavior. . . . However, gradually good customs of the land wore thin, and instead, laws and regulations took prominence, tax assessment increased year after year, and forced labor was applied manifold. Taxable households declined month after month, and farmlands showed deterioration day after day. It was during the reign of Emperor Kimmei (r. 540–571) that Buddhism first reached this nation. This doctrine became widely practiced after the reign of Empress Suiko (r. 593–628). From those who were ministers and functionaries above to those who were of modest circumstances below, if they did not build temples and pagodas they were considered not to belong to the race of man. Thus many squandered their wealth in the building of pagodas. They competed for the honor of discarding their farmland for temple use, and many bought freemen to become servants of temples. When the era of Tempyō (729–749) came, Buddhism was even more cherished, resulting in loss of farmland to build many large temples. The magnificence of the edifices, the enormity of the Buddha statues, the intricacy of the craftsmanship and the rare splendor surrounding them are more like the creation of ghostly spirits than of men.

When Emperor Shōmu (r. 724–749) ordered that a provincial monastery and nunnery be built in each of the provinces of the seven regions, the expense of building these edifices was borne by the public through taxation in each of these provinces. In so doing, five of ten parts of the public fund were expended. Then came the reign of Emperor Kammu (r. 782–806) who moved his capital to Nagaoka. When the work was completed, he again changed the capital [to Heian]. . . . In so doing, three of five parts of the public fund were expended. Then Emperor Ninmyō (r. 833–850) ascended the throne. He had a capricious taste for luxuries . . . and thus stifled development of agriculture and injured the interests of women. His costumes were made in the morning only to be changed in the evening. Every day and every month, there was a change in fashion. The beauty of bed chambers and nightdresses, and the abundance of banquets and festive music and dancing were beyond compare through the ages. In this way, one half of the public fund was expended. . . .

In 893, your subject was named governor of Bichū. In that province, there was a village of Nima in the district of Shimotsumichi. According to the topographical records of that province (*Fudoki*), in the year 660, Empress Kōgyoku [at the time of the Korean campaign], went to Tsukushi, planning to send reinforcement. . . . When an edict was issued to call men to service, there were 20,000 men who responded to the call [from the district of Shimotsumichi]. . . . However, during the reign of Emperor Shōmu when the Minister of Right Kibi no Makibi attempted to take census of this district there were only 1,900 able-bodied men remaining. During the reign era of Jōkan (859–877) the late Minister of Popular Affairs, Fujiwara no Yasunori, . . . took note of the old records which stated that there were 20,000 soldiers from this district, examined the census register only to discover that there were only seventy able-bodied men remaining. When your subject reached this district, he again examined the census, and discovered that there were only two old men [between the ages of sixty-one and sixty-five], four mature men, and three young men [between the ages of sixteen and twenty]. Lately during the eleventh year of Engi [911], when the governor of that province Fujiwara Kimitoshi completed his term and returned to the capital, your subject inquired of him if there were any able-bodied men left in the district. His response was that not a single man was left. . . . This was merely an example of one district. But from this we can infer very clearly how all under heaven have suffered.

Now that your Imperial Majesty is reigning at the most propitious time in a thousand years . . . the country's fortune can be restored in a matter of days. Knowing this, your subject cannot restrain from rejoicing. Therefore, unworthy as he is, . . . realizing that his knowledge is limited, confined in his outlook as if gazing at the heavens from the bottom of a well and can stretch only a few feet, your subject respectfully submits his recommendations as below, leaving them to the acceptance of your heavenly pleasure:

1. The drought should be eradicated to bring good crops. . . .
2. Luxurious living should be proscribed.

During the reigns of the sage emperors, austerity was respected and luxury forbidden. People wore the same clothing over and over again after washing, and ate plain coarse food. These things were praised by the ancients, and were regarded as honorable signs of a well-governed era. However, nowadays, luxury becomes fashionable step by step and the benevolent influence of the Emperor is not appreciated. From officers and functionaries of the government, ladies-in-waiting and other women in the Court, and children of powerful families to those loafers in the capital, all luxuriate in food and clothing. When a host entertains at banquets, costs soar day after day and there is no limit to them. Your subject is simply giving one example to point out how things are going on. Humbly looking into the past, your subject discovers that during the reign eras of Jōkan (859–877) and Genkei (877–885), all imperial princes and court nobles used coarse silk from Tsukushi for unlined summer clothes, . . . nowadays, even the plain functionaries and scribes insist on using the highest grade of white silk for unlined summer clothes, . . . and their wives, daughters and maid servants . . . squander tens of thousands of pieces of money into dyeing their sleeves scarlet. . . .

In the days of old, Zi Lu wore wadded clothes, and was not ashamed before those who wore beautiful clothes made of fox-fur. Zi Si[21] took pride in his

---

[21]Zi Lu and Zi Si were disciples of Confucius. The latter was especially known for his frugality.

honest poverty and still could look down on the ostentatiousness of a carriage drawn by four horses. These are the high standards set by the sage philosophers which common people cannot hope to attain. The common people look for differences between themselves and others, and compete to show off their wealth. If they see someone being frugal they greet him with derision. The rich revel in the fact that they can [consume] to their hearts' content, and the poor are ashamed that they cannot keep up with the rich. Therefore they tailor just one cloth which can bring about bankruptcy for the rest of their lives, and set up a banquet which has to be paid for by several years of their incomes. This has caused the fields to be lain in waste, and bandits to rise in a large number. If these [luxurious practices] are not proscribed, your subject fears that they may damage the benevolent rule of Your Majesty. Therefore, your subject humbly entreats that a dress code be established in accordance with the ranks held by the people, and that the *kebiishi* (police officers) be ordered to enforce the code, punishing those who exceed the limits. As to a code regulating banquets, it has been in existence for some time, but it has been violated by those who are above, and consequently imitated by those who are below. Therefore your subject further entreats that the *kebiishi* be ordered to enforce these existing regulations.

Also there must be established regulations concerning memorial services and funeral expenses, consistent with the ranks held by the people. The regulations must be made applicable alike to ministers and functionaries of the court down to the common people. Nowadays those families in mourning go through seventy-seven days of lecture series [conducted by Buddhist priests] and Buddhist ceremonies at anniversary dates. The people squander their fortunes to give lavish offerings to the dead. The food on one table is spread over ten square feet, and the fees collected by a monk can exceed one thousand gold pieces. To pay for these, some people have to rent out the houses in which they live and others have to sell their houses. Filial sons become fugitives from unpaid debts, and young children unwittingly become victims of hunger and starvation. Anyone who has received the love of the parents in nurturing and protecting him is desirous of remembering that love even after the death of the parents. However, in doing this meritorious observance, one must be governed by a certain limit. How can one expect to acquire merits for the departed parents and ancestors by means of bankrupting their descendants? . . .

3. Each province should be ordered to distribute the *kubunden* (allotment land) only in accordance with the actual number of people living in that province. . . .

4. Stipends should be given to students studying in universities.

Reflecting on this matter, it is said that the way to govern a country is to secure the services of men of talent, and the method of obtaining talent is by providing education. Thus, as of old, the sage kings without fail always established schools to teach virtuous doctrines. . . . Study of our ancient records shows that in our country, universities were first established during the

Taihō period (701–704). Later in the Tempyō period (729–749), Minister of the Right Kibi no Asomi personally taught the students in order to spread the virtuous way and the arts. He ordered 400 students to study the five classics and three histories,[22] the law and arithmetic, or the six arts comprising the Chinese sound system and calligraphy and others. Thereafter under every reign, official encouragement was given. When Ōtomo no Yakamochi committed an offense, his land in Echizen consisting of over one hundred *chō* was confiscated. To this was added over thirty *chō* of public land in Yamashiro and fifty-five *chō* of land in Kawachi to be used for providing food and sustenance for the students. These were then called scholarship fields (*kangakuden*). . . . Another edict also decreed that every year the rice obtained from the original 94,000 sheaves from Hitachi was to be used for multiple cooking purposes in the student dormitory, and the rice obtained from the original 800 sheaves from Tango was to be applied for flavoring and for a sweet taste for the students. Over the years, things changed. During the reign of Jōwa (834–836), Ban no Yoshio appealed the conviction of Yakamochi, and when the latter was found not guilty, his estate appropriated for scholarship fields in the province of Kaga was returned. Later the thirty *chō* of the scholarship fields were divided into four portions, with three portions diverted for use of the medicine and stable offices, and only one portion retained for students' food. As to the land in the province of Kawachi, frequently there were floods, and the land was reclaimed by the river. The sheaves given by the two provinces of Hitachi and Tango were frequently not supplied, and the original amount of sheaves was lost. Consequently there was no rice to be gained from the system. The only thing that is left is . . . seven *chō* of land in Yamashiro. And this small amount must feed several hundred students. Thin rice gruel may be supplied, but it is not sufficient to serve everyone. As to the students, those who have hopes of attaining their goals can forget the hunger and cold and work diligently. Among those who live in the dormitories are those sharp and dull in native intelligence and foolish and smart in talent. Some cannot be taught and are hard to employ, others because of their talent can leave the cocoon. All told, only thirty or forty percent of the students can be considered of medium attainment. If one has talent he is already selected to serve. If one has no talent, he wastes away his youth to become a decrepit old man. For some of the students their old homes become dilapidated and there is no place to which they can return. One can find snowy-haired students starving on the green banks of a river. When this sight is observed by those who are to follow, they simply regard the University as the place to meet unfulfilled dreams and disappointment. To

---

[22]The five classics are the classics of *Change* (*Yi jing*), *History* (*Shu jing*), *Poetry* (*Shi jing*), *Rituals* (*Li Ji*) and *Spring and Autumn Annals* (*Chuan chiu*). The three histories are the *Historical Records* (*Shi ji*), *History of the Former Han Dynasty* (*Han shu*) and *History of the Later Han Dynasty* (*Hou Han shu*).

them it also becomes a place of poverty, hunger and cold. Parents admonish each other not to send their sons to school. Thus the quadrangle between the south and north lecture halls is overrun by wild grass, and there is no one in the east and west study halls. At the time of making recommendations, professors do not take into account the talent of the candidates, but simply glance at a list of students. In this manner the labor of many are wasted, and favoritism arises, causing the unqualified to prosper. Those of us who have benefited from the patronage of some powerful households, or those of us who have been able to gain wings to fly into the blue yonder can only follow the steps of our Master Confucius to lament the dilapidation of our schools. The time is late, restoration is not in sight, and the great schools of the former emperors are quickly becoming ruins.

Reflecting on this matter, your subject is reminded of the saying that man must have food as the basis of his survival. Therefore he humbly recommends that the system of scholarship fields be restored.

It is further recommended that students who are not residing in the dormitories shall not have the right to be recommended for official positions. Even though we had this type of regulation in the past, it was not enforced because no food could be provided [in the dormitories].

The professors and masters of the colleges must be ordered to observe strictly the rule that students from all provinces, even though endowed with talent, cannot be recommended for official positions unless they reside in the dormitories. In this manner, students can be selected rigorously to become our national leaders. And these beautiful people[23] can bring honor and glory to our nation.

5. The number of performers at the five major festivals should be curtailed. . . .

6. Judges should be increased in number in accordance with our old regulations. . . .

7. The salaries and stipends for all the officials should be provided in an equitable manner. . . .

8. The despatch of imperial envoys to provinces should be stopped when there are complaints from minor officials and common people. . . .[24]

9. The number of people exempt from the tax register should be limited at each province. . . .

10. The practice of acquiring positions as *kebiishi* (police officers) in the provinces through purchase should be discontinued. . . .

---

[23]The term "beautiful people" comes from the *Book of Poetry*. Many other terms used in the last paragraph are also taken from the *Book of Poetry*, making various literary allusions. The memorial itself is written in impeccable Chinese.

[24]In order to preserve the reputation and effectiveness of good local officials, the central government should not interfere excessively in purely local affairs.

11. Transgressions committed by monks and brutal acts of violence by official retainers in the provinces should be proscribed. . . .

12. Again it is requested that the port in the province of Harima be repaired. . . .[25]

FIXATION WITH CHINA

The aristocratic class eagerly sought imported goods from China and its surrounding areas. The kingdom of Pohai (713–926, in Korean Parhae and in Japanese Bokkai) was a tributary state of the Tang located in the present day southern and eastern Manchuria and the northeastern corner of North Korea. It traded actively with China, and served as an intermediary for Japan in its trade with Tang. Arrival of its trading missions created excitement and even pandemonium, as traders undercut each other to secure advantages for their masters in the capital city. Document 5 shows how difficult it was to proscribe these activities.

Japan established formal relations with Tang China in 630. Until 894, when the dispatch of envoys was officially suspended, there were 19 plans to send missions of which 15 were actually carried out. These missions performed a number of useful functions. (1) It was certainly desirable for Japan to import aggressively Tang's advanced cultural attainments, technologies and institutions; (2) inasmuch as Tang was the center of the known world, it was imperative to maintain relations with it to obtain information concerning the rest of the world; and (3) it was beneficial to trade directly and officially with Tang.

The proposed 894 mission was planned under Emperor Uda (r. 887–897). If implemented, it would have been the first time in sixty years that such a mission would be sent. Uda's mother was not a Fujiwara, and one of his cherished political goals was to establish direct rule by the emperor without interference by the Fujiwara family. It could well be that this proposed mission was part of that political maneuvering. In counseling for suspension, Sugawara no Michizane (805–903) spoke only of unsettling conditions in Tang China (Document 6). In reality, Japan's own poor financial conditions, threats posed by pirates from Silla (a Korean state), and the availability of private Tang ships for hire for trading purposes should also be considered as reasons. Whatever the reason, the suspension became another sign of the waning of Chinese influence, at least in the political arena.

Education was an area in which the old fixation with things Chinese persisted well beyond the tenth century. Among the aristocratic class, to be educated still meant to be educated in the Chinese classics. Men were given opportunities to

---

[25]The port was reportedly built by the monk Gyōgi (688–749). When its facilities were not available shipwrecks were common in the area.

receive such an education, but not women. To be fully accepted by other ladies in waiting in the imperial court, Lady Murasaki had to pretend that she lacked knowledge of the Chinese classics (Document 7). It was fortunate for Japan that women did not have formal Chinese education. They wrote in the vernacular forcefully and elegantly, producing classics such as The Tale of Genji, *and* Pillow Book of Seishonagon.

5   **Regulations Concerning Trade with Pohai, 828**[26]   On the matter relating to receiving trading missions from Pohai, Minister of Popular Affairs Kiyohara no Mahito Natsuno commands the governor of Tajima and his functionaries to abide by the following regulations:

1. That they supply food and provisions for the guests. . . .
2. That they repair their ships. . . .
3. That they refrain from engaging in private trading.

It is our law not to trade privately in goods brought to our shores by our foreign guests. In spite of this established rule, our people fiercely compete to trade privately because of their love for anything which is foreign (e.g., made in China and its surrounding areas). The governor and his functionaries must strictly enforce the law to avoid recurrence. Violators shall be punished in the following manner. A commoner shall receive one hundred lashes. If a messenger is sent from the capital by an imperial prince or a high ranking official to engage in such a trade, the governor must stop the messenger from doing so and report that fact to us promptly. If the governor himself, to curry favor with those who are above him, engages in private trade, an especially severe punishment will be meted out to him. There must not be opportunities for further violation.

4. That they make copies of communications by the foreign guests and send them to the capital.

6   **On the Advisability of Continuing to Send Envoys to Tang China, 894**[27]   Your subject has studied carefully a report sent last year by Chūkan, a Japanese monk residing in Tang. In it he describes in detail erosion of Tang's power. He informs us that there has been an inquiry from a Tang official concerning Japan's suspension of sending envoys to Tang. The monk further avers that in his personal opinion, no envoy should be sent at this juncture. Chūkan is merely a monk, but his loyalty to your majesty is almost a second nature to him. As for his love for his homeland, it is almost like horses from the north rejoicing

---

[26]From *Ruiju Sandai Kyaku* as quoted in Hashimoto Yoshihiko, ed., *Komonjo no Kataru Nihonshi (Japanese History through Old Documents)*, vol. 2, *Heian (period)* (Tokyo: Chikuma Shobō, 1991), pp. 142–43.

[27]From *Kanke Bunsō (Writings of Sugawara no Michizane)* as quoted in Hashimoto, ed., *op. cit.*, pp. 259–60.

in the north wind, and migrating birds from the south always perching on branches extending to the south.

Your subject and his colleagues have studied old records. There were envoys who were unable to survive rigors of sea journey or were killed by bandits. However, once they touched the shores of Tang their safety was always assured and they did not suffer hunger or cold. In this context, the report of Chūkan gives us grave concern, as we can no longer be certain of their safety [within Tang].

Your subject and his colleagues prostrate and beg of your majesty to circulate Chūkan's report to nobles and learned men, and seek their opinions as to the advisability of continuing to send envoys to Tang. This is a matter of national concern. We are not worried about our own safety as such. We beg of you to render a decision as we humbly present our heartfelt concerns.

Sixth year of Kampyō (894) Ninth month, 14th day, Envoy to Tang, Sugawara no Michizane, et al.

7   Diary of Lady Murasaki, 1008–1010[28]

When my older brother Korechika and I were still young, he received formal lessons in reading [the Chinese classics] while I had to settle for the privilege of sitting nearby. It was almost eerie as I could always recite whatever he was taught. That included those passages he forgot or could not comprehend readily. My father Tametoki was a learned man. He would sigh and say how sad he was that I was not born a boy.

I was told that men who showed off their knowledge were often denied advancement. [As a woman I had to be even more careful.] I always pretended that I did not know how to write a single-stroke word like "one." I learned how not to pay attention to books which I once read. Afraid that someone might find out that I was literate [in Chinese], I refused to read a legend over a picture on a screen.

The imperial consort Shōshi commanded me to read for her pieces from *The Selected Writings of Bo Zhuyi* (772–846). She showed a great deal of interest in a variety of topics. So starting two years ago, when no one else was around, I taught her ancient poems contained in volumes three and four of *Bo Zhuyi*. These were clandestine meetings, and the imperial consort also desired that our secret be kept. Eventually our secret was uncovered by her father [Fujiwara no Michinaga (969–1027)] and by [her husband] Emperor Ichij) (r. 986–1011). . . .

LIFE OF THE NOBILITY

By the tenth century, as a result of the decline in governmental power, the aristocratic families lost much of their contact with the provinces. Their life,

---

[28]From *Murasaki Shikibu Nikki* (*Diary of Lady Murasaki*) as quoted in Ōkubo Toshiaki et al., eds., *Shiryō ni yoru Nihon no Ayumi* (*Japanese History through Documents*), *Kodaihen* (*Ancient Period*) (Tokyo: Yoshikawa Kōbunkan, 1960), pp. 337–38.

which was sustained by the income from their shōen *(see Chapter 4), was largely confined to the Heian capital. It was a life given to the pursuit of the rule of taste, of fun and festivals and of their traditional perquisites. Yet there was a feeling of general decay, as witnessed in the observations of the capital city (Document 8) by one Yoshishige no Yasutane (d. 1002) who discarded his promising career in Chinese literature in favor of the Pure Land belief. The nobility was also given very much to superstition based mainly on the* yin-yang *philosophy imported from China. The admonitions given to his heirs by Fujiwara Morosuke (907–960), founder of the Kujō family, vividly portray their superstitious practices (Document 9).*

8 **Observations on the Heian Capital, 982**[29]   I have been observing the conditions of the eastern and western sections of the capital city for more than twenty years. The western section has lost most of its dwellings, and is now reduced almost to rubble. People have left, but none enters the western section. Houses have crumbled into hovels but no new houses are built. Walking in this area, one finds that only those who do not mind being poor and destitute remain in the area. There are also some who prefer the life of the recluse, who under normal circumstances would have withdrawn into the mountains or returned to the fields, remaining in the western section. As to those who wish to attain riches and work toward that end, they cannot wait a moment to leave the section.

In olden days, there was a great mansion owned by a nobleman, whose many chambers were adorned by vermilion doors and whose garden was full of bamboos, trees, springs and stones. It was a spectacular sight. However, its owner [Minamoto no Takaaki, the Minister of Left] was demoted [in 967 to the position of Vice Governor of the Dazai area (Kyushu, Dazai no Gon-no-sotsu)]. Thereafter the mansion was burned down by a fire. Several tens of families used to have their mansions nearby, but they left the neighborhood one after another. Later the owner returned, but did not repair the mansion. He had many children and grandchildren, but none chose to remain in the area. The gates were closed by thorns and bushes, and foxes and racoon dogs were secure in their holes. Such devastation must be the manifestation of the will of Heaven to destroy the western section. It is certainly caused by the wrongdoings of the people.

In contrast, the eastern section from the Fourth Avenue northward, especially the northwestern and northeastern areas, is congested with people from all walks of life. The gates and buildings of great mansions follow one after another. Smaller buildings are erected so closely that their eaves touch one another. If the neighbor to the east suffers a fire, the western neighbor cannot escape a similar fate. If the neighbor to the south is invaded by armed bandits, the northern neighbor can expect to be affected similarly. . . . The rich are not necessarily

---

[29]From the *Honcho Monzui*, Book 12, in *Kokushi Taikei*, Vol. 29B, *op. cit.*, pp. 298–300.

endowed with virtue, while the poor still retain the sense of shame. Thus those poor people who live close to great families do not enjoy freedom of movement and behave continuously with trepidation. They do not dare replace their torn roofs or rebuild their broken fences. They are unable to laugh when happy or cry loudly when sorrowful. They are no different from sparrows who come near a flock of hawks. Instead of moving to another location to have a larger area to erect their dwellings, these insignificant people build their small dwellings close to each other, and contend for the small space. . . . In extreme instances, families were annihilated because of lack of space. Some foolish people erect their dwellings by the River Kamo and when a flood comes they cast their fate along with fish and tortoises. Others choose to stay in the northern fields where in time of drought, there is not even a drop of drinking water. There is space in the two sections of the capital, yet how stubborn are the people to elect to remain only in a small portion of the capital.

By the River Kamo and on the northern fields, people not only build houses and dwellings but also cultivate fields and gardens. Old farmers toil on the land to create ridges between rice fields and dam up the river to irrigate their fields. But last year there was a flood and the river crested over the dike. The officials in charge of flood control used to boast of their accomplishment, but today they take no actions to rectify the situation. Must the people in the capital be consigned to a fate similar to that of fish? When I study the regulations (*kyaku*), I discover that the western bank of the River Kamo can be cultivated by the Sujin-in only, and no exception is made. This prohibition is necessitated by the frequent flood damage. Furthermore, the banks of the River Kamo and the northern fields are two of the four major suburban areas which are utilized by the Emperor for the imperial outings. Even if people wish to cultivate these two areas, responsible officials must stop them. . . .

I cannot understand why people choose to stay in the congested eastern section which does not even belong to the capital proper while deserting the western section which is within the capital proper. The southern part of the western section is now given to waste where good grain can be produced. Why do people leave fertile soil to go to the infertile one? Is this due to the command of Heaven or due to the folly of the people?

9 Daily Observance, Last Testament of Fujiwara Morosuke, c 960[30]

When you arise in the morning chant seven times the name of the star for the year. Next look at yourself in a mirror. Next consult the calendar to know the fortune for the day. Next use your toothpick and face west to wash your hands. Next chant the name of the Buddha. At the same time you may also chant

[30]From *Kujōdono Ikai* (*Last Testament of Lord Kujō*) as quoted in Ōkubo et al., *op. cit.*, p. 372.

the names of those Shintō shrines to which you are affiliated. Next make your diary entry for yesterday. Next eat your rice-gruel [for breakfast]. Next set your hair (once every three days, not every day). Next cut your finger and toe nails (cut your finger nails on the day of the ox and your toe nails on the day of the tiger). Then select a day to bathe (once every five days). You must consult the fortune before bathing. (It is said in the Biography of the Yellow Emperor that bathing on the first day of the month results in a shortened life. Bathing on the eighth day brings about longevity. Bathing on the eleventh day helps your eyesight, and bathing on the eighteenth day causes suffering from bandits. Bathing on the day of the horse results in the loss of love and respect, and bathing on the day of the boar brings shame. Do not bathe on bad days. The bad days are, the days of the tiger, dragon horse and dog, and the day when the star of the long-nosed goblin comes down to earth to eat the food of the human beings). Next, if you have to go to your office, put your cap and robe on. . . .

When children are grown to the point of knowing what is going on around them, they must be taught to read the classics and important books written by the sages of old. This is done in the morning which is followed by the practice of calligraphy. They may be allowed to play afterwards. They are strictly forbidden to engage in falconry or gambling. After coming of age, and before entering their careers with the government, do likewise. However, all of you are advised to select at an early age your main object of worship (*honzon*). Wash your hands in the water drawn in a wash basin, chant the name of the Buddha who is your main object of worship or chant the miraculous words of the Shingon (True Words, the sect propagated by Kūkai). As to the frequency of this form of worship, use your own discretion. However, if you do not believe, your lives are likely to be cut short, as demonstrated by many former examples. . . . Retain the services of monks who are good believers, pure in spirit and endowed with wisdom. Converse with them when occasion permits. This will not only help you in this world but also create good karmic conditions for future lives. . . .

TALES OF THE COMMON MAN

The setuwa bungaku *or tale literature flourished in the Heian and Kamakura periods. It contained folk tales, oral traditions and legends, and represented Buddhist and secular views of life as perceived by common men. The following selections are taken from the* Uji Shūi Monogatari (A Collection of Tales from Uji), *which along with the larger* Konjaku Monogatarishū (A Collection of Tales of Old and New), *represents the best of the tale literature.*

The exact date of the compilation of the Uji *collection is not known, but it is usually thought to have occurred in the early thirteenth century or during the Kamakura period. However, many of its tales, through internal and linguistic evidence, can be assigned dates earlier than 1070. Thus in many ways, the tales can show the life style of common men during the Heian period. The common people's disdain for dishonest priests is shown in Document 10. The court life, which revelled in trivia and ceremonies, did not escape their close scrutiny. (Document 11). Document 12 gives a fairly representative sample of morality tales. It contains a Buddhist notion of ahimsa or non-injury to living creatures as well as a feeling for just rewards and punishments.*

10 How a Priest Put the Magic Incantation of the Bodhisattva Zuigu into His Forehead[31]

Again, long ago a very dignified-looking mountain priest came into a certain man's house and stood outside the retainers' duty-room, in a small courtyard enclosed by a screen. He had an air of great consequence, with an axe slung on his back and a conch-shell trumpet at his belt and in his hand a staff tipped with rings. When the retainers asked who he was, he replied, "I spent some time on Hakuṣan, then I went to the Sacred Peak and I intended to perform devotions there for another two thousand days, but my goods gave out and so I have come to beg alms. Please inform your master." As he stood there, they observed that in the middle of his forehead he had a scar about two inches long extending up towards his hair, still newly healed and reddish. When one of the retainers wanted to know how he came to have this scar on his forehead, he assumed a tone of great dignity and said, "That is where I put in the magic incantation of the Bodhisattva Zuigu." "What a wonderful thing," said the retainers to each other. "You see many people who have cut off a finger or a toe, say but who would have expected to come across someone who has broken open his forehead and put in the incantation of Zuigu?" Just then a young retainer of about sixteen or seventeen came running out and, taking one look at the priest, he burst out, "Don't make me laugh! A fine one you'd be to put the Zuigu incantation into your forehead! You used to go and sneak into that house belonging to the metal-founder, directly to the east of young Gō's place in the Seventh Ward, and go to bed with the wife—till last summer the metal-founder came home and discovered you in bed with her. You didn't stop for anything, just bolted off up the street heading west. In front of my place you were cornered and had your head split open with a hoe. I saw it myself!" His words quite shocked the retainers, but the priest's face showed no sign of concern whatever. With an air of great solemnity and innocence, he said, "That's when I seized the opportunity to put it in." The whole crowd was convulsed with laughter, and the priest took advantage of this to slip away.

---

[31]From D. E. Mills, *A Collection of Tales from Uji* (Cambridge: Cambridge University Press, 1970), pp. 141–42. Reprinted with the permission of Cambridge University Press. The term "Zuigu" means "according to prayer." This bodhisattva is a metamorphosis of Kannon who sees that all prayers are answered. This magic incantation is a *dharani* from the *Zuigu Darani Kyō*.

11

About Aotsune (Sir Evergreen)[32]   Long ago, during the reign of the Emperor Murakami (946–967), there was a certain scion of an old princely family who was Master of the Office of the Left Division of the Capital. Though he was fairly tall and very much the aristocrat, he looked on the whole rather stupid, and there was a certain awkwardness about him. The back of his head bulged out like a stirrup, so that the strings of his cap swung free and did not even touch his back. His face had a greenish pallor, as if it had been painted with a flower dye, his eyes were sunken, and he had a very prominent bright-red nose. His lips were thin and colorless, and when he smiled his teeth protruded, showing the red of his gums. His beard was red, too, and grew very long. He had a very nasal voice, so loud that when he spoke the whole building shook. He walked with a jerky movement of his body and his shoulders. Because of his green complexion, the young gentlemen of the Court jokingly called him Aotsune no Kimi ('Sir Evergreen'). The young men mocked him so cruelly at every turn that the reports reaching the Emperor's ears could no longer be ignored, and he issued a stern reprimand. "It is very unfair of you to make fun of this gentleman. His father the Prince would surely bear me ill-will if I were not to put a stop to such behavior now that it has come to my attention." The courtiers felt rather abashed at this, and came to an agreement that they would give up making fun of Aotsune, vowing as follows: "In view of His Majesty's disapproval, we swear that henceforth anyone using the name 'Aotsune' shall pay a forfeit by entertaining the rest of us to wine and fruit and whatnot." But it was not long after they had taken this vow that Lord Horikawa,[33] who was at that time still only a Courtier in Attendance,[34] got a back view of the gentleman in question as he was walking along one day, and forgetting his promise, blurted out, "Where is old Sir Evergreen going?" The other courtiers crowded round, all talking to him at once. "Now you must do as we all agreed. Hurry up and send for some wine and fruit and pay forfeit." He brushed their complaints aside, but they were so insistent that eventually he said, "Very well, then, I'll pay my forfeit the day after tomorrow. I want you all to be there then." When the day arrived there was not a single absentee, for everybody was anxious to see Lord Horikawa pay his forfeit, and the courtiers were all sitting in their places waiting when he appeared. He was in informal dress, his face radiant, his clothes exquisitely perfumed, and he fairly oozed charm. Below the beautiful long skirt of his robe could be seen the edge of a green under-robe, filled to a lustrous sheen, while his trousers were also of green. He had dressed his three attendants in green hunting-coats and skirts. One carried a green-painted tray bearing celadon

---

[32]*Ibid.*, pp. 336–38. Aotsune's real name was Minamoto Kunimasa, grandson of Emperor Daigo (r. 897–930).

[33]Fujiwara Kanemichi, died 977, aged fifty-three.

[34]I.e., he had not yet attained the Third Court Rank.

porcelain plates heaped with greenish-yellow *koka* fruit (pear). Another brought in four or five wild pigeons attached to a stick of bamboo, while the third brought in *sake* in celadon porcelain jars, with green paper over the tops. At the sight of these three attendants coming one after another into the audience chamber with these things, the courtiers burst out together in one great shriek of laughter. The Emperor heard them and wanted to know the reason for such a commotion in the audience chamber. "Kanemichi used the name 'Aotsune,' Your Majesty," said one of the ladies, "And he's paying the forfeit that they insisted on." Curious to see what the forfeit was, the Emperor went to his day-time apartment and took a look through the lattice-work screen. Now he realized what the laughter was about, for Kanemichi, himself dressed in green, was paying his forfeit with foods that were all green in color, brought in by servants who were likewise dressed in green. His Majesty himself found it a harmless and very amusing joke.

From then on, since no one made any serious attempt to reprimand them, the courtiers made fun of Aotsume more than ever.

12 How a Sparrow Repaid Its Debt of Gratitude[35]

Long ago, one fine day in spring, a woman of about sixty was cleansing herself of lice when she saw a boy pick up a stone and throw it at one of the sparrows which was hopping around in the garden. The stone broke the bird's leg, and as it floundered about, wildly flapping its wings, a crow came swooping down on it. "Oh, the poor thing," cried the woman, "the crow will get it," and snatching it up, she revived it with her breath and gave it something to eat. At night, she placed it for safety in a little bucket. Next morning, when she gave it some rice and also a medicinal powder made from ground copper, her children and grandchildren ridiculed her. "Just look," they jeered, "Grannie's taken to keeping sparrows in her old age."

For several months she tended it, till in time it was hopping about again, and though it was only a sparrow, it was deeply grateful to her for nursing it back to health. Whenever she left the house on the slightest errand, the woman would ask someone to look after the sparrow and feed it. . . . She kept it till it could fly again, then, confident that there was no longer any risk of its being caught by a crow, she went outside and held it up on her hand to see if it would fly away. Off it went with a flap of its wings. Everyone laughed at the woman because she missed her sparrow so much. "For so long now I've been used to shutting it up at night and feeding it in the morning," she said, "and oh dear, now it's flown away! I wonder if it will ever come back."

About three weeks later, she suddenly heard a sparrow chirping away near her house. "Well I never!" she exclaimed. "What a wonderful thing for it to remember me and come back!" The sparrow took one look at the woman's face, then it

---

[35]*Ibid.*, pp. 209–14.

seemed to drop some tiny object out of its mouth and flew away. "Whatever can it be, this thing the sparrow has dropped?" she exclaimed, and going up to it, she found it was a single calabash-seed. "It must have had some reason for bringing this," she said, and she picked it up and kept it. Her children laughed at her and said, "There's a fine thing to do, getting something from a sparrow and treating it as if you'd got a fortune!" "All the same," she told them, "I'm going to plant it and see what happens," which she did. When autumn came, the seed had produced an enormous crop of calabashes, much larger and more plentiful than usual. Delighted, the woman gave some to her neighbors, and however many she picked, the supply was inexhaustible. The children who had laughed at her were now eating the fruit from morning to night, while everyone in the village received a share. In the end, the woman picked out seven or eight especially big ones to make into gourds, and hung them up in the house.

After several months, she inspected them and found that they were ready. As she took them down to cut openings in them, she thought they seemed rather heavy, which was mysterious. But when she cut one open, she found it full to the brim. Wondering whatever could be inside it, she began emptying it out—and found it full of white rice! In utter amazement, she poured all of the rice into a large vessel, only to discover that the gourd immediately refilled itself. "Obviously some miracle has taken place—it must be the sparrow's doing," she exclaimed, bewildered but very happy. She put that gourd away out of sight before she examined the rest of them, but they all proved to be crammed full of rice, just like the first one. Whenever she took rice from the gourds, there was always far more than she could possibly use, so that she became extremely rich. The people in the neighboring villages were astonished to see how prosperous she had become, and were filled with envy at her incredible good fortune.

Now the children of the woman who lived next door said to their mother, "You and that woman next door are the same sort of people, but just look where she's got to! Why haven't you ever managed to do any good for us?" Their criticism stung the woman into going to see her neighbor. "Well, well, however did you manage this business?" she asked. "Well, it all began when a sparrow dropped a calabash-seed and I planted it." said the other woman. The neighbor now began to keep a sharp lookout in case she too might find a sparrow with a broken leg to tend. But there were no such sparrows to be found. Every morning as she looked out, there would be sparrows hopping around pecking at any grains of rice that happened to be lying about outside the back door—and one day she picked up some stones and threw them in the hope of hitting one. Since she had several throws and there was such a flock of birds, she naturally managed to hit one, and as it lay on the ground, unable to fly away, she went up to it in great excitement and hit it again, to make sure that its leg was broken. Then she picked it up and took it indoors, where she fed it and treated it with medicine. "Why, if a single sparrow brought my neighbor all that wealth," she thought to herself, "I should get a lot more credit from my children than she did from hers." So she scattered some rice in the doorway and sat watching, then when a group of sparrows gathered to peck at it, she threw several stones at them, injuring three. "That will do," she thought, and putting the three sparrows with broken legs into a bucket, she fed them a medicinal powder made from ground copper. Some months later, she took them outdoors and they all flew away. In her own estimation she had acted with great kindness. But the sparrows bitterly resented having had their legs broken and being kept in captivity for months.

Ten days went by, and to the woman's great joy the sparrows returned. As she was staring at them to see if they had anything in their mouths, they each dropped a calabash-seed and flew off . . . picking up the seeds, she planted them in three places. In no time, much faster than ordinary ones, they had grown into huge plants, though none of them had borne much fruit—not more than seven or eight calabashes. She beamed with pleasure as she looked at them. . . . Since there were only a few calabashes, she did not eat any herself or let anyone else eat any, in the hope of getting more rice from them. Her children grumbled, "The woman next door ate some of hers and gave some to her neighbors. And we've got three seeds, which is more than she had, so there ought to be something for ourselves and the neighbors to eat." Feeling that perhaps they were right, the woman gave some away to the neighbors, while she cooked a number of the fruit for herself and her family to eat. The calabashes tasted terribly bitter, and made everyone feel quite nauseated. Every single person who had eaten any, including the woman herself and her children, were sick. The neighbors were furious and came round in a very ugly mood, demanding to know what it was she had given them. The woman and her children, meanwhile, were sprawled out half-conscious and vomiting all over the place, so that there was little point in the neighbors' complaining, and they went away. In two or three days, everyone had recovered, and the woman came to the conclusion that the peculiar things which had happened must have been the outcome of being overhasty and eating the calabashes which should have given rice. She therefore hung the rest of the fruit up in store. After some months, when she felt they would be ready, she went into the storeroom armed with buckets to hold the rice. Her toothless mouth grinning from ear to ear with happiness, she held the buckets up to the gourds and went to pour out the contents of the fruit—but what emerged was a stream of things like horseflies, bees, centipedes, lizards and snakes; she felt no pain, and thought that it was rice pouring over her, for she shouted. "Wait a moment, my sparrows. Let me get in a little at a time." Out of the seven or eight gourds came a vast horde of venomous creatures which stung the children and their mother—the latter so badly that she died. The sparrows had resented having their legs broken and had persuaded swarms of insects and reptiles to enter the gourds; whereas the sparrow next door had been grateful because when it had broken its leg it had been saved from a crow and nursed back to health. So you see, you should never be jealous of other people.

CHAPTER IV

Rise of Feudal Institutions

It was generally conceded by historians that Japan, along with Western Europe, exhibited one of the "only two fully-proven cases of feudalism."[1] Indeed, between 1192 and 1600, Japanese society demonstrated many of the characteristics of "feudalism" which were similar to those developed in Western Europe between 800 and 1200. The purpose of this chapter is to study (1) the origins of *shōen* (private domains or proprietorships). (2) the ascendancy of the warrior class, (3) the coalescence of the two, and (4) the founding of the Kamakura Shogunate, all of which contributed to the development of feudalism in Japan.

The origins of *shōen* can be traced directly to the breakdown of the *ritsu-ryō* system (see Documents 2 and 3, Chapter II), which was fashioned after the codes of China. The Chinese concept of state ownership of land, and a system of allotment of rice fields and their periodic redistribution remained alien to Japanese practices. As Asakawa Kanichi points out, two factors peculiar to Japanese agriculture, namely the comparative absence of pasture, and the cultivation of rice as the chief agricultural industry,[2] contributed to the persistence of the older native institution of individual ownership.

The *ritsu-ryō* system was honored more in its breach than in its observance.

---

[1]Rushton Coulborn, *Feudalism in History* (Princeton: Princeton University Press, 1956), p. 185. Other excellent discussions of Japanese feudalism can be found in John W. Hall and Marius B. Jansen, eds., *Studies in the Institutional History of Early Modern Japan* (Princeton: Princeton University Press, 1968), Kanichi Asakawa, *The Documents of Iriki* (Tokyo: Japan Society for the Promotion of Science, 1955), Minoru Shinoda, *The Founding of the Kamakura Shogunate, 1180–1185* (New York: Columbia University Press, 1960), and John W. Hall, *Government and Local Power in Japan, 500–1700: A Study Based on Bizen Province* (Princeton: Princeton University Press, 1966).

[2]K. Asakawa, "Some Aspects of Japanese Feudal Institutions" in *TASJ*, 1st Ser. Vol. 46 (1918), pp. 92–93.

Even at the inception of the Taika reforms of 645, several concessions were made to the nobility and clan chieftains. There were *iden* (rank-rice fields) and *shikiden* (office-rice fields) whose size depended on the degree of the rank or the importance of the office of the holder, or *kōden* (merit-rice fields) which were granted for meritorious services, and *shiden* (gift-rice fields) freely given by the emperor. These rice fields were, in the strict sense of the word, not private estates and were technically subject to taxation. However, in practice, offices and ranks tended to be hereditary, and *iden* and *shikiden* could thus be held in the same family for generations.

Lands held by shrines (*shinden*) and temples (*jiden*) were also exempt from taxation. With the removal of some of the choice fields from the tax roll and from the allotment system, the government was forced to resort to some other measures. One of its bolder undertakings was to encourage reclamation of new fields (*konden*). However, as soon as it proved an incentive for cultivation—by providing tax exemption for three generations—the system was again open to exploitation by great families and temples. Trends toward further private ownership were confirmed in 743 in a decree which permitted possession of newly cultivated lands by private parties in perpetuity. It was a concession to the claims of the nobility to these lands, and the principle of state ownership of lands was in effect abandoned.

Some of the private estates held by the nobility were called *shōen*, and so were the lands acquired by the great Buddhist temples. By 902 when the government tried to restrict the spread of *shōen*, many of the *shōen* contained the following two fundamental characteristics: (1) They had as their seigniors some powerful nobility, imperial princes, Buddhist orders and/or shrines, and (2) they acquired immunities from taxation and from entry by public officials and thus were able to remove themselves from the encroachment of civil authorities. There were several avenues to acquire such immunities. One was the continuation of the privileges granted to *iden*, *shikiden* and other tax-free estates, and another was through commendation to one or more seigniors.

Proliferation of *shōen* continued, and by the eleventh and twelfth centuries, *shōen* reached its fullest development, acquiring a very complex organization. Travelers in twelfth-century Japan would have discovered the countryside divided into many *shōen* which consisted of farms scattered over rather ill-defined areas. Farming was generally prosperous. Farm implements made of iron such as spades, hoes and plows were owned by the cultivators and/or managers. There was also a noticeable improvement in the farming techniques, such as the use of horses and oxen as draft animals. Use of manure and night soil as fertilizer was widely known, and double cropping was practiced in the Kamakura period. Irrigation works were essential to farming, and each farmer contributed to the maintenance of dikes and embankments or to the digging of ditches. However, the fact that *shōen* boundaries were not always well-defined contributed to many disputes over the right to use water.

Cultivators paid anywhere from thirty to fifty percent of their produce as the annual rent (*nengu*) to their various managers and seigniors. In addition, they had to perform miscellaneous services, and were also subject to miscellaneous exactions. The exact amount of their burden varied from *shōen* to *shōen*, depending on the intricate fee or tax structure that was developed in that particular *shōen*. The cultivators, as a rule, did not pay taxes to the central government, but their burdens were probably heavier than in the periods immediately following the Taika reforms.

The *shōen* was not a subdivision of the civil administration, but a private domain which attained its own financial and judicial autonomy. While it was a "private domain," outright ownership of land was, for all practical purposes, non-existent. A great number of people held certain functions over *shōen*, which in turn gave them rights to recompense for performing such functions. These functions and rights were called *shiki*, and their *shiki* were not mutually exclusive but overlapping. In the ascending order, first there was the small cultivator, who enjoyed the rights of cultivating the land, living on it and consuming whatever was left from the fruits of his labor after the rights of all other concerned parties were satisfied (*saku shiki* or *sakute shiki*, etc.). Then there was the *myōshu* (in the twelfth century), or master of *myōden* (name-rice fields), who owned the basic unit within the *shōen*. His rights were similar to those of the proprietor of a subdivision of *shōen* (*jinushi shiki*), and could also combine the rights of a manager or bailiff (*azukaridokoro shiki*). The *myōshu* had his beginning as a *tato*, who held the right of cultivation which could be transferred. Above them stood the manager or bailiff (*shōkan*) who managed *shōen* in return for a share of its produce (*azukaridokoro shiki*). He was appointed by the *ryōshu* or *ryōke*, who exercised the rights of ownership and of collecting the annual rent (*ryōshu shiki*). A *ryōshu* could be a local magnate who had initially brought the land under cultivation, or an imperial prince, court noble, or abbot of a temple who received a grant of land in one form or another. A *honke*, or a patron, received lands commended to him, and by virtue of his high position, ensured the immunity of *shōen* from taxation and/or encroachment. He could also be an imperial prince, a powerful court noble, or an abbot of a great temple. His *honke shiki* was confined to the right of a certain portion of the annual rent.

The *shiki* was not a fixed tenure, and it was flexible. According to Asakawa Kanichi,[3] the *shiki* was an attempt, perhaps unconsciously at first, by the independent landholders to retain the real possession and use of land and to secure its immunity from public taxation. They had thus resorted to the division and conveyance of detached *shiki* of land. The excessive mobility of *shiki* would thus suggest that "personal property right of cultivated land in Japan" was "already securely entrenched" before the beginning of Japan's feudal formation. This did

---

[3]*Ibid.*, pp. 93–94.

prevent the appearance of a manorial organization, and the encroachment by the seignior upon the freedom of individual possession was resisted. It could well account for the basic difference between the development of feudalism in Japan and in Western Europe.

In its initial development, and before the founding of the Kamakura Shogunate, *shōen* was neither a manor nor a fief. Its transformation into a fief had to await a new organization which could break down the subtlety of the *shiki*. This process could be achieved only with the rise of the warrior class and its confirmation into power.

Rise of the samurai (warrior) class: The central government's power to govern became seriously weakened in the ninth century when its military and police organizations experienced radical changes. In 816 the appointment of a *kebiishi* (metropolitan constable) was made in the capital, and the operations of his office were later extended to the provinces. This was followed by the appointment of officers to assist police officers in apprehending bandits and pirates (*tsuibushi* and *ōryōshi* who could be considered imperial gendarmes). They were emergency organs endowed with excessive powers which eventually subverted the basic functions of the official system.

On military matters, in 792 the government suspended the principle of universal military service (though this was never fully practiced), and replaced it with a system of locally enlisted armies of able-bodied young men (*kondeisei*), selected from among the families of district officers and local magnates. This system proved to be unworkable, and the local magnates, with the economic powers of *shōen* to back them, often converted these armies into their own private armies.

The imperial court required for its own protection a group of professional soldiers, named Takiguchi no Bushi. Its example was followed by the nobility who employed their own private soldiers. These soldiers were called *saburai*, meaning private retainers who were in waiting at the command of their masters. The term took a new form, *samurai*, by which later Japanese warriors were known. The samurai came from provinces to serve in the capital or in the *shōen* to protect the interests of the nobility. They were the ones who could effectuate their reign over the peasantry and protect the scattered private domains. As the police power of the central government diminished, the importance of the samurai rose correspondingly. In the beginning their influence was meager, and their social position was low. But when some former provincial governors decided to stay in the provinces after the expiration of their terms of office, or some noble men sought their fortune in those localities by becoming leaders of the samurai, their positions gradually acquired social respectability to the extent that they could challenge the dominance of the court nobility.

The samurai class experienced the fastest growth in the eastern region (Kantō), where the government called upon them to fight the early border wars. Several other factors also contributed to the rise of powerful local lords. Kantō provided larger tracts of lands which could be converted into larger private domains. The distance from the capital made it possible for the growth of new institutions unencumbered by the old tradition. In addition, local lords could be law unto themselves and unto their own retainers. They were the ones who could provide the most effective protection. The samurai in the eastern region were often banded as *ichizoku*, or *rōtō*, literally "one family" or "retainers" in the service of their master. They were not necessarily related by blood or marriage to their master, but the term is symbolic of their cohesive unity and represented their close ties of personal bondage. This developed into the system of *gokenin* or vassals (literally, member of the household).

In 1091, the Imperial Court prohibited land owners from commending their *shōen* to Minamoto Yoshiie who was the hero of the so-called Nine Years' War (1051–1062) and Three Years' War (1083–1087). To the rank-conscious court nobility, sanctioning the commendations made to Yoshiie would elevate the "upstart," a mere *saburai*, to the same rank as the court nobles, who heretofore had enjoyed the exclusive privilege of being patrons and seigniors of *shōen*. Yoshiie's ascendancy also seriously challenged their potentially lucrative sources of income. However, it was symptomatic of the age that the owners and cultivators preferred Yoshiie over court nobles as their patron and seignior. It was the former who could wield the actual power, and in the face of it the power of the nobility was found wanting. It was in this way that the hold of the samurai over the *shōen* was strengthened steadily over the succeeding years.

The rivalry between the two samurai families of Taira and Minamoto resulted in the eventual victory of the Minamoto family, and in 1192, Minamoto no Yoritomo founded the Kamakura Shogunate. One can cautiously assign to this date the beginning of "feudalism" in Japan.[4] For our purpose, Yoritomo's greatest contribution to Japanese feudalism lies in his regularization of the practices of combining pledges of military allegiance with protection over land holdings. He initiated the *shugo-jitō* (protector-steward) system to provide him with a means of extending his sway over the distant provinces, and of enforcing his powers of tax collection as well as of military protection. However, initially the power of the Kamakura Shogunate was not complete. Some *shōen* continued to be controlled by a system which sought its directions from Kyoto. This dilemma was dissolved in 1221 when the forces of Kamakura defeated the army of the ex-Emperor Go-Toba. The war of Jōkyū, as it was known, extended the *jitō* system to the entire country, and with it the right of interference in the affairs of the imperial court.

The Hōjō Code of judicature (1232) showed the new self-confidence of the victorious Kamakura warriors. Practical reason, and not the customary laws of the Kyoto court, became the guide in the writing of this new legislation. There was an

---

[4]But see John W. Hall, "Feudalism in Japan—A Reassessment," in Hall and Jansen, *op. cit.*, pp. 39ff.

unabashed attempt to create a new law and new society for a new era which was to be governed by the samurai. The code was the first significant step toward attaining an efficient instrument of mental analysis. And like their European counterparts, there was "no longer a divorce between the means of expression and the thought to be expressed" among the Japanese men of action.[5] With their new self-awareness, the samurai created new institutions and a new set of values which dominated Japan certainly until 1600, and beyond that to the end of the Tokugawa period.

PUBLIC VS. PRIVATE OWNERSHIP OF LAND

The ideal of public ownership of land, first espoused by the Taika reforms of 645, can be found in Document 1 which describes the system of land allotment and periodic redistribution. This was an imitation of Tang China's "equal field" system, but the indigenous customary practices of the past persisted. One example was the permission to sell and purchase mulberry gardens [for silk production] and lots on which houses were erected. In addition, lease on mulberry gardens could be continued indefinitely. Thus, once private possession of land was legalized, public ownership of land quickly receded to the background.

Scarcity of allotment land led the government in 722 to seek a means of opening up the one million chō (about three million acres) of wasteland and virgin land (Document 2). It was an ambitious scheme which would have brought land under cultivation to twice the level of that cultivated before the measure went into effect. However, the difficulty of implementing this konden *policy forced the government to adopt a new measure the following year, by permitting cultivators to enjoy the lands they opened up tax-free for one to three generations (Document 3). This was followed in 743 by an edict which permitted private possession of land (Document 4), which proved to be a boon to the nobility and to the great temples. The proscription of 765 was a half-hearted effort to reverse this trend, but it never succeeded (Document 5).*

1   Allotment Land (Kubunden) and Other Land Regulations[6]

a) Allotment Land:

In distributing land, two *tan* shall be given to a man as his allotment land, and

---

[5]See Marc Bloch, *Feudal Society* (Chicago: University of Chicago Press, 1961), p. 108.

[6]In selecting documents for this chapter, I am indebted to Ōkubo Toshiaki et al., eds., *Shiryō ni yoru Nihon no Ayumi (Japanese History through Documents) Kodaihen (Ancient Period)* and *Chūseihen (Mediaeval Period)* (Tokyo: Yoshikawa Kōbunkan, 1960 and 1963). As much as possible reference will be given to these volumes in providing citations. The Ōkubo volumes give further citations to the original sources. This particular document comes from the *Ryo no Gige*, Book 3, Land Regulations, and is in Ōkubo's *Kodaihen*, pp. 141–142.

two-thirds of that amount for a woman. No one shall receive allotment land if he is five years of age or younger. Some localities may or may not have sufficient fields for distribution. In that event, local customs must be consulted. If the land is poor and can be cultivated only in alternate years, then double the regular amounts shall be distributed. After the distribution is completed, the size and the four borders must be minutely recorded.

The land allocation shall be made once every six years, but lands belonging to shrines and temples are not subject to this rule. If a holder of allotment land dies and his land is returned to the state, it will again be placed for the purpose of distribution in the year in which land allocation is made.

. . . Slaves belonging to officials (whether they are allowed to maintain their own household or not) are to be treated as if they were free men for the purpose of receiving allotment land. Private slaves maintaining their own households and common slaves shall receive one third of the amount distributed to free men, subject to the availability of fields in localities.

b) Gardens and Lots on Which Houses are Erected:

Gardens may be allotted to people in accordance with the availability. If a particular household does not have an heir, then the allotted garden is escheated to the state. If an individual wishes to sell or purchase a lot on which a house is to be erected, he must petition the appropriate bureau of the government and receive its approval. Officials and common people (*hyakushō*) must not transfer the title to their housing lots and gardens to temples, either as an act of benevolence or by selling.

c) Lease of Public Fields:

Publicly owned fields in different provinces [which are not included in *iden, shikiden* or *kubunden*] may be leased by the provincial governors in accordance with the prevailing prices of the locality. The rental thus received shall be sent to the Council of State (*dajōkan*) for its miscellaneous use. All rice fields leased shall be limited for a period of one year. Gardens may be leased for an indefinite period, or may be sold. All such transactions must be petitioned to the appropriate governmental bureau and receive its approval.

2   Plan to Cultivate One Million Chō of New Fields, 727[7]

Sixth year of Yōrō [722], second of the fourth month (leap year), 25th day. The Council of State addressed the throne, saying: ". . . It is said that people regard the acquisition of food as one of their highest goals. To govern well, we must establish appropriate plans to foster this end. We therefore respectfully recommend that farming be encouraged, and crops be stored to prepare against dry seasons. Officials shall be entrusted with the task of sending laborers to cultivate good fields in the amount of one million *chō*.

---

[7]*Ibid.*, p. 185. Documents 2 through 5 come from the *Shoku Nihongi.*

"The laborers shall be impressed for service for not more than ten days, during which time their food shall be provided. In addition publicly owned farm implements shall be rented out for their use. . . . If provincial governors (*kuni no tsukasa*) are found not diligent in performing their duties, or unwilling to organize the work for cultivation, they shall be immediately relieved of their positions. . . . If common people under a particular official's jurisdiction reclaim wastelands and idle fields to produce more than 3,000 *koku* of grains by their hard work, the official shall be decorated with the sixth order of meritorious services. If more than 1,000 *koku* are produced, he shall be exempt from taxation for life. Those officials [who have performed well and] who are above the eighth rank shall be given one point of merit to count toward their future promotion. If after such rewards are given, and they remain idle and do not perform their duties, then the additional ranks conferred shall be retroactively cancelled, and the officials shall be demoted to their original station."

3 **Land Held for Three Generations or One Generation (Sanze Isshin no Hō), 723**[8] Seventh year of Yōrō [723], Summer, fourth month, 17th day. The Council of State addressed the throne, saying: "These days, people are increasing in number but fields are becoming scarce. We therefore respectfully recommend that the government decree to all under heaven to open land for cultivation. If there are those who make new irrigation ditches and dams and reclaim new land for cultivation, regardless of the amount involved, they shall enjoy use of such land for three generations [without paying taxes]. If there are those who reclaim new land by using old ditches and dams, they shall enjoy use of such land for life [without paying taxes]."

4 **Private Ownership of Reclaimed Land, 743**[9] Fifteenth year of Tempyō [743], fifth month, 27th day. His Majesty the Emperor decreed, saying: "We have heard that in accordance with the regulations promulgated in the seventh year of Yōrō [723], newly reclaimed land was reverted to the state after the expiration of the time limit, to be placed for distribution. This caused farmers to refrain from performing their tasks, and the newly reclaimed land again became wasteland. Thereafter it is ordered that all newly reclaimed land, irrespective of the provisions of the Three Generations or One Generation Rule, shall become irrevocably the possession of the reclaimers.

"The areas that may be placed under private possession are, however, subject to the following limitations: imperial princes of first rank, or court nobles of first rank, 500 *chō*; imperial princes of second rank and court nobles of second rank,

---

[8]*Ibid.*, p. 185.
[9]*Ibid.*, p. 196.

400 *chō*; imperial princes third and fourth ranks and court nobles third rank, 300 *chō*; court nobles fourth rank, 200 *chō*; court nobles fifth rank, 100 *chō*; persons of sixth to eighth ranks inclusive, 50 *chō*; and those below that rank to the common men, 10 *chō*. . . . Those lands reclaimed by provincial governors are to revert to the state in accordance with the regulations now in effect."[10]

5 Proscription of Private Ownership of Land, 765[11]   First year of Tempyō Shingo [765], third month, 5th day.

The Emperor ordered, saying: "We have heard that in accordance with the decree of the fifteenth year of Tempyō [743], reclaimers could retain as their private possessions lands reclaimed by them irrespective of the provisions of the Three Generations or One Generation Rule. Thus they could retain such lands in perpetuity. In this way people under heaven competed with one another to re-claim new land [for private gains]. Powerful families have exploited the labor of the common people; as a result, poor people no longer have time to sustain themselves for their own well being. Thereafter, all such practice shall be pro-scribed, and no new land shall be reclaimed. However, this restriction shall not apply to temples which wish to continue developing new lands in accordance with the previously set plans. Also common people in the specific localities (*tōdo no hyakushō*) shall be permitted to retain one or two *chō* as their private possession."

GROWTH OF SHŌEN

Several means were employed by holders of shōen *to expand its privileges which in turn insured its phenomenal growth between the tenth and twelfth centuries. One was to gain immunity from taxation (*fuyu) *for the newly-acquired lands which were technically ineligible for such privileges (Document 6). And once immunity from taxation was secured, the* shōen *holders reasoned that it was no longer necessary for public officials to enter the* shōen *in question, since there was no need for investigating the taxable crops or people who could be im-pressed upon to perform certain services. The immunity from entry (*funyū) *was often extended to include denial of entry to police officers (Document 7). Docu-ments grouped together as Document 8 show how the Tōji, belonging to the Shingon sect, successfully extended most of these privileges to all of its landhold-ings to create a powerful* shōen.

Even after these immunities were acquired, if the owner were powerless, the

---

[10]In the year 729 the following regulation was issued: "The lands opened to cultivation by provincial governors during their tenure of office . . . shall all revert to the state, to facilitate their redistribution to local people."

[11]Ōkubo, *op. cit.*, p. 186.

*provincial governor—whose duties included protection of sources of tax reve-
nue—could still cancel the privileges given to a particular* shōen. *Commendation
to a more powerful person was a means of protecting such privileges. Document
9 shows how a series of commendations was made to prevent "lawless encroachment by provincial officials." Note also the different* shiki *which were discussed
in that particular document.*

Just how the proliferation of shōen *could adversely affect the livelihood of
common people is described in Document 10. There is evidence to show that the
imperial proscription of 902 against further spread of* shōen *was implemented,
at least partially. The* shōen *held by middle and lower eschelon nobles were
adversely affected by the proscription and there was a sizable reorganization of*
shōen *holdings. However, those in the highest position, the Fujiwara family in
particular, benefited from the proscription. No provincial governors would dare
challenge them when they violated the proscription, and they could continue to
receive lands in commendations, at the expense of lesser nobles.*

*Document 11 comes from an earlier period, and describes the power of
provincial governors as it affected the growth of* shōen. *Initially, provincial
governors represented the interest of the central government and indirectly that
of the Fujiwara family. In addition, they utilized the opportunities of being governors to serve their own interests as well. They could do so by working closely
with local magnates, which often deterred development of independent cultivators and landholders (see the discussion of* myōshu *and* tato *in the following
section). However, when the interest of governors and of local magnates came
into direct conflict with that of the Fujiwara family, the latter would even tempo-
rarily align with the common peasantry to preserve their own supremacy. Document 11 must be read in this light.*

*Incidentally, in the documents below the terms "shōen" and "shō" are used
interchangeably.*

6 Privilege of Tax Immunity (Fuyu), 951 and 953[12]

a) An Order of the Council of State, Issued to the Provincial Governor of Ise.

On the matter of immunity from taxation for the Sone *shō*, owned by the
Daigoji [temple]. Officials of the *shō* and its inhabitants are also to be exempt
from miscellaneous labor services imposed from time to time.

A certain *shō* which is located in the district (*kōri*) of Ishi on the above matter,
the said temple submitted a brief dated the seventh day of the seventh month
which stated: "Arguments relating to the question of the *shō*'s tax-exempt status

---

[12]*Ibid.*, pp. 261–262. This particular document comes from the records of the Daigo
Temple. Hereafter readers will find many documents related to temple *shōen*. This is not
by design. It is caused by the fact that temple records have been better preserved than
others. Japanese proper names which end with *ji, tera* or *dera* signify temples (e.g., Tōji
for Eastern Temple).

were previously communicated to your office, but we have yet to receive your ruling on this matter." Meanwhile, the officials of the said *shō* submitted a brief dated the ninth day of this month (ninth month) in which they gave the following statement: "There is no precedent under which this *shō* can be subject to taxation. However, the present governor, Fujiwara no Ason Kunikaze is arbitrarily departing from past practices by imposing taxation and miscellaneous labor services on the *shō*. We beg of the Council of State to give us its official document expeditiously, so that the *shō*'s exempt status from tax and from miscellaneous labor services can be clearly established. Only in so doing can we again attend to the business of this *shō*.

The Minister of the Left [Fujiwara Saneyori] declares that, obedient to the imperial command, the petition shall be granted as stated. The province shall be apprised of this decision, and once the official document arrives, must take steps accordingly.

Fifth year of Tenryaku [951], ninth month, 15th day.

b) An Order of the Ministry of Popular Affairs, Issued to the Provincial Governor of Ise.

On the matter of immunity from taxation, the Sone *shō*, owned by the Daigoji, located in the district of Ishi, paddy fields 140 *chō* 100 *bu*.

An official document . . . from the Council of State indicates that it received a communication from the Daigoji, saying that the paddy fields in question belong to the estate of the ex-Emperor Suzaku [r. 930–946, d. 952], which were conveyed to the temple [in 948] by his majesty's decree. In the previous year, the Council of State granted the privileges of tax immunity and exemption from miscellaneous labor services, and ordered the province accordingly (see the above document).

However, the provincial officials continued to impose miscellaneous labor services on the grounds that the precise area of the said *shō* is not recorded and that no official document from the Ministry [of Popular Affairs] is available. The communication petitions that an official document from the Ministry of Popular Affairs be given to the *shō* . . . so that taxation and miscellaneous labor services may no longer be required of it. . . .

The Minister of the Right [Fujiwara Morosuke] declares that, obedient to the imperial command, the petition is hereby approved. Provincial officials are asked to act in accordance with this order once it is received.

Seventh year of Tenryaku [953], eighth month, 5th day.

7   Immunity from Entry (Funyū) by Public Officials, 1056 and 1125[13]

a) The Controller of the Left Gives His Command to the Province of Mino.

On matters relating to the Ōi and Akanabe *shō*, it is decreed that boundary markers shall be erected as before, and the entire land within the markers shall be

---

[13]*Ibid.*, p. 263. These two documents are from the Tōdaiji and Mount Kōya.

held secure, without permitting entry by provincial officials. The two *shō* shall be exempt from miscellaneous labor services, in order to enable them to perform their duties for the temple.

A petition submitted by the Tōdaiji [temple] makes the following statement: "These two *shō* are exempt from taxation either by virtue of their exemption from tax registry or by the official documents issued by the Council of State or by the Ministry of Popular Affairs. However, lately provincial governors have, as a rule, made covetousness their guide and have imposed provincial services on the two *shō*. Whenever they call us to account for the services, the performance of the duties of the temple are neglected. In consulting old records, we find that any material produced by the two *shō* in question is to be used for Buddhist mass and other ceremonial functions, for almsgiving, and for the repair of the temple. Thus no provincial officials are to be permitted to enter the two *shō*, and the two *shō* are to be exempt from performing labor services. . . .

"We therefore petition the Controller of the Left to send his official representatives to the two *shō* and other estates, which are owned by the temple, survey the four boundaries, place markers, and forever prevent provincial officials from entering or ordering performance of labor services. . . ."

The Minister of the Right [Fujiwara Norimichi] orders that in obedience to the imperial command, the above petition is approved, . . . and that the province must without fail act in accordance with this order.

Fourth year of Tenki [1056], second of the leap-year month, 26th day.

b) Inhabitants (*jūnin*) of the *Shō* with Official Documents (*Kanshōfu shō*)[14] Belonging to Kongōbuji [temple] Requesting the Administrative Office (*mandokoro*) of Their Patron (*Honke*) [Mt. Kōya] to Rule on a Certain Matter.

"In studying the old precedents, it is found that the official documents issued by the Council of State and the Ministry of Popular Affairs to this *shō* give it power to expel from its domain such criminals as thieves and murderers. It is thus not necessary to permit provincial officials [to enter this *shō*] to make arrest or imprisonment. . . ."

Second year of Tenji [1125], seventh month, 13th day.

8 Establishment of a Shōen, 845, 920, and 1042[15]

a) An Official Order of the Ministry of Popular Affairs, Issued to the Provincial Governor of Tanba.

---

[14]*Kanshōfu shō*, a *shōen* enjoying immunity from taxation by virtue of having official documents from both the Council of State and the Ministry of Popular Affairs. Its territory was surveyed in the presence of officials of the *shō* and of the province before the immunity was granted. In this case, the term is used as a proper noun to designate those *shōen* which were under the control of Mount Koya.

[15]*Ibid.*, pp. 258, 259, 261.

To contribute in perpetuity for the sustenance of the Tōji [temple] in Kyoto,[16] there are paddy fields and lands comprising forty-four *chō* and 142 *bu*, located in the district (*kōri*) of Taki. Of these, there are: nine *chō* and 144 *bu* of cultivated fields; one pond and ditches extending for a length of seventy *jō*; and thirty-five *chō* of wooded area.

The four boundaries are: the eastern boundary adjoins the public land; the western boundary is the hill of Banzan; the southern boundary is a river; and the northern boundary is the hill of Ōyama.

There is also a tract of land in the county (*gō*) of Kawachi. . . . A document issued by the Council of State, dated the eighth day of the eighth month, previously noted that the lesser sub-abbot, Jikkei, petitioned the government and gave the following statement:

"The Tōji was built [in 796] by the wish of Emperor [Kammu] to preserve treasures of the Shingon sect and to become a center for copying the Tripitaka and regulatory works (*kalpas*). This unprecedented undertaking in our country was completed, and manuscripts were permanently enshrined in an exquisite condition. I, for one, unworthy as I am, devoted all my energy to its completion. Our late teacher, the great abbot Kūkai, also established a school and named it Shugeiin. He developed a curriculum in Chinese classics and history. To sustain its teaching activities, he originally assigned fields and gardens for the school's use. However, death claimed him before he could complete his heart's desires, and times have changed. What he intended to accomplish was singularly a difficult task. His disciples consulted one another, and decided to sell the school, and [using its proceeds] purchased fields and residence halls for the purpose of the propagation of the Law. Since the governmental regulations did not permit purchase of fields by temples [at that time], we decided to sign the names of the parishioners (*danotsu*) of our temple as purchasers in the land-sale documents, and the deeds were so recorded. It was not our intention to conceal anything in this fashion.

"On behalf of our temple, I petition you to show us a special favor by granting the titles to these lands in question to the Tōji, to be used for the sustenance of the sacred scriptures, regulatory works, and doctrinal works. This would enable these works to be preserved for as long as heaven and earth exist, and compete with the sun and moon in their luster. Great are the merits that can be acquired, and there is hardly time to elaborate further on all of their ramifications."

[The Ministry] approves the above petition. The governor's office is hereby notified, and is asked to act accordingly as soon as this order is received.

Twelfth year of Jōwa [845], ninth month, 10th day.

b) A Notification from the Household of the Minister of the Right [Fujiwara Tadahira] to the Governor's Office in Tanba.

---

[16]The temple was built in 796 near the eastern gate of the capital city, and was given to Kūkai in 823 to establish a training center for the Shingon sect.

On the matter relating to the lands claimed by the Tōji for the purpose of propagation of the Law, an area of forty-six *chō*, four *tan* and 156 *bu*, located in the district of Taki. The four boundaries are . . . (see a) above.

Notification: A petition received from the Tōji gives the following statement: "The lands in question are tax-exempt religious fields. That privilege was granted pursuant to a petition by the late sub-abbot Jikkei who claimed that the lands were used for the purpose of propagation of the Law, and in so doing served to protect the nation. In 845, the temple received an official document confirming this. The temple established a *shō* office to manage and receive produce from the lands. Among the lands are eleven *chō* four *tan* and fifty-six *bu* of cultivated fields, thirty-five *chō* of wooded area, and two ponds. The wooded area is gradually becoming cultivated. However, as soon as the *shō* office develops a new field, the provincial governor and district chief claim that it is a public field which must be classified as land left over from the application of the allotment land system [and are thus subject to taxation]. As a result, very little benefit accrues from these fields for the propagation of the Law. The wishes of the departed teacher are thus negated, and can no longer help the advancement of his disciples."

I, the Minister of the Right, am sending this matter to your office for further investigation. If these are proved to be true, return the lands to the temple in accordance with the provisions of the old document. Do not forsake the idea of performing meritorious works for Buddha. I hereby notify you through a messenger from the temple.

Twentieth year of Engi [920], ninth month, 11th day.

c) The Controller of the Left Gives His Command to the Province of Tanba.

On matters relating to the Ōyama *shō*, belonging to the Tōji. Government officials and functionaries must study public documents certifying the title and delimit the four boundaries of the said *shō*.

On the above matter, a petition from the Tōji, dated the tenth of this month gives the following statement: "The *shō* in question has belonged to the temple for a couple of hundred years. However, lately provincial governors have been claiming that the paddy fields are public land, and have assessed miscellaneous taxes, even though they have been familiar with the old documents. This led to our petition of the thirteenth day of the tenth month last, which asked for and was granted that within the four boundaries of the *shō*, no provincial officials shall be permitted to enter and make inspections. However, the provincial governor, Fujiwara no Ason Tomoie, does not comply with the order contained in the document granted by your office. He has lawlessly despatched a number of provincial officials to enter the *shō*, arrested *shō* officials and *tato* (holders of the right of cultivation), subjected them to severe reprimand, and denied them freedom of movement. These are matters of grave concern. We earnestly implore you to grant us an imperial judgment which will order the governmental officials and functionaries to delimit four boundaries of this *shō* in accordance with evidence available in public documents certifying the title. Furthermore, we request that another order be given to the provincial governor, enjoining him from committing this unreasonable act hereafter and forever. . . ."

The Middle Counsellor, Fujiwara Sadayori, declares that in obedience to the imperial command, [the above petition is approved, and] the provincial governor's office must know the content of this order and act accordingly.

Third year of Chōkyū [1042], twelfth month, 25th day.

9 Commendation of Shōen[17]   On the matter relating to Kanokogi (shō).

1. The present holder [of this shō] is the direct descendant of the Buddhist acolyte Jushō, the original ryōshu who first reclaimed the land [whose right was confirmed in 1029].

2. At the time of Takakata, descendant of Jushō, in order to share in the authority wielded by Lord [Fujiwara] Sanemasa, the land was commended to Sanemasa, making the latter the ryōke (lord of the shō). A portion of Takakata's share of the annual rent (nengu) equal to 400 koku was given to Sanemasa, and Takakata became a manager in charge of the shō office with corresponding rights (azukaridokoro shiki). [1086]. . . .

3. Sanemasa's great-grandson Gansai (Fujiwara Takamichi) lost much of his family's influence, and was powerless to prevent the lawless encroachment by provincial officials. This prompted Gansai to commend 200 koku from his share of the annual rent as ryōke to Imperial Princess Kaya-no-In. After the death of the princess [in 1148], he erected a temple of religious merit to pray for the soul of the departed princess, and commended the same 200 koku for that purpose. Thereafter, through the good offices of the princess' mother, Mifukumon-In [consort of Emperor Toba], his commendation was accepted by the Ninnaji [temple]. In this way the Kanokogi shō acquired a honke (patron). . . .

10 Edict to Curtail Spread of Shōen, 902[18]   An order of the Council of State.

The following practices are forbidden: all new cultivation of chokushiden;[19] purchase of fields or houses from the common people by former emperors, imperial princes or court nobles of the fifth rank and above; and petition for cultivation of wastelands or fields.

In examining the documents, it is found lately that the practice of opening up

---

[17]Ōkubo, op. cit., p. 264.

[18]Ibid., pp. 265–266.

[19]Rice fields opened with imperial sanction which could be kept privately and retain their tax-exempt status.

chokushiden is spreading to all provinces. Even though the *chokushiden* may open up wastelands, they deprive the common people of their means of engaging in productive activities. As those who open up *chokushiden* proceed to establish new *shō* offices, and impose a multitude of inordinate burdens on the people, the exactions become too frequent, and threats to the livelihood difficult to bear. The common people who are thus victimized, in order to run away from such burdens, often go to the capital city, and attach themselves to great families [to become their retainers]. Others may falsely state that they are commending their rice fields, or selling their houses. In this manner they get official notifications and set up official markers on their borders.

Provincial officials are cognizant of these devious schemes, but are fearful of the power of great families, and remain silent. They do not dare take action against such deception. Thus on days when taxes are due, they do not accept the taxes, and rely on the powerful families to bail them out of their difficulties. At the harvest time, they store crops in private houses and do not carry them to government storage-houses. It is no wonder that the collection of taxes has become increasingly difficult. . . .

Rice fields are incorporated into the *shō* of powerful families. . . . People lose their means of sustenance as they lose agricultural and mulberry fields. Eventually they have no room on this earth, and become vagabonds in other territories. . . .

The Minister of the Left [Fujiwara Tokihira] declares that obedient to the imperial command, it is ordered that hereafter all new cultivation of *chokushiden* must be stopped and such fields already in existence must be leased to the common people on payment of rentals. All lands belonging to temples, shrines and common people must have their titles examined, and [if titles are found defective] must be returned to the original holders. If the common people are found to be engaged in the selling or commending of their fields or houses to powerful families, they must be subjected to sixty lashes. This punishment must be administered without regard to the positions they hold, high positions, free men or vagabonds. If anyone is found purchasing or accepting such fields or houses, or petitioning to occupy wastelands and houses located therein, in direct violation of this order, the provincial office must immediately record the names of the cultivator owner, of the one who affixes his signature to the document, and of the messenger. All of them shall be charged with the crime of violating the imperial command, and no mercy shall be shown to them. . . . Exception is made for the *shō* offices which have been in existence from past generations and which have legitimate titles to lands, provided they do not interfere with the affairs of the province. This order must be implemented within one hundred days of its arrival, and a full report must be made.

Second year of Engi [902], third month, 13th day.

11 Provincial Governors Not Permitted to Interfere in the Common People's Farming Activities, 784[20]

Third year of Enryaku [784], eleventh month, 3rd day. The Minister of the Right [Fujiwara Zekō], by the command of the Emperor, declared: "People are the basis of the nation, and when that basis is secure, the entire nation enjoys tranquility. Of all that the people rely on for their livelihood, none is as important as agriculture and sericulture. However, we hear reports that many provincial governors are derelict of their duties and engage in many unlawful activities. Shamelessly they depart from their duties of upholding the people, and are only concerned with obtaining private gains. Some of them occupy large tracts of forests and fields, depriving the common people of their use. Others manage their own rice fields and gardens, preventing the common people from engaging in their own productive work. As a result, the common people are enfeebled and wasted away. The entire country is cognizant of [the need for] proscribing such practices and punishing the greedy.

"It is decreed that henceforward, no provincial governors shall be permitted to manage rice fields or dry fields except the public lands. Furthermore they shall not be permitted to open new fields for private cultivation and invade the agricultural and mulberry fields belonging to the common people. Anyone who violates this proscription shall not only have his cultivated fields and crops confiscated but also be dismissed immediately from his position and be charged with insubordination. If any of his colleagues or local magistrates under his jurisdiction knowingly conceal his crime, they shall also be charged with the same crime. If there is anyone who informs on [the offending party's misdeed], the [rice] crop from the offending party's field shall be given to him [as a reward]. Never permit corrupt officials to retain the source of their corruption!"

ORGANIZATION OF SHŌEN

The description of shōen *in the old records usually fell under two categories. One was to describe the area in* chō *and* tan, *the Japanese counterparts (but not equivalent) of acres and square yards. The other was simply to give the four boundaries. The latter was often the device employed by great landholders to encroach on the fields, gardens, and houses of small land owners. And in some instances, publicly owned lands could also be included within the four bound-*

---

[20]From the *Shoku Nihongi*, Book 38, *Kokushi Taikei (Major Compilation of National History)*, Vol. 2 (Tokyo: Yoshikawa Kōbunkan, 1966), p. 502.

aries to which the shōen *laid claim. Document 12 was an attempt to prohibit these practices.*

Initially, the common people had no means at their disposal to counteract the encroachment by local magnates or by the nobility and great temples from Kyoto. However, during the ninth and tenth centuries, the so-called harita *rose in different parts of the country. This conceded the right of ownership of the fields to the* ryōshu, *but simultaneously recognized the cultivation and occupancy rights of the common people. Their rights were at first neither solid nor irrevocable, and annually they had to petition the* ryōshu *to have him confirm their rights in writing (Document 13). These rights were called* azukarisaku-ken *or* sakute shiki. *Gradually through custom, the common people's claim became stronger. They could hold onto their rights without cultivating the fields themselves, and were transformed into landholders who exercised some of the rights of landlords. In this manner a powerful class of farmers developed, who were called* tato. *Document 14 comes from a fictitious story, but it does provide a glimpse of the life-style of an affluent* tato. *Note that the* tato *owned his own farming implements, and was able to repair them.*

In Europe, "the legal system of the first feudal age rested on the idea that what has been has ipso facto *the right to be."[21] A similar process can be detected in Japan in the evolution of the cultivation and occupancy rights into the* myō *(right attached to name). The* myō *was first accepted by provincial governors as a basic taxable unit within their domain, and later by the* ryōshu *as a basic rent-paying unit of* shōen. *The applicable lands were called* myōden *(name rice fields), and the holders of the rights to these fields,* myōshu *(holders of the* myō*). Document 15 shows one of the earliest instances of the use of the term* myō. *There the fee paid to confirm his rights as the* myōshu *was paid by third parties. It was a clear indication that it was immaterial whether or not the* myōshu *cultivated his own lands. What mattered was that his* myōden *should remain a taxable unit. The* myō *in the process of its development created a concept of freely disposable property. Simultaneously, among the* ryōshu *group, it became legally impossible to prevent sale of lands to persons other than members of the family, which in effect confirmed the existence of this concept. And without this concept, the later granting of land in fief would not have been possible. In that sense, it was an important link to Kamakura feudalism.*

To counteract the semi-autonomous farming activities of the myōshu *and* tato, *the* ryōshu *held a portion of his* shōen *as* tsukuda, *or directly operated fields. For its maintenance, all of the people within his domain, including the* myōshu *and* tato, *had to contribute miscellaneous labor services and taxes. There were different categories of* shō *officials who managed the affairs of the*

---

[21]Bloch, *op. cit.*, p. 113.

shō *which included the overseeing of* tsukuda, *and collection of annual rent* (nengu) *and other taxes.*

12 Lands Occupied by Private Parties Must Be Measured by the Area in Chō and Tan, 811[22]   Second year of Kōnin [811], second month, 3rd day.

The Minister of Popular Affairs [Fujiwara Sonohito] . . . addressed the throne, saying: "According to the edict of the fifteenth year of Tempyō [743, Document 4] anyone who wishes to open and occupy a new field must first receive an official permission before engaging in developing the field. Such permission cannot be granted for the fields where the new cultivation may interfere with the [legitimate farming] activities of the common people. Furthermore, after the land is granted for three years, if no cultivation takes place, the state can entertain requests for cultivation by others. Lately those who petition the government simply give the four boundaries without giving the exact measurement of the area in *chō* and *tan*. When one investigates such a claim, often the four boundaries contain official residences and common dwellings. If one carefully ascertains the exact measurement of the area in *chō* and *tan*, the total area thus obtained can never fill the four boundaries described. How unreasonable this is. Your subject respectfully submits that henceforward, all petitions for cultivation of a new field must give the exact measurement of the area in question in *chō* and *tan*, and not by the four boundaries. Encroachment upon others' properties and interference with the farming activities of the common people must be proscribed. In obedience to the imperial command, your subject, the Minister of Right [Fujiwara Sonohito, who assumed this office in 812] makes this recommendation."

13 Emergence of Tato, 859 and 1091[23]

a) A Report of the Inspection of Paddy Fields by Inspector of Rice Fields of the Echi *Shō* in the Province of Ōmi.

. . . the two tracts of land in question were originally certified in medium-grade fields. However, when the new inspection was made, they had to be classified as high-grade fields. This being the case, the inspector called the *tato* by the name of Hata no kimi Yasuo, who previously served as governor of Ise, to give full account of the situation. The inspector inquired why these fields which were obviously of high-grade continued to pay only the amount of rent (*jishi*)[24]

---

[22]From the *Ruijū Sandaikyaku (Collection of Laws of Three Reigns)* in *Kokushi Taikei, op. cit.*, Vol. 25 (Tokyo: Yoshikawa Kōbunkan, 1965), pp. 442–443.

[23]Ōkubo, *op. cit.*, pp. 270–271. These documents are from the Tōdaiji.

[24]Normally under the *rityu-ryō* system, the amount of rent (*jishi*) was 20 percent of the harvested amount.

due from medium-grade fields. This was in effect a crime against the three treasures of Buddhism.[25] The *tato* answered, saying that the classification was made long ago, and there was no desire to default on his part, and no crime was thus committed. The inspector insisted that even though he might not be bright, he could not allow the mistakes to continue, and it was incumbent upon the *tato* to make the correct assessment and treat his fields as of high-grade. The *tato* answered that he could not go against this reasoning, and would consider the fields as of high-grade, and would pay his rent accordingly. . . .

First year of Jōkan [859], twelfth month, 25th day.

b) Respectfully Submitted for Your Consideration on the Matter of the Land Belonging to the Tōjaiji [temple].

Altogether the tract contains two *chō* five *tan* and 140 *bu*, located in the village of Minase, district of Shima-no-kami, Province of Settsu.

The petitioner holds *sakute shiki* (rights of cultivator) to the above-mentioned estate. Therefore, he makes this formal petition [to reconfirm these rights]. Concerning the amount of rent (*jishi*) to be paid, a request is made that you examine the proceeds from the land which can serve as the basis of determination. These items are written here for your consideration.

Fifth year of Kanji [1091], fourth month, 5th day.

14 Management of Shōen by Tato[26]

The husband of the third daughter is a man by the name of Tanaka Hōeki. He is diligent in his farming occupation and entertains no other ambition. He owns several *chō* of land, and is called the *daimyō-tato*.[27] He provides his own spades and hoes to cultivate rich and poor fields, and prepares ahead for dry seasons. He repairs his own domestic-style and Chinese-style plows. He is skillful in handling his workers. He provides recompense for work done by farmers in fixing dikes and embankments, digging ditches, or preparing foot-paths between rice fields. He also rewards the work of those men and women who come to help in busy planting seasons. Whatever he plants, such as the late crops, rice, and glutinous rice, he harvests far more than other people. The amount he realizes from pounding the crop at the millstone also increases year after year. This is, however, only part of the story. When he plants barley, wheat, soy bean, cowpea, millet, buckwheat and sesame, they grow in number and become ripe for harvest. In spring he wastes not a single grain of seed, but in the fall, he receives ten thousandfold in return. From the time he begins planting in the spring to the time he completes his harvest in the fall, he commits not a single faulty step. . . .

---

[25]The holder of this *shō* is a Buddhist temple, Gangōji.

[26]*Ibid.*, pp. 271–272. This is taken from *Shin Sarugaku Ki*, an exaggerated story about people who came to the Sarugaku theater.

[27]Here note the word "*daimyō*" appearing alongside the word "*tato*."

15 Establishment of Myōden, 1000[28] Receipt Issued by the Office in Charge of Lamp Oil of the Tōdaiji.

Examining six quarts (*shō*, not to be confused with *shōen's shō*) of oil donated.

Three quarts were contributed by Hiromi Shōren and the other three by Taguchi Shunin.

The said lamp oil is contributed by them as this year's fee, for the recognition of their rights to the *myō*, which bears the name of Tamate Yasukichi. It is submitted to us in good order, and for this reason, this receipt is given.

Second year of Chōhō [1000], eleventh month, 22nd day.

RISE OF THE WARRIOR (SAMURAI) CLASS

When in 792 the government decided to abandon the conscript army in favor of the kondei *system—a system of locally enlisted armies of able-bodied young men—it unwittingly created an irreversible trend toward the rise of the warrior class in Japan (Document 16). Selected as they were from among the private following of local magnates, the* kondei *had their first loyalty toward their masters and were bound to them by personal ties. Gradually they became private soldiers defending the interests of* shōen. *The ninth century saw the erosion of the police power of the central government. The appointment of local police commissioners and other police officers (*shokoku kebiishi, tsuibushi, *and* ōryōshi) *only accelerated the existing trend. Services in localities often proved to be attractive to the dissatisfied nobles—especially those of non-Fujiwara origin—who chose to take up their domiciles in localities and become samurai (Document 17). And without the aid of the samurai—some of them unruly—provincial governors found themselves incapable of discharging their duties (Document 18b).*

The shōen's *somewhat ill-defined dual system of control over land and people also helped to bring about the emergence of the samurai class. Essentially the relationships which governed the* shōen *were based on the* shiki *that each held to the land. Personal relationships did develop from this but they were incidental to the control of the land as expressed in the* shiki. *This duality made it possible for some* shōen *officials to serve concurrently as retainers of a samurai lord (Document 18a). The thought that they might possibly be serving two masters would have escaped them, for the simple reason that the personal relationship which bound the samurai, including their military obligations, could be easily divorced from the basically eco-*

---

[28]*Ibid.*, p. 272. This document comes from the Tōdaiji.

nomic relationship of the shōen *controlled by the* shiki *of the land. This mentality also eased the process of conversion of former provincial governors and former Kyoto nobles into samurai.*

The tato's *contribution to the emergence of the samurai class must not be overlooked. As Document 14 above demonstrates, the* tato *were independent cultivators who owned their own farm implements and had strong claims over the land they cultivated. They utilized the labor of semi-slave workers. However, in the eleventh century, the semi-slave workers increasingly assumed postures of independence, rendering the* tato's *position vulnerable and forcing them to seek a new profession by becoming samurai.*

In the preceding section, we discussed that the myō *in the process of its development created a concept of freely disposable property, and that a* ryōshu *could not legally prevent the sale of lands to persons other than members of the family. However, there was a countervailing force at work to preserve the landholdings of a specific family. That was by the application of a modified form of primogeniture. It was not a pure form of primogeniture in that the eldest son did not have the exclusive right of inheritance, nor did he always enjoy preferential treatment over all other heirs. However, at the death of a* ryōshu, *all of his property was often added together and the major portion was given to the eldest son. In this manner, the economic and even military power of the family could be preserved.[29] A Japanese term,* ienoko, *which appears in Document 18b2, denotes members of the household who are from the families of children other than the first-born and other relatives as distinguished from the family of the first-born. It gives proof to the practice of this modified form of primogeniture.*

The relationship between the samurai lord and his followers resembled that of the master-servant relationship, whose ties were presumed to be as close as those of kinsmen. When Minamoto no Yoritomo attained power, he codified this relationship by giving his followers the title gokenin *(vassals, literally, members of the household) who had to subordinate themselves and were tied to him by the personal bond. And symbolic of their subordination was the submission of their names (Document 19). In return the vassals were rewarded either by the confirming or awarding of landholdings (Document 20). The feudalistic lord and vassal relationship was thus complete.*

---

[29] A commentary to the Yōrō Code's *Koryō* or household registry regulations section contains the following passage: "Question: Is there any restrictions as to the assigning of the legal heir (*chakushi*)? Answer: If one is of the eighth rank or above, he may assign a legal heir. Others are not permitted to do so, and his property must be divided evenly among his heirs. However, those who have accumulated great wealth over generations may be permitted to be treated as if they were of the eighth rank or above." *Ryōshūge*, Book 10, in *Kokushi Taikei, op. cit.*, Vol. 23, p. 293.

If the above can be accepted at its face value, Japan practiced a modified form of primogeniture among its nobility and the wealthy as early as 718.

16   The Kondei System, 792[30]   An Official Order of the Council of State.

On the matter relating to the recruitment of the *kondei* (physically able).

Thirty people from the province of Yamato.

Thirty people from the province of Kawachi.

Twenty people from the province of Izumi[31]. . . .

Previously [on the seventh day of this month], the Minister of the Right [Fujiwara Tsugunawa] declared that in obedience to the imperial command [all military divisions consisting of] conscript soldiers stationed in the provinces should be abolished with the exception of those in the important border areas. The munitions depots, outposts, and governmental offices which were previously defended by them should be defended by the *kondei* to be sent to those positions. We now order that you select those physically able from among the sons of district chiefs (*kōri no tsukasa*), and place them to serve on these posts on a rotating basis.

Eleventh year of Enryaku [792], sixth month, 14th day.

17   Proscription Against Heian Nobility's Becoming Local Samurai, 891[32]   An Order of the Council of State.

On prohibiting people from Kyoto to reside outside of the capital region (*kinai*).

Lately, those people whose domiciles are in the capital city [of Heian], and who are children and heirs of princes and of important court officials, reside outside the capital region. Some intermarry [with people from outer provinces], and others engage in agriculture or commerce and are no different from the people in the provinces. There are also reports that vagabonds form gangs and treat villages as if they were their own possessions. They oppose provincial governors and local officials and make threats on poor people. They not only hinder normal functioning of provincial affairs, but also create a climate detrimental to public morality. The Minister of the Right [Minamoto Tooru] therefore declares: "In obedience to the imperial command, an order must be given to supervise strictly [their activities]. They must withdraw from the outer provinces before the seventh month of the coming year. If they persist in their disobedience and do not mend their ways, regardless of any connection they may have, they must be banished to distant places. There shall be no exception made to our previous order that no governmental official be permitted to remain in his post

---

[30]Ōkubo, *op. cit.*, p. 278. This and the following documents are from the *Ruiju Sandai Kyaku*.

[31]Levies from 48 other provinces omitted from the translated version.

[32]Ōkubo, *op. cit.*, p. 282.

after expiration of his present term. If the governmental officials in charge of this matter do not indict those who commit this offense, they must also be dealt with as if committing the similar offense. . . ."

Third year of Kanhei [891], ninth month, eleventh day.

18   Master of His Retainers, 1114:

a) on the third day of the eighth month, I went to the Prime Minister's Office. . . . I was commanded by the widow of the late Prime Minister (*Dajōdaijin*) Kujō [Fujiwara Nobunaga] that there were two *shō* officials in the province of Shimotsuke, who served as arresting officers (*shimobe*) for the police commissioner (*kebiishi*). They became *rōtō* (followers, or members of a group or household) of Minamoto no Tameyoshi. They must be called in [to account for their indiscretion], and be expelled from the *shō*.[33]

b) On Matters Relating to the Business of Province[34]

1. Preventing riotous behavior.

When a newly appointed governor travels to the province to which he is assigned, some of his *rōtō* and other followers either rob things from other persons or engage in quarrels among themselves. It is therefore ordered that a newly appointed governor must select from among his *rōtō*, pure and strong persons who can engage in the task of stopping this kind of behavior.

2. Do not permit members of your household (*ienoko*) to speak ill of others, and prevent unruly actions of your high ranking *rōtō*.

If on reflection one does not stop those conditions which lead to the use of foul language, and permit one's *rōtō* to engage freely in slandering or heaping abuse on others . . . as these things continue to multiply, people will start ridiculing you. When you take the responsibility of serving the public, you are really performing something good for yourself too. But if you do not put a stop to the abuse that some of your followers—whether they be your own most beloved children or *rōtō*—heap on others, and let this continue [those who are the object of abuse will not serve you]. In this way, you may not be able to collect taxes and send them to the central government. You will then gain the reputation of being an ineffectual governor. If your children and *rōtō* cannot uphold one another and also help you, your term of office will be one of emptiness. If all your followers will pursue their own follies, you will be left with no followers day and night. Then what benefit is there [of becoming a governor]?

---

[33]Ōkubo, *op. cit., Chuseihen*, p. 11. This document comes from *Chiu Yu Ki*, the diary of Middle Counsellor Nakamikado Munetada, which gave accounts of festivals, rituals, social and political conditions between the reigns of Emperors Horikawa and Sutoku (1087–1138).

[34]*Ibid.*, p. 15. This selection comes from *Choyagunsai*, being a compendium of official documents and poems and prose writings completed in 1116 by Miyoshi Tameyasu.

19 Establishment of Relationship Between Lord and Vassals (Gokenin), 1184[35]   [First year of Genreki, 1184] ninth month, 19th day. [Yoritomo sends Tachibana Kiminari to Sanuki to secure the support of local lords.]

Following the destruction of the Ichinotani fortification in Settsu Province in the Second Month, members of the Heike have been plundering the various provinces in the west, and Genji troops have been sent into the region to check the Heike. One of the means employed has been the sending of Tachibana Kiminari and his men as an advance column into Sanuki Province to secure the support of local lords. They have since submitted to the Minamoto, and a roster containing their names has been transmitted to Kamakura. Today, His Lordship has sent instructions to the local lords of Sanuki to take their orders from Kiminari.

[Yoritomo's monogram]

"Ordered to: Immediate vassals of Sanuki Province

"To submit forthwith to the command of Tachibana Kiminari and to join in the Kyushu campaign.

"At this time when the Heike are plundering your lands, you have indicated your submission to me. A roster of your names has been submitted to me. It is indeed a most loyal act on your part. Submit forthwith to the command of Kiminari and conduct yourselves in a loyal and meritorious manner. Thus ordered."

Genreki first year [1184], ninth month, nineteenth day. "Immediate vassals of Sanuki Province:

"The following is a roster of immediate vassals of Sanuki, in which province, at Yashima, the Heike are presently established, who have renounced the Heike for the Genji and who are now in service in Kyoto. They are Tō no taifu Sukemitsu [thirteen others including his sons, younger brother and others]. The aforementioned, having served the Genji in Kyoto, are vassals of the Lord of Kamakura, as indicated."

First year of Genreki [1184], fifth month.

20 Rewarding the Vassals, 1180[36]   Fourth year of Jishō [1180], tenth month, 23rd day. [Yoritomo rewards his vassals for their services.]

His Lordship has arrived at the provincial capital of Sagami [Kamakura] and,

---

[35]Minoru Shinoda, *The Founding of the Kamakura Shogunate, 1180–1185.* (New York: Columbia University Press, 1960), p. 277.

[36]*Ibid.,* p. 191. Those who were rewarded had been Yoritomo's followers from the very beginning of his campaign. Changes made on the basis of Book 1 of the *Azuma Kagami* as quoted in Ōkubo, *op. cit.,* p. 205.

for the first time, he had made awards to his men for meritorious services rendered in his behalf. The men whose present holdings were confirmed or to whom new grants were made were: Lord Hōjo, Takeda Nobuyoshi, Yasuda Yoshisada, Chiba Tsunetane, Miura Yoshizumi, Taira Hirotsune, Wada Yoshimori, Doi Sanehira, Adachi Morinaga, Tsuchiya Munetō, Okazaki Yoshizane, Kudō Chikamitsu, Sasaki Sadatsuna, Sasaki Tsunetaka, Sasaki Moritsuna, Sasaki Taketsuna, Kudō Kagemitsu, Amano Tōkage, Ōba Kageyoshi, Usami Sukemochi, Ichikawa Yukifusa, lay priest Katō Kagekazu, Usami Sanemasa, Ōmi Iehide, and Iida Ieyoshi. In addition Yoshizumi was confirmed as vice governor of Miura and Yukihira as *shō* official of Shimokōbe.

RULE BY THE KAMAKURA SHOGUNATE

Minamoto no Yoritomo's assertion of power over Kantō came in different stages. While he was still a minor power in Izu, he successfully captured a shrine estate, and denied continuation of commission to the previous corrupt holder. In this, he skillfully used a secret edict issued by Prince Mochihito to impress on others the legitimacy of his claim (Document 21). He won his victory over the Heike in 1183, and the following year he established his capital in Kamakura. The establishment of Samurai-dokoro *(which was charged with the task of controlling the* gokenin, *and had jurisdiction over military and police affairs, Document 22),* Kumon-jo *(which kept public documents, and had jurisdiction over political affairs, Document 23, renamed* Mandokoro *in 1191), and* Monchū-jo *(court of judicature, Document 24) followed. These were at first his private house organs, but eventually developed into the core of the* bakufu *organization.*

*Kamakura successfully extended its sway over the entire country by gaining the right to appoint Protectors (*shugo) *and Stewards (*jitō) *outside of Kantō (Document 25). In this way, Kamakura could administer or otherwise interfere in the affairs of* shōen *across the country, giving the former both a stronger economic base and greater political power.*

One of the most outstanding achievements of the Hōjō regents was the issuance in 1232 of a code of judicature, called either Goseibai Shikimoku *or* Jōei Shikimoku *(Document 26). About the* Shikimoku, *its main author Hōjō Yasutoki wrote two letters to his brother in Kyoto, Shigetoki, explaining its intent.*[37]

*"We have decided to record the detailed procedure in order to render impartial verdicts without discriminating between the high and the low. These rules may deviate from the teachings of the existing laws in some minor points. However, the ancient codes and regulations (*ritsu-ryō *and* kyakūshiki) *are like complicated Chinese characters, understood only by a very few people. They are rendered useless to those who understand only Japanese syllabary (*kana). *This*

---

[37]Ōkubo, *op. cit.*, pp. 131–132.

shikimoku *is presented in such a way that the great majority of the people can take comfort in it—just as there are many people who can understand Japanese syllabary, so must this shikimoku be* uniformly *known. "*

In another passage of the letter Yasutoki stressed the importance of dōri, *which means practical reason or sensible solution to matters, over the application of old codes or customary laws. There was a clear rejection of the values that the nobility in Kyoto cherished, and a host of questions were answered from the new perspectives of the feudal samurai.*

*Articles 3 through 6 dealt with the functions of Protectors and Stewards. The succeeding two articles dealt with the tenure of fiefs (*shoryō*) by vassals. Of special interest to historians are the provisions of Article 8 which confirmed the right of a holder if the property remained in his hands for twenty years. Articles 18 and 26 granted to the father the right of revoking an assignment to his son or daughter, and Article 23 gave women the right to adopt their own heirs. Article 42 gave under certain circumstances, an option to a farmer to continue to live in the fief or go elsewhere—a far more enlightened measure than the practice prevalent in the Tokugawa period. These provisions (Articles 18, 23, and 42), incidentally, went counter to those of the ancient codes (*ritsu-ryō*).*

The reader's attention is also called to the solemn oath attached to the shikimoku. *It swore that the decisions rendered should be the decisions of the "whole council in session." It also affirmed the superiority of the council as against that of an individual, no matter how bright or well-intended one might be.*

The shikimoku *was, in effect, a declaration by the Hōjō regents to provide equal justice to their vassals. Questions such as the rights on land remained one of the fundamental issues, and the success of the Kamakura government depended on its ability to protect the interests of its* gokenin, *whose feudal services were the cornerstone of the power of the shogunate.*

21 **Proclamation of Yoritomo's Rule over Kantō, 1180**[38] The clerk fifth rank Tomochika, a relative of Kanetaka, has been inclined to commit unwarranted outrages on the people at Uraya estate (*mikuri*) where he resides. Yoritomo commanded him through Kunimichi to cease such acts. This is the beginning of His Lordship's administration of Kantō. His Lordship's directive reads:

"Ordered to: The local gentry of Uraya shrine estate (*mikuri*):

"That the commission of the clerk fifth rank Tomochika cease forthwith. It is manifestly clear in the language of Prince Mochihito's pronouncement that the public and private domains in the provinces in the east are within His Lordship's jurisdiction. The attention of residents of this region is directed to this order and

---

[38]Shinoda, *op. cit.*, pp. 163–164.

they are advised to take steps to have their holdings confirmed. Thus ordered, in accordance with His Lordship's instructions."

Fourth year of Jishō [1180], eighth month, 19th day.

22 Establishment of the Samurai-dokoro, 1180[39] [Fourth year of Jishō, 1180], eleventh month, 17th day. . . . Wada Tarō Yoshimori has been appointed president of the *Samurai-dokoro*. Yoshimori had requested the office in the eighth month during the flight from Ishibashi Mountain when His Lordship's safety was uncertain. Now His Lordship has given his consent and has issued instructions today to reserve this office for Yoshimori.

23 Building for the Kumon-jo, 1184[40] [First year of Genreki, 1184], eighth month, 24th day. A new building is to be constructed for the *Kumon-jo*. Today the ceremony of the raising of the pillars and beams was held. The commissioners in charge are the lay priest clerk Yasunobu and the secretary of the Bureau of Statistics Yukimasa.

Tenth month, 6th day. . . . At 9 A.M. the ceremony of the first writing for the newly constructed *Kumon-jo* was held. The scribes for the occasion were the secretary of the Bureau of Statistics Fujiwara Yukimasa, the secretary of the Right Horse Bureau Adachi Tōmoto, Kai Shirō, Onakatomi Akiie, and the secretary Kunimichi. The first document, which was opened before His Lordship by Hiromoto, was written by Kunimichi. Then matters pertaining to shrine lands and to Buddhist temples were attended to, following which a banquet was given by the vice governor, Chiba. His Lordship, who attended, presented gifts of horses to the higher officials and swords to the lower officials.

24 Establishment of Monchū-jo, 1184[41] [First year of Genreki, 1184], tenth month, 20th day. With the assistance of Toshikane and Moritoki, His Lordship attended to rendering decisions on cases brought by various persons. The writing of the decisions was assigned to Miyoshi Yasunobu. Two rooms on the east side of His Lordship's residence have been set aside for this purpose and designated the *Monchū-jo*.

25 Appointment of Protectors (Shugo) and Stewards (Jitō), 1185[42] [First year of Bunji, 1185], eleventh month, 12th day. [Ōe Hiromoto proposes the posting of Protectors and Stewards.]

---

[39]*Ibid.*, p. 196.
[40]*Ibid.*, p. 275.
[41]*Ibid.*, p. 279.
[42]*Ibid.*, pp. 349–350, 353–354, 361–362.

. . . Because of the seriousness of Kantō of the present developments, and because the constant attention which these developments require is a source of great inconvenience, the ex-official of Inaba, Ōe Hiromoto has addressed Yoritomo as follows: "The country has fallen into decadence. Men possessed of the devil run rampant. There are rebels in our land whom it has not been possible to destroy. But in the eastern provinces peace and order have been achieved because of Your Lordship's presence. Elsewhere, however, violence is apt to occur. It would be a detriment to the people and an expense to the provinces if, in each instance, soldiers from the east must be sent out to restore order. Accordingly, if, on this occasion, Your Lordship could take action in the provinces and appoint Protectors and Stewards for each provincial office and *shōen*, there would be nothing to fear. Such a request should be made immediately to the throne." Yoritomo was greatly pleased, and it was decided to pursue this proposal. This wise counsel has strengthened the bond between His Lordship and his minister.

28th day. [The right to post Protectors and Stewards and to levy a commissariat rice tax is requested of the ex-sovereign.]

The evening Lord Hōjō made a representation to the court through Yoshida Tsunafusa, regarding the appointment of Protectors and Stewards uniformly in all provinces, and the levying of a commissariat rice tax of 5 quarts (*shō*) per *tan* on all lands [i.e., 0.05 of a bushel on every 0.245 of an acre], whether public or private. As for the latter, the levy would apply irrespective of their ownership by powerful officials or influential families.

Twelfth month, 21st day. [Yoritomo elaborates on the role of Stewards.] It has been declared that private domains in the various provinces shall come entirely under the control of Kantō. Previously those who called themselves Stewards were probably retainers of the Heike who had assumed the role without imperial approval. Or they had been given this title by the Heike and were stationed on the lands of the Heike. Also, civil governors and *ryōke* have been known to station Stewards on their lands as a personal favor to their retainers. As a result the governors and *ryōshu* who have dispensed private favors are now empty-handed and dismayed. Now that the control of *shōen* is uniform throughout the provinces, there need be no anxiety among *ryōshu* and legal guardians of *shōen*.

26 Goseibai Shikimoku—Formulary for the Shogun's Decision of Lawsuits, 1232[43]

1. The shrines of the gods must be kept in repair; and their worship performed with the greatest attention. . . .

---

[43] Adapted from John Carey Hall, "Japanese Feudal Law: The Institutes of Judicature: Being a Translation of 'Go Seibai Shikimoku' (A.D. 1232)" in *TASJ*, 1st Ser. Vol. 34 (1906), pp. 16–44. Satō Shinichi et al., *Chūsei Hōsei Shiryōshū (Documentary Collection on Mediaeval Legal and Institutional History)* Vol. 1, *Kamakura Bakufuhō* (Kamakura Laws) (Tokyo: Iwanami Shoten, 1957), pp. 3–55.

2. Temples and pagodas must be kept in repair and the Buddhist services diligently celebrated. . . .

3. Of the duties devolving on Protectors (*shugō*) in the provinces. In the time of the august Right General [Yoritomo's] House, it was settled that those duties should be the calling out and despatching of the Grand Guard for service at the capital, the suppression of conspiracies and rebellion and the punishment of murder and violence (which included night attacks on houses, gang robbery and piracy). Of late years, however, deputies (*daikan*) have been taken on and distributed over the districts (*kōri* or *gun*) and counties (*gō*) and these have been imposing public burdens (*kuji* or all forms of taxation) on the villages. Not being Governors of the provinces (*kuni no tsukasa* or *kokushi*), they yet hinder the work of the province: not being Stewards (*jitō*) they are yet greedy of the profits of the land. Such proceedings and schemes are utterly unprincipled.

Be it noted that no person, even if his family were for generations vassals (*gokenin*) of the august House of Minamoto, is competent to impress [people] for military service unless he has an investiture [to the land] of the present date.

On the other hand, it is reported that inferior officials (*geshi*) and managers of *shōen* in various places make use of the name of vassals (*gokenin*) of the august House as a pretext for opposing the orders of the Governor of the province or of the *ryōke*. Such persons, even if they are desirous of being taken into the service of the Protectors, must not under any circumstances be included in the enrollment for service in the Guards. In short, conforming to the precedents of the time of the august General's House, the Protectors must cease altogether from giving directions in matters outside of the hurrying-up of the Grand Guards and the suppression of plots, rebellion, murder and violence.

In the event of a Protector disobeying this article and intermeddling in affairs other than those herein named, if a complaint is instituted against him by the Governor of the province or the *ryōke*, or if the Steward or the folk aggrieved petition for redress, his downright lawlessness being thus brought to light, he shall be divested of his office and a person of gentle character appointed in his stead. Again, as regards deputies, not more than one is to be appointed by a Protector.

4. Of Protectors confiscating the property of persons on account of offenses, without reporting cases of crimes.

When persons are found committing serious offenses, the Protectors should make a detailed report of the case [to Kamakura] and follow such directions as may be given them in relation thereto; yet there are some who, without ascertaining the truth or falsehood of an accusation, or investigating whether the offense committed was serious or trifling, arbitrarily pronounce the escheat of the criminal's [fields, gardens, houses and other property] and selfishly cause them to be confiscated. Such unjust judgments are a nefarious artifice for the indulgence of license. Let a report be properly made to us of the circumstances of each case and our decision upon the matter be respectfully asked for, any further persistence in transgressions of this kind will be dealt with criminally. . . .

5. Of Stewards in the provinces detaining a part of the assessed amounts of the annual rent (*nengu*).

If a plaint is instituted by the holder of the rights to *shōen* (*honjo*), alleging that a Steward is withholding the annual rent (*nengu*) payable to him, a statement of account will be at once taken, and the plaintiff shall receive a certificate of the balance that may be found to be due to him. If the Steward be adjudged to be in default, and has no valid plea to urge in justification, he will be required to make compensation in full. . . . If the amount be greater than he is able to pay at once, he will be allowed three years within which to discharge completely his liability. Any Steward who, after such delay granted, shall make further delays and difficulties, contrary to the intention of this article, shall be deprived of his post.

6. Governors of provinces and *ryōke* may exercise their normal jurisdiction without referring to the Kantō [authorities].

In cases where jurisdiction has heretofore been exercised by the Governor's office, by *shōen*, by Shintō shrines or by Buddhist temples on behalf of the holder of the rights to *shōen* (*honjo*), it will not be necessary for us now to introduce interference. Even if they wish to refer a matter to us for advice, they are not permitted to do so. . . .

The proper procedure in bringing a suit is for the parties to come provided with letters of recommendation from their own *honjo*. Hence persons who come unprovided with such letters, whether they be from a province, a *shōen*, a shrine or a temple, have already committed a breach of *dōri* (propriety or practical reason) and henceforth their suits will not be received in judicature.

7. Whether the fiefs (*shoryō*) which have been granted since the time of Yoritomo by the successive *Shōgun* and by Her Ladyship the Dowager Masako are to be revoked or exchanged in consequence of suits being brought by the original owners.

Such fiefs having been granted as rewards for distinguished merits in the field, or for valuable services in official employment, have not been acquired without just title. And if judgment were to be given in favor of someone who alleged that such was originally the fief of his ancestors, though one face might beam with joy, the many comrades could assuredly feel no sense of security. A stop must be put to persons bringing such unsettling suits.

In case, however, one of the grantees of the present epoch should commit a crime, and the original owner, watching his opportunity, should thereupon bring a suit for recovery of possession, he cannot well be prohibited from doing so. . . .

8. Of fiefs which, though deeds of investiture are held, have not been had in possession the actual right (*chigyō*) through a series of years (*nenjo*).

With respect to the above, if more than twenty years have elapsed since the present holder was in possession, his title is not to be inquired into and no change can be made, following herein the precedent established by the Yoritomo House. And if anyone falsely alleging himself to be in possession, obtains by deceit a deed of grant, even though he may have the document in his possession it is not to be recognized as having validity.

11. Whether in consequence of a husband's crime the estate (*shoryō*) of the wife is to be confiscated or not.

In cases of serious crime, treason, murder and maiming, also banditry, piracy, night-attacks, robbery and the like, the guilt of the husband extends to the wife also. In cases of murder and maiming, cutting and wounding, arising out of a sudden dispute, however, she is not to be held responsible.

14. When a crime or offense is committed by deputies, whether or not the principals are responsible.

When a deputy is guilty of murder or any lesser one of the serious crimes, if his principal arrests and sends him on for trial, the master shall not be held responsible. But if the master in order to shield the deputy reports that the latter is not to blame, and the truth is afterwards found out, incriminating him, the former cannot escape responsibility and accordingly his fief shall be confiscated. In such cases the deputy shall be imprisoned. . . .

Again, if a deputy either detains the annual rent (*nengu*) or contravenes the laws and precedents even though the action is that of the deputy alone, his principal shall nevertheless be responsible. . . .

15. Of the crime of forgery.

If a samurai commits the above, his fief shall be confiscated; if he has no investiture he shall be sent into exile. If one of the lower class commits it, he shall be branded in the face by burning. The amanuensis shall receive the same punishment. . . .

18. Whether, after transferring a fief to a daughter, parents may or may not revoke (*kuikaeshi*) the transfer on account of a subsequent estrangement.

A group of legal scholars avers that though the two sexes are distinct as regards denomination, there is no difference between them as regards parental benefactions and that therefore a gift to a daughter is as irrevocable as to a son. If, however, the deed of assignment (*yuzurijō*) to a daughter were held to be irrevocable she would be able to rely upon it, and would have no scruples about entering upon an undutiful and reprehensible course of conduct. And fathers and mothers, on the other hand, forecasting the probability of conflicts of opinion arising, must beware of assigning a fief to a daughter. Once a beginning is made of severing the relation of parent and child, the foundation is laid for disobedience and insubordination. In case a daughter shows any unsteadiness of behavior, the parents ought to be able to exercise their own discretion accordingly. When the question is understood to rest on this foundation the daughter, induced by the hope of the deed of assignment being confirmed, will be loyal [to the *bakufu*] and punctilious in the discharge of her filial duty; and the parents, impelled by the desire of completing their fostering care, will find the course of their affection uniform and even throughout.

19. Of persons, whether related or not, who have been reared and supported,

afterwards turn their backs on the descendants of their original masters.

. . . When persons have rendered some loyal service to their masters, the latter, in their abounding appreciation of the spirit so displayed have in some cases handed them an allocation-note and in other cases have granted them a deed of enfeoffment. Yet they pretend that those grants were merely free-will gifts and take a view of things opposite to that taken by the sons or grandsons of their first master, with the result that the tenor of the relations to each other becomes very different from what it ought to be. . . . When such persons forget all at once the predecessor's benefaction, and act in opposition to his son or grandson, the fiefs which were so assigned to them are to be taken from them and given back to the descendant of the original holder.

20. Of the succession to a fief when the child, after getting the deed of assignment, predeceases the parents.

Even when the child is alive, what is to hinder the parents from revoking the assignment? How much more, then, are they free to dispose of the fief after the child has died; the thing must be left entirely to the discretion of the father or grandfather.

21. Whether when a wife or concubine, after getting an assignment from the husband, has been divorced, she can retain the tenure of the fief or not.

If the wife in question has been repudiated in consequence of having committed some serious transgression, even if she holds a written promise of the bygone days, she may not hold the fief of her former husband. On the other hand, if the wife in question has a virtuous record and was innocent of any fault and was discarded by reason of the husband's preference for novelty, the fief which had been assigned to her cannot be revoked.

22. Of parents who when making a disposition of their fief, pass over a grown-up son whose relationship with the parents has not been severed.

When parents have brought up their son to man's estate, and he has shown himself to be diligent and deserving then, either in consequence of a stepmother's slanders or out of favoritism to the son of a concubine although the son's relationship has not been severed, suddenly to leave him out and without rhyme or reason make no grant to him, would be the very extreme of arbitrariness. Accordingly when the designated heir comes of age, one-fifth of his fief must be cut off and assigned to any older brother who is without sufficient means. . . .

23. Of the adoption of heirs by women.

Although the spirit of the [ancient] laws does not allow adoption by females, yet since the time of the General of the Right [Yoritomo] down to the present day it has been the invariable rule to allow women who had no children of their own to adopt an heir and transmit the fief to him. And not only that, but all over the country, in the capital as well as in the rural districts there is abundant evidence of the existence of the same practices. It is needless to enumerate the cases. Besides, after full consideration and discussion, its validity has been recognized, and it is hereby confirmed.

25. Of vassals in the Kantō who married their daughters to Court nobles (*kuge*) and assigned fiefs to them, thereby diminishing the sufficiency of the public services.

As regards such fiefs, although they were assigned to daughters and thus became alienated, nevertheless the assessment for public services must be imposed thereon in accordance with the holders' rank and standing. Even though when the father was alive the son-in-law's fief may have been, as a matter of favor, exempted, after his death, service must be insisted on. If presuming on the dignity of his position, the holder of such a fief omits to perform personal service, the said fief must be for long withheld from him. In general, there must be no obstinacy as regards public services, which are equally required of all in the Kantō. . . . After this, if anyone still makes difficulties, he is not to have the right (*chigyō*) to the fief.

26. Of revoking an assignment to one son, after a *bakufu* writ of assurance (*ando no kudashibumi*) has been granted and then making the assignment to another son.

That matters of this kind are to be left to the discretion of the parents has been already practically laid down in a preceding section. Hence even when a *bakufu* writ of assurance has been granted to confirm the intent of the first deed of assignment, yet if the father changes his mind and decides to assign the fief to another son, it is the subsequent deed of assignment which is to take effect, and an adjudication for that purpose is permitted.

37. Of vassals of the Kantō applying to Kyoto for side offices such as the superintendentships (*uwatsukasa*) of estates.

This practice was strictly forbidden in the time of the Minamoto House. Of late years however, some persons, following the bent of their own ambitions, have not only disregarded the prohibition, but have entered into competition with others seeking to obtain the same appointment. Henceforth anyone found indulging in such ill-regulated ambition shall be punished by the escheating of the whole of his fief.

38. Of Steward General (*sōjitō*) hindering the functions (*shiki*) of the *myōshu* who were properly within their own domains.

When one who has been placed in general charge of a district as Steward General endeavors to encroach upon villages which are distinct and separate therefrom, under the pretext of their being within the district under his charge, will be deemed culpable. In such a case, an Instruction will be issued to him stating that, . . . if the Steward forms unlawful designs against the *myōshu*, and places unjustifiable hindrances in the way of his performing his functions (*shiki*), an Instruction will be issued to the *myōshu* empowering him to pay the taxes to the Government directly (i.e., bypassing the Steward altogether).

39. That those desirous of obtaining office or rank [from Kyoto] must have a written recommendation from the Kantō.

That those who have performed a meritorious service and are desirous of being raised in rank therefore should be recommended [by us to the Emperor] is an established and impartial mode of proceeding; and there is consequently no need to prescribe regulations about it. . . .

40. Of Buddhist clergy within the Kamakura Domain striving at their own option to obtain ecclesiastical positions and rank.

Inasmuch as it leads to the deranging of the due subordination in the hierarchy, the practice of applying at will [to Kyoto] for preferment is in itself a source of confusion and furthermore entails undue multiplication of higher ecclesiastical dignities. . . .

Henceforth if anyone should in the future apply for preferment without first having received our permission he shall, if he be the incumbent of a temple or shrine, be deprived of his benefice. Even if he belongs to the clergy specially attached to the chaplaincies of the *shōgun* he shall nevertheless be dismissed.

Should, however, one of the Zen Sects make such an application, an influential member of the same sect will be directed to administer a gentle admonition.

41. Of slaves and unclassed persons.

[In cases of dispute respecting the ownership of such persons] the precedent established by the august Right General's House must be adhered to; that is to say, if more than ten years have elapsed without the former owner having asserted his claim, there shall be no discussion as to the merits of the case and the possession of the present owner is not to be interfered with. Concerning the children born to the slaves, although certain qualifications were established by the previous laws, the precedent set at the time of Lord Yoritomo must be adhered to, i.e., a boy is to be awarded along with his father, and a girl may be awarded along with her mother.

42. Of inflicting loss and ruin on absconding farmers under the pretext of punishing runaways.

When people living in the provinces run away and escape, the *ryōshu* and others, proclaiming that runaways must be punished, detain their wives and children, and confiscate their property. Such a mode of procedure is quite the reverse of benevolent government. Henceforth such must be referred [to Kamakura] for adjudication, and if it is found that the farmer is in arrears as regards payment of his annual rent (*nengu*) and levies, he shall be compelled to make good the deficiency. If he is found not to be so in arrears the property seized from him shall be forthwith restored to him, and it shall be entirely at the option of the farmer himself whether he shall continue to live in the fief or go elsewhere.

48. Of buying and selling fiefs.

That those who have inherited a private estate from their ancestors may under stress of necessity dispose of it by sale is a settled law. But as for those persons who either in consequence of accumulated merit or on account of their personal exertions have been made the recipients of special favors from the *bakufu*—for them to buy and sell such at their own pleasure is a proceeding that is by no means blameless. Henceforth, it certainly must be stopped. If nevertheless, any person, in disregard of the prohibition, disposes of a fief by sale, both the seller and the buyer shall be equally dealt with as guilty.

Solemn Oath

That questions of right or wrong shall be decided at meetings of the Council (*hyōjōshū*).

Whereas a simple individual is liable to make mistakes through defect of judgment, even when the mind is unbiased; and besides that, is led, out of prejudice or partiality, whilst intending to follow reason (*dōri*), to pronounce a wrong judgment; or again, in cases where there is no clue, considers that proof exists; or being cognizant of the facts and unwilling that another's shortcomings should be exposed, refrains from pronouncing a judgment one way or the other; so that intention and fact are in disaccord and catastrophes afterwards ensue.

Therefore, in general, at meetings of the Council, whenever questions of right or wrong are concerned there shall be no regard for ties of relationship, there shall be no giving-in to likes or dislikes, but in whatever direction reason (*dōri*) prevails and as the inmost thought of the mind leads, without regard for companions or fear of powerful Houses, we shall speak out. Matters of adjudication shall be clearly decided and whilst not conflicting with reason (*dōri*) the sentence shall be a statute of the whole Council in session. If a mistake is made in the matter, it shall be the error of the whole Council acting as one. Even when a decision given in a case is perfectly just, it shall be a constitution of the whole Council in session. If a mistake is made and action taken without good grounds, it shall be the error of the whole Council acting as one. . . .

Furthermore, when suitors having no color of right on their side fail to obtain a trial of their claim from the Court of the Council and then make an appeal to one of its members, if a writ of endorsement is granted by him it is tantamount to saying that all the rest of the members are wrong. Like as if we were one man shall we maintain judgment. Such are the reasons for these articles. If even in a single instance we swerve from either to bend or to break them, may the gods Brahma, Indra, four Deva Kings, and all the gods great and small, celestial and terrestrial of the sixty odd provinces of Nippon, and especially the two Incarnations of Buddha (*gongen*) in Izu and Hakone, Mishima Daimyōjin, Hachiman Daibosatsu and Temman Dai Jizai Tenjin punish us and all our tribe, connections and belongings with the punishments of the gods and the punishments of the Buddhas; so may it be.

Accordingly we swear a solemn oath as above.

First year of Jōei [1232], seventh month, 10th day.

(Signed by) Hōjō Musashi no Kami Taira Ason Yasutoki (and twelve other Council members).

CHAPTER V

Kamakura Buddhism

"The sound of the bell of Gion Shōja (temple) echoes the impermanence of all things. The hue of the flowers of the teak tree declares that they who flourish must be brought low." So goes the *Tale of Heike* in its famous opening passage. It captures the spirit of the Kamakura period, which was preoccupied with the thought of the impermanence of things.

With the advent of the Kamakura period, old privileges and positions waxed and waned. The Heian patrician society was replaced by the samurai society. And within the samurai class, many great families rose and fell. First there was the Taira family who enjoyed a brief moment of glory only to be supplanted by the Minamoto family. The latter, in turn, quickly lost their power to the ingenious device of regency begun by the Hōjō family. The establishment of feudal institutions to replace the old order was a long and arduous process. Meanwhile, disorder and social changes fostered an attitude of questioning antiquated values. And along with this came challenges to Heian Buddhism, which was esoteric in nature, and which in the final analysis became nothing more than an aesthetic cult, catering to the whims of the privileged.

Even during the latter part of the Heian period, there were several discernible tendencies toward reform of Buddhism. There was widespread belief that the Latter Degenerate Days (*mappō*) had come and that it was necessary to return to the purity of the original doctrines. Then there were some worthies who were either called *hijiri* (saints) or *shōnin* (superior men) who departed from the teachings of the established sects to preach a simple gospel of faith to the common people in cities and village huts.

The precursor to these reform movements was the monk Genshin (942–1017). His popular work *Ōjō Yōshū* (*Essentials of Salvation*, Document 1) depicted the horrors of hell and contrasted them vividly with the bliss of the Western Paradise. To attain rebirth in this paradise, Genshin stressed faith in the efficacy of the original vow of Amida Buddha (Amitabha). This could be manifested in the practice of *nembutsu*, by reciting the sacred name of Amida Buddha in the formula *Namu Amida Butsu* (Hail to the Name of Amida Buddha).

By stressing faith and dependence on the power of another (*tariki*), Genshin brought a totally new concept to Japanese Buddhism. The sequel to his teaching was to deny, as a means of salvation, dependence on one's own strength (*jiriki*) as practiced in traditional Buddhism, be it in the form of ascetic observance, in spiritual and metaphysical exercises, or in performing good works. By simplifying the creed, he also opened the gate of paradise to the reach of common men.

The way that was paved by Genshin was brought into fruition by Hōnen (1133–1212), who became the founder of the Pure Land (Jōdo) Sect in Japan (around 1175). Hōnen taught absolute efficacy of *nembutsu*, and departed in some points from the teachings of Genshin. For example, Genshin maintained that in invoking the sacred name Buddha, one ought to form a mental image of Amida Buddha, and meditate on it. Hōnen rejected meditation or complete comprehension as unnecessary (Documents 2–6).

Shinran (1173–1262) moved Hōnen's teachings of the absolute efficacy of *nembutsu* one step further and to its logical conclusion. In traditional Pure Land beliefs, such as those advocated by the Chinese monk Shandao and by Hōnen, the awakening of faith required diligent observance of prayers to the Three Treasures. Thus there was an element of acquiring faith by one's own power. To Shinran "faith is a gift freely given" by all the Buddhas. He maintained that faith as well as the thought of Amida Buddha was transferred to or conferred upon all sentient beings to ensure the latter's salvation. And since salvation was dependent on the work of Amida Buddha: "If a good man can attain salvation, even more so a wicked man." (Document 8a)

After his death, Shinran's followers were organized into a new sect calling themselves the True Pure Land Sect (Jōdo Shin Shiu or simply Shin Shiu). The inevitable schism set in, but today Shin Shiu remains one of the two most important Buddhist sects in Japan.

The Pure Land faith appealed chiefly to farmers, city dwellers and other common people. Some samurai also became devotees of the new faith. However, samurai were by upbringing and training self-reliant and could not always find themselves comfortable in the teachings which stressed dependence on other's power (*tariki*). To their spiritual quests, the newly formed Rinzai and Sōtō sects of Zen provided the needed reassurance.

The word *Zen* is a Japanese rendition of the Chinese term *chan* which in turn is derived from the Sanskrit *dhyana*, meaning meditation. There is no doubt that its doctrine is inspired by the early Buddhist precepts, such as enlightenment experience (Sk. *sambodhi*, or in Japanese *satori*). However, Zen is a peculiarly East Asian product and contains the mystic tradition of Taoism with a lesser extent of pragmatic Confucian teachings blended in with Buddhist ideals. Tradition has it that its first patriarch was an Indian monk named Bodhidharma who arrived in China in 520. His teachings were transmitted to Huike (487–593) (Document 9c). By the time of the sixth Patriarch Huineng (638–713) the Zen group had split into the northern and southern schools, with the former adhering to the doctrine of gradual enlightenment and the latter to sudden enlightenment. The southern school, founded by Huineng, prospered and by the ninth century, seven sects could trace their teachings to this school. Two of these sects continued to exert great influence on Buddhist thinking in the later Tang and Song periods. They were Linji and Caodong, which were transmitted to Japan by Eisai (1141–1215) and Dōgen (1200–1253) to become the Rinzai and Sōtō sects in Japan.

It is the Zen belief that every individual has a Buddha-nature within him, and it is not necessary to go outside of one's self to discover the Buddha-nature. Introspection and self-understanding, rather than scriptural or other external authorities, are the keys to enlightenment. Truth can be known, if one's mind is cleansed of old habits and prejudices. And a rigorous application of meditation is necessary to permit the mind to make its own discovery. To this end, different methods have been devised, and two are still commonly used today. One is *kōan* or "public theme," which consists of a question and an answer between the master and his disciple.

Another widely used method is *zazen* or "sitting in meditation." Both Eisai and Dōgen stressed the importance of *zazen*, but the latter did so by minimizing the importance of *kōan*. (Document 9e) Unlike *kōan*, "sitting in meditation" means without any specific problem in mind and without any thought for achieving enlightenment. Thus there is a sense of self-abatement.

Both the Rinzai and Sōtō sects taught the value of introspection, tight discipline and self-reliance, which found favor among the samurai. By teaching the possibility of sudden enlightenment, without waiting for the moment of death, they also gave a new meaning to the life to be lived on this earth. They maintained close contact with the Southern Song and became the agent for importing the latter's cultural attainments, such as the new style of painting. Tea, incidentally, was brought back to Japan by the monk Eisai, who also wrote a book, *Kissa Yōjōki* (*Drinking Tea for Longevity*), to encourage its use. In later years, Zen Buddhist monks were found in government services and in trade negotiations with China.

Another Buddhist tradition which developed in the Kamakura period was that of the sect begun by Nichiren. Nichiren received his training at Mt. Hiei and also studied Jōdo and Zen doctrines. He came to the conclusion that only the *Lotus Sutra* contained the true doctrine, and if that sutra could be propagated, the world could yet be saved from the turmoils of the Latter Degenerate Days. Thus convinced, he began his crusade in 1253 at the age of thirty-one, and went to the street corners in Kamakura to preach the efficacy of the *Lotus Sutra*. His watchwords were *namu hōrengekyō* or "hail to the name of the *Lotus Sutra*." In its simplicity, it was similar to calling on the name of Amida Buddha, but in its fierceness, it was distinct from the *nembutsu* practices. Nichiren termed both the Jōdo and Zen sects as heretical teachings, and claimed that as long as the heretical teachings were allowed in the country, the country would be stricken by disasters. The earthquakes, drought, a long spell of rain, and later the Mongol invasion seemed to bear out his prophecy, and gained him adherents. In 1274, the year when he was allowed to return from one of his many banishments, he started a new sect, calling it the Hokke (lotus) or Nichiren sect.

Nichiren was the first Buddhist thinker to emphasize the unique position held by Japan in Buddhism. Indeed Buddhism was begun in India and transmitted to China and then to Japan. Yet it was in Japan that the true and superior teaching was to be maintained, he asserted (Document 13).

Initially Nichiren attracted samurai as his adherents. Gradually farmers and merchants also came into his fold. During the next period, Nichiren's militant doctrine gave voice and solace to the farmers and merchants who were suppressed by the samurai class. The tradition which was set at that time is continued today. In fact the Sōka Gakkai and Risshō Kōseikai, the two militant Buddhist groups in contemporary Japan, both trace their origins to Nichiren's teachings. Their believers come mainly from the lower middle class people who do not share fully in the current economic prosperity. The superior organization, cultural events, militant pronouncements, and self-assertiveness these groups provide give voice to the disenchanted, and a sense of belonging.

From Jōdo to Zen to Nichiren, the Kamakura sects were variegated groups. However, there were some distinct similarities as well. For one thing, they all began as a movement to bring Buddhist teachings closer to the people, and all shared the mark of popular religion. They also attempted to remove the superficiality of the immediate past, by preserving and restoring Buddhism's pristine purity. For example, right behavior, right meditation, and application of discipline in Dōgen were purely a means to return to the original purity of Buddha's time. With the exception of Nichiren—whose teachings bordered on fundamentalism and on the literal interpretation of the *Lotus Sutra*—all sects shared some degree of disdain for scriptures. Zen preferred *mondo*, oral transmission or question and answer, over written materials. By advocating the practice of *nembutsu*, Jōdo sects also relegated the importance of learning the scriptures to a secondary place.

There was also a coalescence of secular and spiritual pursuits. If one could attain sudden enlightenment (*satori*) in his own lifetime, or could chant the name of Amida Buddha or of the *Lotus Sutra* to gain salvation, then it followed that it was not necessary for one to forsake his secular pursuits in favor of things spiritual. A samurai could remain a samurai and attain his *satori*, and a merchant could say *nembutsu* to gain his salvation, all in their present states.

The Kamakura sects in the process of their development became truly Japanese Buddhism. There was an unmistakable sign of the waning of Chinese influence. The writings of the great thinkers of this age were done in the "mixed *kana*" script, combining indigenous Japanese words with Chinese terminologies. Inevitably more and more of thoughts germane to Japan were expressed. In the actual doctrines, Nichiren was nationalistic and even xenophobic, and the supremacy of Japan was taught unabashedly. Only the Zen sects retained their visibly close ties to China.

As a movement, Kamakura Buddhism was nationwide in scope. The travels of the evangelists of that period, from Kamakura to Kyoto and other areas of Japan, ensured that their teachings would not remain regional ones. The new sects keenly reflected the feelings of the people of that age. They also provided new sets of values and cultural traditions. From the drinking of tea to the militant political works of Sōka Gakkai, present-day Japan can still feel the pulse of the forces which were at work in Kamakura Buddhism.

SALVATION THROUGH NEMBUTSU

The Ōjō Yōshū was completed in 985 by the scholarly monk Genshin (942–1017) from Mt. Hiei. The work was the first systematic exposition of the doctrine of Pure Land (Jōdo) in Japan, and received the rare distinction of being exported to Sōng China. It showed the longing of sentient beings for the joys of the Western paradise and their desires to be extricated from the disgusting conditions of their world. As to the means of attaining salvation, Genshin counselled others to turn to the "one gate of nembutsu," or to recite the name of Amida Buddha. The horrors of hell and pleasures of paradise were contrasted in a vivid manner. In this way, the work also contributed to the rise of Jōdo art, which portrayed hell and paradise in a manner described by Genshin to sustain the faith of believers.

1 Ōjō Yōshū, or the Essentials of Salvation[1]

Preface

The teaching which shows how to obtain birth into Paradise and the easy way of training for becoming a Buddha, is for the sinners of this dark world just as easy as seeing with one's eyes or walking with one's feet. As it is such a blessed teaching, shall not who seek with an earnest heart enter this way, priests and laymen, men and women, the noble and the ignoble, the wise and the foolish? Only the revealed and the hidden teachings are comprehensive, and the causes

---

[1]From A.K. Reischauer, tr., "Genshin's Ōjō Yōshū: Collected Essays on Birth into Paradise" in *TASJ*, 2nd Series. Vol. 7 (1930), pp. 25, 59–67, 70, 92–94.

and circumstances and the religious disciplines are numerous, but these are not difficult for the clever and wise who can easily understand things. But what about myself, one who is only a foolish man? I cannot comprehend these difficult things and walk in this hard way. That is why I have turned to the one gate of *nembutsu*. I have now peace of heart and so have decided to set forth briefly in outline the teaching of the scriptures in regard to this matter. . . .

General Summary of Disgusting Conditions in the Six Ways

In taking a general view of these disgusting conditions it may all be regarded as a box of suffering. Let us therefore be careful not to be ruined by pleasures, for mountains from all four sides close in on us and there is no escape. But the spirit of covetousness and even of love enmesh the heart and it is captivated by the five lusts[2] and it continually dotes on inconstant things regarding as pleasure that which is not real pleasure. . . .

When once we have died, father and mother, brothers and sisters, wife and children, friends, servants and property—not one of these comes near to befriend us. Only our evil *karma* constantly pursues us and only Yamaraja, ruler of the realm of departed spirits, says to the victim: "I do not ascribe one extra sin to you. You have come here in consequence of the sins you yourself have committed. Deeds and their rewards follow each other and there is nothing to take the place of your sins. Your father and mother, wife and children cannot save you. Only you yourself can work out the cause of your deliverance. Therefore cast away the evil works which fetter your hands and neck. Leave behind the evil way and seek peace."

It is also said in a poem of a sermon by the Bodhisattva Nagarjuna[3] addressed to King Zandaka: "As for this body, impurity flows incessantly from its nine openings like the water in the rivers and oceans. A thin skin covers it and makes it appear as pure, and it is decorated with brocade and embroidery, but every wise man, knowing that all this is a deception, flings away all lust. It is like a person with a scab on his body who approaches the fire and at first feels comfortable but afterwards finds that it only increases his pain. Thus it is with all forms of passion: at the beginning they give pleasure but at the end they cause great suffering." To know that the real state of the body is impurity is to understand that it is vanity and that the self is not real. He who disciplines himself with this thought obtains his reward. He who is superior in form and who has great

---

[2]The unlawful desire for carnal pleasures. According to one view, they are regarded as operating through the five senses: (1) sight, (2) sound, (3) smell, (4) taste, and (5) touch. According to the second view, they mean passion for (1) property, (2) the opposite sex, (3) eating and drinking, (4) fame, and (5) sleep.

[3]One of the promoters of Mahayana Buddhism. He was a Brahman by birth and lived in Southern India during the second century A.D. He was the author of some twenty-four works. Almost all the Mahayana sects of Buddhism trace their doctrinal lineage back to him.

knowledge but does not practice the commandments and does not have real wisdom is still a beast. But one may be ugly in outward appearance and know little and yet if he is disciplined in the commandments and has the true wisdom he is called superior. . . . A believing heart, keeping the commandments, giving alms, hearing many things, wisdom, a feeling of shame and uprightness—these seven laws are called the Holy Treasure; these are truly treasures with which nothing is to be compared. They are the golden words of Tathāgata[4] and they surpass all the rarest treasures of the world. If one knows how to be content he is truly rich even though he may be poor. And one who has many desires is truly poor even though he may possess great wealth. Where there is great wealth there is also much suffering. It is like the dragon with many heads—the more heads the more poison. Let us realize that delicious things are really like poison and, therefore, let us purify ourselves with the waters of wisdom. Though we must eat in order to sustain this body, still let us not covet rich foods to satisfy our palates and stomachs and so do injury to the heart. Let us not seek satisfaction in the little things of life and thereby lose the big things. Also Mencius said: "Even coarse clothing covers the body and keeps out the cold." Why, then, should we covet showy garments and be proud? In general it may be said that one who has a true regard for the virtue of the heart is indifferent to external appearance. He does not envy people who wear brocades and is not ashamed of his own simple clothes. Therefore it is said in the *Analects* of Confucius: "He who is seeking the Way but is still ashamed of wearing poor clothes and eating simple food is not worthy to talk with." . . . Let us be diligent and seek the way to the highest *nirvana*. First let us harmonize this body and be at peace, and after this let us purify ourselves. The three other periods, namely, the beginning, middle and end of the night, are for meditation on life and death and for seeking understanding. Do not pass the time in vain.

It is, for example, like putting a pinch of salt into the river Ganges which, of course, would not make the river salt water. So it is when a little evil is mixed with the various good deeds; it is dissipated and disappears. Even though we may receive the pleasures of separation from our passions in Brahma,[5] we shall nevertheless fall again into the sufferings of the immeasurable flames; and though we may be in the heavenly palace and our bodies radiate brilliant light we shall afterward enter again into the black dark hell. In the so-called Black-Rope-Hell and in the Hell-of-Repetition eight hells burn fiercely and continuously, and this is the punishment for the evil deeds of all living beings. It is impossible to paint, put into words, read or think about the condition of such sufferings. What,

---

[4]In Japanese Nyorai. It is a name for the Buddha and literally means one who has "thus come," to lead the way.

[5]In Japanese Bonten. A Brahman god adopted by Buddhism as one of its guardian deities. He was looked upon not as the creator as in Brahmanism, but as a transitory Deva, surpassed by every saint, as soon as the latter obtains *bodhi* or enlightenment.

then, must be the tortures of these victims: If we compare the suffering of even a single thought about the Hell-of-No-Interval with that of a man cutting his body with three hundred swords the latter will not be one billionth as severe. The suffering in the Realm of the Beasts is immeasurable. They are bound with ropes and beaten with whips. Some of them are injured for the sake of the bright pearls, feathers, horns, tusks, bones, hair, skin and flesh which they yield.

The suffering in the Realm of Hungry Spirits is also like this. Though the beings here seek various kinds of satisfaction they cannot be satisfied in heart. Enduring hunger, tortured by heat and cold, tired and exhausted, their sufferings are boundless. . . . They lament over the agony of the hot flames even in the pure cool of the autumn moon, and they suffer from the cold even in the warm days of spring. When they happen to come to an orchard the various fruits suddenly disappear, and when they approach a pure stream of water this quickly dries up. As a result of their evil *karma* their life drags on and for fifteen thousand years they suffer various tortures and continually receive poison without intermission. In this Realm of Hungry Spirits the swift river of passion carries the beings along according to the law of Cause and Effect. The fire of an evil mind and anger rages furiously and consumes both body and mind. If anyone would extinguish such various evil works let him walk in the way of real deliverance. Forsaking the law of worldly fame, let him obtain the place of purity and permanence. If there is any mind for disliking the departing from this evil world, it is like Bodhisattva Asvagōsha's resuscitation when he heard the singers' song which runs as follows: "The various phenomena of existence are like a vision and like an illusion. In all relations of the Three Worlds there is not one that can be relied upon. Kingly rank, high fame and the wielding of power—none of these can remain when impermanency comes over them. A floating cloud seems to be there but suddenly it disappears and becomes nothing. This body is an empty illusion and like a plantain. It is an enemy and a thief and cannot be trusted. It is like a box full of vipers. No human being can be loved with pleasure. For this reason all the Buddhas continually mortify the body."

In the above passage we have in detail the teachings about impermanency, suffering, the void, and the non-Atman. Those who hear this doctrine understand the Way. . . .

Pleasures of the First Opening of the Lotus

What is called the pleasures of the first opening of the lotus is this: When a believer is born into the realm of Paradise we speak of it as the time of the first opening of his lotus. All his pleasures are increased a hundred thousand times above what they were before. Such a one is like a blind man who has for the first time received his sight, or like a man from the country who has suddenly been transported to a palace. As he looks at his own body his skin becomes radiant with golden rays. His clothes are made of natural treasures. . . . Living beings from all parts of the universe are born into this place like showers of rain. Saints like the grains of sand on the Ganges for their number come from the innumerable Buddha lands. Some ascend into the palaces and live in the sky. Some, sitting in a place in the sky, read and explain the scriptures. Others, sitting in silence in the sky, are enjoying the ecstasy of meditation. Also on the ground among the trees of the forests such sights are common. Here and there are some wading and bathing in the streams while others are singing and scattering flowers. There are still others who are walking to and fro among the palaces and halls, worshipping and praising the Tathāgata. In such ways the innumerable heavenly beings and saints enjoy themselves, each one according to his heart's desire. How impossible it is, then, to given all the names of the incarnate Buddha and Bodhisattvas who fill Paradise like a cloud of fragrant flowers.

The Pleasures of Making Progress in the Way of Buddha

The pleasures of making progress in the way of Buddha are as follows: In this present world it is hard to practice the way and obtain the fruit. The reason is that the one who suffers is always sad and the one who obtains pleasures is always captivated by them. Therefore whether it be pleasure or pain, both are far removed from the way of deliverance. Whether one is prosperous or in misfortune, both are alike bound to the wheel of change. Even the few whose mind is converted and who practice good works find it difficult to succeed. Evil passions break out from within and evil circumstances pull one from without. . . . That Mokuren backslid, though he tried for sixty *kalpas*,[6] was due to this fact. Only the Tathāgata, Lord Shakamuni, was able to pile up merit and virtue through hard and painful works for numberless *kalpas*. He sought after the way of the Bodhisattva and never ceased for even a moment. Looking around the three thousand great worlds, there is not to be found a particle as small as a poppy seed for which this Bodhisattva did not sacrifice his body. All this he did in order to save living beings. Thus disciplining himself he was able to achieve the way of understanding. All other beings who attempted to establish themselves failed in practicing the discipline. With them it was like a baby elephant being killed by swords and arrows because of its weakness. . . . But the beings in this Paradise Land do not backslide because they have abundant favorable causes surrounding them. They make progress in the Buddha Way. These favorable causes are the following: (1) They are ever sustained by the power of the mercy of Amida Buddha; (2) The light of Amida Buddha constantly shines upon them so that the mind of right understanding is ever increasing; (3) The water, birds, trees, tinkling of bells by the breezes and other sounds constantly remind them of the nembutsu, the Law, and the priesthood and so develop their

---

[6]*Kalpa* is the general term for a long period which cannot be defined by months or years.

hearts; (4) The various Budhisattvas are their friends and so there are no evil external circumstances and all doubts within are removed; (5) Their lives are as long as the eternal *kalpas* and equal to that of a Buddha so that they are not interrupted by birth and death and thus are enabled naturally to calm their minds and achieve the Way of the Buddha. We read in a poem of the *Flower Wreath Sūtra (Kegon* or *Mahāvipulya-buddhāvatamaska sūtra)*: "If a being looks but once upon a Buddha he will without fail be purified from all evil." If it is true that but one glance will have this effect, then how much greater must be the effect when one constantly beholds the Buddha! Even the effects of evil deeds committed throughout countless hundred millions of *kalpas* would pass away like a spring snow or dew drops and frost in the sunshine. Thus, because of the various favorable circumstances, the hearts of the beings in Paradise are in no way like our hearts. In their going and coming, in their advancing and in their resting they are not at all troubled in their minds. All these beings obtain hearts of great love and mercy. It is natural for them to make progress in the Way of Buddha and to understand the doctrine of non-birth and non-death. Ultimately and without fail they obtain the position of an Isshofushō[7] Buddhahood and are able for the sake of living beings to reveal themselves in eight forms, or in accordance with circumstances they can go to the land of sublimity and purity and there turn the wheel of the marvelous Law and so save various beings. That today I desire Paradise and wish to have all beings obtain the same and that I am going throughout the ten directions to draw living beings unto myself, is just like Amida Buddha's great vow of mercy. Is not such grace joy? Truly the affairs of this life are in the interval of a dream. Why then not fling away everything and seek after the Paradise of the Pure Land? May all believers beware of being idle.

In a poem by Nagarjuna we read: "In Amida's infinite and accommodating realm there is no bad purpose or foolish wisdom. There is no illumination in evil causes but only natural progress in the Buddha Way. If one once obtains birth he will be unmoved and he will attain full enlightenment. Therefore I accept Amida Buddha and worship him. If I should tell about his virtues, his goodness is as wide, great and limitless as the waters of the great ocean. Oh that I might obtain the good root and purity and that I might together with other beings obtain birth in that land: May we together with all beings be born into the Pleasant Land of Peace!"

HŌNEN AND THE FOUNDING OF THE JŌDO SECT

Hōnen (1133–1212) entered Mt. Hiei and studied Tendai doctrines at the age of fifteen, and later went to Nara to acquire knowledge of the Kegon and Hossō sects. However, he became increasingly dissatisfied with the teachings which

---

[7]One who attains Buddhahood by one truth and passes through all realms of existence unhindered.

stressed learning and ascetic exercises which, in the final analysis, sought salvation through one's own efforts (jiriki). After reading Genshin's Ōjō Yōshū (Document 1), he decided to found a new sect based on the nembutsu (Document 3). He vigorously claimed that his new doctrines were as valid as any of the established ones (Document 2). The shorter letter (Document 4) contains the essence of his teachings. The catechism (Document 5) shows his deep commitment to the nembutsu. As to the position of women (Document 6), Hōnen assured them of their eventual salvation by taking the form of men, which was a step forward, but still showed the bias of a male-dominated society.

The new Jōdo sect became a powerful force, gaining for its converts such people as ex-Emperor Goshirakawa, Kampaku Kujō Kanezane, famed samurai, as well as many common men. The hostilities of established sects led to his banishment in Tosa (1207), but he utilized this opportunity to spread his teachings to the common man. In 1211 he was allowed to return to Kyoto, but died the following year.

2   The Ancients Not Necessarily Our Superiors[8]

"There is a saying that we should reverently expect posterity to surpass the great of the present, and so we may say that the teacher is not necessarily in advance of his pupil. Five hundred years after the death of the Buddha, five hundred enlightened priests (Sk. *Arhats*) met together and composed the *Abhidharma-mahāvibhāssa-śāstra* [a doctrinal treatise of the Sthāvira school of the Hinayana Buddhism], and nine hundred years after his death, Vasubandhu appeared and wrote the *Abhidharma-kośa-śāstra* [a fifth-century work which became the standard book of the Kusha sect, one of the six Nara sects of Japan], thus overturning those teachings. We see therefore that the antiquity of a doctrine cannot of itself decide whether it be true or false."

3   Nembutsu and the Founding of a New Sect[9]

.... Hōnen was well acquainted with the doctrines of the various sects of the Holy Path. ... Nevertheless he was still troubled about the way of attaining salvation, and ill at ease. So with a view to the discovery of the path leading thereto immediately after death, he read the whole of the Buddhist Scriptures through five times. He dwelt long and intently upon every trace he could find of what Shakamuni himself had taught during his life-time, only to find one difficulty after another presenting itself to his mind. At last he found a book called *Ōjō Yōshū*, written

---

[8]Adapted from Harper H. Coates and Ryugaku Ishizuka, *Honen, the Buddhist Saint: His Life and Teaching* (Kyoto: Chionin, 1925), pp. 161–162.

[9]*Ibid.*, pp. 183–184. The Coates and Ishizuka volume is a translation of a biography of Hōnen by the monk Shunjo which was completed around 1300. This document is a description by Shunjo, and does not contain Hōnen's words.

by Genshin, based upon a commentary by the venerable Shandao on the Meditation Sūtra. While pursuing this book, it occurred to him to examine Shandao's commentary. He found that the writer earnestly inculcated the principle that by the practice of the *nembutsu*, even the ordinary man, with all his distractions, may understand how he may be born into the Pure Land immediately at death, and thus the way of deliverance was made very easy. Although he had noticed it every time he turned over the pages of Scripture, he read this again three times with special attention, and finally came to the following passage:—"Only repeat the name of Amida with all your heart. Whether walking or standing, sitting or lying, never cease the practice of it even for a moment. This is the very work which unfailingly brings forth salvation, for it is in accordance with the Original Vow of that Buddha." Through this passage he was led to the conclusion that the common man, no matter how far removed from the age of the Buddha, may by the repetition of Amida's name, by virtue of Buddha's Original Vow, of a certainty attain birth into the Pure Land. And so in the spring of the fifth year of Jōan [1175], when he was forty-three years of age, he unhesitatingly abandoned all other forms of religious discipline, and applied himself exclusively to the practice of the *nembutsu*.

4   **The Short Letter (Isshi Koshōsoku)**[10]   Once Hōnen wrote an outline of the Jōdo doctrine on a sheet of paper, which runs as follows: "I have carefully examined the qualifications necessary in these Latter Degenerate Days for all sentient beings to attain birth into the Pure Land of Perfect Bliss, and I find that no matter how meager one's religious practices may be, he should not give way to doubt, for ten repetitions of the sacred name are quite enough, indeed even one. And it matters not how great a sinner a man may be, he should not give way to doubts; for, as it says, Amida does not hate a man, however deeply stained with sin he may be. And though the times be ever so degenerate, let him not doubt. For even sentient beings, who will live in the period after the Law has perished, can be born into the Pure Land. How much more men of our own times! Even though we be indeed unclean, we need not doubt the possibility of attaining *Ōjō*, for it is specifically stated that we are but ordinary mortals, painted with evil passions.

"There are indeed many Pure Lands in the ten quarters of the universe, but we seek the Pure Land in the West, because it is in this one that all sentient beings, who have committed the ten evil deeds and the five deadly sins, can find *Ōjō*. The reason for giving ourselves up to Amida alone among all the Buddhas is that He welcomes those who have repeated His sacred name, even three or five times. And the reason we choose the *nembutsu* out of all the other forms of religious discipline is because it is the one prescribed in the Original Vow of that

---

[10]*Ibid.*, pp. 402–404.

Buddha. If we are but born into the Pure Land by embarking upon Amida's Original Vow, then none of our cherished desires remains unfulfilled. And this embarking upon the ship of the Original Vow depends upon our faith.

"It is a joy beyond all other joys to have attained all these things that are so difficult of attainment, first of all being born a human being, then coming into contact with the Original Vow, then having one's religious aspirations aroused, then getting free from the long round of transmigrations, and finally being born into the Pure Land. While believing that even the man who is so sinful that he has committed the ten evil deeds and the five deadly sins may be born into the Pure Land, as far as you are concerned, be not guilty even of the smallest sins. And if a sinful man may thus be born into that land, how much that ten repetitions, yea even one, will never be in vain, and so continually practice it without ceasing. If by repeating the *nembutsu* once a man may thus reach *Ōjō*, how much more so if he repeats it many times!

"As Amida Buddha has already verified the words of His Vow, 'unless it happens as I vow, I shall not accept enlightenment,' and is now in reality in that blissful land, as He said, He surely will come and meet us when we are about to die. . . .

"Let your joy, therefore be as high as the heavens above and as deep as the earth beneath. Let us then whether walking, standing, sitting or lying, or wherever we are, always be returning thanks for the great blessedness of having in this life come in contact with the Original Vow of the Amida Buddha. It is in these words of the Vow where He graciously says, 'Or even ten times calling' that we should above all put our trust, and it is to the clause where Shandao says that of a certainty we shall be born into the Pure Land, that we should above all else direct our faith."

5   A Catechism[11] [A man once asked Hōnen some hundred and forty-five questions on the preparation needed for attaining *Ōjō*, and he answered them all. Below is a transcription of a few of them.]

Question 1. Is it possible for a man to enter the Pure Land simply by concentration of mind and the repetition of the *nembutsu*, and doing nothing else, even though his heart undergoes no change?

Answer:—It is the rule with common men for their hearts to be in a state of confusion, and it cannot be helped. The only thing is that if men do concentrate their minds upon Amida, and call upon his name, their sin will be destroyed, and they will attain *Ōjō*. Even sins more grievous than that of mental confusion disappear, if men practice the *nembutsu*.

Question 2. Even if we do not fix the number of times for repeating the *nembutsu* as our daily task, is it not all right to do it as often as one can?

---

[11] *Ibid.*, pp. 422–427.

Answer:—It is better to fix the number, lest you yield to laziness.

Question 3. Ought we to practice the *nembutsu* after eating leeks, onions or venison, while the scent of them still remains in the mouth?

Answer:—There is nothing whatever in the world that should interfere with the practice of the *nembutsu*.

Question 4. How many repetitions of the sacred name should one regard as a day's work?

Answer:—Well, the number of *nembutsu* repetitions may begin with ten thousand, and then go on to twenty, thirty, fifty, sixty or even a hundred thousand. Everyone should in his own heart and according to his own will, determine the number within these limits.

Question 5. They say that the cord with the five-colored strands is put into the Buddha's left hand, but in which of my hands should it be put, and how drawn (when I come to die)?

Answer:—It should be drawn by both hands.

Question 6. Is there any merit in fasting from noon till dawn, and ought one to do it?

Answer:—There is merit in such fasting especially on the six days of fasting appointed for each month. But in case there is some matter of great importance, or one is ill, it is not necessary to do it, but only to repeat the *nembutsu*, and one will thereby get free from the transmigratory round and attain *Ōjō*.

Question 7. Even if one does not see a Buddha, or fasten a cord from one's hand to the Buddha's, or even call upon the sacred name oneself, is it possible to be born into the Pure Land at death merely by listening to others repeating the *nembutsu*?

Answer:—It is not always necessary to fasten the cord to one's hands, nor to meet the Buddha face to face, but by means of the *nembutsu* alone can one attain *Ōjō*. And so long as one has a very deep faith, it is enough to listen to other men's repetitions of the *nembutsu*.

Question 8. Though one may wish to be eternally free from the experience of birth and death, and never to be born again into this three-fold world, is it true, as some say, that, even after one has become a citizen of the Land of Perfect Bliss, the *karma* which has brought him there loses its efficacy, so that he may be born again here into this three-fold world? Now I have no wish to be so reborn, even though I might be born a king, or born into the so-called heavenly world above. My one wish is to get entirely free from this world, and never return here, and so to this end what should I do?

Answer:—Such ideas are entirely wrong. If one is once born into the Land of Bliss, he will never return to this world, but every such one will attain Buddhahood. Only in case one wishes to come back to save others, he may indeed do so, but by so doing, he does not again return to the round of birth and death. There is nothing better than the practice of the *nembutsu* to get safely out of this three-fold world and be born into the Land of Perfect Bliss. So you ought to practice it most diligently.

Question 10. Is it a sin to drink *sake* (Japanese rice wine)?

Answer:—Indeed one ought not to drink, but (you know) it is the way of the world.

Question 12. When one is about to die, is it enough, in order to attain *Ōjō*, to repeat the *nembutsu* as one ordinarily does, without calling a religious adviser?

Answer:—Even though no religious adviser comes in, and one is not able to die as painlessly as he desires, he will attain *Ōjō* if only he repeats the *nembutsu*.

Question 13. When evil thoughts will keep arising within the mind, what ought one do?

Answer:—The only thing to do is to repeat the *nembutsu*.

Question 18. Is it all right to make up on one day for religious duties that were neglected on another day? And may one store up merit now, so as to be forehanded for the future?

Answer:—It is all right to make up for past losses. But to be laying up for the future (forgetting the present) would tend to laziness.

Question 19. Is there any merit in bringing offerings to a lawless or ignorant priest?

Answer:—We ought in these latter days to do honor to a lawless and ignorant priest even as to the Buddha.

6 **On the Salvation of Women**[12] In Hōnen's Commentary on the Larger Sūtra, in dealing with the thirty-fifth of the forty-eight Vows, namely the one about woman's birth into the Pure Land, he explains it as follows:—"The vow of birth into the Pure Land by means of *nembutsu*, as above mentioned, refers to both men and women, without distinction. If so, what then is the special significance of this vow? On careful reflection, we must admit that there are great hindrances in the way of woman's attaining enlightenment, so that unless she be dealt with in a special way, she may become a victim of doubts. The reason is that her sin is grievous, and so she is not allowed to enter the lofty palace of the great Brahma, nor to look upon the clouds which hover over his ministers and people. She is always taken down to a lower seat than the soft-cushioned one of the divine Indra, and she can never behold the flowers in his thirty-three-citied Heaven. . . . No matter what Sūtra or Shāstra (commentaries) you look at, she is always spoken of in terms of scorn, and everywhere despised. There is no place for her to go but to the three painful states and the eight misfortunes, and there are no shapes for her to assume but those of the six ways and the four modes of birth. Even in Japan, too, woman is refused admission to holy places and buildings. Around the sacred places on Mount Hiei, founded by Dengyō Daishi, he himself set boundaries by valleys and mountain peaks, within which women were forbidden to enter. From this we see that over the top of the mountain of the

---

[12]*Ibid.*, p. 351.

One Vehicle [i.e., the one and only true way of salvation in all the worlds, according to the Tendai doctrine], the clouds of the five obstacles cannot be overspread, and in the depth of the valley of the ineffable sweetness, the stream of the three obediences cannot flow. Mount Kōya is also a mountain peak set apart by Kōbō Daishi, where flourishes the Superior Vehicle of the Shingon. There the moonlight of the three secrets shines over everything, and yet not over the incapacity of woman. The water of wisdom stored in the five vessels flows everywhere over the mountain, but it does not wash away woman's uncleanness. The gold and bronze image of Vairocana, one hundred and sixty feet high, erected by the Emperor Shōmu, may be worshipped by women at a distance, but they are not allowed to go inside the door. . . . Alas! woman! Though thou has two feet, there are mountains of the Law which thou mayst not ascend, and courtyards of the Buddha which thou mayst not tread. Shame though it be, while possessed of two eyes, there are sacred places upon which thou mayst not look, and holy images which thou mayst not worship! . . . . How then, can you ever possibly draw near to the Buddha of the ten thousand transcendent virtues in the Pure Land of countless treasures? It is no wonder that women doubt the possibility of attaining birth into the Pure Land.

"This is the reason that the Buddha Amida made a separate vow particularly for women. The following is the venerable Shandao's interpretation of it:—By virtue of the merit of Amida's great Vow, women who call upon the sacred name, may, when they come to the end of life here, have their bodies changed into those of men. Amida holds out His hands to them, and the Bodhisattvas help them to seats upon a lotus stand, on which they are carried into the Pure Land. Amida Himself goes before them, so that they are admitted into His great community, and at length attain that state of *nirvana*, wherein they transcend the experience of life and death. Apart from the power of the great Vow of Amida, a woman cannot have her body changed to that of a man in a thousand *kalpas*, as there are sands in the river Ganges. This expresses the beneficent power of Amida's merciful Vow, by which woman may escape pain and receive the gift of blessedness!"

SHINRAN AND DEPENDENCE ON AMIDA'S PURE GRACE

Shinran (1173–1262), entered the Buddhist priesthood at the age of nine and studied at Mt. Hiei. In his late twenties, he was converted to Hōnen's belief in the nembutsu and in the efficacy of the original vow of Amida Buddha. When Hōnen was exiled to Tosa, Shinran also drew a sentence to be exiled to Echigo, the present-day Niigata on the Japan Sea side. After his pardon, he went to the Kantō region to propagate his new doctrine. He taught the simple doctrine of transcendence from ascetic discipline and dependence on Amida's pure grace, which appealed to the farmers and other common folk.

In his real life Shinran departed from the traditional monastic vow of celibacy. If salvation depended on the efficacy of Amida's original vow, then celibacy had no bearing on ultimate redemption. The fact that Shinran was able to face honestly problems associated with conjugal love and the passion which could destroy the whole person and was able to find a realistic solution to these problems, probably contributed to the further success of his new doctrines.

In its simplicity, and in its avocation of faith in the efficacy of the original vow, there was none which equalled Shinran's writings. An excerpt from a letter entitled, "Doubts expressed by a believer of nembutsu *in Kasama" (Document 7) reaffirms that the Tathāgata would indeed meet a true believer at his deathbed to escort him to the Pure Land, thus allaying the fear of his followers who would otherwise revert to the practice of ascetic discipline. This particular letter, written when Shinran was eighty-three, testifies to the vital energy, intellectual capacity, and deep faith of the man.*

The next selection (Document 8) comes from the Tannishō, *which consists of nineteen short chapters assembled from Shinran's sayings after his death by Yuien and other disciples. Here the logical consequences of the doctrine of* tariki *comes through very clearly in the words: "If a good man can attain salvation, even more so a wicked man." However, like Paul in his epistles, Shinran was mindful of the fact that profession of faith was not a license for believers to engage in evil deeds. The* Tannishō *also includes a short passage which suggests that no matter how much one gives to a temple or to a good cause, "if there is no faith, his act is in vain."*

7 Doubts Expressed by a Believer of Nembutsu in Kasama[13]

At the heart of the teaching of the True Pure Land (Shin) Sect is the differentiation between *tariki* (dependence on another) and *jiriki* (dependence on one's own power) in the basic intellect and emotion of those who seek salvation. This point was already explicated by the great teachers of India and by the founders of the Pure Land Sect in China.

First, *jiriki* consists of the acts of calling on the names of Buddhas other than Amida, and the desire to attain the basic goodness as taught by other sects in accordance with the *karma* the seekers have acquired. They rely on themselves, use their own judgment, and by their own efforts attempt to extricate their minds from the confusion of action, language, and thought. Thus cleansing themselves, they hope to be born again into the Pure Land. This is what we call *jiriki*.

Second, *tariki* consists of faith in the efficacy of the specially selected eighteenth Original Vow of the Buddha Amida which promises that salvation can be attained by the practice of *nembutsu*. The holy teacher Hōnen mentioned that

---

[13]From *Shinranshū (The Writings of Shinran)* in *Nihon Koten Bungaku Taikei (Major Compilation of Japanese Classics)*, Vol. 82 (Tokyo: Iwanami Shoten, 1964), pp. 117–120.

since salvation is traced to the Original Vow of the Tathāgata, *tariki* can make just one who is unjust. When we speak of being made just, we are actually referring to the process of being justified. When a seeker is justified by his own effort, by *jiriki*, then that is called a scheme to attain justification. In the case of *tariki*, faith in the efficacy of the Original Vow insures salvation, and such a scheme becomes unnecessary.

However, one may doubt that the Tathāgata will come to welcome him at his deathbed to escort him to the Pure Land if he has been a wicked person. Bear in mind that man is ingrained with all evil desires, and must be regarded as a wicked one. Nor can one feel the certainty of his salvation because of the goodness of his heart. A man who depends on the scheme arising from his *jiriki* cannot expect to reach the True Pure Land. I have heard that any seeker who is confident of his own *jiriki* can attain his salvation in the periphery of the Pure Land inhabited by those who doubt the wisdom of the Buddhas. They profess belief in the *nembutsu*, but cannot eradicate their doubts, and their mentality is close to that of an unborn baby.

To fulfill his eighteenth Original Vow, Bodhisattva Dharamākara became Amida Buddha (Amitābha) and showed his countenance to his believers and gave them countless blessings. . . . Therefore, salvation can be attained by everyone regardless of being good or wicked, and no partiality is shown to the state of earthly desires. In describing his belief in the *nembutsu* which derived from the Original Vow, Genshin stated in his *Ōjō Yōshū*, "whether walking or standing, sitting or lying, never cease the practice of *nembutsu* for a moment." He clearly stated that all true believers can be surrounded by the light of the Amida Buddha. In this manner even though they may be unenlightened and are still troubled by their desires, they can attain their salvation in the Pure Land of Perfect Bliss. It is decreed by Shakamuni Tathāgata that all can in this manner gain perfect understanding to move toward Buddhahood. . . . According to the commentary of the venerable Shandao, Shakamuni, Amida and all the Buddhas are of the same mind, abiding by all sentient beings who are believers of the *nembutsu*, as inseparably as shadows are from the bodies. Thus, Shakamuni Tathāgata rejoiced in the believers, claiming that they are his close friends. Indeed those who are blessed with this faith are the true disciples of Buddha. . . . They are foreordained to attain salvation in the right manner. [In the matter of gaining enlightenment], they are no different from Maitreya [the Buddha who is called the Loving One]. They attain true faith, which is followed by salvation in the Pure Land of Bliss. One must know that to gain his faith is a gift freely given by Shakamuni, Amida, and all the Buddhas. Therefore you must not speak ill of the teachings of Buddha other than Amida, or of their devotees. Nor can you deride the training they undergo to attain the basic goodness. Some people may hate and vilify believers in the *nembutsu*, but it does not follow that those believers can hate and vilify them in return. Be compassionate, and of an understanding heart, as we are taught by the saints of the past. How true it is, how true it is. The grace of the Buddha is so profound that even if one finds himself at the periphery of the Pure Land and is still engulfed with confusion, he can still attain salvation in the True Land of Recompense,[14] and being enlightened, become one with *nirvana*. This is possible because of the compassionate pleas contained in the nineteenth and twentieth vows. Indeed there is no limit to the grace of Buddha. You must make every effort to understand the grace of Buddha. This is a great doctrine, not what my chief disciple Shōshinbō, or I, Shinran, myself try to teach you without any basis, [for it is written in the scriptures].

Seventh year of Kenchō [1255], tenth month, 3rd day.

Written by Shinran at the age of eighty-three.

8 From the Tannishō[15]

(a) Salvation for the Wicked

We proclaim: "If a good man can attain *Ōjō*, even more so a wicked man." However, most people in this world will say: "If a wicked man can attain salvation, even more so a good man." This latter statement seems reasonable on the surface, but it is against the spirit of our belief in the efficacy of Amida's Original Vow (*hongan tariki*). Let me explain. The man who is depending on his own power to do good (*jiriki sazen*) is lacking in the aspiration to depend on another's power (*tariki*), and is led astray from the Original Vow of Amida Buddha. However, if he repents of his desire to depend on his own power (*jiriki*) and becomes solely reliant on *tariki*, he can then attain salvation in the True Land of Recompense.

We are encumbered by our worldly passions, and whatever religious austerities we may observe, we still cannot be freed from the cycle of birth and death. It is he, Amida Buddha, who took compassion on us of our miseries, and made his vow with the intention of bringing wicked men to attain Buddhahood. A wicked man who is cognizant of his own shortcomings, and depends on *tariki*, is the prime object of true salvation. Therefore Shinran teaches that: "If a good man can attain salvation, even more so a wicked man."

(b) Evil Deeds Committed by *Nembutsu* Devotees

If one does not fear evil, because he cannot understand the mystery of the Original Vow of Amida, or if one believes that he cannot attain salvation by

---

[14]True Land of Recompense is used almost synonymously with the term "Pure Land," or "Pure Land of Perfect Bliss." It is in recompense to the Original Vow of Amida and not to any particular individual's act of faith.

[15]From *Shinranshū, supra.*, pp. 194–195, 203–206, 211–212.

merely taking advantage of the Original Vow, then he is a doubter of the efficacy of the Original Vow. He is also one who is ignorant of the past karmic formations of good and evil. The awakening of the mind to goodness is caused by good karmic formations of the past. The proclivity toward evil also comes from bad karmic formations of the past. . . . Once Shinran spoke to his disciples: "Now assume that I ask you to kill one thousand people, so that you can be assured of your own salvation. . . ." One of his disciples answered: "Even though this is indeed the command of my master, none of us in our present disposition can kill a man." Shinran responded by asking if his disciples were trying to contradict him, and continued: "Now, listen to this, if you simply follow the dictates of your intention, and if you are told that for the sake of attaining salvation, you have to kill a thousand, you can kill. However, you will not harm anyone because your karmic formation will not permit you to kill a single person. It is not because you are pure in your intention that you do not commit the act of killing. On the other hand, even though you may not wish to harm anyone, you may end up killing a hundred or even a thousand people." Once we discern our intention to be good, we think it is good, and if our intention is bad, we think it is bad, without gaining the knowledge of the miraculous power that aids us from the Original Vow. This is what our teacher Shinran wanted to convey to us.

Some time ago, a certain man was possessed by the mistaken notion that the Vow was a vow which was intended to save those who committed wicked deeds. Thus he deliberately committed wicked deeds to lay claim to his eventual salvation. When talks of his misdeeds spread and became known to Shinran, he wrote the man by saying that "just because you have the necessary antidote does not mean that you can freely take poison." In this way. Shinran wanted to correct his mistaken notions.

This is not to say that wicked deeds in themselves hinder one's own salvation. "If my belief in the Original Vow consists only of observance of the Law, how can I expect to be freed from the cycle of birth and death? Unworthy as I am, yet I am saved by the power of the Original Vow, and can now securely rejoice in it. However, I cannot create wicked deeds, unless there have been past karmic formations which make them possible."

Shinran also said, "For the purpose of obtaining salvation, there is no difference between those who cast their nets or rods to fish in the sea and river, or those who hunt animals and fowls in the fields and mountains to obtain their means of sustenance, and those who engage in trade or farm in the paddy fields and gardens to obtain their livelihood. Had it not been for karmic formations of the past, these people might have taken up different occupations." But nowadays, there are many who pretend to be seekers of the future life, and claim that the *nembutsu* is the exclusive domain of good men. They put posters on the walls of the public halls of the seminaries where *nembutsu* believers congregate, and insist that people who have done thus and thus are to be excluded. They wear the mask of diligent disciples of the Buddha. But they are liars and hypocrites.

If one has committed wicked deeds while relying on the efficacy of the Original Vow, he has done so because of his past karmic formations. This being the case, one must eradicate from his mind the desire to do good or evil in order to obtain salvation. Simply rely on the Original Vow. That is the true way of *tariki*. . . .

It may be proper not to take advantage of the Original Vow, if one can say that he can believe in the Vow only after he has cleansed himself of his wicked deeds and worldly passions. But the one who is able to rid himself of worldly passion is already a Buddha. This being the case [since a Buddha does not require salvation], all the meditation that the Amida Buddha did for five *kalpas* in arriving at his vows will be in vain. Those people who criticize the ones who take advantage of the Original Vow must also be aware that they are also encumbered by all the worldly passions and impurities. Are they not also the ones who must take advantage of the Original Vow? Judge not if others are taking advantage of the Original Vow by committing wicked acts. It seems clear that those who are quick to judge are the immature ones. . . .

(c) On Offerings to the Temples

There are some who say that the amount of offerings made determines the large or small stature one attains when becoming a Buddha. This teaching is anathema, and ridiculous beyond comparison.

First, how can one measure the precious body of a Buddha in terms of largeness or smallness? Our Master, Amida Buddha's measurement is given in one scripture, but it is done in order to allow us mortals to have a perception of his being. Once we gain enlightenment and acquire Buddha nature, we shall not take the shape of long, short, round or square, or the coloring of blue, yellow, red, white, or black. Is there any yardstick we can use to measure the body of a Buddha? No, there is none.

One scripture suggests that "by saying *nembutsu* one can see the likeness of a Buddha, the larger the voice the larger the likeness, the smaller the voice the smaller the likeness." Using this phrase as a textual basis, [some devotees of *jiriki* may have] created this unsound doctrine [of the amount of offering as the determinant] of Buddha's shape.

The offerings given to the temples are similar to the act of alms-giving [in the Brahmanic practices]. However, no matter how much one brings his treasures unstintingly to the altar of the Buddha, or to Buddhist teachers, if there is no faith, his act is in vain. One may not provide a single sheet of paper or one-half a pence for the sustenance of a Buddhist order, yet if he is endowed with profound faith and is dependent on *tariki*, he is the one for whom the intent of the Original Vow can be fulfilled.

[If someone continues to ask for large donations] and threatens fellow devotees of *nembutsu* by appealing to different doctrines, he is doing so for his own enrichment and shows his passion for worldly matters.

DŌGEN AND THE MEANING OF ZEN

Dōgen (1200–1253) first studied the Tendai doctrines, but later moved to the Kenninji to study Zen. In 1223 he went to Song China, and upon his return in 1227, became the founder of the Sōtō sect of Zen in Japan.

Like Eisai (1141–1215) before him, his efforts met hostile reception from the established Tendai sect, but unlike Eisai he avoided patronage from temporal powers. In 1243 he established the Eiheiji in Echizen (the present-day Fukui), away from Kyoto, and insisted on the application of rigorous discipline in the training of his disciples.

Among his works are the Shōbō Genzō (Collection of the True Law), *a monumental work in 100 volumes, which contains his view of the truth concerning Zen Buddhism. A smaller work, the* Shōbō Genzō Zuimonki (Occasional Conversations on the True Law), *contains the conversations of Dōgen, as recorded by his disciple Ejō, who was a few years his senior. His dedication to Zen, to austerity, and to right living is well reflected in the following selections from the* Zuimonki (Conversations). *Note also his mastery of the Confucian classics, and his skillful use of Confucian precepts for the propagation of Zen. Often Zen is said to be influenced deeply by Buddhism and Taoism. But in this and in other instances, the cultural influence of Confucianism should not be overlooked.*

9   Conversation with the Master[16]

(a) Knowing the Way in This Life

At an evening conversation, the Master, Dōgen, said: "Confucius once said, 'If one gains knowledge of the Way in the morning, there will be no regret in dying the same evening.' Anyone who is studying the Law of Buddha today must have a similar resolution. In the immemorial *kalpa* of times, we experience many existences, being born vainly and dying vainly. This time we have the rare opportunity of being born as human beings, and being able to hear the teachings of Buddha. If we do not gain enlightenment this time, how can we expect to gain enlightenment in the many, many incarnations that may follow. One may hold his life dear and aspire to live forever. But that is not an attainable goal. If this is the life with which we must part one day, is it not better to spend every available

---

[16]Dōgen, *Shōbō Genzō Zuimonki*, ed. by Yoshida Shōkin (Tokyo: Kadokawa Shoten, 1960), pp. 109–110, 113–134, 165–167, 186–243.

moment for the sake of the teachings of Buddha, which will bring joy forever?"

"Regrettable is the one who thinks only of the future and of the livelihood for tomorrow. Such thoughts bind him to this world which he must renounce, and prevent him from pursuing his training in Buddhism. Thus he aimlessly wastes away the remaining days and nights of his life. Abandon thoughts for tomorrow. Come death by starvation or from freezing. Even if there is no means of survival for tomorrow, it is better to hear the teachings of Buddha and share in his wisdom today and perish, than to forsake the teachings. This determination is called religious awakening. With it one can gain understanding of the teachings of Buddha. Without it, no matter how long he may train in the Way of Buddha, he still cannot attain enlightenment. He may give an appearance of renouncing the world, and study the teachings of Buddha, but without a positive commitment. Secretly he may be more concerned with the clothing for summer and winter, or with the livelihood for tomorrow and for the next year. People who have taken this attitude are not unknown to us. It is obvious that this is not the way to understand the teachings of Shakamuni."

(b) On Good Deeds

At an evening conversation, the Master said: ". . . The one who does good deeds and expects to be appreciated, does something better than committing a bad deed. However, he does so for his own benefit and not for others. A truly righteous man does good deeds without letting his beneficiary know of his deeds. He does good deeds freely and does not expect that someone will recognize his deeds. A monk must have a resolve far greater than this. In teaching all sentient beings, he must not discriminate between those who are close to him and those who are scarcely known to him. He must be able to treat everyone equally for the sake of his salvation. In doing something helpful either for the laity or for the priests, he must not think of his own benefit. People may not recognize or appreciate his work, but he must with the singleness of heart do good for them. Furthermore, if he has this resolve, he must not let others know that this is his resolve.

"Traditionally a monk renounces not only the world but also himself. If he has truly renounced himself, how can there be a desire to be recognized or appreciated by others? This does not mean that one can freely commit malicious acts, irrespective of the feelings of others. That is, of course, against the will of Buddha.

"I beseech all of you to do good for others, without having thoughts for recompense or for attaining fame. If you can selflessly dedicate yourselves for the sake of others, you have taken the first step toward effacing yourselves. And to attain this first step, first think of the impermanence of life. The one cycle of birth and death is like a dream, and time fritters away. Life is evanescent like a dew-drop, and time passes without waiting for men. Take heed that all of us are [on this earth] but for a moment. Thus even on the least of things do good to others, in order to follow the will of Buddha."

(c) Transmission of Zen Teachings

On New Year's eve, the second year of Katei [February 3, 1237], Ejō was installed as the chief abbot of the Kōshōji. . . . On that occasion, Dōgen gave the following sermon. . . .

"I shall now discuss with you how the teachings of Zen Buddhism are transmitted to us. The first patriarch, Bodhidharma, arrived in China and resided in the Shaolin temple in Mt. Song, sitting in meditation (*zazen*) and gazing at the walls, to await the arrival of a propitious time. On the twelfth month of that year, venerable Huike (487–593) became his disciple. The first patriarch, aware of the superior talent of Huike, gave him all the necessary training, and in recognition of the latter's attainment of enlightenment, transmitted his robe and the Law, [and made him the second patriarch]. Thereafter the transmission was made to the succeeding patriarch, and the Law is widely spread today.

"Today we are establishing a new temple, and are welcoming to its honored place the first chief abbot, to let him represent me in teaching the priests. Do not worry if there are only a few novices. Nor must you be unduly concerned because this happens to be your first experience. Shanzhao of Song was said to have only six or seven disciples, and Weiyan (751–834) of Tang had less than ten. However, all followed the teachings of Shakamuni, and while the number was small, the monasteries prospered.

"One monk gained his *satori* by hearing the sound of a bamboo hitting against roof tiles. Another attained his enlightenment by observing the opening of peach blossoms. Can a bamboo differentiate between sharpness and dullness or between doubt and enlightenment? Can a flower distinguish between shallowness and depth or between wisdom and folly? Flowers open year after year, but people who gaze at them do not necessarily attain their *satori*. Bamboos make their sound from time to time, but those who hear them are not always led to enlightenment in the Way of Buddha. Enlightenment comes to those who have for a long period of time attended to their training, studied the Way, and diligently performed their duties. When they gain enlightenment, it is not because of the sharpness of sound coming from the bamboo, or because of the deep coloring of the flower. No matter how mysterious the sound of a bamboo may be, it does not come of its own, without assistance from the roof tiles. No matter how exquisite the coloring of a flower may be, it cannot blossom of its own without assistance from the spring wind. The study of the Way is very much like this.

"Everyone of us is endowed with the ability to study the Way, but to gain the Way each of us requires help from others. Each one of us has certain wisdom, but to be trained in the Way, each of us must have cooperation of a group.

Therefore you must become of one mind, and of uniform resolve, and join in the performance of Zen rituals, in the studying of and in the diligent searching for the Law. A stone must be cut and polished to become a jewel. A man can gain his poise and character by assiduous training. Is there any uncut stone that can have a sparkle, or is there any uneducated person who can claim wisdom? You must work diligently to attain the goals you have set for yourselves. You must humble yourselves and must not be delinquent in studying the Way.

"The ancient sage said that time must not be wasted. I now ask you this question. Can we stop time, by wishing it would not go away? Or would time flow regardless of our desires? Time does not waste itself. It is man who wastes it away. Therefore man must not waste either himself or time, and must study diligently the Way. This is the spirit of the saying of the ancient sage.

"Again I beseech you to be of one mind and participate in the training of Zen and in the study of the Way. It is not easy to handle this task alone. The founder of Buddhism always asked his followers to assemble together. There were some who studied directly under Shakamuni Tathāgata, and there were others who studied under his disciple Ānanda to gain their enlightenment. My dear disciple Ejō, since you are now installed as the chief abbot, do not be so self-effacing as to say you are not equal to the task. When the abbot, Shaochu of Song was asked by a monk about the nature of Buddha, he replied, 'Jute three pounds.' He then posted the question and answer as a *kōan* (public theme) to let his priests study. You can perhaps follow his example too."

After saying this Dōgen left the pulpit. Drums were beaten, and Ejō again ascended to the pulpit to give his sermon. This was the first ceremony at the Kōshōji. At that time Ejō was thirty-nine years of age.

(d) Studying the Law with Diligence

The Master gave the following talk:

"There are many people in this world who are desirous of studying the Law, but they stray because they fear that this is the period of the Latter Degenerate Days (*mappō*), and that people are depraved. Finding themselves unable to practice rigorous religious austerities, they take the easier way of relying on the karmic conditions and expect to attain their *satori* in the coming reincarnation. This kind of thinking is based on completely mistaken assumptions.

"It is true that in Buddhism there are three periods assigned: First there is the period of the True Law (*shōbō*), then comes the period of the Reflected Law (*zōbō*), and finally the period of the Latter Degenerate Days of the Law (*mappō*). However, these three periods are assigned only for convenience. The period when Shakamuni Tathāgata was with us can certainly be called the period of the True Law. Yet it does not follow that all the priests of that time were superior. Even in that mysterious age, there were some utterly depraved ones. And unless there were such depraved ones, Buddha would not have given his commandments. One cannot say that because our age belongs to the Latter Degenerate Days, all the people living now are depraved. All men have the capacity to know the Law, and there is no such person who is incapable of doing it. If a man practices religious austerity, he can see the sign. He is endowed with a mind that can discern between good and evil. He has his hands and feet, and without any difficulty can press his palms together in prayer (*gasshō*) or walk to perform his religious duties. Indeed there is no such thing as lack of facilities in the performance of religious austerity. To be born as a human being means to be endowed with the ability of studying the Law. This is the privilege denied to all other beings. Those of you who study must not think of tomorrow. This day and this time shall be your only thought as you practice religious austerity in accordance with the Law."

(e) On *Zazen*

The Master gave the following talk:

"The most important means in the study of the Way is to sit in meditation (*zazen*). Many people in Song China attained *satori* through the power of *zazen*. By engaging in *zazen*, and through its merit, a person who is unable to answer a single question, and who has no particular talent or education can prove to be superior to a man who is clever and has studied for a long period of time. Therefore anyone who desires to study the Way must not divert his attention from *zazen*. The way of the founder of Buddhism is merely *zazen*. Once this is done, all the rest will follow."

Upon hearing this, the chief disciple Ejō inquired: "If one simultaneously sits in meditation and studies the scriptures, he can understand at least part of the sayings of a public theme (*kōan*). But when one merely performs *zazen*, those [enlightening] signs are absent. Must one still sit in meditation to the exclusion of all others?"

Dōgen answered: "One can gain little knowledge by digesting only part of a *kōan*. That can create a condition which hinders one from understanding the Way of the founder of Buddhism. If one sits in meditation and lets the time pass, it can lead to the Way of Shakamuni. The wise men of old did recommend simultaneously reading of scriptures and *zazen*, along with performance of *zazen* alone. There are some who have attained *satori* through *kōan*. But the very inspiration for his religious awakening came from *zazen*. Indeed, the merit which brings about *satori* comes from *zazen*."

LOTUS, BUDDHA, AND NATIONALISM

Nichiren was born in 1222 in the household of a fisherman. After completion of his study at Mt. Hiei, he established a new Hokke sect, which claimed that belief in the efficacy of the Lotus Sutra—*which was also the basic text of the Tendai sect in Mt. Hiei—would enable man to become one with the eternal Buddha. Nichiren propagated his new belief by preaching at the street corners of Kamakura, and warned against beliefs in the doctrine of other sects, which he termed uniformly as heretical. He also asserted that unless the nation followed his true belief, the country would be invaded. This he wrote in his treatise,* Rissho Ankoku-ron (On Establishing the Right and Bringing Peace to the Nation), *and submitted to the Regent Hōjō Tokiyori in 1268. His prophetic stance was proven correct when the Mongols invaded Japan in 1274. However, his zeal for proselytizing, and his contempt for other sects led to his exile first in Izu and later to the island of Sado.*

Nichiren did not look to China or India for inspiration but claimed that Japan should become the center of Buddhist beliefs. In this fashion, a fierce belief in the Lotus Sutra was transformed into a nationalist credo (Document 13).

Nichiren's appeal during his lifetime was concentrated among the middle and lower echelon samurai and among the common people. In modern days, his teachings continue to serve as the basis of new Buddhist sects, such as Sōka Gakkai and Rissho Kōseikai.

10   Nichiren's Letter to Lord Nanjo[17]

There are many in Japan who read and study the Lotus of Truth; there are, again, many who are attacked because they have conspired against others; but there is none who is abused because of [his revering] the Lotus of Truth. Thus, none of the men in Japan who hold to the Scripture have yet realized what is stated in the Scripture [since everyone who really holds to it must encounter perils on that account]; the one who really reads it is none other than I, Nichiren, who put in practice the text, "We shall not care for bodily life, but do our best for the sake of the incomparable Way." Then, I, Nichiren, am the one, supreme one, the pioneer of the Lotus of Truth.

11   Efficacy of Simple-Hearted Faith

If you desire to attain Buddhahood immediately, lay down the banner of pride, cast away the club of resentment, and trust yourselves to the unique Truth. Fame and profit are nothing more than vanity of this life; pride and obstinacy are simple fetters to the coming life. . . . When you fall into an abyss and someone has lowered a rope to pull you out, should you hesitate to grasp the rope because you doubt the power of the helper? Has not Buddha declared, "I alone am the protector and savior?" There is the power! Is it not taught that faith is the only entrance [to salvation]? There is

---

[17]All selections from Masaharu Anesaki, *Nichiren, The Buddhist Prophet,* 2nd. ed. (Cambridge, Massachusetts: Harvard University Press, 1916), pp. 46–47, 50, 66–67, 124–125.

the rope! One who hesitates to seize it, and will not utter the Sacred Truth, will never be able to climb the precipice of *Bodhi* (Enlightenment). . . . Our hearts ache and our sleeves are wet [with tears], until we see face to face the tender figure of the One, who says to us, "I am thy Father." At this thought our hearts beat, even as when we behold the brilliant clouds in the evening sky or the pale moonlight of the fast-falling night. . . . Should any season be passed without thinking of the compassionate promise, "Constantly I am thinking of you?" Should any month or day be spent without revering the teaching that there is none who cannot attain Buddhahood? . . . Devote yourself whole-heartedly to the "Adoration to the Lotus of the Perfect Truth," and utter it yourself as well as admonish others to do the same. Such is your task in this human life.

12   **The Lotus of Perfect Truth**   What I call the Heritage of the Great Thing Concerning Life and Death is none other than the Scripture, the Lotus of the Perfect Truth. For the Sacred Title of the Lotus was handed down from the two Buddhas, Shakamuni and Prabhūtra-ratna, to the Bodhisattva Viśista-cāritra, when the Buddhas appeared in the Heavenly Shrine, and from eternity the heritage has been kept without interruption. "Perfect" represents death,[18] and "Truth," life; while life and death make up the essence of the ten realms of existence—the essence identical with that of the Lotus. . . . All that is born and dies is a birth and death of the Scripture (Truth), the Lotus in its ultimate reality. . . . Then, to utter the Sacred Title of the Lotus with the conviction that the three are one—the Three, that is, Shakamuni, the Buddha who from eternity has realized Buddhahood; the Lotus of Truth, which leads all beings, without exception, to Buddhahood; and we, beings in all the realms of existence. To utter the Sacred Title is, therefore, the Heritage of the Sole Great Thing Concerning Life and Death. This is the essential key to [the religious life of] Nichiren's disciples and followers, namely, adherence to the Lotus of Truth. . . .

Whenever Nichiren's disciples and followers utter the Adoration of the Lotus of the Perfect Truth—being united in heart, even in separate existences, like the association existing between fish and water, there lies the Heritage of the Sole Great Thing Concerning Life and Death. This is the essence of what is promulgated by Nichiren. If it should be fulfilled, the great vow of propagating [the Truth throughout the Latter Days] over the whole world would be achieved.

Will the Bodhisattva Viśista-cāritra appear in these Latter Degenerate Days to open wide the gateway of the Truth, or will he not appear? The Scripture tells

---

[18]Nichiren interpreted the word "Perfect" (Sanskrit, *sad*) to mean reincarnation, the mysterious continuity and perpetuity of life through births and deaths. In this sense death is but a phase in the perpetual flow of life, a step to another manifestation of life. Therefore, this interpretation. Compare Marcus Aurelius, "Death, like birth, is a revelation of nature." [Mr. Anesaki's footnote]

us so; yet will it surely happen? Will the Bodhisattva appear, or not? At any rate, I, Nichiren, have now accomplished the pioneer work.

Whatever may happen to you, arouse in yourself a strong faith and pray that you may, at the moment of death, utter the Sacred Title in clear consciousness and with earnest faith! Do not seek besides this any Heritage of the Sole Great Thing Concerning Life and Death. Herein lies the truth of the saying that there is *Bodhi* even in depravities, and *nirvana* even in birth and death.[19] Vain it is to hold the Lotus of Truth without this heritage of faith!

13   Buddhism with Japan as Its Center   That India was called the country of the Moon-tribe[20] was prophetic of the appearance of Buddha [in the country]. Our Fusō[21] is called Japan, the Land of Sunrise. Must it not be the country where the [predestined] Sage should appear? The transit of the moon shifts from west to east; this symbolizes the transmission of Buddha's religion to the East. The sun rises in the east and sets in the west; this is an omen that the Buddhist religion shall return from the Land of Sunrise to the country of the Moon-tribe. The moon is not bright all the time, and justly so [Buddha proclaimed the Perfect Truth] only during eight years of his life.[22] The sun surpasses the moon in brilliance, and in like manner [the light of the eastern Sage] is destined to illumine the dark ages after the fifth five hundred years.

---

[19]This does not mean to nullify the distinction between enlightenment and illusion, but to emphasize that truth is not be to sought beyond what we deem this life of vices and the realm of birth and death. The point may be seen in the synthesis of "vacuity" and "phenomenal reality," in the "Middle Path." [Mr. Anesaki's footnote]

[20]That is, Yuezhi. The idea that India was the country of the Moon-tribe was combined with another tradition identifying the name India with Indu, the moon.

[21]The name of a certain kind of tree called Fusō was sometimes employed by the Chinese as an appellation of Japan.

[22]Buddhist tradition puts the preaching of the Lotus of Truth in the last eight years of Buddha's ministry.

This final-Jōmon-period pottery, unearthed from the Ōmori shell mound, was a lamp. It attests to the rich variety of lifestyles possible in Japan from around 1,000 B.C. to 250 B.C. (see Chapter 1). (Courtesy of Edo Tokyo Museum.)

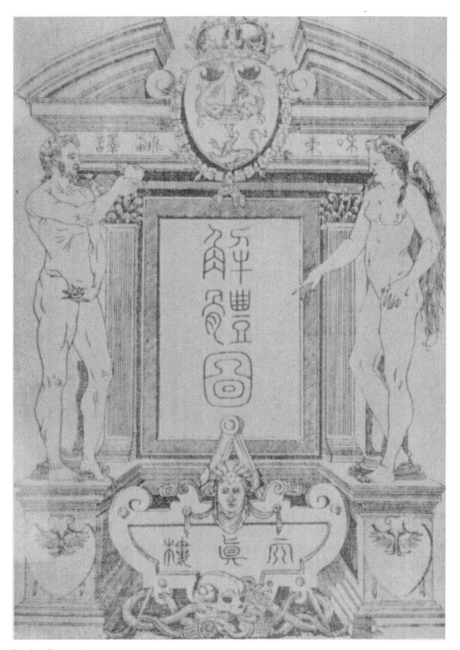

Sugita Gempaku's *Kaitai Shinsho*, a translation of *Tabulae Anatomicae*, published in the fall of 1774 (see pp. 263–66). (Courtesy of Edo Tokyo Museum.)

In 1792, Shiba Kōkan published this map of the world (Western Hemisphere not shown). It was based on a 1787 French map obtained by his friend Ōtsuki Gentaku in Nagasaki. Knowledge about the rest of the world trickled into Japan even during this long period of isolation (compare pp. 225–27). (Courtesy of Edo Tokyo Museum.)

With snow-capped Mt. Fuji as the backdrop, Hokusai captured this New Year's day scene of Echigoya (see page 228) around 1832. The signboards state that the store trades in cash only and does not charge inflated prices. The kite has an inscription "Longevity." (Courtesy of Edo Tokyo Museum.)

CHAPTER VI

The Development of Feudal Institutions through the Muromachi Period

Emperor Godaigo's Kemmu Restoration in 1333 was an anachronistic venture. He was able to destroy the power of the already weakened Hōjō family in Kamakura only because a significant number of the warrior class supported him for reasons of their own. To the warriors, the Restoration provided opportunities for redistribution of feudal privileges and for aggrandizement of their domanial holdings. Thus when the issue of rewards was ineptly handled, there was a sizable defection.

In 1336 Ashikaga Takauji enthroned Emperor Kōmyō from the rival northern branch, and had himself named the new *shōgun*. Thus was begun another period of rule by the warriors. However, unlike Minamoto no Yoritomo before him, Ashikaga Takauji did not enjoy near-monopoly of power. Emperor Godaigo and his heirs tenaciously held onto their right to occupy the throne, and the country was divided into the Northern Court and the Southern Court for the next 57 years. Most of the warriors sided with one of the courts. The question of legitimacy was not a significant issue for them except when it served their purpose. The rivalries of the two courts again gave the warriors opportunities to aggrandize and secure their domanial holdings. During this period several trends began to surface.

Among the warriors, the kinship and blood-ties which bound them so closely during the Kamakura period became a thing of the past. Members of the same family could be found on both sides of the struggle between the Northern and Southern Courts. Gradually warriors would be bound by common interests and geographical factors. However, the emergence of domanial lords with well-defined geographical boundaries and control over the territory and populace would have to wait for several more centuries (see Chapter VII).

Several factors were at work since the latter part of the Kamakura period to make this gradual transition. The decline in the power and prestige of the court nobles and of the great temples and shrines was reflected in their diminished ability to lay claim to or to have control over the *shōen*. This in turn facilitated the encroachment upon the *shōen*, first by the *jitō* and then by the *shugo*. Using their military power effectively, the *jitō* and *shugo* were able to enter into agreement with the *ryōshu* (lords of *shōen*) which permitted the former to share in the rights of proprietorship over the *shōen*, and enjoy economic advantages derived from them. Such agreements often called for remitting of a specific sum or a portion of the produce as annual rent to the *ryōshu* while allowing the remainder to be kept by the *jitō* or *shugo*.

Initially the *shugo* were appointed by the Ashikaga *bakufu* to serve as military governors, as subordinates of the *shōgun*. With the decline in the imperial bureaucratic system, they exercised concurrently the powers of civil governors (*kokushi* or *kuni no tsukasa*), who after the Kemmu Restoration were often not appointed.

Increasingly, along with the economic strength they maintained through their rights to proprietorship in the *shōen*, the *shugo* became the final authority on local affairs, preparing the way for the emergence of the *shugo daimyō*. The Ashikaga depended on the *shūgo* to enforce their decrees and policies, but were in no position to curtail the *shugo*'s self-aggrandizing schemes.

The Muromachi period also saw a very substantial improvement in agricultural technology which caused the emergence of new classes of lower and middle farmers. Quest for adequate irrigation facilities often resulted in the creation of new village communities without regard to the traditional *shōen* boundaries. The cohesiveness of village communities made it possible for the villages to engage in certain forms of "political" activities, such as submission of petitions to lighten their burdens or even to band together in peasant uprisings. The spread of a money economy, the establishment of semipermanent market places (*ichi*), and the growth of *za* or merchant guilds brought forth surprisingly vigorous economic activities. The *ichi* and *za* sought special privileges and monopolistic rights, and depended on court nobles, regional rulers and temples and shrines for protection. They enjoyed the privileges of exemption from corvée-type duties, and of free passage through barriers. In return they performed certain duties and paid their dues to their lords who protected them. In the Muromachi period, the established *za* were often challenged by the new *za* formed by those who previously traded in subordinate positions with the established *za*. At times the *daimyō* found it convenient to allow the merchants in his castle towns to form new *za*, and make them his tax-collection agencies. To cope with these challenges, the established *za* often became more traditional, insisting on the hereditary principles in the allocation of seats available in a given *za*. This, in turn, created a counter move from the *daimyō* to abolish *za* as an economic institution altogether. Examples of such a move are found in the free-market (*raku-ichi*) and abolition-of-*za* (*raku-za*) policies of Oda Nobunaga (see Chapter 7).

The economic conditions of this period were also responsible for the gradual adoption of the practice of primogeniture. It started slowly as a means of protecting the meager inheritance which when further subdivided would have caused hardship to everyone concerned.

The legacy of the Muromachi period is not confined to its institutions. In the cultural fields, the Nō theater prospered under the benign protection of the Ashikaga, and so did the Chinese studies pursued by the Zen monks of the five major temples (*gozan bungaku*). The tea ceremony, the art of *ikebana* (flower arrangement), and the monochrome paintings of Sesshū and others which we consider as genuinely Japanese have their origins in the Muromachi period. These, however, are not the subjects of this chapter. The spirit of the Muromachi culture is often described by the term *yūgen* which can be roughly translated as mystic or subtle elegance. Cultural forms of the period were not overt but subdued. Their simple exteriors hid some of the more profound meanings. In the study of the social institutions of the age, we must also look beneath the surface. In appearance they were feudalistic, but in reality they contained some elements of modernity. Thus they paved the way for the emergence of Tokugawa society which in many respects can be considered the first modern society in East Asia.

JITŌ'S ENCROACHMENT UPON SHŌEN

During the Kamakura period, jitō *often utilized their military power to encroach upon the rights held by* ryōshu *or lords of* shōen, *regardless of whether they were of nobility or temples and shrines. Their encroachment took the form of withholding of annual rent due the* ryōshu, *or an outright illegal occupation of the land. Disputes over land titles, annual rent, and jurisdiction were frequent. And to avoid such disputes, several compromises were effected. One such method was* jitō uke *or* jitō ukedokoro, *as seen in Documents 1 and 2. (1) It bound the* jitō *to pay a certain set amount of annual rent each year to the* ryōshu *irrespective of rich or poor harvest, and (2) in return, it granted the* jitō *the powers of management and maintenance of the* shōen. *His powers were almost exclusive because entry by the officials of the* ryōshu *was no longer permitted.*

The second method was one called shitaji chūbun, *as described in Document 3. The word* shitaji *is a composite term for the lands which could provide any form of income including annual rent and miscellaneous services (*nengu *and* shōeki). *Such lands included not only fields and gardens, but also hills and forests and* salt farms. These lands were then divided into one half, or one third and two thirds between the ryōshu and jitō, with each having jurisdiction over its part and pledging not to invade the other's territory.

Both of these methods greatly enhanced the power of the jitō. The Kamakura bakufu encouraged these types of compromise for the purposes of enhancing the power of the jitō, and of speedy settlement of disputes.

1 Jitō Ukedokoro, 1308[1]   Settlement (wayo):

Dispute between zasshō (shō official, more specifically, officer in charge of miscellaneous affairs) Michisuke and jitō Yamanouchi Sudō Saburo Michisuke, District of Yasumoto, Province of Bingo.

The above suit was brought by zasshō Michisuke. Even though the briefs by the plaintiff and the defendant were already discussed, the parties now wish to settle the matter by compromise. The questions at issue include inspection (kenchū), annual rent (nengu), and division of land into respective areas of responsibility (chūbun). Now there shall be no further litigation by the zasshō on these matters.

The agreement is essentially as follows: Management of the land in this district shall become the responsibility of the jitō in perpetuity. On the matter relating to the payment of annual rent to the ryōke (lord of the shōen, there shall be no entry [into the shōen] by the representative of the ryōke.

Effective next year, that is the second year of Enkei [1309], of the annual rent due the ryōke, which is forty-five kan,[2] twenty-five kan shall be paid within the year the rent is due, and the remaining twenty kan by the second month of the following year. This amount is fixed and regardless of poor harvest or not, the jitō shall be responsible for its payment, and shall without delay consign the rice or remit the money of Kyoto. However, if there is a serious crop failure nationwide, the jitō may send a massenger to the ryōke, requesting the latter to send an inspector to the shō office, and determine the amount of the annual rent due in accordance with the conditions of the crop. . . . This is the settlement the two parties have agreed to. If the ryōke violates this agreement and breaks this contract (ukedokoro), of the amount of annual rent which is forty-five kan, the jitō may withhold one half of it. If the jitō shall act contrary to the provisions of this document, and fail to consign or transmit the annual rent, then he may be relieved from this contract (ukedokoro), and a suit may be

---

[1] Yamanouchi Sudō-ke Monjo, as quoted in Ōkubo Toshiaki et al., Shiryō ni yoru Nihon no Ayumi (Japanese History through Documents), Vol. 2, Chūseihen (Mediaeval Period) (Tokyo: Yoshikawa Kōbunkan, 1958), pp. 146–147.

[2] The term kan was used most commonly to signify a unit of money which was equal to 1,000 mon. Mon was the smallest basic unit. However, during the Muromachi period the term was used also to denote a certain amount of crops that could be harvested from a field held by the samurai (chigyō).

instituted against him to handle the matter. In such an event, the *zasshō* may enter the *shō* office to discharge his responsibilities (*azukaridokoro zasshō*). This being the case, we request that the agreement be made known to others as soon as possible, and let this serve as a precedent for future reference.

First year of Enkei [1308], twelfth month, 18th day.

Jitō, Fujiwara Michisuke, *monogram*

Zasshō, Michisuke, *monogram*

2   On Matters Relating to the Annual Rent Due the Ryōke of Tomida Shō in the Province of Owari, 1327[3]   On the matter of annual rent related to the above *shō*, it is to be handled in accordance with the document (*ukebumi*) signed by Regent Hōjō in the fifth year of Jōgen [1211] [accepting the existing *jitō uke*]. However, there have been instances of withholding of annual rent, and suits have been brought against the *jitō*. Now a document is issued by the *jitō* stating that each year during the eleventh month, an amount of one hundred and ten *kan* will be delivered to Kyoto. Therefore the suit is cancelled and the entry of inspectors [sent by the *ryōke*] is stopped. However, the fields directly operated by [the representatives of] the *ryōke* are from the beginning not covered by the document, and the *zasshō*'s control of these fields shall not be open to question. If anyone acts contrary to the provisions of this document, [the *jitō uke* shall be cancelled and] the control of this *shō* shall revert directly to the control of the *ryōke*, or the provisions of the original document issued during the reign period of Jōgen [1211] shall become applicable.

This paper is issued for future reference.

Second year of Kareki [1327], fifth month, 18th day.

3   Shitaji Chūbun (Division of Lands in One Half for Administrative Purposes), 1318[4]   Settlement:

In re: Management of lands in Kamizaki *shō*, Province of Bingo.

The above named *shō* has as its *ryōke*, Kongō Sanmai In (temple) belonging to Mr. Kōya. Its *zasshō* Yukimori had a dispute over the management of the *shō* and its lands with *jitō*, Ano Suetsugu. The dispute was brought to trial and briefs by the plaintiff and defendant were presented and argued three times. However, it is agreed that as long as the *shō* remains in the possession (*chigyō*) of this temple, taking into consideration the special circumstances, a settlement shall be effected as follows: That the wet and dry fields, hills and rivers and all other lands shall be divided into one-half, and each party shall manage its respective

---

[3]*Engakuji Monjo*, in Ōkubo, *op. cit.*, p. 147.

[4]*Kongō Saumai In Monjo*, in Ōkubo, *op. cit.*, p. 148.

sphere with the exclusion of the other. These are the terms of the settlement as recorded.

Second year of Bunpō [1318], second month, 17th day.

Acting *Jitō* Saemon jo Sukekage, *monogram*

Zasshō Yukimori, *monogram*

TOKUSEI—FORGIVING OF DEBTS

Prior to the Kamakura period the term tokusei *was used to signify forgiveness of taxes due in the event of natural calamity. However, the Kamakura and Muromachi* bakufu *utilized the term to signify a policy intended to solidify the foundation of their governments. The most famous* tokusei *edict of 1297 was issued as an emergency measure to rescue retainers (or vassals) of the* bakufu *from their financial difficulties which became more pronounced after the Mongol invasion. The edict had the unintended effect of cutting off the supply of money to needy retainers, and resulted in great financial confusion. It was abandoned the following year, but the same type of measure was reissued from time to time. During the Muromachi period most of the* tokusei *edicts were issued either in response to the demands of peasant uprisings or for the purpose of strengthening the financial position of the* bakufu *(as against that of its retainers).*

4   The Tokusei Edict of Einin, 1297[5]

a) The Law Promulgated in Kantō (Kamakura)

1. Mortgaged land. Fifth year of Einin [1297], third month, 6th day.

The above, if the land was acquired by the *jitō* or *gokenin* (retainers or vassals of the *shōgun*), it need not be returned to the original owner if the transfer has been in effect for more than twenty years, and if it has been done in accordance with these provisions. However, if the land was acquired by those other than the *gokenin* and by the commoner (*bonge*) [referring to usurers operating the *dozō* and the like], then it must be returned to the original owner, irrespective of the number of years involved.

b) Laws Sent from Kantō (Kamakura) to Rokuhara (Kyoto)

1. Prohibition against Appeals.

Appeals have increased year after year, and those who have lost a case have often resorted to an appeal without considering the merit of the case. Thus those who have won the litigation cannot obtain assurance (*ando*). This is the root

---

[5]*Tōji Hyakugō Monjo*, in Satō Shinichi et al., eds., *Chūsei Hōsei Shiryōshū (Documentary Collections on Mediaeval Legal and Institutional History)*, Vol. 1, *Kamakura Bakufu Hō (Laws of the Kamakura Bakufu)* (Tokyo: Iwanami Shoten, 1955), pp. 295–297. For a discussion of this *tokusei* see Delmer M. Brown, "The Japanese *Tokusei* of 1297," in *Harvard Journal of Asiatic Studies*, Vol. 12 (1949), pp. 188–206.

cause of many unhappy experiences. It is therefore decreed that this practice shall be prohibited. . . .

2. Mortgaging and Selling of Land.

Many retainers suffer difficulties by mortgaging or selling their land. Hereafter, such practices are prohibited. As to the land already sold, it must be returned to its original owner. However, this prohibition does not apply if the land was initially sold with the permission of the *bakufu*, which was confirmed by an official document (*okudashibumi* or *gechijō*), or if the land has been held (*chigyō*) for more than twenty years by the present owner, irrespective of whether the land is owned publicly or privately. If anyone disobeys this prohibition and acts lawlessly, he shall be punished.

With regard to land on which a non-retainer or commoner presently holds mortgage or title, it must be returned to the original owner, irrespective of the passage of years.

3. On the Matter of Lending Money for Interest.

When a person is in need of money, without regard for ill-advised expenditures, he incurs heavy debts from which he cannot extricate himself. In this way, the rich monopolize the benefit coming from high interest payments and the poor have no place to turn. Hereafter such debts cannot be recovered through litigation. Even if a creditor claims that his loan was certified by an official document (*gechijō*) and has not been paid and appeals [to the *bakufu*], no hearing will be granted.

With regard to pledging articles of value at a pawnshop (*kura*), such practice cannot be prohibited.

CRITICISM OF THE KEMMU RESTORATION

The writer of the following scribbling may have never expected this impromptu writing which he left on the dry river bed of Nijō in Kyoto to survive into the twentieth century. But it proved to be one of the best satires of the new government of Emperor Godaigo and of the Japanese society under him. The lack of law and order, the declining prestige of the Imperial Court, the arrogance of the new samurai, inequity existing in the Emperor's reward system, and the resulting confusions were all symptomatic of the age. It was no wonder that within two years after the start of the Kemmu Restoration (1333), the new government for all practical purposes was supplanted by the Askikaga.

5   Scribbling on the Dry River Bed of Nijō[6]   These are the kinds of things which are in vogue in this Capital City (Kyoto): burglars at night, false imperial

---

[6]*Kemmu Nenkanki (Records of the Kemmu Era)* in Kasahara Kazuo et al., eds., *Seisen Nihonshi Shiryōshū (Selected Documents on Japanese History)*, rev. ed. (Tokyo: Yamagawa Shuppansha, 1970), pp. 81–82.

scripts; prisoners, rapid horses to indicate trouble some place, false alarms; nuns returning to secular life to become prostitutes, or people becoming priests without going through regular ordination procedures; one who is lost in the street after experiencing a moment of glory as *daimyō* only to lose it, or starting unnecessary wars just for the sake of having titles to their estates reassured or of receiving rewards; litigants who leave their home provinces to converge on the claims court in the capital, carrying their documents in letter boxes; Zen monks and those monks without official ranks who use flattery and informing on others to gain the favor of the government; upstarts who supplant their superiors; appointments to the court of claims without regard to their ability or suitability; samurai who are unused to court ceremonies wearing the full regalia, including caps and wooden maces, pretentiously participate in the rituals of the Imperial Palace; appointment secretaries at the Court who pretend to be wise men, who as the middle men deceive both the Court and those who come to the Court, but whose falsehood cannot long remain hidden; . . .

Samurai who have to pawn away armors and repay their debts on a day-to-day basis; samurai from the Kantō region going to their offices in palanquins; man's divided silk shirts for ceremonial wear normally not allowed for use by plebians are worn by many without discrimination between the high born and the lowly born; inability of the samurai to discard their suits of armor because peace is still not here; samurai who cannot master the art of archery, who busily chase dogs, and who fall from their horses many more times than the number of arrows they possess; . . . the court nobles of the Capital City and samurai of Kamakura mixing together trying to have a meet of link verses (*renga*) only to see complete dissonance, and wherever a *renga* meet is held, people always prefer to become judges; really there is no distinction between those who are well accomplished in the arts, and those upstarts who want to claim authority without foundation. This is an age of licentiousness and disorder. There used to be a time when samurai obeyed the laws promulgated by Shōgun Minamoto no Yoritomo who subjugated the entire country. Nowadays, those once proud samurai are reduced to ones without backbones. This is a time of change, and those who rendered meritorious services and had many horses and cows in the morning, can find all of their wealth taken away in the evening. That is what is happening today. Then there are some who are not particularly loyal or distinguished by service, yet can attain rapid promotion to higher ranks. There must be some inequity existing, and the credibility of what is happening is certainly open to question. Somehow this is a strange way to unify the country. Being born in this day and age, what I can hear and see are often difficult to account for. But I am sharing with others at least one tenth of what the children in Kyoto are humming with certain tunes today.

ASHIKAGA TAKAUJI'S RISE TO POWER

After he was securely placed in the position of authority in Kyoto, and after successfully enthroning Emperor Kōmyō of the Northern Branch, Ashikaga

Takauji issued the following formulary consisting of seventeen articles (1336). It made reference to the Hōjō family who controlled the Kamakura bakufu, and showed clearly the intent of the Ashikaga to become the successors to the powers of the Kamakura bakufu. The articles were written by the monk Zeen. They cannot be considered the basic law by the Muromachi bakufu, but rather a series of injunctions. Until the Eisei period (1504–1520) numerous additions were made to the Kemmu Shikimoku in response to the changing conditions and to the needs of a given moment. The number of these additions exceeded 200 articles.

6   **Kemmu Shikimoku, 1336**[7]   Should the *bakufu* remain in Kamakura as before, or should it be moved to another location? . . . If the people desire moving of the *bakufu* from Kamakura to Kyoto, then should not the government follow the wishes of the people?

The way of government, . . . according to the classics, is that virtue resides in good government. And the art of governing is to make the people content. We must therefore set the people's hearts at rest as expeditiously as possible. These are to be decreed immediately, but its rough outline is given below:

1. Frugality must be universally practiced.

2. Drinking and wild frolicking in groups must be suppressed.

3. Crimes of violence and outrage must be stopped.

4. Private houses which are owned by former enemies of the Ashikaga are no longer subject to confiscation.

5. The vacant lots existing in the capital city must be returned to their original owners.

6. Pawnshops and other financial institutions may be re-opened for business with protection from the government.

7. In selecting *shugo* (protectors) for different provinces, men with special talents in administrative matters shall be chosen.

8. The government must put an end to interference by men of power and by nobility, as well as by women, Zen monks, and monks holding no official ranks.

9. Men in public offices must be told not to be derelict in their duties. Furthermore they must be carefully selected.

10. Under no circumstances can bribery be tolerated.

11. Presents received from different quarters while in or out of office must be returned.

12. Retainers who serve closely must be carefully selected.

13. Strive to attain decorum.

14. When men of integrity, righteousness and honor are found, reward them accordingly.

---

[7]*Kemmu Shikimoku* in Satō Shinichi et al., eds., *Chūsei Hōseishi Shiryōshū (Documentary Collection of Mediaeval Legal and Institutional History)*, Vol. 2, *Muromachi Bakufu Hō (Laws of the Muromachi Bakufu)* (Tokyo: Iwanami Shoten, 1957), pp. 3–7.

15. Litigations brought by the poor and the inexperienced must be listened to with compassion.

16. Litigations brought by shrines and temples may or may not be heard depending on their merits, and must be carefully scrutinized [with large shrines and temples placed under the tightest scrutiny].

17. The date for the issuance of a formulary on litigation must be set.

The above seventeen articles are described briefly. . . . If we can emulate the virtuous rule of the sacred emperors Daigo and Murakami during the Engi (901–923) and Tenryaku (945–957) eras in the olden days, and if we can follow the more recent examples set by the father and son team of Hōjō Yoshitoki (1163–1224, second regent of the Kamakura period) and Hōjō Yasutoki (1183–1242, third regent), we shall then be able to govern in such a way as to gain adulation from all the people, which shall serve as the basis of peace within the four seas.

SHUGO AS DOMANIAL LORDS

By the middle of the fourteenth century, it became a common practice for the shugo *to acquire fiscal rights in all non-military* shōen *within the areas under their jurisdiction. Along with the military and other responsibilities they acquired previously, they became the sole authorities in their provinces. This section shows their gradual transformation into the* shugo-daimyō, *who held sway over their own extensive territorial holdings, almost independently of shogunal control. The earlier emphasis placed on the functions of the* shūgo *as officials of the* bakufu *is given in Document 7. Document 8 prohibited the encroachment upon* shōen *held by temples and shrines, and also banned other illegal activities. Thus the two documents together show the dilemma that faced the Ashikaga government, namely the necessity to strengthen the position of the* shugo *in order to make them viable members of the Ashikaga* bakufu, *but in the process the latter also had to guard against their illegal activities including territorial acquisitions. Document 9, which was an edict of 1346, shows the continued encroachment upon* shōen, *and transformation of the samurai within specific provinces as private retainers of the* shugo. *In this way, militarily, politically, and economically, the* shugo *quickly completed their tasks of converting the territories under their jurisdiction as their own domains. The continued turmoil in the country, the adoption of the law of sharing rent between* shugo *and those who held proprietary rights to the* shōen (hanzei) *(Document 10), and the practice of permitting the* shugo *to submit only a set amount of the annual rent in return for the actual control of the* shōen *(Document 11) completely eroded the bases on which the* shōen *could survive. And with the demise of the* shōen *came the further enhancement of the powers of the* shugo-daimyō *as domanial lords.*

The demise of the shōen *also brought about economic difficulties for court nobles who were supported by the* shōen. *Their relative position vis-à-vis the samurai is reflected in Document 12.*

7   **Appointment of Shugo, 1336**[8]   In selecting the *shugo* for different provinces, men with special talents in administrative matters shall be chosen. The past practice has been to name to the *shugo*'s position those who have served loyally in the military, and as a means of assigning the *shōen* to those who deserve rewards. However, the position of *shugo* is similar to the ancient position [of provincial governor (*kuni no tsukasa*)]. Whether a province can be governed well or not depends on this position. Therefore by appointing to this position only those who are talented, we shall be able to pacify the people.

8   **On Matters Relating to Shugo of Various Provinces, 1338**[9]   Issued on the fifth year of Kemmu [1338], seventh month, 29th day.

The rationale behind the appointment of *shugo* is to let them govern the provinces and to comfort the people. Thus only men of virtue must be appointed to these positions. Those who do not benefit the provinces must be replaced. Some may say that their positions are granted to them as reward for their meritorious service or that their positions have been in their families for generations. Some of them have encroached upon the proprietary rights of the original *shōen* protected by major temples and shrines. They have assumed the functions of various *jitō*, stationed their own troops, and filled [key] positions with their own retainers (*kenin*). These things are not supposed to be done. The provisions of the *Jōei Shikimoku* must be closely observed. The duties of the *shugo* as stated in the *Shikimoku* are three [see Chapter 6, Document 26, Article 3], and in all other matters, the *shugo* must not interfere. However, in recent years, without the authority of directives which are given from above and which are recorded, and without bothering to petition the higher authorities, an innumerably large number of *shugo*—whose conduct is of grave concern to us—in a short span of time, have moved in groups from one location to another over lands and rivers to press their demands. The circumvention of the administrative law and disturbance of established order are caused by their actions. Whatever infraction of law that exists must be rectified. It is hereby decreed.

9   **Increase in the Powers of Shugo, 1346**[10]   Matters which must not be performed by the *shugo* of various provinces.

1. With the exception of the three major duties (described in the *Jōei Shikimoku*) and the two additional duties of prohibiting harvesting of another's

---

[8]From *Kemmu Shikimoku jō jō* in *ibid.*, p. 5, being an explanation of Article 7 of Document 6 above.

[9]From *Kemmu Irai Tsuika*, in *ibid.*, pp. 11–12.

[10]From *Kemmu Irai Tsuika*, in *ibid.*, pp. 23–24.

fields when there are disputes, and of sending of retainers to oversee disputes in the fields, no *shugo* shall interfere in any other matters or gain proceeds from rent due others, all of which can be injurious to the *jitō* and to the retainers of the *shōgun*.

5. The *shugo* shall not contract marriages [with the families of *jitō* and of retainers of the *shōgun*,] as a means of forcibly making them allies.

6. The *shugo* shall not falsely claim that he has the right to collect rent from *shōen*, or use another's name, to gain financial control of those *shōen* protected by major temples and shrines.

7. The *shugo* shall not falsely state that he has orders from the provincial governor or the *ryōke* to collect rent without delay or that the rent he is collecting is for the use of temples and shrines. He is enjoined from sending his messengers to collect rent from common people's households.

8. The *shugo* shall not confiscate property from the common people under the pretext of using it for military purposes, or of borrowing it from them.

9. The *shugo* shall not acquire bonds of debts from others under a false pretext and use them to harass debtors.

10. The *shugo* shall not divide the tax allocated to him to those *jitō* and *gokenin* (retainers of the *shōgun*) residing in his domain, [thus transferring his tax burdens to others].

11. The *shugo* shall not erect new barriers and assess transit (or harbor) taxes on products coming from mountains, fields, and rivers, thus inconveniencing travellers.

It is said that these items prohibited are widely practiced these days. However, if any one of the above prohibitions is violated, that person shall be immediately relieved from the position of *shugo*. If the *shugo* is not aware of the crime committed, and it is proven beyond any shadow of doubt that the crime is committed by his deputy (*daikan*), in that case, the latter's estate (*shoryō*) shall be confiscated. If the latter possesses no estate, then he shall be condemned to banishment.

10   Adoption of the Law of Sharing Rent (Hanzei no Hō), 1352[11]   On matters relating to estates protected by temples and shrines. Instructions issued on the third year of Kannō [1352], seventh month, 24th day.

As a result of recent disturbances, temples and shrines are lying in ruins, and patrons of the *shōen* (*honjo*) are deprived of their regular sources of income. This phenomenon has increased two-fold in recent years. In the provinces where there is no warfare, invasion of the *shōen* and seizure of annual rent by samurai are frequently observed. Therefore it is decreed that the *shugo* shall undertake the responsibilities of notifying the due dates of annual rent which are set in accor-

---

[11]From *Kemmu Irai Tsuika*, in *ibid.*, pp. 28–29.

dance with the proximity or distance from the capital. If anyone disobeys this decree, one third of his estate (*shoryō*) shall be confiscated. If he has no estate, then he shall be condemned to banishment. If anyone, after initially obeying this decree, changes his mind and again disobeys, then the *shugo* may, without prior approval from the *bakufu*, mobilize the *jitō* and *gokenin* in his own province, move immediately to the locality, mete out the punishment, and place a deputy (*zasshō*, meaning *daikan*) as before to handle the matters of that particular *shōen*. Thereafter, the *shugo* must make a detailed report to the *bakufu*. If the *shugo* is derelict in this, he must be removed from his position.

In the three provinces of Ōmi, Mino, and Owari, one-half of the annual rent shall be assigned for use as military provisions. The crop harvested this year, and this year's only, shall be deposited with the military forces. (The administration and disbursement of the crop shall be left in the hands of the *shugo*.) The *shugo* must be notified of this matter. One-half of the annual rent must be turned over to the patrons of the *shōen* (*honjo*). If those who receive the crop in consignment on one pretext or another refuse to return the crop to the rightful owner, then the application of this law of sharing one-half of the rent shall be cancelled and everything must be returned to the patron of the *shōen*.

11 Shugo-uke (Contract for Shugo), 1402[12]

On matters relating to the estate belonging to Mt. Kōya, located in Ōta *shō* and the Kuwabara region in the province of Bingo: The estate which is now managed by Onomichi Kurashiki who as a holder of the functions of *jitō* (*jitō-shiki*) is entitled to a certain portion of the rent (*chigyō*).

Henceforth all basic works shall be performed by Yamana Hirotsune (the *shugo*), who has agreed to submit to this temple one thousand *koku* each year as its share of the annual rent. It is ordered that this fact must be made known immediately, and I am sending this notice accordingly.

Ninth year of Ōei [1402], seventh month, 19th day.

Shami [Kanrei (commissioner) Hatakeyama Motokuni],

monogram

To the monks of this temple.

12 Contrast Between the Prosperity of Samurai and Poverty of Court Nobles[13]

Court nobles (*kuge*) have become so poor that they squat near a ditch

---

[12]From *Kōyasan Monjo* in Ōkubo et al., *op. cit.*, p. 280. The term *Shugo-uke* signifies a contract under which the *shugo* assumes the duties of collecting rent and administrative responsibilities. This *shō*'s annual revenue was about 1,800 *koku*, thus this *shugo-uke* was contracted at slightly over one-half of its annual revenue.

[13]From the *Taiheiki*, Vol. 33, in *Nihon Koten Bungaku Taikei (Major Compilation of Japanese Classics)*, Vol. 36 (Tokyo: Iwanami Shoten, 1952), p. 252.

or wonder around in the street. In contrast the wealth of the samurai has multiplied day after day. They wear the best silk, and have eight different kinds of delicacies on their tables. When Hōjō Takatoki (1303–1333, the last regent) was Regent governing the country, the *shūgo* discharged only three basic duties and had no other responsibilities, Now, whether it be large or small, everything pertaining to the governing of a province is handled by a *shūgo*. He treats the *jitō* and *gokenin* (*shōgun*'s retainers) as if they were his own personal followers (or retainers, *rojū*), and controls the estates belonging to temples and shrines, sharing in one-half of their annual rent (in order to pay for the stipends of his own retainers). His authority is as great as the *tandai* (commissioners) stationed in Rokuhara (Kyoto) or Kyushu. In the Capital City, there are many *daimyō* headed by Sasaki Dōyō. These *daimyō* like to congregate together in a tea ceremony. Whenever they get together, they make merriment. All the treasurers from overseas and from our homeland are there. Every room is exquisitely decorated, and their chairs are covered by the furs of leopards and tigers. . . .

AGRICULTURAL DEVELOPMENT AND VILLAGE COMMUNITY

The late Kamakura period witnessed a substantial improvement in agricultural technology. This included the introduction of double cropping (and in some cases triple cropping), deep cultivation, use of draft animals (horses and oxen), nurturing of seedlings before planting, use of ashes and other fertilizers, and prevention of insect damage, all of which contributed to a sharp rise in productivity.

One of the results of these technological changes was further subdivision of the shiki *and of farming classes. Those who were in the subordinate positions became small and middle farmers. As a result the traditional* myōshu shiki *(see Chapter 6, under Organization of Shōen) was transformed into either an outright ownership or the right to share in a portion of the yields of the land. The existence of money economy facilitated transfer of such rights and examples are found in Documents 13 and 14.*

The technological improvement was closely related to irrigation, and access to water or water rights became one of the most important issues of the day. Traditionally, the shōen *were bound by political and economic factors, and some of them existed in noncontiguous areas. With the necessity for community action in order to gain access to water, artificial boundaries created by the* shōen *were often disregarded, and in the place of* shōen, sō, *or village communities, were born. The problems relating to water rights were often simply described, and no document is given in this chapter. However, Document 15 shows the organization of the* sō. *There was a sense of solidarity and they could bind themselves together against undue exactions (Document 16).*

In this manner the shōen *received another blow to its continued existence.*

13 Matters Relating to the Sale of Title Deeds (Rikken) to Fields, 1321[14] Altogether one *tan* of land.

The four boundaries are as described in this title deed (*rikken*). . . . The above fields are privately owned and are inherited by Yukisada from his forefathers. However, now that he is in need [of money], he is selling the land at the cost of five *kan* of money, which act is completed with the transmission of seven copies of this deed including the original. Thus there shall be no interference from any quarters. As to the fields thus sold, Yukisada will remain as cultivator (*sakunin*), who promises to pay to the *jitō* and to the state the special taxes (*kujizeni*) [in kind or in cash, which are paid in addition to the annual rent] due them, and also to pay to the landlord eight *to* of rice as rent each year. However, if in the future he can redeem the full purchase price, a new title deed on the land may be issued [in Yukisada's favor].

First year of Genkyō [1321], sixth month, 26th day.

Seller, Yukisada, *monogram*
Purchaser, Monk (of Mt. Kōya)

14 Sale of Hyakushō Shiki (Rights of Farmers Residing on Land) on Certain Fields, 1480[15] Altogether two *tan* of land.

The above fields, even though privately owned by Matsuzaki Gorōbe, and his son Jirō Tarō, because of their need [for money], the *hyakushō shiki* (farmer's *shiki*) of these fields, which yields six *to* of rice each year, is now being sold in perpetuity at the cost of three *kan*. . . .

Seller, residing near the Matsuzaki Shrine
Gorōbe no jō
Same as above, his son
Jirō Tarō

15 A Covenant for the Sō (Village Self-Governing Association), 1489[16] Regulations commonly agreed to by the people of the village of Imahori, dated first year of Entoku [1489], eleventh month, 4th day.

1. Anyone who receives his right to residence from the *sō* (village self-

---

[14]From *Kōyasan Monjo*, in Ōkubo et al., *op. cit.*, p. 330. Here the sale of Yukisada's *myōshu shiki* to Mt. Kōya was involved.

[15]*Ibid.*, pp. 330–331. Hereafter the term *hyakushō* is translated as "farmer" or "farmers." The original meaning of the term was "the common people." But the great majority of people were farmers, and gradually the term became synonymous with "farmers." The purchaser was Daitokuji.

[16]From *Hiei Jinja Monjo*, in Kasahara, *op. cit.*, p. 92.

governing association) will not be permitted to board anyone from outside of this village.

2. No one from other villages will be permitted to reside in this village, unless someone from this village serves as his guarantor.

3. If there is any boundary dispute between privately owned land and land owned by the *sō*, the matter must be settled with the payment of money.

4. No one will be permitted to keep dogs.

5. From the common fund of the *sō*, an amount of one *kan* will be paid each year for the performance of *sarugaku* to be held on the sixth day of the second month.

6. Anyone who sells his house must pay to the *sō* three *mon* out of one hundred *mon*, and thirty *mon* out of one *kan* realized from the sale. Anyone who disobeys this rule shall be expelled from the *za* (in this instance, *za* signifies worshipper's group of the village shrine).

7. Anyone who conceals the amount of the sale price of his house shall be punished.

8. No house shall be built to the east of the moat.

16   Joint Petition by Farmers, 1407[17]   A Petition rendered on the fourteenth year of Ōei [1407], twelfth month, 15th day.

We beg your indulgence in the following matters:

1. We request that the rice offered to the temple which is earmarked for festivals be distributed to the farmers.

2. We further request that the expenses of the office of the *shōen*, which now amount to one *koku* three *to* of rice, may no longer be borne by the farmers....

3. We wish to report that the flood damage has resulted in a reduction of eight *koku* and four *to* in rice production, and there is an additional damage of three *koku* and one *to* of rice.

4. On account of poor crops or abandonment of land, you previously ordered us to pay one half of the rent due from Nishidai (part of Ōyama *shō*, which amounts to twenty-four *koku*, eight *to* and three *shō*. However, cultivators of these fields come from other distant *shō*, and we cannot force them to work. Therefore, this year please count this as a complete loss.

7. The bribe due the *shugo* in the amount of three *kan* five hundred *mon* is submitted to you....

8. After having paid our annual rent, we wish to report that those farmers who absconded have now returned.

9. The illegal acts of the deputy (*daikan*) were the root cause of the absconding of the farmers in the way they did, after exhausting all available means [to

---

[17]In Ōkubo et al., *op. cit.*, p. 337. This was a direct appeal by the farmers addressed to the Tōji, which was the *ryōshu* of the *shōen*.

fight against such illegal acts]. Relying on the help you are granting us, they have returned. However, if the deputy continues to occupy his position, then their return will be in vain. We venture to speak out in this manner, because the sinful and illegal deeds of the deputy are many. If [a new] deputy can be dispatched from the temple, it will benefit the farmers greatly. We have heard that the *ryōshu* of Ōyama *shō* is consulting with the *shugo* to summon the farmers [for additional duties]. We are very much surprised. This makes us to have no other recourse but to think of [moving to] other provinces.

May we submit our humble thoughts?

With trepidation, respectfully

Farmers from Kazuidani

To the Chief of the Administrative Department (*bugyōsho*) [of Tōji].

RISE OF A MONEY ECONOMY

The use of money became so pervasive in the fifteenth century that it infiltrated the shōen, *further eroding the latter's economic bases. Document 17 shows substitution of money for the payment of annual rent in kind, and Document 18 shows the method used in determining the monetary value of rice. Document 19 shows how a money draft sent from one region could be honored in another region. Document 20 shows the inevitable consequence of infiltration of money economy which forced some farmers to sell their farms, while those who purchased farms gained wealth for themselves. Note also the frequency of utilization of pawnshops which charged usurious rates of interest.*

The existing inequity thus led to the occurrence of peasant uprisings as seen in Document 21. Their primary targets were the pawnshops which had done them wrong, and their demands often included deliverance from their debts in the form of another tokusei *(Document 22; compare Document 4).*

17   **Substitution of Money to Pay Taxes, 1353**[18]   Petition from Yano *Shō*, Province of Harima, Submitted to Nishi no Onkata, on Tax (*kuji*) Matters.

If rice received as annual rent (*nengu*) is to be submitted to you in kind, boats must be utilized for its transportation, and we must also impose forced labor on the farmers. There are many difficulties connected with transportation by water. If money can be substituted for the payment of annual rent [it will facilitate the matter considerably]. We can sell rice at acceptable market price, and if it meets your approval, the money can be transmitted through *shugo* Akamatsu. We hereby beg your acceptance. . . .

Second year of Bunwa [1353], eleventh month.

---

[18]*Tōji Hyakugō Monjo*, in Ōkubo et al., *op. cit.*, pp. 351–352.

18 Determination of Equivalent Money Value for Rice, 1361[19]   We have received your communication of the tenth month, 16th day.

On the matter of selling rice received in payment for annual rent at an acceptable market price, on the first day of the tenth month at the Naha market in the presence of the lower *shō* official (*jige bantō*) and farmers, the agreed price (*washi*) for the rice for annual rent payment previously transported was set at one *koku*, two *to* and three *shō* [of rice] for one *kan* [of money]. Of this your messenger was aware. Thereafter on the first day of the eleventh month, at the Naha market in the presence of your messenger, the agreed market price was set at one *koku* and three *shō* [of rice] for one *kan* [of money]. . . .

> Suketada, *monogram*
> Nobuhiro, *monogram*

19 Money Draft, 1468[20]   On Matters Relating to Draft (*warifu*) from Shinmi. Second year of Ōnin [1468], first month, 12th day.

Money to be exchanged.

Seal   Altogether ten *kan*

This is to certify that the above amount of money may be issued to Sakabe Jirō-Shirō. We appreciate your response in due course.

Twelfth month, 13th day.

> To Mr. Hikogorō   *Seal*

20 Land Owners and Pawnshops, 1471[21]   From the Five *Shō* Located in the District of Sumiyoshi, Settsu Province.

Irrigated field in front of the archery practice field, cultivated by or its *saku shiki* (cultivator's *shiki*) owned by Taiseiji. Three *tan* and sixty *bu*.

Eastern boundary, provincial boundary.

Southern boundary, granary.

Western boundary, Nishi Kōenji.

Northern boundary, upper and middle cultivated fields.

[Hereafter description of four boundaries omitted]

Purchased on the eighteenth year of Ōei [1411], second month, 17th day, from Taiseiji. Two copies of the official title deed. Original tax (*eki*) on the public land leased for rental (*kuden*), three *to*. Spring and autumn rental (*jishi*), one hundred *mon* each.

---

[19]*Ibid.*, p. 352. Again the document was directed to Tōji, the *ryōke*.
[20]*Ibid.*, p. 353.
[21]*Daitokuji Monjo*, in Ōkubo et al., *op. cit.*, pp. 353–354. This document contains the same information found in a land register (*tsubosuke*). The latter contains the following information for each parcel of land: type, location, cultivator, size, boundaries, and history.

Irrigated field in front of the archery practice field, cultivated by Rokurō Shirō. One *tan* and sixty *bu*.

A forfeited pawn on thirty-second year of Ōei [1425], second month, 29th day. Took possession of the land which did not come under the *tokusei* decree of 1428. Later in accordance with the judgment rendered by the *bakufu*, returned to the original owner. Original title deed reportedly lost in a fire, but a copy was taken and there is a bond of debt.

Irrigated field with night soil pond, cultivator's title deed. Two and one half *tan*, of which thirty *bu* in [vegetable] gardens.

A forfeited pawn from the exercise hall, on the fifth year of Eikyō [1433], second month, 17th day. Three copies of the original title deed.

Original tax on the public land leased for rental, three *to*, official levy one hundred *mon*, to be paid twice (annually). Also other levies. . . .

Altogether one *chō* nine *tan* and seventy-five *bu*.

Executed in accordance with the last will of Wagamagokoya.[22]

Dōkin, *monogram*

Third year of Bunmei [1471], tenth month.

21 Peasant Uprisings (Tsuchi Ikki, or Do Ikki), 1428[23]

The first year of Shōchō [1428], in the ninth month, an uprising of *domin* [a composite term for peasants, other common people, and lower samurai] broke out. They claimed *tokusei* and went on to destroy wine shops, pawn shops (*dozō*), and temples which engaged in usury. They took anything they could lay their hands on, and cancelled the debts. Kanrei (commissioner) Hatakeyama Mitsuie suppressed this. There is nothing more than this incident to bring about the ruin of our country. This is the first time since the founding of Japan that an uprising of *domin* ever occurred.

22 Fighting for Tokusei, 1441[24]

(a) On the third day of this month (ninth month of the first year of Kakitsu, 1441), *domin* all around this area rose in revolt. They called their uprising *tsuchi ikki*, claimed *tokusei*, and burned or broke those things they borrowed [e.g., bonds and mortgages] from others, and went to pawnshops to redeem their goods with only a portion of the amount due. All of this started in Ōmi. . . . The government forces with a large number of men commanded by the *Samurai-dokoro* (Office of Samurai Affairs) engaged in a defensive fight, but the *domin* were far more numerous, numbering in the tens of thousands, and the government forces could not hold their positions. . . .

---

[22]Wagamagokoya was possibly a merchant engaged in usury.

[23]*Daijōin Nikki Mokuroku* and *Kennaiki* in Kasahara et al., *op. cit.*, p. 93.

[24]*Kennaiki*, in Kasahara et al., *op. cit.*, p. 94.

On the tenth day, an association of pawnshop keepers (*dozō isshū*) submitted to Kanrei Hosokawa Mochiyuki a sum of 1,000 *kan* to bribe him into suppressing the uprising. Initially there was a letter of agreement stating that he would stop the disorder and engage in a defensive fight. However, he could not make his stand, and there were many *daimyō* (such as Hatakeyama, who did not agree with Kanrei Hosokawa since they were also heavily in debt and welcomed another enactment of *tokusei*). Thus the *kanrei* had to return the 1,000 *kan* of money and abandoned his defensive operations.

On the 14th day, *tokusei* was decreed, saying that it should be equally applicable throughout the country.

(b) Articles of *Tokusei*, limited to the first year of Kakitsu [1441]. [A Decree of the *Bakufu*]

1. On lands which are sold in perpetuity: in accordance with the provisions of the *tokusei* decree of Einin [Document 4], if a piece of land changed hands before the last twenty years, the purchaser shall claim full title to it. If the transfer has occurred within the past twenty years, the land shall be returned to the seller. However, if the transaction has taken place only between common men, irrespective of the time limit described above, the purchaser must consult [the seller].

DEVELOPMENT OF ICHI AND ZA

*One of the outstanding developments in the economic history of Japan was the rise of markets (*ichi*) in the Muromachi period. They became collection and distribution centers. In the course of their development, they formed their own boundaries, which were distinct from those of the* shōen. *As the markets became semi-permanent fixtures, the domanial lords or patrons attempted to impose their control over them. Document 23 shows not only the boundary limits of the market, but also the power of control exercised by the patron over the affairs of the market.*

*During this period, most marketing was done by merchants who owned a specific seat (*za*) in a certain market which was usually placed under the protection of a nobleman, temple, or domanial lord. Collectively, those merchants who belonged to the same trade formed an association known as the* za, *which bore some resemblance to the European trade guild. Unless a merchant belonged to a* za, *he could not trade anywhere. Document 24 shows disputes between two contending* za *for their rights to engage in a similar type of commerce.*

23   Rise of Ichi (Market) c. 1415[25]   Regulations Regarding the Takaama Market (*ichi*) Posted. . . .

1. The four boundaries of the *ichi* shall be within the confines of one *chō*, as

---

[25]*Kasuga Jinja Monjo*, in Ōkubo et al., *op. cit.*, p. 356. The Kasuga Shrine and the Kōfuku Temple in Nara were administered together during this period.

noted in the map showing the respective locations of houses and grounds.

2. Anyone who is not a member of this *ichi* cannot sell or purchase within the confines of this one *chō*.

3. Within the market place, only samurai and officials connected with the temple shall be permitted to receive orders and perform their duties. Lower officials and servants are not permitted to reside within the confines of the *ichi*.

4. Every year, fees for exhibiting merchandise at the *za*, and rental for the houses and grounds must be paid.

5. Judgment regarding right and wrong can be rendered by any of the monks (of the Kōfukuji) who specialize in studying. There shall be no further confusion concerning the jurisdiction exercised by us.

24 Disputes between Two Za, 1405[26]

Respectfully submitted, that punishment from heaven be meted out.

The case above is related to the purchase and transportation of sesame, and the suit is brought by representatives (or attorneys or spokesmen, *yoribito*) for the Fuzaka *za*. It avers that henceforward, at whatever market, no one may dispute with the Fuzaka *za* representatives and purchase sesame. However, after these representatives have made their purchases, the remaining sesame may be bought by others. Furthermore, the suit asks that the principle of such sesame not being sold outside of the province be reaffirmed. In that event, [the Fuzaka *za* is] agreeable to the sale of one horseback load or one load carried on the shoulders between two persons. But it cannot permit five or ten horseback loads to be sold.

If these conditions are not observed, those who disobey will suffer punishment from these deities: Brahma, Indra, Four Deva Kings, Amaterasu Ōmikami, chief deity of Hachimangū, especially Kasuga Daimyōjin, with seven halls and three treasures, and in addition, Kanjizaizon of Nanendō, and all the deities, great and small, in more than sixty provinces of Japan. We make our case as described.

Twelfth year of Ōei [1405], ninth month, 14th day.

Endō et al., each with his seal.

THE SŌRYŌ SYSTEM AND PRIMOGENITURE

During the Kamakura period, divided patrimony was still the rule, but the sōryō (literally the oldest son) was usually given the largest share of the estate, and exercised control over the property of all family members. For the purposes of serving Kamakura and of paying taxes, the sōryō was the unchallenged representative of his family (of kinship association). This practice is recorded in Document 25, which had the date of 1240.

Most of the samurai estates were held in the form of jitō shiki over the shōen,

---

[26]*Daijōin Jisha Zōjiki*, in Ōkubo et al., *op. cit.*, pp. 356–357.

and they were often scattered in different parts of the country. In a period of turmoil, from the end of the Kamakura period through the Muromachi period, fewer and fewer samurai were able to exercise control of their jitō shiki *in those scattered areas. Along with this, there was the tendency of those children other than the first son to maintain independent households. Meanwhile in the family of the* sōryō, *primogeniture became the accepted practice. Document 26, which was dated 1330, shows one of its earlier examples. Voluntary renunciation of individual inheritance in favor of the fittest to succeed to the entire estate to preserve its financial integrity is shown in Document 27. The story was given in the collection of Buddhist stories entitled* Shasekishū *which was compiled in 1279.*

25 Sōryō System of Divided Patrimony, 1240[27]   Division of the Estate (of the late Ōtomo Takanao).

The share of the first son, Oinosuke Nyūdō:

Jitō shiki [rights and income from *jitō*'s functions] and *gōshi shiki* [right and income from *gōshi*'s functions, the latter meaning official of a *gō*, or county] in the county of Ōtomo, province of Sagami.

The share of the second son, Takuma Bettō:

One half of the *jitō shiki* of the village of Shiga in the Ono *shō*, province of Bungo.

The share of Yamato Tarō Hyoenojō:

One half of the *jitō shiki* of the upper village in the same *shō*.

The share of Hachirō:

One half of the *jitō shiki* of the village of Shiga in the same *shō*.

The share of Kurō Nyūdō:

One half of the *jitō shiki* of the lower village in the same *shō*. However, this includes the income realized from the rights pertaining to the caring for the grave of the late father.

The share of daughter Inu Gozen:

Jitō shiki of the middle village in the same *shō*.

The share of daughter Mino no Tsubone:

One half of the *jitō shiki* of the village of Kami in the same *shō*.

The share of the widow of his late son, Takewaki Zaemon no jō. Several sons were born in this marriage.

Yasutada *myō* in the middle village of the same *shō*.

The above estate truly belongs to the late official of the province of Buzen, Takanao Ason who received letters of grant from the offices of successive *shōgun*. However, they were deeded to me, the Nun, Shinmyō, by my late father

---

[27]*Shiga Monjo*, in Kasahara et al., *op. cit.*, pp. 69–70.

Takanao, and were placed under my management through a letter of grant from the *shōgun*'s office. Now, in accordance with the last will of Takanao, his estate is divided in this manner on behalf of his children. It is divided in accordance with the principle of equal division, and must be placed under the management of each without fail. However, in the event the Kamakura *bakufu* issues an order for the payment of different taxes, everyone must submit to the control of the first son, Oinosuke Nyūdō, each sending to him the amount due from his estate depending on the size [so that the tax owned by the family may be paid together]. For future reference, this document of division is written.

The Nun, Shinmyō, *monogram*

Second year of Ennō [1240], fourth month, 6th day.

26   A Deed of Transfer by Yamanouchi-sudō Michitada, 1330[28]

In view of the fact that my estate is limited, in other words, only insignificant, I am therefore transferring the deed only to one legitimate heir. This is done even though it is customary to divide the estate among all children. Hereafter, the estate thus deeded must be inherited by only one of my descendants.

Dated the second year of Gentoku [1330].

27   Voluntary Renunciation of Inheritance, c. 1279[29]

There was a certain domanial lord in the province of Tanba. He owned an estate not too large, but lived comfortably without experiencing poverty. As he became old, he wrote his will to divide his estate among his sons and daughters. He stated that his will should not be opened until after a period of forty-nine days of mourning was over.

After the period of mourning was past, the will was opened, and it divided the estate by giving the eldest son, who was the legitimate heir, the largest share, and on a descending scale in the order of birth, every child received a share. This was the customary way of dividing an estate. However, the oldest son said:

"We cannot challenge what has already been decided by our late father, but I still question the wisdom of his will. Our late father skillfully conducted his affairs, which made it possible for him to serve with distinction in Kyoto and Kamakura at the courts of the emperor and of the *shōgun*. However, if each of us attempts to serve our masters with the estate given to us which is so minutely divided, it will only cause great difficulties. Even though I am the first born, I

---

[28] As quoted in Satō Shinichi, *Nanbokucho no Dōran (Struggles between the Northern and Southern Courts)*, Chūō Kōronsha, *Nihon no Rekishi (A History of Japan)*, Vol. 9 (Tokyo: Chūō Kōronsha, 1965), p. 192.

[29] From the *Shasekishū*, as paraphrased in Kuroda Toshio, *Mōko Shūrai (Mongolian Invasion)*, Chūō Kōronsha, *op. cit.*, Vol. 8, pp. 384–385.

lack talent. Therefore I wish to join a Buddhist order, say my *nembutsu* to attain salvation in my after-life. Thus I suggest someone who is talented inherit the household and manage the entire estate. Others may [follow my example by] entering a Buddhist monastery or nunnery, and rent fields from the heir to gain livelihood."

After consultation, it was decided that the fifth son, being talented, should inherit the household, and all others renounced the world.

CHAPTER **VII**

From Civil Wars to Unification

The Ōnin War rendered the already weakened Ashikaga *bakufu* so powerless that it existed in name only. This also presaged a radical change in the politics of Japan, bringing about new power alignments. Most of the great *shugo daimyō* ceased to exist, with the notable exceptions of the Takeda and Imagawa in the East and the Ōtomo and Shimazu who were securely entrenched in the island of Kyushu. The *shugo daimyō* were replaced by the *sengoku daimyō* who consolidated economic and military power bases within their own domains to embark on their own ambitious courses of conquest of the nation. Not all of the *sengoku daimyō* survived to the end of the warring period. It was a period of *gekokujō*, or the lower supplanting the upper, and they in turn were often replaced by their own subordinates.

Among the more successful *sengoku daimyō*, one could find the names of Hōjō in Kantō, Date in Tōhoku, Uesugi in the Japan Sea region, Arima in Kyushu, Chōsokabe in Shikoku, Uragami, Ukita, Mōri, and Amako in Chūgoku, and Asai, Asakura, Saitō, Oda, and Tokugawa in the regions near the capital provinces. The earlier *sengoku daimyō* failed largely because they lacked the means to curtail the power of their insubordinate vassals. These more successful ones, in contrast, were able to exercise effective control over their vassals and economic resources. A number of house laws reproduced here show how diligent these *sengoku daimyō* were in the control they exercised over their *kashindan* (corps of retainers). They attempted separation of the military from agriculture, and gradually acquired direct control over the farmers and agricultural resources.

Their exactions from the farmers were extremely harsh. From the traditional formula of five shares to the public (taxes), and five shares to the private (to be retained by the cultivators, etc.), the ratio between the tax and the amount to be retained changed to two to one. In addition there were military and corvée duties. Farmers were strictly forbidden to abscond, and a rule of solidarity was imposed whereby tax burdens of those who absconded would have to be borne by the neighbors or fellow villagers.

The *sengoku daimyō* also adopted measures to protect commerce within their own domains. These included, for example, introduction of the free market and abolition of the *za*. During the Muromachi period, most marketing was done by merchants who owned a specific seat (*za*) in a certain market which was usually placed under the protection of a nobleman, temple, or domanial lord. Collectively, those merchants who belonged to the same trade formed an association known as the *za*, which bore some resemblance to the European trade guild. Unless a merchant belonged to a *za*, he could not trade anywhere. However, as more merchants sought seats in the *za* and more *za* were created, both the protection functions of the patrons and the monopolistic privileges of the *za* were weakened. A further erosion in the *za*'s monopolistic privileges came when some of the *daimyō* established free markets (*rakuichi*) in their castle towns, post stations, or harbors. The free market permitted, usually for a limited time only, freedom to trade without being members of a *za*. This system aided the *daimyō* in obtaining needed financial resources, and the *daimyō* did not find it inconsistent to open a free market in one locality and license special privileges to a *za* nearby. Generally the free market was confined to a small region, and markets in other regions remained under the control of the *za*. Thus, to encourage trading at the free market, the *daimyō* often had to force travelers to come to that particular free market. The next logical step in this movement toward freer trade took the form of the abolition of the *za* (*rakuza*), which also had an effect of strengthening the control of the *daimyō* over commercial activities.

In the early sixteenth century, trading areas became enlarged, and many of them encompassed more than one domain of a *sengoku daimyō*. Oda Nobunaga's military might was closely tied in with the fortunes of the merchants of Sakai, who supplied him with nitrate of soda and lead needed for organizing his superior fire power, which in turn facilitated his quest for unification.

Nobunaga was an absolute ruler, who disallowed the authority of religions to stand in the way of his rule. Personally, as observed by the Jesuit Luis Frois, he was nominally of the Hokke sect, but did not believe in the creator, in the immortality of soul, or in life after death. His secularism—or an attempt for apotheosis—was well demonstrated in the erection of his Nijō castle for which he ordered many stone idols to be pulled down, and had them dragged to the site to be used for the construction. The burning of Mt. Hiei (Document 8) further confirmed his role as an absolute secular ruler.

Separation of farmers from warriors under the regime of Hideyoshi opened the way for stratification of status. Warriors had to stay in the castle towns in the service of their lords, and farmers were tied to the lands they cultivated. In the edict of 1591 (Document 15) samurai were forbidden to become merchants or farmers, and farmers were not permitted to engage in commerce, and the stratification became complete. Hideyoshi cadastral surveys (1582–1598) were an attempt to destroy once and for all the duplicating set of *shiki* over the land and to identify clearly the actual cultivators as the persons responsible for bearing the tax and corvée labor burdens.

An efficient standing army was built which, unlike their warrior counterparts of the mediaeval age, did not depend entirely on their own lands for sustenance. They received supplies such as firearms and powder and provisions from centralized storages maintained by Hideyoshi. On the other hand, the vassals did not enjoy full right to their *chigyō* (stipends or possession). They were enfeoffed to specific lands on which Hideyoshi exercised supreme proprietary overlordship. The amount of stipends assigned to an individual vassal was as a rule the sum total of his income from annual rent (*nengu*, which could be spent for his own use) and the right to maintain his own samurai retainers (over whom Hideyoshi retained control). In the matter of *daimyō*'s expenditures, Hideyoshi attempted to regulate the amounts that could be retained by the *daimyō*, and the amounts which could be spent for other purposes. All of these had one single purpose, that of centralizing power in his own hands. However, frequent interference in the financial affairs of the *daimyō* was in part responsible for the disaffection toward the Toyotomi regime which proved fatal after Hideyoshi's death.

The coming of Christian missions to Japan is in itself a fascinating chapter in the history of meetings between the East and the West. The rapid social changes through the Sengoku period provided a fertile ground for the spread of religions appealing to the masses. This was witnessed by the continued vitality of the Zen sects which won many adherents among the samurai, and by the acceptance of the Shin sect by farmers and of the Nichiren sect by city dwellers. As for Christianity, the Japanese people's natural curiosity toward things alien and their questioning of traditional values provided the necessary point of contact. In Kyushu, especially, a large number of conversions were found among the farmers. Some *daimyō* also were fascinated by the newly found doctrine and also by the incidental trade advantages brought about by the foreigners. The Jesuits generally favored a system of evangelization from the top to bottom which, by first converting or influencing the ruler, could bring about mass conversions of those who were ruled. Luis Frois' friendly relations with Oda Nobunaga must be interpreted in this light. Like de Tocqueville on America, the Jesuits were astute observers of Japanese affairs, and some of their impressions of the Japanese people are contained as final selections in this chapter.

DENIAL OF TRADITIONAL AUTHORITY

Denial of the traditional authority represented by the emperor, court nobles, temples and shrines, and even shōgun *came from the* shugo daimyō *and samurai who enjoyed military power. Document 1 is a record of a conversation which presumably took place between one Yamana Sōzen (1404–1473) and a court noble during the Ōnin war (1467–1477). Yamana was one of the* shugo daimyō *who was responsible for igniting that conflict. Arrogant, and self-reliant, he settled all disputes by means of his military power. His attitude represented the phenomenon of* gekokujō. *Against this new tide, the traditional authority could only cite precedents or the wrath of the Buddha (Document 2) which were totally ineffective in preserving their power.*

1 **Challenging Traditional Authority**[1]   My Lord, what you say appears to be reasonable, but you cannot continue to rely on precedents [to win an argument]. Hereafter, you must replace the concept of precedent with a concept consistent with our own times. . . . Do not forget that the contemporary world can create precedents for posterity. The basic principles which govern politics are unchanging through the ages, and precedents can be drawn [to illuminate certain principles]. However, I cannot understand why precedents must be drawn to explain other matters. We have witnessed declining fortunes of many great families who adhered too strictly to precedents and without taking heed of the signs of the times. They lost most of their family incomes, and competed for available official positions without regard to knowledge or integrity. In this manner they had to suffer the humiliation of losing control of the nation to the samurai, and had to be placed in the position of ingratiating themselves to the samurai. If we should follow the age-old precedents, I, Sōzen, as lowly born as I am, could never address your Lordship as an equal as I am doing now. Where can you find a precedent for this? Indeed this must be another sign of the times. . . . Hereafter, my Lord, do not cite the so-called precedents of yours to a mindless barbarian like me. On the other hand, if you can make yourself understand the changing times, unworthly as I am, I, Sōzen, shall be happy to defend the Emperor and the court nobles.

2 **Seizure of Shōen**[2]   As we reflect on the matter carefully, this past disturbance [referring to the Ōnin War] was the cause of the downfall of the laws of

---

[1] Ōkubo Toshiaki et al., eds., *Shiryō ni yoru Nihon no Ayumi (Japanese History through Documents), Kinseihen (Early Modern Period)* (Tokyo: Yoshikawa Kōbunkan, 1955), p. 1.
[2] *Daijōin Jisha Zōjiki* in Kasahara Kazuo et al., eds., *Seisen Nihonshi Shiryōshū (Selected Documents on Japanese History)*, rev. ed. (Tokyo: Yamagawa Shuppansha, 1970), p. 91.

Buddha, the laws of the State, and of aristocratic families. . . . Lately many *daimyō* and their retainers using the threat of their military power, seized at will many *shōen* which had temples and shrines as their patrons. Their actions are based on selfish motives, and they hold the authority of the *shōgun* in contempt. This lawlessness and lack of order must not be tolerated. In fact they act more like animals. From now on, those retainers residing in Yamato [where this temple is located] may also attempt to seize our *shōen*. Lately, with fair frequency, irregular and unusual happenings come to our notice. These must be the doings of those retainers. They are certain to incur the wrath of Heaven, and cannot escape from it. How deplorable that is! How dreadful that is!

SENGOKU DAIMYŌ AS DOMANIAL LORDS

The following five documents show the control exercised by five different sengoku daimyō *over their domains. With the exception of the fifth (Document 7) which deals with military service to be rendered by the farmers and samurai, the documents are excerpts from house laws. There are several common features in these house laws. First, even though the* sengoku daimyō *might have been rebels before, once they were placed in a position of authority, they all insisted on the observance of law, and often expounded the Confucian ideals. They exhorted their retainers to set up good examples for the people of their domains to follow. They urged their retainers to respect the temples and shrines which cultivated a subservient attitude useful in their administration of the domains. With the exception of Takeda Shingen, the* sengoku daimyō *generally permitted different sects to live harmoniously together in their domains. Centralization with themselves at the helm was encouraged. The* daimyō *increasingly assumed the position of lawgiver on purely private affairs and behavior of the people. Document 6 contains excerpts from the 100–article house law of the Chōsokabe family which survived in Tosa under a different family into the Tokugawa times. It is included here as providing the best example of an attempt to legislate public morality with legal sanctions by the* sengoku daimyō.

The Asakura House Law

Asakura Toshikage (1428–1481) became Shugo of Echizen in 1481, and became one of the most important daimyō *in the Japan Sea area. He became more mindful of the art of government and invited to his domain scholars from different areas. The following seventeen-article injunction was given to his successor Ujikage and constituted one of the best examples of the house laws of the* sengoku daimyō. *In the injunction he stressed the necessities of centralized control within the domain (Article 15), filling of positions based on merits (Arti-*

cles 1 and 2), impartial rendering of justice (Articles 14 and 17), encouragement of indigenous domanial culture (Article 5), and constant preparedness against enemies (Articles 3, 4, and 11). There was a stress on rationality instead of superstition (Article 13). In spite of their good organization and administrative skills, in the end the Asakura aligned with the wrong party and the last of the Asakura, Yoshikage, committed suicide in the year 1573 after a decisive defeat at the hands of Oda Nobunaga.

3 The Seventeen-Article Injunction of Asakura Toshikage, c. 1480[3]

1. The Asakura family must not appoint anyone to the rank of elder. But instead utilize the services of men of ability and loyalty [without regard to the positions they hold].

2. Do not give a command post or an administrative position to anyone who lacks ability, even if his family has served the Asakura family for generations.

3. Post intelligence agents (*metsuke*) in both near and distant provinces, even if the world may be at peace. In so doing you can spy on the conditions of these domains without interruption.

4. Do not excessively covet swords and daggers made by famous masters. Even if you can own a sword or dagger worth 10,000 pieces (*hiki*, equivalent of 10 *mon*), it can be overcome by 100 spears each worth 100 pieces. Therefore, use the 10,000 pieces to procure 100 spears, and arm 100 men with them. You can in this manner defend yourself in time of war.

5. Refrain from frequently bringing from Kyoto actors of the four schools of *Nō* (Komparu, Kanze, Hōshō, and Kita) for performances. Instead, use the money needed for that purpose to select talented local actors of *sarugaku*, and train them in the basic elements of *Nō* (*shimai*) for the perpetual enjoyment of this province.

6. Performances of *Nō* shall not be given within the castle at night.

7. Do not send messengers to Date and Shirakawa [in the present-day Fukushima prefecture in the northeast, famed for breeding fine horses] to procure fine horses and falcons on the pretext that it is part of the duties of the samurai. Naturally special considerations may be given to [horses and falcons] arriving from other areas. However, after three years, they must be passed on to some other family. To hold on to them for a long time will inevitably bring forth regret.

8. Members of the Asakura family must by their own example cause all the retainers to adopt quilted cotton clothing *nunoko* as ceremonial dress at the New

[3]Satō Shinichi et al., eds., *Chūsei Hōsei Shiryōshū (Documents on Mediaeval Legal and Institutional History)*, Vol. 3, *Bukekahō (Laws of Military Households)* (Tokyo: Iwanami Shoten, 1965), pp. 335–338; occasionally a slightly different version from pp. 339–343 is substituted in this translation.

Year's celebration. For this purpose, one's family crest must be affixed. If a member of the family wishes to display his wealth by dressing extravagantly, rural samurai from every corner of this province will be forced to follow suit. However, knowing that [their wealth will not permit them to dress up], they will plead illness and absent themselves from their duties for one year and then for two years. In the end, the number of samurai who pay homage to the Asakura family will be reduced.

9. Those retainers who lack special talent or positions, but who are steadfast, must be treated with compassion and understanding. Those who are effeminate may still be used as attendants or messengers if their demeanor is outstanding, and they must not be dismissed lightly. However, if they lack both [steadfastness and good deportment], then it is useless to retain them.

10. If you treat those retainers who have served you faithfully in the same way as those who have not, how can the former be encouraged to continue serving you faithfully?

11. Do not appoint a *rōnin* (masterless samurai) from another province as your keeper of records, unless you are pressed for such services.

12. Do not allow men with special talent, whether monks or laymen, to serve other families. However, this proscription does not apply to those who have no desire of serving [the Asakura family] and only wish to peddle their skills.

13. Regrettable is the practice of selecting an auspicious day or considering a lucky direction in order to win a battle or take a castle, and even shift the time and date accordingly. No matter how auspicious the day may be, if you set sail your boat in a storm or confront a great host alone, your effort will come to naught. No matter how inauspicious the day may be, if you can discern between truth and falsehood, prepare for orthodox and surprise attacks secretly, be flexible in all situations, and depend on a good stratagem, then your victory is assured.

14. Three times a year, select men of ability and honesty, and send them on inspection tours of the province. They must listen to the views of the common people and farmers, and collect information concerning incidences of misgovernment. It will also be advisable for you yourself to go on an inspection tour, provided you wear a light disguise.

15. Do not permit any castle other than that of the Asakura to be built in this province. Move all high-ranking retainers without exception to Ichijōgatani (the Asakura castle). Permit their deputies (*daikan*) and lower officials (*gesu* or *shitazukasa*) to remain in their districts and villages [to measure their estates].

16. When you pass a temple, monastery or town dwelling and the like, rein in your horse for a moment. If the place is attractive, give some words of praise. If the place is damaged, show your concern by expressing your sympathy. These people who consider themselves unworthy will be overjoyed by the fact that you have spoken to them. They will repair the damages expeditiously and pay continued attention to preserve the beauty [of those which you praised]. In this way, without effort on your part, you can keep your

province beautiful. Remember that all of these depend on your own resolve.

17. When a suit is brought to you for your direct decision, do not bend an iota between reason and unreason. If you hear that an official has acted arbitrarily [for private gain], and that fact is well established, you must impose the same penalty on the offending official which was originally meted out to the losing party by him. If you can govern your own domain judiciously and compassionately, there is no need to fear whatever mischief may be committed by the lawless bands of warriors from other domains. If a rumor is spread that there exists in your domain favoritism and unfair discrimination and that rules and behavior codes are violated, other domains may intervene in your affairs.

A famous monk once said that a master of men must be like the two Buddhist deities of Fudō (Sk. Acala) and Aizen (Sk. Rāga-Rāja). Although Fudō carries a sword, and Aizen carries a bow and arrows, these weapons are not intended for slashing or for shooting, but for the purpose of subjugating devils. In their hearts, they are compassionate and circumspect. Like them, a master of samurai must first rectify his own way, and then reward his loyal subjects and soldiers and eliminate those who are disloyal and treacherous. If you can discern between reason and unreason and between good and evil and act accordingly, your system of rewards and punishments is deemed compassionately administered. On the other hand, if your heart is prejudiced, no matter how much you know the words of the sages and study the texts, they all come to naught. You may observe that the *Analects* [of Confucius in I, 8] contains a passage saying that "A gentleman who lacks steadfastness cannot command respect." Do not consider that the term "steadfastness" represents only heavy-handedness. It is essential that you conduct yourself in such a way that both heavy-handedness and leniency can be applied flexibly as the occasion demands.

It will be of no value to you if you take the above articles lightly. I, now a member of a Buddhist order, began my career as a young man and alone. By a determined effort, miraculously I became lord of this domain. Day and night, without closing my eyes, I have made plans. I have preserved in my ears the words of those who are well-known in their crafts. I have commanded the soldiers, and now our domain is free from turmoil. If my descendants will adhere to these precepts, obey and consider them as something akin to the teachings of the deity of Hie Hachiman, the province can be preserved and the Asakura name can be maintained. If there is anyone at the end of our lineage who will conduct himself capriciously, he may not live long enough to regret it.

The Hōjō House Law

From an obscure origin, Hōjō Sōun (1432–1519) became one of the leading daimyō *of the* sengoku *period by his sheer fortitude, cunningness, and ambition. After intervening in two succession disputes, he gained control of the entire province of Izu and built his castle in Nirayama. Later he extended his sway to the major areas of Kantō. As a domanial lord, Hōjō Sōun was an enlightened despot. He needed the loyalty of his people to guard against invasion by other domanial lords, and as a means of gaining their adherence, he reduced annual taxes to forty percent (in place of the traditional fifty percent) of the farm produce and insisted on nonexploitation of farmers by his subordinates. His twenty-one injunctions were one of the earliest house laws by the* sengoku daimyō, *which clearly reflected his philosophy of hard word and of ruling by example.*

4   Hōjō Sōun's Twenty-One Article Injunction for His Vassals, c. 1495[4]

1. Make every effort to rise early in the morning. If you rise late, even your servants will become inattentive, and may not obey your command. In this way you cannot attend to your public duties or private needs. As a result your master, the *daimyō*, may forsake you. Take heed of this injunction.

2. In the evening, go to bed before eight. Night thieves without exception come during the hours between midnight and the first crow of the cock. If you engage in lengthy conversations in the evening, and go to bed after midnight and become sound asleep, and allow the thieves to steal your household goods, what will that do to your reputation? Save on the firewood and lump oil which you otherwise consume unnecessarily and get up at dawn. Cleanse yourself, and worship the deities, make yourself presentable, and give orders for the chores to be performed to your wife and retainers, and go to your office before six. An ancient saying states that one must retire by midnight and rise at dawn. However, that depends on individuals. In any event everyone will benefit by getting up at dawn. If you linger in your bed until your breakfast time or mid-morning, then you cannot go to your office to serve your master. Nor can you then attend to your own business. How impossible that can be, the day can be simply wasted.

7. Say not a false word to anyone regardless of the person with whom you may deal, high or low. Even on a trivial matter, be exact in your presentation. If you say something without foundation, it becomes a habit, and people will question it. Eventually they will forsake you. If someone corrects your falsehood, consider it the shame of your life.

The House Law of Takeda Shingen

Takeda Shingen (1521–1573) was one of the most colorful sengoku daimyō *who, but for his untimely death, could have been the first unifier of Japan, replacing the glory that was exclusively claimed by Oda Nobunaga. As a youth, he proved*

---

[4]*Ibid.*, pp. 345–350.

*himself to be an excellent military commander. When he discovered that his
father was losing the respect of the people in his domain, he expelled his father
and supplanted him. That was in 1541, and thereafter he continuously engaged
in wars of expansion, first northward toward Shinano from his home province
Kai, then westward toward Hida, and finally southward toward Suruga. Just
prior to his death, he defeated the troops commanded by Tokugawa Ieyasu, who
later became the founder of the Tokugawa bakufu. Shingen was not a mere field
commander. He was well-versed in Buddhist scriptures, and held a rank in the
Tendai sect (compare Article 24). He was also known for his interests in literature. His policy within his domain was essentially one of "Rich Country, Strong
Army," his house law consisted of 99 articles, and here only those which are not
duplicated in other house laws are translated. Note the distinct tendency toward
centralization under his own power. In this respect, his house law clearly antici-
pated the Tokugawa laws of the later period.*

5 **Takeda Shingen's Control of Kai, 1547**[5]   The *jitō* (vassals)[6] of this
province have been confiscating lands for their own private benefit, averring that
the confiscation was undertaken to punish a crime, but if the criminal is a
retainer (*hikan*) of Harunobu's (Takeda Shingen's), the *jitō* is not permitted to
interfere. In disposing of other cases, fields and gardens belonging to the criminal must be transferred to another person after securing an order from the
daimyō. In such an event, the annual rent (*nengu*) and other services (*yaku*) must
be remitted to the *jitō* as compensation. As to the land granted by the *daimyō*
(*onchi*), the title is not to be recorded in favor of the criminal [thus allowing it to
revert to the *daimyō*]. As to the houses, fields and gardens which constitute a
taxable unit (*zaike*) and wives, children, and household goods belonging to the
criminal, they must be transferred to the duly appointed authorities.

3. Without a secret understanding with the *daimyō*, no one is permitted to
send messages and letters to another province. However, of necessity, communications by the samurai residents (*kokujin*) of the Province of Shinano may be
continued, as long as it is known to us that they are engaged in devising a
stratagem. Those who live on the border, who are accustomed to exchanging
letters, need not be prohibited from doing so.

4. Anyone who marries someone from outside the province creates causes for
great disturbance, as he may agree to take possession of her estate (*shoryō*) and
send his retainers to serve her family. Therefore such a marriage is strictly
forbidden. If anyone disobeys this injunction, a severe reprimand will be administered.

---

[5]*Ibid.*, pp. 200–206. William Rohl's complete translation is contained in *Oriens Ex-
tremus*, VI, (1959), pp. 210–235.
[6]Here the term *jitō* means vassals of Takeda Shingen.

10. Concerning the land granted by the *daimyō* (*onchi*), even if it may have undergone two phases of a natural disaster, both flood and drought, one must not expect a change of land. One must serve the *daimyō* diligently and in proportion to the amount produced from his land (*bunryō*). Even placed in adverse conditions, if one can discharge his duties exceptionally well, he may then be given suitable land [in its place].

12. It is clearly established that there is a prohibition on the sale of the fief granted by the *daimyō* (*onchiryō*), from which privately held *myōden* (name fields) are exempt. However, this regulation may be modified if details of extenuating circumstances are reported, and after the passage of a set period, the land can then be sold.

14. Exchanging oaths privately by relatives and retainers is tantamount to treason. However, on the battlefield, it is permissible to enter into a compact, so as to encourage loyalty.

22. The Pure Land Sect and the Nichiren Band (*tō*) are not permitted to engage in religious controversy within the borders of our domain (*bunkoku*). If there are people who encourage such controversies, both the priests and their parishioners will be punished.

The Chōsokabe House Law

The Chōsokabe family, unlike many other contemporary sengoku daimyō, *traced its pedigree to at least 1180 which was before the founding of the Kamakura* bakufu. *The family became a contender for the local hegemony in Shikoku during the Ōnin War, when the Hosokawa who held the hereditary position of* shugo *could no longer provide adequate local attention. Chōsokabe Motochika (1538–1599) succeeded to the family leadership (*katoku*) in 1560. Starting in 1570 he began a series of military campaigns which culminated in the battle of 1583 against the Kawano, which enabled him to become the lord of the entire Shikoku. However, he fought against Toyotomi Hideyoshi and was defeated by the latter in his Shikoku campaign. Thereafter he swore fealty to Hideyoshi and received the latter's assurance that he could keep Tosa in the southern part of Shikoku as his domain. He fought for Hideyoshi in the two Korean campaigns which was disastrous for the economic well-being of his domain. After his death the family sided with Hideyoshi's heir against Tokugawa Ieyasu, and the last of the* Chōsokabe *was executed after the defeat in the battle of the Osaka castle which took place in 1615.*

Among the major accomplishments of Chōsokabe Motochika was his cadastral survey which was begun in 1587 and completed in 1598. The survey identified those farmers—who were separated from military duties—and who were responsible for the payment of a set amount of taxes. Note the articles reproduced below which deal with payment of taxes in the event no owner of the land was listed, or with the settlement of dispute over the titles of the lands. Note also an attempt to legislate morality which was often accompanied by imposition of heavy penalties.

6   The Hundred Article Code of Chōsokabe, 1597[7]

6. Lords and vassals, priests and laymen, noble and mean, high and low, must all keep from allowing the rules of humaneness, righteousness, and propriety to suffer disgrace, but should on the contrary keep them constantly in mind.

7. It should be the primary concern of everyone to train himself unceasingly in military accomplishment. Those who tend to excel their fellows in this should be given additional income. Particular attention should be paid to musketry, archery, and horsemanship. The military code is contained in a separate document.

9. You should try to live up to the teachings of the various (Buddhist) sects. In things like literary studies, those who excel their fellows, according to their achievements, can nourish hopes in whatever their area, whether worldly prosperity or religious life.

10. With regard to (Buddhist) priests: (a) those who return to lay life without reporting this to the lord of the province will promptly be executed, (b) They will no longer go out at night unless there is a compelling reason, and (c) their misconduct, when reported, will bring special reward for the informer. Violations of these points will bring punishment of exile or death, depending on the gravity of the offense.

17. It is only natural that services are demanded of those who hold fiefs, and they must be carried out to the letter regardless of whether they are large or small. Anyone late for logging or construction work will be required to repeat the duty period as punishment. And anyone who comes short of the food and provisions requested of him for work detail without excuse will be required to supply as much again.

18. In regard to those who abscond: offenders must be punished whatever their excuse and so also their relatives. Proper reward should be given neighbors or friends who report anyone whose behavior causes suspicion that he is planning to desert. Those who have knowledge of such intent and fail to report it will receive the same punishment as the offender. Furthermore, a man who reports late for lumbering or construction and leaves without getting permission from the magistrate will have his land declared forfeited. If a man deserts directly to another province, punishment will also be imposed on his relatives. Similarly, if

---

[7]Selection from Marius B. Jansen, "Tosa in the Sixteenth Century," in John W. Hall and Marius B. Jansen, *Studies in Institutional History of Early Modern Japan*, with an introduction by Joseph R. Strayer, pp. 102–114. Copyright © 1970 by Princeton University Press. Reprinted by permission of Princeton University Press.

a man's retainer (*hikan*) deserts [from labor duty], the master will be penalized threefold.

25. Quarreling and bickering are strictly forbidden. Whether in the right or wrong, begin with restraint and forbearance. If in spite of this, men resort to violence, then both parties should be punished, regardless of the right or wrong of the matter. If one party only raises his hand against the other, regardless of his reasons for having done so he will be punished.

32. Heavy drinking is prohibited for all people, high and low, to say nothing of all magistrates. Furthermore: With regard to drunkards, the fine for minor offenses will be three *kan* of coins, and appropriate punishment (*seibai*) will be imposed for severe offenses. A man who cuts or strikes others [while drunk] will have his head cut off.

33. As to illicit relations with another's wife: Although it is obvious, unless the guilty pair kill themselves, both of them should be executed. If approval of relatives is obtained, revenge may be undertaken, but unnatural cruelty will constitute a crime. If the husband fails to kill the man, or if he is away at the time the offense becomes known, the people of the village should kill the offender. In addition: If a woman has a reputation, the [marriage] contract is to be broken.

34. When there is not a man in the house, no males—masseurs, peddlers, traveling *sarugaku* performers and musicians, solicitors for religious contributions (*banjin*), or even relatives—shall set foot in the house. If someone is ill and if the relatives approve, a visit may be made, but then only in daytime. Even the magistrate must carry on his business outside the gate. However, this does not apply to parents, sons, and brothers [of the household head].

35. Also, when a man is not present, a woman is not to go visiting Buddhist temples or Shintō shrines or sightseeing. Furthermore: The annual and monthly rites [for deceased relatives] should be held at the temple.

36. Also, in the absence of a man: It is absolutely forbidden for a priest to go in and out of the house. Furthermore: This does not apply to devotional services.

43. Law suits over *kōryō* (*daimyō* domain) and *myōden* (private, name fields) must stop. Furthermore: Land purchases will be validated by special decree, while the quality of service performed will be the criterion for [transfer] of land for which no validation papers previously exist.

44. It is a punishable offense to convert rice paddy fields into dry fields or house sites. Where this has been done the taxes will be kept at the same rate as those for paddy.

45. With regard to purchasing land: Even if someone has a contract providing for transfer in perpetuity, if the rice produced [by the plot] is less than ten *hyō* (about one acre of normal paddy) the land remains redeemable [by the seller]. Even if it is claimed that a plot was clearly sold permanently, if there is no documentary evidence to support this the plot can be reclaimed by its seller [with restitution of price]. And if despite claims there is no documentary evidence to establish even such redeemable status for land, the land will be considered as

toshige [redeemable from crop yield]. The above rules were established in accordance with previous regulations. When a contract provides that land will be held in pledge at the rate of one *tan* per borrowed *hyō* of rice (about one fifth the yield of average paddy), if the lender has enjoyed crop rights for three years the original owner will no longer be required to repay the loan; he is also entitled to the return of his land. Furthermore: Land alienated under provisions of perpetual or of conditional sale will revert to the original owner if the purchaser's family dies out. But if someone succeeds to this family within ten years the land must again be returned to the purchaser. If, however, it is more than ten years before a successor takes over, their claims lose effect and the land will be considered part of the original owner's fief. The same rule holds for lenders and loans. Furthermore: If the seller's family dies out, except for lands specially registered earlier, all three classifications—perpetual sale, conditional transfer, and terminal option—are to be declared forfeit and confiscated.

46. With regard to abandoned and wasteland throughout the realm: *Shōya* (village heads) in the area must warn their people against letting it grow rank. If the *shōya* is unable to deal with it alone he should consult the magistrate about initiating reclamation measures. If the abandonment has been caused by negligence, the *shōya* of that place must assume responsibility for paying the tax in place of the tillers.

47. As to fiefs throughout the realm: The crop yield, as ascertained by the fall survey of the fields ready for harvest (*kemi*) should be apportioned, two-thirds to the vassal samurai (*jitō*) and one-third to the farmer. If farmers object to this, the samurai will have to use his own judgment. He must, at any rate, take care lest the land be abandoned and ruined.

50. As for the paddy, dry, and dwelling fields which came in dispute at the time of the land survey: As long as these are unresolved, the *shōya* of those areas will have to deliver the exact amount of tax due.

51. With regard to irrigation duty: The irrigation magistrate and *shōya* of the areas concerned must place particular emphasis on allowing nothing to obstruct the irrigation channels. If large-scale damage beyond the capacity of the people dependent on the water takes place, it should be reported to the magistrate, who, after consultation, should call out all the people to repair the damage.

52.   Whoever discovers that anyone, whether vassal or farmer, is concealing the existence of [untaxed] fields and reports it to the lord, will be rewarded strikingly. Acting on such information, the magistrate will base his ruling on the land survey register. If it becomes clear that a vassal concealed the field, he will be severely punished. And if it is a farmer who concealed it, he will be forced to pay double the tax due since the land survey, after which he will be banished. If he pleads hardship at this, he will have his head cut off.

53. With regard to disputes over property lines: In all cases such disputes will be decided in accordance with the register of the land survey. After a case has been heard with the arguments of both parties stated, the person found to be at fault will

be fined five *kan* (i.e., 5000 copper coins) to punish him for his carelessness. If both parties refuse to listen to reason, the disputed area will be confiscated.

60. With regard to farmers throughout the realm: The *jitō, shōya,* and magistrates must foster them solicitously in their official capacity. Do not require extra taxes and work in addition to the regular exactions from them. But of course, the regular annual tax must be paid strictly. If it comes even a little short, *shōya* and land owners of the lord's own domain will receive prompt and severe punishment.

63. With regard to a magistrate or *shōya* anywhere in the realm who shows favoritism or partiality or indulges in any other unjust practices whatever, it makes no difference whether complaints come from someone in the offender's area [of jurisdiction] or not. Details should be forwarded to the authorities, and they will be rewarded. After an investigation, punishment will be meted out.

82. With regard to family succession: It is necessary to notify the lord and receive his permission, even if the heir is the head's real child. It is strictly forbidden to decide succession matters privately. Furthermore: One must also request permission to become a guardian for a minor.

83. Anyone who succeeds to two houses without getting the approval of higher authority will be punished as soon as it becomes known.

84. As regards family name and succession designation for loyal retainers: If a vassal commits a crime and has to be punished, his family name will not be affected if the offense was a minor one. But if he commits a major crime, his punishment should include the loss of his family name.

85. With regard to the marriage of samurai: It is strictly prohibited for samurai who receive over 100 *koku* to arrange a marriage without the lord's approval. Supplement: Whether one's status be high or low, matters of marriage must not be broached at any time if the understanding of both families has not been arranged.

86. Private contract is prohibited in all matters.

92. As to false accusations: Punishment will depend on whether the offense is minor or serious. If it is a minor matter, the fine will be three *kan* of coins.

93. Regardless of rank, the practice of dismounting [in deference to a superior] should be stopped. However, when an envoy or deputy from above (i.e., Hideyoshi) passes, he should receive this courtesy.

Military Conscription

The following document was issued in 1587 by a minor deputy of Hōjō Ujimasa (1538–1590), who was an ally of Oda Nobunaga and Tokugawa Ieyasu in 1582 against the forces of Takeda Katsuyori, heir to Shingen (see Document 5). His victory in this encounter confirmed him as one of the major powers in the Kantō region. After the murder of Oda Nobunaga in the same year, he found himself aligned against the ascending power of Toyotomi Hideyoshi, and had to prepare for a siege by the superior forces of Hideyoshi which took place in 1589–1590.

In this document, the common people and samurai were mentioned separately and were treated equally for the purpose of drafting for military services. It was the policy of sengoku daimyō *to separate warriors and farmers and to reduce the power of the* ji-samurai, *a class of people who held the status of samurai but were also entrenched in the localities as cultivators or land-holders. Yet the Hōjō family was not successful in this regard, and their conscripted army was no match for Hideyoshi's professional army.*

7 Compulsory Military Service Decreed by Hōjō Ujimasa, 1587[8]

1. All men, without distinction as to being of the samurai class or of common people, in this county (gō) are ordered to come and register for the service of this province in an emergency. Of these, eight [are to be drafted].

2. They are to bring with them any of the following three weapons: an arrow, spear, or gun. However, a spear, whether its shaft is made of bamboo or wood, is useless if it is shorter then two *ken* [about twelve feet]. Even if one claims to be an official of the higher authorities, and does not follow the above injunctions, he must still be treated the same as merchants or petty artisans. The registration applies to all men from fifteen to seventy years of age.

3. Those who respond to the call must prepare their daggers and military emblems in such a way as to make them look like worthy warriors.

4. If an able-bodied man is deliberately left behind, he and the one who has ordered him to remain will be beheaded immediately by the Minor Deputy (*shō-daikan*) of the county upon hearing of it.

5. Anyone who abides by the provisions of this circular diligently, whether he be of the samurai class or of common men, can expect to receive rewards.

The above provisions describe the need in time of emergency. Everyone is directed to complete preparation of their implements of war by the end of the eighth month. The names of those who register must be submitted by a responsible party by the twentieth day of the next month. The above provisions must be widely circulated within the county.

Fifteenth year of Tenshō [1587], last day of the seventh month.
To the Minor Deputy and People of Iwase Village.

ODA NOBUNAGA'S ROAD TOWARD UNIFICATION

In 1586 Oda Nobunaga (1534–1582) entered Kyoto, accompanied by Ashikaga Yoshiaki, pretender to the position of shōgun. *He successfully placed Yoshiaki as* shōgun, *and obtained de facto control of all political matters. However, the*

---

[8]*Sōshū Monjo* in Ōkubo et al., *op. cit.,* p. 8.

*relationship between Yoshiaki and Nobunaga deteriorated, and the former
aligned himself with other sengoku daimyō such as the Asai, Asakura, Takeda,
and Mōri families and with the Honganji (temple). In 1570 Nobunaga decisively
defeated the combined forces of Asai and Asakura, and the following year burnt
down the university-monastery complex at Mt. Hiei on the pretext that it aided
the Asai forces.*

*Document 8 is an account given by Luis Frois, S.J. (1532–1597), a Jesuit
missionary who came to Japan in 1563 and, in the course of his missionary
activities, gained the confidence of Nobunaga. It described the thoroughness
with which Nobunaga destroyed Mt. Hiei, and also showed Nobunaga's disre-
spect and distrust of deities and buddhas. The destruction of Mt. Hiei was partly
a military move, in that monk soldiers had been a source of concern and threat
to the security of the capital city for many centuries. They utilized their privileged position as monks and interfered in politics with impunity. They also
exercised disproportionately large power because they were in the position to tip
the balance of power among contending military families. Nobunaga's destruction of Mt. Hiei, along with the destruction of Ishiyama Honganji in 1580,
signified the end of the military power of great monasteries. It also meant destruction of idols and of old religions, and symbolically suggested the end of
l'ancien régime in Japan.*

*An effective unification policy called for creating better traveling and trans-
portation facilities and for establishing a stronger and more viable economic
system. The sengoku daimyō did remove barriers within their domains to facilitate travel, and Nobunaga extended this policy to a much wider scale (Document
9). Document 10 shows the practice of promoting the free market and of abolish-
ing the za.*

8 Nobunaga's Destruction of Hieizan, 1571[9]

On his arrival at Sakamoto
he realized that as he was accompanied by an army of 30,000 men he was in a
good position to take revenge on the bonzes (monks) of the universities of
Hieizan, and so he assembled his whole army to overcome the monks. When the
bonzes learnt of his intention and saw that there was no other expedient, they
sent word offering him 300 bars of gold (each one worth 45 silver taels) and 200
bars were sent from the town of Katata. But not one of them would Nobunaga
accept, declaring that he had not come there to enrich himself with gold but to
punish their crimes with all severity and rigor. When the satraps of the universities heard this reply, although they knew that Nobunaga had but scant respect for
the *kami* (Shintō deity) and *hotoke* (Buddha), they still did not believe that he

---

[9]Michael Cooper, ed., *They Came to Japan: An Anthology of European Reports on
Japan, 1543–1640* (Ann Arbor: Center for Japanese Studies, University of Michigan,
1955 edition), pp. 98–99. Reprinted by permission of the editor.

would destroy the idol of Sannō, for it was greatly venerated and its punishments were no less feared. And so for this reason they all decided to gather in the temple (which is on top of the mountain) and to abandon all the other monasteries and their treasures. At the same time the bonzes persuaded the people of the town of Sakamoto to go up as well with their womenfolk and children.

Knowing that he had them all on top of the mountain, Nobunaga immediately gave orders to set fire to Sakamoto and to put to the sword all those found within the town. This was on September 29th of this year, 1571, the Feast of the Dedication of the glorious St. Michael. And in order to show the bonzes who were upon the mountain the little regard he had for the chimeras (which they had described to him) and for the punishments of Sannō, the second thing that he did was to burn all the temples of this idol which were below the foot of the mountain: he also destroyed by fire the seven universities so that nothing at all was left of them. Then deploying his army of 30,000 men in the form of a ring around the mountain, he gave the order to advance to the top. The bonzes began to resist with their weapons and wounded about 150 soldiers. But they were unable to withstand such a furious assault and were all put to the sword, together with the men, women, and children of Sakamoto, which is near the foot of the mountain.

The next day, the last in September and the Feast of the glorious St. Jerome, they burnt down the large temple of Sannō, which, as I have said, was on top of the mountain. Then Nobunaga ordered a large number of musketeers to go out into the hills and woods as if on a hunt; should they find any bonzes hiding there, they were not to spare the life of a single one of them. And this they duly did. But Nobunaga was not satisfied with this victory and desired to slake his thirst for vengence even more and to increase his fame. So he commanded his whole army to go and plunder the remaining houses of the bonzes and to burn down all the four hundred odd temples of those famous universities of Hieizan. And on that same day all of them were destroyed, burnt down and reduced to ashes. Then he ordered the army to the town of Katata, which was unable to offer resistance and was also laid waste by fire. They told me that there had perished about 1,500 bonzes and the same number of layfolk, men, women, and children.

9 **Removal of Barriers, 1568**[10] On the tenth month of the eleventh year of Eiroku [1568] . . . [Oda Nobunaga] abolished many, many barriers and levies (*yaku*) existing in his domain (*bunkoku*). This was done in part for the benefit of the entire domain, and in part in consideration of the welfare of travelers going to and returning from one province to another. All the people, high and low, were very pleased and felt grateful [to Nobunaga].

---

[10]*Nobunagokō ki* in Kasahara et al., *op. cit.*, p. 105.

10 Free Market and Abolition of Za, 1577[11]   Regulations for Azuchi Yamashita Machi:

1. Since this place is established as a free market (*rakuichi*), all *za* are abolished and the market is hereby exempt from all levies (*yaku*) and miscellaneous taxes (*kuji*).

2. Merchants who are traveling must not use the Kamikaidō. Anyone who comes to or leaves Kyoto must come through this town (Azuchi) to stay overnight. . . .

3. This town is exempt from supplying horses for official transportation purposes.

4. Any *tokusei* decrees promulgated in the domain (*bunkoku*) shall not apply to this town.

5. People coming from other domains and other towns, once they establish their domicile in this town shall be treated equally with those who have been in this town before. No objection shall be raised with regard to their former affiliation with other lords. If anyone claims to be a retainer of Nobunaga, and attempts to impose temporary taxes or services [on others in town], that must be stopped.

6. The following are strictly forbidden: engaging in quarrels and disputes; entering into an agreement which involves seizure of property for non-payment of debts (this proscription is applicable to all agreements whether they be made applicable to particular provinces, localities or counties); forcing a purchase at a lower price, forcing a sale; and forcing a person to stay in a particular inn.

7. Horse merchants must come to this town, and all sales and purchases of horses in this domain must be conducted here.

If anyone violates any of the above provisions, he shall be punished expeditiously.

Fifth year of Tenshō [1577], sixth month.

UNIFICATION BY TOYOTOMI HIDEYOSHI

When the news of Oda Nobunaga's assassination reached Toyotomi Hideyoshi, he quickly concluded a favorable peace with the Mōri family and returned to the capital region to avenge the death of his master. With a combination of decisiveness, military skills, and good fortune, Hideyoshi quickly rose to the predominant position among former followers of Oda Nobunaga, and by 1590 completed unification of the country by destroying the last major opponents, the Hōjō. While military campaigns were going on, Hideyoshi adopted numerous measures to effect stratification of society which would provide the basis for forming a stable centralized government under his domination.

---

[11]*Hachiman Machi Kyōyū Bunsho* in Kasahara et al., *op. cit.*, pp. 104–105.

In an agrarian society in which farmers comprised eighty percent of the population, the need for effective control of the farmers was paramount. To insure adequate production of foodstuff, and to maintain sources of annual taxes and of corvée labor, Hideyoshi resorted to the policy of separating farmers from warriors, and decreed that farmers should not move from one village to another to seek another master (1586). In this attempt he was far more successful than the sengoku daimyō *before him. The prohibition of owning swords by the peasantry must be understood in this light (Document 11).*

Cadastral surveys were conducted by Oda Nobunaga between 1568 and 1582, and this policy was continued by Hideyoshi. The latter improved on the policy by applying it to the entire country and by providing a uniform system of measurement. Document 12 shows the determination with which Hideyoshi pursued this policy. Document 13 is divided into five articles and holds an enormous significance in the history of the land system in Japan. By decreeing that 300 bu *should be considered a* tan, *instead of the previous 360* bu, *it increased the number of taxable units by twenty percent. And for the first time a unified unit in measuring rice both for commercial transactions and for the payment of taxes was provided. Once the survey was completed, the data were recorded in triplicate which served as the basis of taxation and of rural control. Technically the cadastral surveys recognized only the right of the cultivator (*saku shiki*), and rejected the rights of landholders to part of the produce (*myōshu shiki*). If this policy were implemented to its logical conclusion it could have given impetus to the creation of small owner-cultivators. However, various compromises were made, and in effect,* saku shiki *and* tokubunken *(the right to share in part of the produce) were granted to landowners who agreed to pay a fixed amount of taxes. For the application of a cadastral survey in Tosa, see Document 6.*

An edict for census-taking was issued in 1591, a year after the completion of unification of the country. This census-taking was in part designed to gain accurate statistical data in preparation for the Korean war which began the following year. However, the main significance of the census-taking is found in Articles 2 and 3 of Document 14. They were intended for the stratification of society, including prohibition of moving from one village to another and of changing from one occupation to another. Change of status was further defined in Document 15. This edict included prohibition of acquiring new masters without permission from the old masters. The first two articles of the edict made separation of peasantry from the warriors complete.

The regime Hideyoshi established was a military regime, but when compared to the Tokugawa bakufu *which followed his, it was relatively weak in its power to control the vassals. The* daimyō *subordinated themselves to Hideyoshi, but in most cases retained most of their old domains and powers. In Document 16 the status of the* daimyō *was clearly defined, and their forming alliances through marriage or otherwise was strictly forbidden.*

In religious matters, Hideyoshi's policy toward Buddhism was milder than the one pursued by Nobunaga. He could warn Mt. Kōya not to follow the example of Mt. Hiei (see Document 8), and at the same time regulate its affairs to his own satisfaction. The monastery in turn could receive assurance of retaining its temple land (Document 17). In contrast, Hideyoshi was suspicious of Christianity, and while declaring that one could become a Christian if his conscience so dictated, he attempted to limit its propagation (Document 18), and missionaries were ordered to be deported (Document 19). Note the extreme interest Hideyoshi showed in foreign trade, by repeating that black ships could continue to come to the Japanese shores.

11 Collection of Swords, 1588[12]

(a) The Edict:

1. Farmers of all provinces are strictly forbidden to have in their possession any swords, short swords, bows, spears, firearms, or other types of weapons. If unnecessary implements of war are kept, the collection of annual rent (*nengu*) may become more difficult, and without provocation uprisings can be fomented. Therefore, those who perpetrate improper acts against samurai who receive a grant of land (*kyūnin*) must be brought to trial and punished. However, in that event, their wet and dry fields will remain unattended, and the samurai will lose their rights (*chigyō*) to the yields from the fields. Therefore, the heads of provinces, samurai who receive a grant of land, and deputies must collect all the weapons described above and submit them to Hideyoshi's government.

2. The swords and short swords collected in the above manner will not be wasted. They will be used as nails and bolts in the construction of the Great Image of Buddha. In this way, farmers will benefit not only in this life but also in the lives to come.

3. If farmers possess only agricultural implements and devote themselves exclusively to cultivating the fields, they and their descendants will prosper. This compassionate concern for the well-being of the farmers is the reason for the issuance of this edict, and such a concern is the foundation for the peace and security of the country and the joy and happiness of all the people. In China, in olden days, the sage ruler Yao pacified the country and converted precious swords and sharp knives into agricultural implements. But there is no precedent for such an act in this country. Thus, all the people must abide by the provisions of this edict and understand its intent, and farmers must work diligently in agriculture and sericulture.

All the implements cited above shall be collected and submitted forthwith.

Vermilion seal of Hideyoshi
Sixteenth year of Tenshō [1588], seventh month, 8th day.

---

[12]*Kobayakawa-ke Monjo* and *Tamonin Nikki* in Ōkubo et al., *op. cit.*, p. 38.

(b) Commentary

All the swords possessed by farmers in this country have been collected for the ostensible purpose of making nails for the erecting of the Great Image of Buddha. For this world, this can prevent unnecessary killings resulting from disturbances involving the use of swords. For the next world, merits can be acquired through the use of the nails. It is decreed that the collection of swords will benefit all the people. But truthfully, this is a measure specifically adopted to prevent occurrence of peasant uprisings (*ikki*). Indeed various motivations are behind this.

12 Toyotomi Hideyoshi's Vermilion Seal Letter to Asano Nagamasa on Cadastral Survey, 1590[13]

Concerning your surveying of the lands, on matters such as determination of the expected amount to be harvested (*todai*), you must follow the intent of this vermilion seal letter, as you were commanded to do so the day before yesterday. In everything, given scrupulous care. Do not make a careless mistake, nor go beyond the authority which is given you.

I hereby command that you thoroughly communicate to local samurai (*kokujin*) and farmers, so that they can understand [the intent of this measure]. If there is anyone who does not obey this order, if he is a master of a castle, besiege him in his castle, and after due deliberation amongst you, have everyone in his castle killed. If disobedience is spread even among the farmers, slaughter every one of those living in one or two counties (*gō*). This order is to be strictly obeyed in the more than sixty provinces of this country, and no careless mistake is to be permitted even in [such remote provinces as] Dewa and Ōshū. It is acceptable if [pursuant to this order] lands without cultivators are created. You must understand the intent of this letter, and do your utmost in the places as far as the deepest reach of the mountains and the farthest point the oars can go in the seas. If you slacken your efforts, the Kampaku (Hideyoshi) himself will come to oversee the matter.

It is hereby ordered. Answer immediately if it can be done accordingly.

Eighteenth year of Tenshō [1590], eighth month, 12th day.

Vermilion seal of Hideyoshi

Asano Nagamasa dono.

13 Cadastral Survey, 1598[14]

Criteria for the survey [Preamble missing]. . . .

The following articles must be observed in surveying the land.

---

[13]*Asanoke Monjo* in Ōkubo et al., *op. cit.*, pp. 34–35.

[14]*Saifukuji Monjo* in Ōkubo et al., *op. cit.*, p. 33.

1. A pole with the length of six *shaku* three *sun* shall be regarded as one *ken*. Henceforth, one *tan* shall be 300 *bu*, consisting of an area five *ken* by sixty *ken*.[15]

2. The grades of the wet and dry fields (*tahata*) and houses and accompanying fields (*zaike*) shall be carefully investigated, and classified as upper, middle, and lower, and the expected amount to be harvested (*todai*)[16] set accordingly.

3. The amount of rice set aside in repayment of the amount expected to be lost in transit shall not exceed two *masu* full for each *koku* of rice.[17] No other miscellaneous exactions shall be imposed.

4. All annual taxes (*nengu*)[18] shall be paid with the *masu* in use in Kyoto as the measuring unit. All purchasing and sale of rice shall also use the same *masu*.

5. In transporting rice in payment of annual tax (*nengu-mai*), the farmers are responsible for the first five *ri*.[19] Thereafter, deputies, as persons receiving land from the *daimyō* (*kyūnin*), shall be responsible for its transportation.

Third year of Keichō [1598], seventh month, 18th day.

Kimura Sōzaemon no Jō, *monogram*

To the Sōbyakusho (all the farmers in the *sō*, or village) in care of Haramura Jirōuemon

14 Census-Taking, 1591[20] We are quickly transmitting to you the following:

1. The Kampaku (Hideyoshi) has ordered that a census be taken in the sixty-six provinces. . . .

2. The number of households, and the number of people, men, women, old, and young, must be reported on a village to village basis. Addendum: Those retainers (*hōkōnin*) must be noted as retainers, townsmen (*chōnin*) as townsmen and farmers (*hyakushō*) as farmers, and their occupations must appear along with their names. . . .

3. Residence by people from other provinces or other counties is not permitted.

---

[15]Previously no set standard was available for the length of *ken*. *Tan* was normally 360 *bu* before, but with Hideyoshi's edict, it was reduced to 300 *bu*. One *ken* equals 1,818 meters or 1,987 yards. One *tan* equals 9.915 ares or 0.245 acre.

[16]*Todai* means the amount that is expected to be produced by each *tan* of land belonging to a specific grade. In this way, the amount of tax can be fixed without resorting to the equivalent monetary valuation by *kan*, to the size of the land expressed in *chō*, *tan*, or *bu*, or to the exact amount harvested each year.

[17]*Masu* is a measure containing one *shō*, which is about 1.638 quarts. One *koku* of brown rice is about 5.01 bushels.

[18]Hereafter the term *nengu* is translated as annual tax or taxes, reflecting the nature of the payment which by this time was no longer the rent paid to those who held certain rights (*shiki*), but a tax paid to the central and local authorities.

[19]One *ri* traditionally represented about four-tenths of a mile. (Today, the same term represents 2.445 miles.)

[20]*Kikkawa-ke Monjo* in Ōkubo et al., *op. cit.*, pp. 39–40.

Addendum: However, if he has a guarantor, he may write an oath before a deity and deposit it with a seal of blood, stating that while remaining [in the village, etc.], he will behave responsibly. Further addendum: The reasons for persons from other provinces taking up residence and the number of years involved must be clearly stated.

The seventh month of last year shall serve as the basis, and no one who has entered after that time shall be permitted to remain [in the new place]. . . .

Nineteenth year of Tenshō [1591], third month, 6th day.

Ankokuji Ekei, *monogram*

Sase Motoyoshi, *monogram*

15   Edict on Change of Status, 1591[21]

1. If there should be living among you men who were in military service including those who served Hideyoshi (*hōkōnin*), higher ranking warriors of the *daimyō* (samurai), those who took their order from samurai (*chūgen*), lowest ranking warriors (*komono*), and those who performed miscellaneous chores for samurai (*arashigo*)—who have assumed the identity of a townsman (*chōnin*) or farmer after the Ōshū campaign which took place the seventh month of last year, they must be expelled. The townsmen and farmers must investigate [to see that this order is carried out]. If anyone as described is kept concealed, the entire town or village shall be held responsible and punished accordingly.

2. If any farmer abandons his wet and dry fields and engages in trade or offers himself for hire for wages, not only is he to be punished, but also his fellow villagers. If there is anyone who neither serves in the military nor cultivates land, it is the responsibility of the deputies and other local officials to investigate and expel him. If they do not take action, those local officials shall be stripped of their posts on account of negligence. If a townsman is disguised as a farmer, and that fact is concealed, that county or town shall be regarded as committing a culpable offense.

3. No employment shall be given to a military retainer—be he a samurai, or *komono*, the lowest rank of warrior—who has left his former master without permission. In employing a retainer, you must investigate thoroughly his background, and insist on having a guarantor. If the above already has a master and that fact is discovered, he shall be arrested for not following this provision, and shall be returned to his former master. If this regulation is violated, and the offender is willfully set free, then three persons shall be beheaded in place of the one, and their heads sent to the offender's original master. If this threefold substitution is not effected, then there is no alternative but to punish the new master.

These are the provisions, as set forth, in the above articles.

Nineteenth year of Tenshō [1591], eighth month, 21st day.

Vermilion Seal of Hideyoshi

---

[21]*Kobayakawa-ke Monjo* in Ōkubo et al., *op. cit.*, pp. 40–41.

16 Control of Daimyō, 1595[22]   An Edict:

1. The *daimyō*, when contracting marriage among their houses, must first receive the approval [of Hideyoshi], and then proceed to complete the arrangement.

2. The *daimyō* and *shōmyō* (lesser lords) are gravely warned that it is strictly forbidden to enter into contract or swear an oath among themselves.

3. If a quarrel or dispute arises among you, let forbearance be your guide to allow reason to settle the matter.

4. If someone falsely accuses another, and brings a suit before you, ask both parties to be present, and investigate the matter thoroughly.

5. Those who are permitted to use a palanquin are: Tokugawa Ieyasu, Maeda Toshiie, Uesugi Kagekatsu, Mōri Terumoto, Kobayakawa Takakage [all except the last named are members of the five elders], old court nobles, priests in charge of Zen monasteries, other famous monks, and those who took the tonsure. All others, even if they are *daimyō*, cannot use a palanquin. However, if the *daimyō* are young they may go on horseback. If they are over fifty years of age, and if the distance to be traveled is over one *ri*, they may be permitted to use a palanquin. When ill, they may be permitted to use a palanquin.

If there is anyone who disobeys the articles above, he must be punished very severely forthwith.

> Fourth year of Bunroku [1595], eighth month, 3rd day.
> Names of the five elders and their monograms.

17 Control of Mt. Kōya, 1585[23]   Aide Mémoire:

1. The lands which belong to Mt. Kōya, whose title is clearly established through a document written by Kōbō Daishi, may continue to be treated as a temple estate (*jiryō*).

2. If Mt. Kōya invades another's estate, the provisions in the document written by Kōbō Daishi shall become no longer applicable. Thus anyone attempting such an act can cause the demise of Mt. Kōya. Use good judgment in this matter.

3. It is said that temple priests, those engaged in ascetic exercises, and other monks who do not have a taste for study resort to the use of weapons, guns, and the like. There is no greater treachery or misdeed than these.

4. As set forth in the regulations by Kōbō Daishi, temple priests, those engaged in ascetic exercises, and all others must encourage one another to concentrate their efforts on Buddhist masses and other religious services.

5. The temple is forbidden to offer sanctuary to traitors and other criminals who regard the entire country as their enemy. While they may claim to be the

---

[22]*Asanoke Monjo* in Ōkubo et al., *op. cit.*, p. 31.
[23]*Kōyasan Monjo* in Ōkubo et al., *op. cit.*, pp. 46–47.

ones who are forsaking the world, if they kill their parents and children, what use is there for the lord? If the mountain (Mt. Kōya) harbors someone who is disgraced and has to cut off a paper-cord which ties his hair and thus loses his manly appearance, will it not be an embarrassment for Mt. Kōya?

6. Mt. Hiei and Negoroji were destroyed by making the nation their enemy. This you have witnessed. Therefore use your good sense in these matters.

7. The above articles as described, if fully accepted by all the monks and by those who engage in ascetic exercises, then each of them must write a letter guaranteeing his own conduct. If the monks and all others can without reservation accept these articles, Hideyoshi will do his utmost to protect and maintain Mt. Kōya.

Thirteenth year of Tenshō [1585], fourth month, 10th day.

Hideyoshi, *monogram*

18   Limitation on the Propagation of Christianity, 1587[24]

1. Whether one desires to become a follower of the padre is up to that person's own conscience.

2. If one receives a province, a district, or a village as his fief, and forces farmers in his domain who are properly registered under certain temples to become followers of the padre against their wishes, then he has committed a most unreasonable illegal act.

3. When a vassal (*kyūnin*) receives a grant of a province or a district, he must consider it as a property entrusted to him on a temporary basis. A vassal may be moved from one place to another, but farmers remain in the same place. Thus if an unreasonable illegal act is committed [as described above], the vassal will be called upon to account for his culpable offense. The intent of this provision must be observed.

4. Anyone whose fief is over 200 *chō* and who can expect two to three thousand *kan* of rice harvest each year must receive permission from the authorities before becoming a follower of the padre.

5. Anyone whose fief is smaller than the one described above may, as his conscience dictates, select for himself from between eight or nine religions.

8. If a *daimyō* who has a fief over a province, a district, or a village, forces his retainers to become followers of the padre, he is committing a crime worse than the followers of Honganji who assembled in their temple [to engage in the Ikkō riot]. This will have an adverse effect on [the welfare of] the nation. Anyone who cannot use good judgment in this matter will be punished.

10. It is illegal to sell Japanese people to China, to the South Seas, or to Korea [as slaves]. Henceforth, sale of persons in Japan is forbidden.

Fifteenth year of Tenshō [1587], sixth month, 18th day.

Vermilion Seal

---

[24]*Goshuin shishiki kokaku* in Ōkubo et al., *op. cit.*, pp. 50–51.

19   Expulsion of Missionaries, 1587[25]

1. Japan is the country of gods, but has been receiving false teachings from Christian countries. This cannot be tolerated any further.

2. The [missionaries] approach people in provinces and districts to make them their followers, and let them destroy shrines and temples. This is an unheard of outrage. When a vassal receives a province, a district, a village, or another form of a fief, he must consider it as a property entrusted to him on a temporary basis. He must follow the laws of this country, and abide by their intent. However, some vassals illegally [commend part of their fiefs to the church]. This is a culpable offense.

3. The padres, by their special knowledge [in the sciences and medicine], feel that they can at will entice people to become their believers. In so doing they commit the illegal act of destroying the teachings of Buddha prevailing in Japan. These padres cannot be permitted to remain in Japan. They must prepare to leave the country within twenty days of the issuance of this notice. However, the vassals must not make unreasonable demands on the padres, which shall be treated as a culpable offense.

4. The black [Portuguese and Spanish] ships come to Japan to engage in trade. Thus the matter is a separate one. They can continue to engage in trade.

5. Hereafter, anyone who does not hinder the teachings of Buddha, whether he be a merchant or not, may come and go freely from Christian countries to Japan.

This is our wish, and so ordered.

Fifteenth year of Tenshō [1587], sixth month, 19th day.

JAPAN'S CHRISTIAN CENTURY

St. Francis Xavier (1506–1552), the apostle to India, came to Japan in 1549 and opened a new chapter in the history of Christian missions. He was favorably impressed by the Japanese (Document 20), and so was Cosme de Torres, S.J. (d. 1570), whom Xavier left as Superior of the Japanese mission. He believed that the Japanese were governed by reason, and showed enormous optimism for the success of the Japanese mission (Document 21). Alessandro Valignano, S.J. (1539–1606), who visited Japan three times in 1579–1582, 1590–1592, and 1583–1603, thought the Japanese were prudent (Document 22) and patient (Document 23), but were too addicted to sensual pleasures and sins (Document 24).

---

[25]*Matsuura Monjo* in Ōkubo et al., *op. cit.*, p. 51. For an account of this event by the missionary, Luis Frois, see C.R.B. Boxer, *The Christian Century in Japan, 1549–1950* (Berkeley: University of California Press, 1951), pp. 148ff.

*Soon optimism gave way to the recognition that Japanese were all too differ-
ent, and as João Rodrigues, S.J. (1561–1634), who served as interpreter for
Hideyoshi and Ieyasu, described it, the Japanese could not be trusted (Document
25). Oda Nobunaga's dislike of Buddhism and Shintō, and his friendship to the
missionaries helped Christianity to penetrate into the central part of Japan, but
it met strong resistance from the established religions and then later from secular rulers. Its proscription is treated elsewhere (Documents 18 and 19 in this
chapter, and Document 12 through 14 in Chapter VIII).*

20 St. Francis Xavier's View of Japanese, c. 1550[26]   The Japanese have
a high opinion of themselves because they think that no other nation can compare with them in regard to weapons and valor, and so they look down on all
foreigners. They greatly prize and value their arms, and prefer to have good
weapons, decorated with gold and silver, more than anything else in the
world. They carry a sword and dagger both inside and outside the house and
lay them at their pillows when they sleep. Never in my life have I met people
who rely so much on their arms. They are excellent archers and fight on foot,
although there are horses in the country. They are very courteous to each
other, but they do not show this courtesy to foreigners, whom they despise.
They spend all their money on dress, weapons, and servants, and do not
possess any treasures. They are very warlike and are always involved in wars,
and thus the ablest man becomes the greatest lord. They have but one king,
although they have not obeyed him for more than 150 years, and for this
reason internal wars continue.

21 Cosme de Torres on Japanese Receptivity, c. 1550[27]   These Japan-
ese are better disposed to embrace our holy Faith than any other people in the
world. They are as prudent as could be desired and are governed by reason just
as much as, or even more than, Spaniards; they are more inquisitive than any
other people I have met. No men in the wide world like more than they to hear
sermons on how to serve their Creator and save their souls. Their conversation is
so polite that they all seem to have been brought up in the palaces of great
nobles; in fact, the compliments they pay each other are beyond description.
They grumble but little about their neighbors and envy nobody. They do not
gamble; just as theft is punished by death, so also is gambling. As a pastime they
practice with their weapons, at which they are extremely adept, or write couplets,
just as the Romans composed poetry, and most of the gentry occupy themselves in
this way....

---

[26]Cooper, *op. cit.*, p. 41.
[27]*Ibid.*, pp. 40–41.

22 Alessandro Valignano on Japanese Prudence and Discretion, c. 1580[28]

They are very prudent and discreet in all their dealings with others and they never weary anybody by recounting their troubles or by complaining or grumbling as people do in Europe. When they go visiting, their etiquette demands that they never say anything which might upset their host. And do they never come and talk about their troubles and grievances, because as they claim to suffer much and always to show courage in adversity, they keep their troubles to themselves as best they can. When they meet or go to visit somebody, they always appear cheerful and in good spirits, and they either do not refer to their troubles at all, or, if they do, at most they just mention them with a laugh as if they did not worry about such unimportant matters. As they are so opposed to every kind of gossip, they never talk about other people's affairs or grumble about their princes and rulers, but instead they speak on topics in keeping with the times and circumstances, dwelling on them only for as long as they think they can afford pleasure and contentment for their hosts.

For this reason (and also in order not to become heated in their dealings with others), they observe a general custom in Japan of not transacting any important or difficult business face to face with another person, but instead they do it all through messages or a third person. This method is so much in vogue that it is used between fathers and their children, masters and their servants, and even between husbands and wives, for they maintain that it is only prudent to conduct through a third person such matters which may give rise to anger, objections, or quarrels. As a result they live in such peace and quietness that even the children forbear to use inelegant expressions among themselves, nor do they fight or hit each other like European lads; instead, they speak politely and never fail to show each other respect. In fact they show such incredible gravity and maturity that they seen more like solemn men than children.

23 Alessandro Valignano on Patience and Resignation, c. 1580[29]

The people are incredibly resigned to their sufferings and hardships; often enough one sees great and powerful kings and lords banished from their realms and dispossessed of all they own, yet they live quietly and contentedly in their misery and poverty as if they had not lost a thing. It seems that much of this is due to the fact that such changes in station are common and frequent in Japan, for in no other country in the world does the wheel of fortune turn so often as here. One frequently sees nonentities become powerful nobles and, on the contrary, great

---

[28]*Ibid.*, p. 43. All of his writings selected are from his *Historia del Principio y Progresso de la Compania de Jesus en las Indias Orientales 1542–1564*, Josef Wicki, S. J., ed. (Rome, 1944).

[29]*Ibid.*, pp. 44–45.

men reduced to nothing with all their property confiscated. This is, I say, such a common and ordinary event among them that all hold themselves in readiness for such a change in fortune; and when it happens to them, they take the blow well as if it were something expected and quite ordinary.

They are also moderate in their emotions and never show them outwardly, even though they may feel them in their hearts. They keep their anger and rage so tightly under control that rarely does anybody show any vexation. For this reason neither in the streets nor in the very houses is there any shouting or brawling such as can be heard in other countries. Husbands do not beat or shout at their wives, neither do fathers their sons, nor masters their servants. On the contrary they outwardly appear very calm and deal with each other either by the messages that they send or by the cultured words that they speak; in this way, even though they may be exiled, killed, or thrown out of their homes, everything is done quietly and in good order.

Finally, although two men may be deadly enemies, they will both smile at each other and neither will fail to perform any of the customary courtesies towards each other. Their conduct in such cases is beyond both belief and understanding; things reach such a pass that when they are most determined to take revenge and kill somebody, they show him much affection and familiarity, laughing and joking with him. Seizing their chance when he is completely off his guard, they draw their heavy swords, which are as sharp as razors, and so attack him that generally he is killed by the first or second blow. Then they replace their swords quietly and calmly as if nothing had happened and do not give the slightest indication of passion or anger either by word of mouth or change of expression. And thus they all give the impression of being very mild, patient, and well disposed, and it cannot be denied that they are superior to all other peoples in this respect.

24 Alessandro Valignano on Sensual Vices and Meager Loyalty, c. 1580[30]

Their first bad quality is that they are much addicted to sensual vices and sins, a thing which has always been true of pagans. The men do not pay much attention to what their wives do in this respect because they trust them exceedingly, but both husbands and relatives may kill an adulterous wife and her partner at will. But even worse is their great dissipation in the sin that does not bear mentioning. This is regarded so lightly that both the boys and men who consort with them brag and talk about it openly without trying to cover the matter up. This is because the bonzes teach that not only is it not a sin but that it is even something quite natural and virtuous and as such the bonzes to a certain extent reserve this practice for themselves. They are forbidden under grave penalties by ancient laws and customs to have the use of women and so they find a

---

[30]*Ibid.*, pp. 46–47.

remedy for their disorderly appetites by preaching this pernicious doctrine to the blind pagans. They are certainly past masters in this teaching and so they are worse and more openly involved in it than other people. But their great influence over the people, coupled with the customs handed down by their forefathers, completely blinds the Japanese, who consequently do not realize how abominable and wicked is this sin, as reason itself plainly shows.

The second defect of this nation is the meager loyalty which the people show towards their rulers. They rebel against them whenever they have a chance, either usurping them or joining up with their enemies. Then they do a turn-about and declare themselves friends again, only to rebel once more when the opportunity presents itself; yet this sort of conduct does not discredit them at all. As a result, none of the lords (or very few of them) are secure in their domains and, as we can see, there are many upheavals and wars. These in turn bring about many deaths and betrayals of friends and relations because it is impossible for the rulers to succeed in any other way. The chief root of the evil is the fact that the people are no longer subjects to the Emperor (*dairi*), who was once the true and traditional ruler. There was a rebellion against him and Japan was divided up among so many usurping barons that there are always wars among them, each one trying to grab for himself as much territory as he can. The government of the country is far less centralized than that of Europe, and the power and sway of the nobles is so different from what we find in Europe that it is no wonder that there is so much treachery and unrest. The bonzes have no little responsibility for this because ambition prompts them to become the chief instigators and agents of these rebellions.

25 João Rodrigues on Japanese Craftiness, c. 1610[31] They are so crafty in their hearts that nobody can understand them. Whence it is said that they have three hearts: a false one in their mouths for all the world to see, another within their hearts only for their friends, and the third in the depths of their hearts, reserved for themselves alone and never manifested to anybody. As a result all order decays here for everyone acts merely according to the circumstances and occasion. But they do not use their double-dealing to cheat people in business matters, as do the Chinese in their transactions and thievery, for in this respect the Japanese are most exact; but they reserve their treachery for affairs of diplomacy and war in order not to be deceived themselves. And in particular when they wish to kill a person by treachery (a stratagem often employed to avoid many deaths), they put on a great pretense by entertaining him with every sign of love and joy—and then in the middle of it all, off comes his head.

---

[31] *Ibid.*, p. 45. Rodrigues entered the Society of Jesus in Japan in 1580 and remained there until his expulsion in 1612. Among his works were *Historia da Igreja de Japan*, and *Arte da Lingoa de Japan*.

CHAPTER VIII

Tokugawa: Era of Peace

"Great Peace throughout the Realm," or *Tenka Taihei*, was the phrase used to describe the peaceful conditions which prevailed over two and a half centuries. There were intermittent peasant uprisings and disturbances connected with masterless samurai, but altogether the mood of peace and prosperity prevailed during the entire period when the Tokugawa family governed the country.

The long-lasting stability did not come by accident. It was a result of the deliberate policies adopted by the Tokugawa *bakufu* when it formally took power in 1603. Tokugawa Ieyasu improved on Hideyoshi's policy of indirect rule through the familiar *daimyō* system, by establishing three major categories of *daimyō*. There were the *shimpan* which consisted of collateral descendants of the Tokugawa *shōgun*, the *fudai* which were comprised of descendants of those loyal to Tokugawa Ieyasu before the battle of Sekigahara in 1600, and the *tozama* or outer *daimyō* who were enemies or allies of Tokugawa Ieyasu at the time of the battle of Sekigahara and became Tokugawa vassals only after the battle. In the assignment of domains, care was taken to reward the Tokugawa vassals and allies, and to ensure loyalty of the *tozama*. The *bakufu* possessed the power of reassigning domains or confiscating them. An effective system of surveillance was maintained through the *metsuke* (inspectors). *Daimyō* families were not allowed to contract marriages without approval from the *bakufu*, and major *daimyō* families were bound to the Tokugawa through marriages. A system of leaving hostages in Edo became compulsory in 1634, and the following year the system of alternate attendance (*sankin kōtai*) became institutionalized (Document 1 through 3).

The domains where the *daimyō* ruled were called *han*. They maintained governments which were replicas of the Tokugawa *bakufu*. The Japanese historians often call this juxtaposition of the *bakufu* and *han* governments the *baku-han* system. On the one hand was the *bakufu*, representing the centralizing power, and on the other hand, the *han*, representing the remnants of feudalistic tendencies. Yet the system did work. If the *bakufu* realized no tax revenues from the *han*, it was nevertheless relieved of the burdens of local government by the latter. It could also order the *han* governments to engage in the building of the Edo castle and other civil engineering duties or to perform military services. The existence of the *han*, which numbered as many as 295 in the early Tokugawa period, ensured the continuation of local diversity. This in turn served to infuse vitality in the cultural attainment of the period.

The economic basis of both the *bakufu* and *han* governments was in agriculture. Thus control of the rural area became of paramount importance. The Tokugawa legislation generally aimed at controlling farmers and the lands. The cadastral surveys conducted by Hideyoshi and the later ones under Tokugawa served as the basis of taxation. The Tokugawa *bakufu* directly controlled one-fourth of the lands, and its magistrates (*daikan*), working under the *kanjō bugyō* (commissioner of finance), came into close contact with the day-to-day affairs of the rural areas (Documents 4 through 9).

In spite of their generally agrarian oriented mentality, control of major urban areas was not neglected, and two *machi bugyō* (town commissioners) each were assigned to Edo, Osaka, and Kyoto. (Documents 10 and 11). Buddhist temples, along with Shintō shrines, were also placed under a rigid system of control, and the Buddhist temples were made an arm of the government in its system of surveillance of its citizens (Document 12).

The decision to close the country was a momentous one. The pros and cons of that decision cannot be debated here. However, suffice to say, it did contribute to the stability and peace that the Tokugawa rulers sought from that decision (Documents 13 through 17).

The Tokugawa peace, in turn, brought forth prosperity. The rich varieties of commercial activities experienced during this period are contained in Documents 18 through 22. Students of economic history may find in the training of apprentices, described in Document 20, practices akin to the training of employees undertaken by modern Japanese corporations. Some of today's famed Japanese management practices, such as *nemawashi* and corporate philosophy, can also find their precursors in the Tokugawa period. They are included as Documents 23 and 24. Growth of commerce gave the *chōnin* class an opportunity to redefine their role in society. Documents 25 and 26 relate to this subject.

CONTROL OF VASSALS

In 1611, Ieyasu felt strong enough to exact an oath of fealty from the daimyō *of central and western Japan, and in 1612 he imposed a similar covenant of submission on the* daimyō *of the northern provinces. The initial oath was taken by the* daimyō *at the Castle of Nijō in Kyoto. At that time the Toyotomi forces were in Osaka, and the capture of Osaka Castle was still four years away. In exacting these terms, Ieyasu had especially in mind the loyalty of those* tozama daimyō *who had been vassals of the Toyotomi. The oath was the first ordinance which defined the duties of the Tokugawa vassals. (Document 1).*

*Buke Shohatto (Document 2) was issued in 1615, a year before Ieyasu's death. It laid down fundamental rules for the conduct of the entire military class. It was amended frequently, and here the amendments of Kanei (1635) which gave specific instructions on the system of alternate attendance (*sankin kōtai*) are reproduced (Document 3). Otherwise the substance of* Buke Shohatto *remained the same and was reaffirmed on the accession of each new* shōgun. *It enjoined the samurai to the virtues of obedience, sacrifice, and frugality. Its attempt to lay down standards of dress and food reminds one of similar attempts made by Yoritomo, the Hōjō Regents, and the* sengoku daimyō *(see Documents 3 through 6 in Chapter 7). Each of the articles was accompanied by comments drawn from earlier authorities, such as historical works and old laws. Frequently these comments consisted of appropriate quotations from the Confucian classics. The document was drafted by the Zen monk, Sūden (1569–1633) in collaboration with other scholars. After approval by Ieyasu who was in his retirement, the document was sent to Shōgun Hidetada. The second* shōgun *in turn promulgated the laws in Fushimi Castle before the assembly of the* daimyō *who had also come to witness a performance of* Nō.

1 Oath of Fealty, 1611[1]

1. We will respect the laws and formularies established by the *bakufu* for generations since the time of the General of the Right (Yoritomo); out of concern for our own interest, we will strictly obey any regulations which may be issued by Edo hereafter.

2. If there will be anyone who violates the laws and regulations or goes contrary to the instructions given from above (Edo), we will not harbor any such person in our respective domains.

3. If any samurai or other subordinate officer in our employ is found guilty of rebellion or homicide, and that fact is reported to us, we pledge to each other that we shall not take the offender into our employ.

In case any of the foregoing articles is violated, upon investigation conducted by Edo, we shall be immediately liable to be severely dealt with in accordance with the laws and regulations.

Sixteenth year of Keichō [1611], fourth month, 16th day.

Jointly signed by the *daimyō* in Kyoto

---

[1]Ishii Ryōsuke, *Gotōke Reijō (Codes and Regulations Issued by the Tokugawa Bakufu)*, in *Kinsei Hōsei Shiryō Sōsho (A Compendium of Documents on Early Modern Legal and Institutional History)*, Vol. 2 (Tokyo: Sōbunsha, 1959), p. 1.

2   Laws of Military Households (Buke Shohatto), 1615[2]

1. The study of literature and the practice of the military arts, including archery and horsemanship, must be cultivated diligently.

"On the left hand literature, on the right hand use of arms"[3] was the rule of the ancients. Both must be pursued concurrently. Archery and horsemanship are essential skills for military men. It is said that war is a curse. However, it is resorted to only when it is inevitable. In time of peace, do not forget the possibility of disturbances. Train yourselves and be prepared.

2. Avoid group drinking and wild parties.

The existing codes strictly forbid these matters. Especially, when one indulges in licentious sex, or becomes addicted to gambling, it creates a cause for the destruction of one's own domain.

3. Anyone who violates the law must not be harbored in any domain.

Law is the foundation of social order. Reason may be violated in the name of law, but law may not be violated in the name of reason. Anyone who violates the law must be severely punished.

4. The *daimyō*, the lesser lords (*shōmyō*), and those who hold land under them (*kyūnin*) must at once expel from their domains any of their own retainers or soldiers who are charged with treason or murder.

Anyone who entertains a treasonous design can become an instrument for destroying the nation and a deadly sword to annihilate the people. How can this be tolerated?

5. Hereafter, do not allow people from other domains to mingle or reside in your own domain. This ban does not apply to people from your own domain.

Each domain has its own customs different from others. If someone wishes to divulge his own domain's secrets to people of another domain, or to report the secrets of another domain to people of his own domain, he is showing a sign of his intent to curry favors.

6. The castles in various domains may be repaired, provided the matter is reported without fail. New construction of any kind is strictly forbidden.

A castle with a parapet exceeding ten feet in height and 3,000 feet in length is injurious to the domain. Steep breastworks and deep moats are causes of a great rebellion.

7. If innovations are being made or factions are being formed in a neighboring domain, it must be reported immediately.

Men have a proclivity toward forming factions, but seldom do they attain their goals. There are some who [on account of their factions] disobey their masters and fathers, and feud with their neighboring villages. Why must one engage in [meaningless] innovations, instead of obeying old examples?

---

[2]*Ibid.*, pp. 1–3.
[3]Traditionally left takes precedence over right.

8. Marriage must not be contracted in private [without approval from the *bakufu*].

Marriage is the union symbolizing the harmony of *yin* and *yang*, and it cannot be entered into lightly. The thirty-eighth hexagram *kuei* [in the *Book of Changes*], says "Marriage is not to be contracted to create disturbance. Let the longing of male and female for each other be satisfied. If disturbance is to take hold, then the proper time will slip by."[4] The "Peach Young" poem of the *Book of Odes* says "When men and women observe what is correct, and marry at the proper time, there will be no unattached women in the land." To form a factional alliance through marriage is the root of treason.

9. The *daimyō*'s visits (*sankin*) to Edo must follow the following regulations:

The *Shoku Nihongi (Chronicles of Japan, Continued)* contains a regulation saying that "Unless entrusted with some official duty, no one is permitted to assemble his clansmen at his own pleasure. Furthermore no one is to have more than twenty horsemen as his escort within the limits of the capital. . . ." Hence it is not permissible to be accompanied by a large force of soldiers. For the *daimyō* whose revenues range from 1,000,000 *koku* down to 200,000 *koku* of rice, not more than twenty horsemen may accompany them. For those whose revenues are 100,000 *koku* or less, the number is to be proportionate to their incomes. On official business, however, the number of persons accompanying him can be proportionate to the rank of each *daimyō*.

10. The regulations with regard to dress materials must not be breached.

Lords and vassals, superiors and inferiors, must observe what is proper within their positions in life. Without authorization, no retainer may indiscriminately wear fine white damask, white wadded silk garments, purple silk kimono, purple silk linings, and kimono sleeves which bear no family crest. Lately retainers and soldiers have taken to wearing rich damask and silk brocade. This was not sanctioned by the old laws, and must now be kept within bounds.

11. Persons without rank are not to ride in palanquins.

Traditionally there have been certain families entitled to ride palanquins without permission, and there have been others receiving such permission. Lately ordinary retainers and soldiers have taken to riding in palanquins, which is a wanton act. Hereafter, the *daimyō* of various domains, their close relatives, and their distinguished officials may ride palanquins without special permission. In addition, briefly, doctors and astrologers, persons over sixty years of age, and those who are sick or invalid may ride palanquins after securing necessary permission. If retainers and soldiers wantonly ride palanquins, their masters shall be held responsible. The above restrictions do not apply to court nobles, Buddhist prelates, and those who have taken the tonsure.

---

[4]In arriving at this interpretation, I have consulted Honda Hitoshi, *Eki (Book of Changes)* (Tokyo: Asahi Shimbunsha, 1965), pp. 284–285.

12. The samurai of all domains must practice frugality. When the rich proudly display their wealth, the poor are ashamed of not being on a par with them. There is nothing which will corrupt public morality more than this, and therefore it must be severely restricted.

13. The lords of all domains must select as their officials men of administrative ability.

The way of governing a country is to get the right men. If the lord clearly discerns between the merits and faults of his retainers, he can administer due rewards and punishments. If the domain has good men, it flourishes more than ever. If it has no good men, it is doomed to perish. This is an admonition which the wise men of old bequeathed to us.

Take heed and observe the purport of the foregoing rules.

First year of Genna [1615], seventh month.

3 **Amendments of Kanei to Buke Shohatto, 1635[5]**   It is now settled that the *daimyō*, and *shōmyō* are to serve in turns (*kōtai*) at Edo. They shall proceed hither (*sankin*) every year in summer during the course of the fourth month. Lately the numbers of retainers and servants accompanying them have become excessive. This is not only wasteful to the domains and districts, but also imposes considerable hardship on the people. Hereafter suitable reductions in this respect must be made. However, if they are ordered to go to Kyoto, follow the instructions given. On official business, however, the number of persons accompanying him can be proportionate to the rank of each *daimyō* or *shōmyō*.

13. When an occasion arises that the hostages given by subvassals to their lords can be punished by banishment or death, that punishment must not be meted out before receiving a consent order from the above (the *bakufu*). If the circumstances are such as to necessitate instant execution of a hostage, a detailed account must be given to the higher authority (*bakufu*).

15. The roads, post horses, ferries, and bridges must be carefully attended to ensure continuous service. Do not permit any impediment to efficient communication.

16. No private toll bars, or new toll bars over river crossings or harbors may be erected.

17. No vessels of over 500 *koku* burden are to be built.

METHODS OF RURAL CONTROL

The official policy of the Tokugawa bakufu *was to emphasize agriculture to the neglect of commerce and industry. This in its idealized terms placed the samurai at the helm with farmers—who were primary producers—as second in the social*

---

[5]Ishii, *op. cit.*, pp. 3–4.

hierarchy of four classes. In reality, farmers were nothing but pawns in the bakufu*'s and* daimyō*'s quest for economic stability, and different measures were adopted to control them.*

*Document 4 was an order issued by the domanial lord of Echizen in 1632. It sought to establish a group of five (*goningumi*), which was given joint responsibilities in mutual surveillance to prevent crimes and absconding, and in the payment of taxes. In a modified form this was widely practiced throughout the country, including the urban areas (see Document 10). Document 5, dated 1603, gave the farmers the rights to move from one district to another, and to appeal to the higher authorities directly, if there were any wrongdoing committed by the domanial lord or the magistrate. In this way, farmers could be utilized to inform on the offending officials, and thus strengthen the control of the* bakufu *over them. Meanwhile the* bakufu *could continue to collect a set amount of annual taxes from the peasantry. An example of how the peasants were treated by their domanial lord and magistrates can be found in Article 7 of the same document.*

The two proscriptions of 1643 against the sale of lands in perpetuity are given in Document 6. These measures were issued in an attempt to prevent the appearance of large farmers who could in turn reduce small owner-cultivators into minor tenant farmers. The same fear of creating a large number of tenant farmers, and of rendering a once productive farm desolate, led the bakufu *to issue an order prohibiting parcelization of land (Document 7). The commentary gives a rationale similar to the ones which advocated the institution of primogeniture (see Documents 26 and 27 of Chapter 6).*

The main concern of the domanial lords was to have good farm workers who could bring in sufficient tax revenue for them. They would ask the farmers to work hard, and also ask the wives and family members to serve producing members in such a way as to ensure high productivity. Document 8 was written by one Naoe Kanetsugu, a retainer of the daimyō *of Aizu by the name of Uesugi, in 1619. His injunctions show the attitudes of the lords over the peasants. There was no regard for their rights, and if the peasant's wife was not useful as a worker, a divorce was strongly suggested. The regulations for villagers (Document 9) issued by the* bakufu *in 1643 give in minute detail what the peasants could wear and what they could eat. There was no room for luxury which would endanger the peasants' ability to pay taxes. Included in the categories of luxury was consumption of rice by the peasantry.*

4 The Group of Five (Goningumi), 1632[6]

1. If there is anyone in the group of five who is given to malfeasance, that fact must be reported without concealing anything.

---

[6]Tōdai Bungakubu nai Shigakukai, ed., *Shiryō Nihonshi (A Documentary History of Japan)*, Vol. 2 (Tokyo: Yamagawa Shuppansha, 1952), p. 39.

2. If there is anyone in the group of five who fails to pay his annual taxes or perform the services required, other members of the group must quickly rectify the situation.

3. If there is anyone in the group of five who runs away, those who are remaining must quickly search for and return him [to the original domicile]. If the return of the runaway cannot be secured, the group of five will be rendered culpable.

4. No one in the group of five may ask to work outside the domain, or to work in a mine elsewhere. Even if he wishes to work within the domain at places such as Maruoka, Oné . . . he must secure permission from the authorities ahead of time.

5. If there is anyone in the group of five who is exceptionally strong, that fact must be reported.

6. Members of the group of five must not permit anyone who absconds, or any stranger who is not beyond suspicion regardless of being man or woman, to lodge in his house. Nor can they provide lodging for any single person. However, if the stranger is an express messenger, lodging may be provided after his letter box is examined.

If there is anyone who violates any of the provisions above, that fact must be reported to the office of the village head (*shōya*) without delay. The village head must report the same to the *tedai*'s (minor magistrate's) office immediately. If there is any violation of the above rules, we [as members of the group of five] shall be deemed to be culpable, and at that time we shall bear no grudges.

In witness whereof, we have jointly affixed our seals for the group of five.

5 Farmers and Annual Tax, 1603[7]

1. If farmers leave the domains directly controlled by the *bakufu* or by the *daimyō*, because of wrongdoing by the magistrates (*daikan*)[8] and domanial lords, even if their former lords make report of the fact, they shall not be returned to the original domiciles arbitrarily.

2. If there is any tax due which has not been paid, the commissioner's office (*bugyōsho*) shall determine the amount due by considering the rates established for neighboring villages. And once that payment of the tax is completed the farmer may be permitted to reside elsewhere.

6. If there is wrongdoing by the magistrates, without any prior report [to the local magistrate], a brief (*meyasu*) may be addressed directly to higher authorities.

7. It is forbidden that farmers be killed without cause. Even if a farmer has

---

[7]Ishii, *op. cit.*, p. 152.

[8]The term "*daikan*" refers to magistrates of those areas under direct Tokugawa control (*chokkatsuryō* or *tenryō*).

committed a crime, he must be arrested first and be placed under the judgment of the magistrate's office, before a sentence can be pronounced.

The above articles are communicated thus by the order of our superiors.

Eighth year of Keichō [1603], third month, 27th day.

Naido Shuri no suke

Aoyama Hitachi no suke

(Jointly Commissioners of Edo and of Kantō).

6   Sale of Land in Perpetuity Forbidden, 1643[9]

(a) Proscription Against Sale of Wet and Dry Fields in Perpetuity:

3. In view of the fact that those farmers who are well-off may purchase more wet and dry fields and become even wealthier, and those farmers who are not in good health are forced to sell their wet and dry fields, hereafter sale and purchase of wet and dry fields is forbidden while farmers are unable to tend to their own personal affairs.

(b) Penalties for the Sale of Wet and Dry Fields in Perpetuity:

1. The seller shall be expelled after a period of imprisonment. If the seller is dead his son shall be punished in the same manner.

2. The purchaser shall be imprisoned in lieu of other penalties. If the purchaser is dead, his son shall be punished in the same manner. However, the wet and dry fields so purchased shall be confiscated by the magistrate (*daikan*) or fief holder (*jitō*).[10]

3. The one who witnesses the sale shall be imprisoned in lieu of other penalties. However, if the witness is dead, his son shall not be punished.

4. If someone acquires lands as a result of default of a mortgage, and takes away all the yields, and places the burden of payment of annual taxes on the mortgager, then the penalties shall be the same as for the sale of land in perpetuity. . . .

Twentieth year of Kanei [1643], third month.

7   Proscription on Parcelization of Land, 1672[11]

(a) An Order by the *Bakufu*, 1672:

No one is permitted to divide his land willfully by the amount of *koku*, if his landholdings do not produce approximately twenty *koku* in the case of a

---

[9]Kodama Sachita et al., eds., *Kinsei Nōsei Shiryōshū (Documents on Early Modern Agricultural Administration)*, Vol. 1, *Edo Bakufu Hōrei (Laws and Regulations of the Tokugawa Bakufu)*, part 1 (Tokyo: Yoshikawa Kōbunkan, 1966), pp. 30–31.

[10]During the Tokugawa period the term *jitō* referred to those fief holders, including the *hatamoto* and those vassals under the *daimyō*, who exercised the right of collecting rent or taxes. They administered the lands granted to them.

[11]Ōkubo Toshiaki et al., *Shiryō ni yoru Nihon no Ayumi (Japanese History through Documents), Kinseihen (Early Modern Period)* (Tokyo: Yoshikawa Kōbunkan, 1955), pp. 92–93.

village headman, or ten *koku* in the case of a plain farmer. If anyone disobeys this, he is liable to be prosecuted. Notify all concerned.

(b) Exposition of the Above

Altogether the proscription [against parcelization of land] by farmers owning land which produces less than ten *koku* has been in force for some time. This is done in order to prevent division of land into small lots for children who are brothers. Otherwise, the position of the head family will be weakened, and later, all the brothers will become destitute peasants. This fact is understood initially, but as one gets older, he becomes indiscreet and wishes to divide land. The oldest son may have little discretion, and may feel that to contradict his father's unorthodox views, even for a moment, is to engage in an unfilial act. With this kind of mentality, he fails to warn his younger brothers, and the land which produced ten *koku* is divided into three portions, with the oldest son receiving five *koku*, the second son three *koku*, and the third son two *koku*. Meanwhile, the oldest son assumes the responsibility for ten *koku*, and on festive occasions everyone comes to him for gifts. There is no benefit accruing from the fact of inheritance. The second and third sons become independent and hold small pieces of land, and sooner or later they cannot maintain themselves. The same lot awaits the eldest son. Unless they can work together, their relations will be strained. If one must sell his own land, and become a tenant farmer, and receive scorn from other people, that comes from the old man's division of the land. . . .

8   Injunctions for Peasants, c. 1619[12]

1. Consider the Lord of your domain, the sun and the moon. Respect your fief holder (*jitō*) or magistrate (*daiken*) as the patron deity (*uji gami*) of your place. Treat your village head (*kimoiri*) as if he were your own father.

2. During the first five days of the new year, pay respect to those around you in accordance with your position. Within the first fifteen days, make more than enough ropes needed to perform your major and minor public services (corvée labor for the year). After the first fifteen days, when mountains and fields are covered with snow, accumulate all the firewood needed for the year. Use a sleigh to pull nightsoil on the fields. At night make sandals for horses. Daughters and wives must sew and weave China-grass to make clothing for their menfolk. If there is a housewife who makes an excessive amount of tea to entertain others, visits around in the absence [of menfolk], and gossips, then she must have a hidden lover. Even if a man has a child with her, that kind of woman must be sent away. . . .

5. During the fourth month, men must work in the fields from dawn to dusk and make furrows as deep as the hoe can penetrate. Wives and daughters must make meals three times, put on red headbands and take the meals to the fields.

---

[12]*Ibid.*, p. 94.

Old and young alike must put the meals in front of the men who are soiled from their work. By seeing the wives attired in red, men, old and young alike, can be so encouraged . . . to the extent of forgetting their fatigue. Once men are home after dusk, give them bath water, and let them wash their feet. Sisters-in-law and female cousins must put the chapped feet of the man on the stomach of his wife and massage them. Let him forget the toil of the day.

Near the end of the fourth month, put a harrow on the horse and rake the fields. Cut miscanthus grass from nearby mountains and put them on the China-grass field. If the field is located near a house, always check how the wind is blowing before burning the miscanthus grass. If time is appropriate, sew millet, barley, and wheat seeds.

13. During the twelfth month, if there is a notification from the fief holder or magistrate about a tax overdue, quickly make the payment. For this favor he renders you, send a bowl of loach fish soup accompanied by a dish of fried sardines. Although, according to the regulations, all that is expected of a farmer on such an occasion is a bowl of soup and a dish of vegetables, the ones [just suggested] are more appropriate. If no tax is paid after the due notice, you can have your precious wife taken away from you as security. Do not forget that in your master's house there are many young minor officials and middlemen who may steal your wife. To make sure that kind of thing never happens to you, pay all your taxes before the end of the eleventh month. Take heed that this advice is adhered to. You are known as a man of lowly origin. But even so, you do not wish to see your precious wife exposed to wild winds (misfortunes), being taken away from you, and stolen by younger men. In this fashion you may lose the support of the way of heaven, come to the end of the rope, be scorned by your lowly peer groups, and regret the incident forever. Always remember that such a misfortune can befall you. Be diligent in delivering your annual tax rice and in doing work for the magistrate. Once all the annual taxes are paid, prepare for the coming of the new year. Make the remaining rice into rice cake (*mochi*), brew same *sake*, buy some salted fish, and add another year to your life happily. New Year is the time you must be able to chant along with others: I set sail on this journey of longevity. May the moon also accompany me!

9 Regulations for Villagers, 1643[13]

1. Hereafter, both the village headman (*shōya*) and higher village officials (*sōbyakushō*) may not build houses which are not consistent with their stations in life. However, town houses (*machiya*) may be built under the direction of the fief holder (*jitō*) or magistrate (*daikan*).

2. Concerning farmer's clothing, in accordance with the previous *bakufu* edict, the village headman and his family may wear silk, pongee, linen, and

---

[13]Ishii, *op. cit.*, pp. 154–155.

cotton; lower village officials (*wakibyakushō*) may wear only linen or cotton. Other materials may not be used to make the neckband (*eri*) or waist sash (*obi*).

3. Neither the village headman nor the higher village officials may dye their clothing purple or crimson. Other colors may be used to dye clothing for wear but no design is permitted.

4. Farmers must be told that their normal meals must consist of grains other than rice and wheat. Rice especially must not be consumed indiscriminately.

5. In villages, hot noodles, thin noodles, buckwheat noodles, bean-jam buns, bean curds, and the like may not be traded. This is to prevent wasteful use of the five grains.

6. *Sake* (rice wine) must not be brewed in villages. Nor can it be brought from elsewhere to be sold locally.

7. Do not go to market towns to drink freely.

8. Farmers must be told that they must take good care of their wet and dry fields, and weed them attentively and conscientiously. If there are insolent farmers who are negligent, the matter will be investigated and the offenders duly punished.

9. If a single farmer is unmistakably overburdened, and cannot carry on his share of farm work, not only his five-man group (*goningumi*) but also the entire village must [in the spirit of] mutual help, assist in his rice planting, and otherwise enable him to pay his annual taxes (*nengu*).

10. From this year on, planting of tobacco on either old fields or new fields is strictly forbidden, because its cultivation wastes the lands that can be used to grow the five grains.

11. The village elders (*nanushi*) and higher village officials, both men and women, are forbidden to use any kind of conveyance.

12. Farmers must be told that no shelter can be given in the district to anyone who comes from another village and does not cultivate the fields, and is not reliable. If any farmer gives shelter to such a person, the gravity of his offense is to be investigated, and he becomes subject to arrest and imprisonment.

13. Wet and dry fields may not be sold in perpetuity.

14. Farmers may not, on account of disputes involving annual taxes and other matters, desert their places and take refuge with those who have absconded. Anyone who violates this, after an investigation, may be considered as committing a culpable offense.

15. If the *jitō* or *daiken* administers the area so poorly that the farmers find it impossible to endure it any longer, they may first pay up all the annual taxes, and leave the village. They may even establish their residence in a neighboring county. If there is no tax overdue, the *jitō* or *daikan* cannot punish them with banishment (*kamae*).

16. Even in the matters of Buddhist ceremonies and religious festivals, over-indulgence beyond one's own status must be avoided.

17. Within the city limits of Edo, no one is to ride on top of a horse loaded with wood, hay, goods in straw sacks, and the like.

The above articles must be made known to all the villages, to secure immediate observance of their intent. Care must be taken continuously to conform to these injunctions.

Twentieth year of Kanei [1643], third month, 11th day.

CONTROL OF THE URBAN AREAS

Edo, the present-day Tokyo, was an insignificant fishing village in 1457 when Ōta Dōkan set out to build a castle there. In 1590 it became the headquarters for the Tokugawa, and in 1603 it became the political center of the country when the Tokugawa bakufu was established. It was inhabited by the retainer groups (kashindan), wives, and children of the tozama-daimyō who remained there as hostages, as well as the merchants who served them. In the Kanei period (1624–1643) the system of alternate attendance (sankin kōtai) became formalized and mansions for the daimyō were built along with houses to accommodate their retainers and families.

The bakufu also regulated the establishment of over three hundred chō (wards—or units within the city). The inhabitants of each of the chō (or machi) often consisted of traders or artisans of the same occupation. Initially the bakufu moved the merchants and artisans from Mikawa and other old domains belonging to the Tokugawa. These merchants and artisans in turn called other merchants and artisans from other domains to come and join them in Edo. The bakufu gave lands and official positions (machidoshiyori, or town elders and/or goyō shōnin, or merchants by appointment to the bakufu to the leading merchants and artisans. They served under the town commissioners (machi bugyō), and became part of the system of control of commerce and industry imposed by the bakufu. This system was also employed in other castle towns and urban areas.

Document 10 contains regulations issued by the town commissioners of Edo. Note the functions played by the machidoshiyori and the group of five as well as the detailed regulations on family relations and on inheritance. Document 11 contains regulations on lawsuits which without fail favored those who were in the position of authority.

10 Regulations for the Residents of Edo, 1655[14]

1. Parties engaged in public brawls and quarrels are punishable by death according to the law irrespective of whichever party is in the right or at fault.

If a murderer escapes, people in his township (*chōnin*) and his guarantor (*ukenin*) must find him.

Anyone who is beaten by another is asked to forebear it and report the matter

---

[14]*Ibid.*, pp. 143–144, also Ōkubo, *op. cit.*, pp. 107–109.

to the commissioner's office (*bugyōsho*). After an investigation, the judgment can be quickly pronounced. If anyone else is implicated in the same crime, his sentence shall be the same as the original culprit.

2. If an official commits the crimes of public brawling and stealing, these crimes must not be imputed to his master. If there is no guarantor for the official, he must be arrested. After an investigation if he is found wanting, he must be placed under the custody of his master. If he runs away, people in his township and the relatives of the master must find him.

3. Quarrels between children need not be punished, and the parents of both parties may restrain them. However, if the parents enter the disputes, their acts shall be treated as culpable offenses.

4. If a child unintentionally kills his friend, he need not be put to death. However, if he is over thirteen years of age, he cannot escape the punishment.

5. Anyone who follows his own silly will, without consulting the town elders (*machidoshiyori*) and the group of five, is considered to have committed a culpable offense. However, if the town elders are at fault, the entire town may submit a petition. After an investigation, the judgment will be quickly pronounced.

6. If a person dies leaving behind accounts payable and other debts, officials on duty and middlemen may ask for repayment. If there is no document of proof, then no claim can be made. If there is a son who is the heir, he shall be the one to make the repayment. It is natural that the father's debts be paid by the son. On the other hand, the father is not responsible for the debts incurred by his son. However, if the father directly places his seal [on the son's bond of debt], then he cannot escape from his obligation of making repayment.

7. Anyone who does not abide by his father's and mother's words of restraint or by the opinion of the town elders and of the group of five, will be called to our presence and be imprisoned. Thereafter if he does not change his mind, the parents shall disinherit him and banish him. If he still holds a grudge against his parents, he may be arrested by the people of the entire township and sent to us to be put to death.

8. A dispute involving a father and a son may be dealt with by the relatives and people of the township. However, if there is no consensus, and a brief is filed with the higher authorities and the two parties confront each other, after an investigation, if the father is found guilty, an appropriate judgment will be given. If the son is found guilty, depending on the father's disposition, he may be punished as one who is not filial, and either be imprisoned or disinherited and banished.

9. When a dispute arises between brothers, it shows that they lack respect for each other and that they are not given to reason. Thus once the two parties confront each other, the party who is found not given to reason must be quickly reprimanded.

10. In a dispute involving a husband and wife, as written in the regulations of former years, a divorced woman must quickly return whatever belongs to her husband, including the money from his store and clothing items he purchased for her. If she makes this difficult, then she is to be deemed as committing a culpable

offense. If the woman dies, and there is a dispute over the disposition of money belonging to the store and over other matters, it can be treated in accordance with previous regulations.

11. When a merchant and his employee become involved in a dispute, they may file a brief with the higher authorities and confront each other. However, these acts will be regarded as lacking in respect for the relationship governing the master and servant. If the employee is found guilty, he shall be sentenced to imprisonment, and in addition, depending on the disposition of the master, other judgments may be rendered.

12. If the family property is first bequeathed to the oldest son and then again bequeathed to the second son, it is usually caused by the alienation of the oldest son from his father while the latter was living. Therefore, when the oldest son brings a suit, if the youngest brother has a document giving a later date, the father's will must be respected. However, if on account of the stepmother's slander the oldest son has been disinherited without having committed an unfilial act, then the family property must be equally divided.

13. If the father and mother do not agree [on the disposition of their property], and the daughter without reason steals from her parents and otherwise commits all sorts of questionable acts, then the man [in her life] must be reprimanded.

14. If a wife receives her husband's family property, she must adopt one of her husband's relatives as her son, or otherwise find an heir for the husband. If a widow seeks a second husband not long after [the death of the first husband], it is to be considered one of her most unrighteous acts. However, if a widow is still young, the relatives and township may consult each other to determine what may be permissible for her.

15. If a husband dies without leaving an heir, the widow may remain in the house. If she commits adultery with an employee soon after her husband's death, it is a clear sign that she is a woman ungrateful to her late husband, and is not respectful of her relatives. She must be expelled from the town, and the husband's relatives may decide who may inherit the household.

16. In case a man is seeing another man's wife secretly, and the man and woman are found together, then without any further ado, bring forth clearly other available evidence. After an investigation, both the man and the woman may be punished with the same punishment. This being the case, a private revenge is not permitted.

17. Arson is a crime originating in one man's malice which can give hardship to many people, and it is one of the worst crimes. Especially if a person first commits robbery and then engages in arson, heavy penalty must be imposed. In accordance with the precedents set, the culprit's father, sons, and brothers may also be punished with the same punishment.

18. When a lawsuit (*kuji*) is brought to the township and both parties do not wish to abide by [its verdict] and an appeal is brought forth, render a judgment as soon as possible after both parties confront each other. This is a means to show justice to the disagreeing parties.

19. If there is anyone who engages in forgery to documents and seals, as soon as that crime is reported, a severe punishment must be given. Of course, the person who helps in the writing of such documents will be punished with the same punishment.

First year of Meireki [1655], tenth month, 13th day.

11 Regulations Regarding Lawsuits (Kuji), 1633[15]

1. On matters relating to the succession to a townsman's (*chōnin*) profession, during the lifetime of the said townsman, the group of five (*goningumi*) must be consulted, and the decision must be put in a record book before three town elders (*machidoshiyori*). If the heir proves to be insolent, again the succession issue may be brought up for decision. At the deathbed, the townsman must not make his last will inconsistent with reason.

2. Any dispute arising between a master and his servants must, of course, be judged in favor of the master. However, if the master is found to be culpable in certain respects, then judgment may be rendered in accordance with reason.

3. Any dispute arising between a parent and a child must be judged in favor of the parent. However, if the parent is found to have committed an unrighteous act, he must be duly reprimanded according to reason.

5. After the seal on the back of a brief (*meyasu*) by the plaintiff has been affixed for so many days, and after being notified in writing [of the pending lawsuit], if the party does not appear, then he is to be imprisoned. However, five days must be allowed to elapse before witnesses can be summoned to confront each other.

9. Briefs (*meyasu*) involving retainers (*kyūnin*) of the office of the magistrate (*daikansho*) and townsmen and farmers must be judged by the commissioner (*bugyō*), magistrate, or their retainers in the same jurisdiction, and their judgment must be accepted. If their judgment is found improper, an appeal may be made to Edo. However, if a suit is not first brought before the commissioner, magistrate, or their retainers, even though reason may be on his side, no judgment can be given.

10. Briefs involving retainers and townsmen and farmers under the jurisdiction of domanial lords may be settled by the domanial lord of that particular domain.

11. Briefs involving farmers residing in territories belonging to shrines and temples are to be brought to the magistrate in the same jurisdiction, and his judgment must be accepted. If his judgment is found improper, an appeal may be made to Edo. If a suit is not first brought to the magistrate, no judgment can be rendered.

12. Disputes involving temples must be settled in accordance with the judg-

---

[15]Ishii, *op. cit.*, pp. 250–251, Ōkubo, *op. cit.*, pp. 105–106.

ment rendered by the main temple. If the judgment of the main temple is found improper, an appeal may be made [by a branch temple] to Edo. If a suit is not first brought to the main temple, even though reason may be on its side, no judgment can be given.

13. Without making an objection [at the time of the trial], and later making an appeal on the ground of unreasonableness is an offense punishable by death or imprisonment in the jurisdiction [in which the suit is brought].

16. Anyone bearing false witness may be subjected to the death penalty or to imprisonment, in accordance with the gravity of the offense.

Tenth year of Kanei [1633], eighth month, 13th day.

CONTROL OF BUDDHIST TEMPLES

Memories which were still fresh when the Tokugawa bakufu came into existence were those of monk soldiers, economic and spiritual powers exercised by religious institutions, along with the threat they posed against the temporal power. Thus exercising strong control over the temples became one of the important tasks for the bakufu. It did so (1) by restricting the right held by the imperial court to grant the highest Buddhist ranks (purple robes, and the title of shōnin) after 1615, making temples and monks far more responsive to the will of the Tokugawa bakufu, and (2) by eroding the financial bases of the major temples. Strict regulations were also imposed on the conduct of monks, which are given in Document 12 below.

On the other hand, the temples were given the function of keeping census records, which had the effect of making them an administrative subdivision of the government. Initially, the idea of registering with the temple of one's own faith was put forward as a means of suppressing Christianity (see Document 16). However, in later years the original intent was lost and the temple registry simply noted the parishioners' names, dates of births and deaths, marriages, and movements from one place to another. While this measure nominally increased the rolls of the temples, it had very little religious significance. Most of the temples were made economically dependent on their parishioners. Article 4 of the document given below must be read in this context.

12 Regulations for Temples in Different Domains, 1665[16]

1. The doctrines and rituals established for different sects must not be mixed and disarranged. If there is anyone who does not behave in accordance with this injunction, an appropriate measure must be taken expeditiously.

2. No one who does not understand the basic doctrines or rituals of a given

---

[16]Ishii, *op. cit.*, pp. 70–71, Ōkubo, *op. cit.*, p. 101.

sect is permitted to become the chief priest of a temple. Addendum: If a new rite is established, it must not preach strange doctrines.

3. The regulations which govern relationships between the main temple and branch temples must not be violated. However, even the main temple cannot take measures against branch temples in an unreasonable manner.

4. Parishioners of the temples can choose to which temple they wish to belong and make contributions. Therefore priests must not compete against one another for parishioners.

5. Priests are enjoined from engaging in activities unbecoming of priests, such as forming groups or planning to fight one another.

6. If there is anyone who has violated the law of the land, and that fact is communicated to a temple, it must turn him away without question.

7. When making repairs to a temple or a monastery, do not make them ostentatiously. Addendum: Temples must be kept clean without fail.

8. The estate belonging to a temple is not subject to sale, nor can it be mortgaged.

9. Do not allow anyone who has expressed a desire to become a disciple but is not of good lineage to enter the priesthood freely. If there is a particular candidate who has an improper and questionable background, the judgment of the domanial lord or magistrate of his domicile must be sought and then act accordingly.

The above articles must be strictly observed by all the sects. . . .

Fifth year of Kanbun [1665], seventh month, 11th day.

CLOSING OF THE COUNTRY

Between 1633 and 1639, the Tokugawa bakufu *issued a series of edicts which effectively closed the country from the outside world—with the exception of the Dutch and the Chinese—until 1853 when Commodore Perry reached the shores of Uraga. Fear of the spread of Christianity and the belief that Christianity was the vanguard of aggression by the Spaniards and Portuguese were among the reasons which prompted the* bakufu *to embark on the policy of seclusion, which lasted for 214 years.*

The desire to monopolize all the benefits from foreign trade in the hands of the bakufu *also played a part. Nagasaki was directly governed by the* bakufu, *and a strict monopolistic control was enforced there. The* bakufu *could set the price on the raw silk it acquired from foreign traders, and then set quotas for its distribution to merchants from five cities (the* ito wappu *system). In 1609 the western* daimyō *were forbidden to maintain large ships. In 1635, prohibition of Japanese ships going overseas became total (Document 13).*

Playing on the bakufu's *fear of the subversive nature of Christianity, the Dutch skillfully maneuvered the* bakufu *into taking the position of excluding all*

*their trading rivals. The British earlier found their Japan trade not profitable
and closed their factory (1623), while the Spaniards found themselves expelled
from the country (1624). The Portuguese were excluded from Japan in 1639
(Document 14), and when they sent an embassy from Macao in a futile hope of
regaining trading privileges, the envoys were put to death (Document 15). The
fear the Japanese felt toward Christianity is well reflected in the renunciation of
the Christian faith reproduced in Document 16.*

*Incidentally, the prohibition of Japanese ships to trade overseas (Document
13) did eliminate one important source of competition—the Japanese-run overseas commerce—against the Dutch trade, and Dutch duplicity in this respect
must be noted. The nature of the Dutch trade is given in an account by Engelbert
Kaempfer (1651–1716) (Document 17), a German doctor, who served the Dutch
traders at Dejima between 1690 and 1692.*

13 The Edict of 1635 Ordering the Closing of Japan: Addressed to the Joint Bugyō of Nagasaki[17]

1. Japanese ships are strictly forbidden to leave for foreign countries.

2. No Japanese is permitted to go abroad. If there is anyone who attempts to
do so secretly, he must be executed. The ship so involved must be impounded
and its owner arrested, and the matter must be reported to the higher authority.

3. If any Japanese returns from overseas after residing there, he must be put
to death.

4. If there is any place where the teachings of padres (Christianity) is practiced, the two of you must order a thorough investigation.

5. Any informer revealing the whereabouts of the followers of padres
(Christians) must be rewarded accordingly. If anyone reveals the whereabouts of
a high ranking padre, he must be given one hundred pieces of silver. For those of
lower ranks, depending on the deed, the reward must be set accordingly.

6. If a foreign ship has an objection [to the measures adopted] and it becomes necessary to report the matter to Edo, you may ask the Ōmura domain to
provide ships to guard the foreign ship, as was done previously.

7. If there are any Southern Barbarians (Westerners) who propagate the
teachings of padres, or otherwise commit crimes, they may be incarcerated in the
prison maintained by the Ōmura domain, as was done previously.

8. All incoming ships must be carefully searched for the followers of padres.

9. No single trading city [see 12 below] shall be permitted to purchase all
the merchandise brought by foreign ships.

10. Samurai are not permitted to purchase any goods originating from foreign
ships directly from Chinese merchants in Nagasaki.

11. After a list of merchandise brought by foreign ships is sent to Edo, as

---

[17]Ōkubo, *op. cit.*, pp. 128–129.

before you may order that commercial dealings may take place without waiting for a reply from Edo.

12. After settling the price, all white yarns (raw silk) brought by foreign ships shall be allocated to the five trading cities and other quarters as stipulated.

13. After settling the price of white yarns (raw silk), other merchandise [brought by foreign ships] may be traded freely between the [licensed] dealers. However, in view of the fact that Chinese ships are small and cannot bring large consignments, you may issue orders of sale at your discretion. Additionally, payment for goods purchased must be made within twenty days after the price is set.

14. The date of departure homeward of foreign ships shall not be later than the twentieth day of the ninth month. Any ships arriving in Japan later than usual shall depart within fifty days of their arrival. As to the departure of Chinese ships, you may use your discretion to order their departure after the departure of the Portuguese *galeota* (galleon).

15. The goods brought by foreign ships which remained unsold may not be deposited or accepted for deposit.

16. The arrival in Nagasaki of representatives of the five trading cities shall not be later than the fifth day of the seventh month. Anyone arriving later than that date shall lose the quota assigned to his city.

17. Ships arriving in Hirado must sell their raw silk at the price set in Nagasaki, and are not permitted to engage in business transactions until after the price is established in Nagasaki.

You are hereby required to act in accordance with the provisions set above. It is so ordered.

Kaga no-kami Hotta Masamori et al., seals.
To: Sakakibara Hida no-kami, Sengoku Yamoto no-kami

14   Completion of the Exclusion, 1639[18]

1. The matter relating to the proscription of Christianity is known [to the Portuguese], however, heretofore they have secretly transported those who are going to propagate that religion.

2. If those who believe in that religion band together in an attempt to do evil things, they must be subjected to punishment.

3. While those who believe in the preaching of padres are in hiding, there are incidents in which that country (Portugal) has sent gifts to them for their sustenance.

In view of the above, hereafter entry by the Portuguese *galeota* is forbidden. If they insist on coming [to Japan], the ships must be destroyed and anyone aboard those ships must be beheaded. We have received the above order and are thus transmitting it to you accordingly.

---

[18]*Ibid.*, pp. 129–130.

The above concerns our disposition with regard to the *galeota*.

Memorandum

With regard to those who believe in Christianity, you are aware that there is a proscription, and thus knowing, you are not permitted to let padres and those who believe in their preaching to come aboard your ships. If there is any violation, all of you who are aboard will be considered culpable. If there is anyone who hides the fact that he is a Christian and boards your ship, you may report it to us. A substantial reward will be given to you for this information.

This memorandum is to be given to those who come on Chinese ships. (A similar note to Dutch ships.)

15 The Fate of the Embassy from Macao, 1640, by Antonio Cardim, S.J.[19]

Because many serious crimes have been committed over a number of years by the propagation of the Christian religion in defiance of his decree, the *shōgun* last year forbade under grave penalties all voyages from Macao to Japan, laying down that if any ship were to come to Japan despite this prohibition, the vessel would be burnt and the sailors and merchants executed. This edict was promulgated both summarily and in detail. Nevertheless, these man have blatantly violated the aforesaid decree by their voyage and are seriously at fault. Furthermore, in spite of their assertion that on no account will they send hereafter ministers of the Christian religion to Japan, the ambassadorial letters from Macao are silent on this point. Since, therefore, the *shōgun* has prohibited such voyages on account of the Christian religion and since no mention of this matter is made in these letters, it is quite evident that the entire legation is but a pretence. For this reason, all who have come hither in this ship are to pay the extreme penalty.

It has accordingly been decided that the ship shall be consumed by flames and that the principal ambassadors shall be put to death along with their companions so that nothing may remain of this harbinger of evil. Thus the example which the *shōgun* has made of them will be noticed abroad in Macao and the home country; as a consequence, all will learn to respect the rights of Princes and Kings. We nevertheless desire that the rabble among the crew be spared and sent back to Macao. But should any other ship come hither by force of adverse circumstances or for any other reason whatsoever, let it be known that, in whatsoever port it may call, one and all will be put to death.

Given on the 3rd day of the 6th moon of the 17th year of the Kanei era, that is, the 25th day of July in the year 1640.

At the same time they also asked what they would say about this punishment

---

[19]Michael Cooper, ed., *They Came to Japan: An Anthology of European Reports on Japan, 1543–1640* (Ann Arbor: Center for Japanese Studies, University of Michigan, 1955 edition). Reprinted by permission of the editor.

to foreign peoples in the Orient and even in Europe, if by chance they should go thither. They replied that they would tell the truth; to wit, that the *shōgun* of Japan had put the Portuguese ambassadors to death and had set fire to their ship because they professed the Christian religion and had disobeyed his edict, and that they, to the number of thirteen, had been spared this punishment and sent back so that they could recount what had happened; but they added that the kings and all the peoples of the world would most certainly condemn what had been done as a crime against international law.

They were then taken thence to the mount of execution in order to identify the heads of the executed men, which they found affixed to boards in three groups. The heads of the ambassadors were set apart from the rest; they did not appear pale or washed out, but rather the freshness and beauty of their features well indicated their fate. Now they were set up near a large pole, from the top of which hung the Tyrant's proclamation. Not far away they espied a house wherein the corpses had been buried and cairns of immense stones had been set up over them; thus if at any time the Japanese should be silent about these men, the very stones would speak.

Inscribed on a pole which emerged from the midst of these stones was the name of the legation and the reason for the executions; it was indeed their monument for posterity and an everlasting trophy of their glory. With unfeeling barbarity the Tyrant had added this inscription: *A similar penalty will be suffered by all those who henceforward come to these shores from Portugal, whether they be sailors, whether they come by error, or whether they be driven hither by storm. Even more, if the King of Portugal, or Shaka, or even the GOD of the Christians were to come, they would all pay the very same penalty.*

16 Renouncing the Kirishitan Faith, 1645[20]   *Vow of Namban* (Southern Barbarians): We have been Kirishitans for many years. But the more we learn of the Kirishitan doctrines the greater becomes our conviction that they are evil. In the first place, we who received instructions from the padre regarding the future life were threatened with excommunication which would keep us away from association with the rest of humanity in all things in the present world, and would cast us into hell in the next world. We were also taught that, unless a person committing a sin confesses it to the padre and secures his pardon, he shall not be saved in the world beyond. In that way the people were led into believing in the padres. All that was for the purpose of taking the lands of others.

When we learned of it, we "shifted" from Kirishitan and became adherents of Hokkekyō while our wives became adherents of Ikkōshū. We hereby present a statement in writing to you, worshipful Magistrate, as a testimony.

---

[20]Yosaburo Takekoshi, *The Economic Aspects of the History of the Civilization of Japan* (New York: Macmillan, 1930), Vol. 2, pp. 88–89.

Hereafter we shall not harbor any thought of the Kirishitan in our heart. Should we entertain any thought of it at all, we shall be punished by Deus Paternus (God the Father), Jesus (His Son), Spirito Santo (the Holy Ghost), as well as by Santa Maria (St. Mary), various angels, and saints.

The grace of God will be lost altogether. Like Judas Iscariot, we shall be without hope, and shall be mere objects of ridicule to the people. We shall never rise. The foregoing is our Kirishitan vow.

Japanese Pledge: We have no thought of the Kirishitan in our hearts. We have certainly "shifted" our faith. If any falsehood be noted in our declaration now or in the future, we shall be subject to divine punishment by Bonten, Taishaku, the four deva kings, the great or little gods in all the sixty or more provinces of Japan, especially the Mishima Daimyōjin, the representatives of the god of Izu and Hakone, Hachiman Daibosatsu, Temman Daijizai Tenjin, especially our own family gods, Suwa Daimyōjin, the village people, and our relatives. This is to certify to the foregoing.

The second year of Shōhō [1645]

Endorsement

To the Honorable Magistrate.

To step on the image of Christ, after "shifting" from the Kirishitan and giving such a pledge, is a rare thing never heard of before in any country. How, and for what reason, can such persons return to the faith again? They will not be reinstated as Kirishitans except through the mediation of a padre. They will not be able to return of their own accord.

Chuan Bateren, converted in Namban.

Ryojun and Ryohaku Bateren, converted in Japan.

I hereby certify that the foregoing Kyūsuke and his wife have truly become Ikkōshū converts.

The second year of Shōhō [1645].

Shusan of the Seishōji

17 Of the Dutch Trade in Japan, 1692[21] The Dutch, allured by the advantageous trade of the Portuguese, resolved, not long after the establishment of their East India company, and in the very infancy of their navigations into the Indies, to make proper settlements in Japan.... The then reigning *shōgun*, Ieyasu, granted the Dutch, in the year 1601, a free trade to all his dominions by an express *Goshuin* (vermilion seal letter)....

---

[21]Engelbert Kaempfer, *The History of Japan*, tr. by J.G. Scheuchzer, F.R.S., Vol. 2 (Glasgow: James MacLehose and Sons, 1906), pp. 170–174, 195, 209–210, 215.

In the year 1638 [the Dutch] were commanded by the *shōgun* (Iemitsu) to demolish the factory and warehouse, which has been lately built by them upon the Island Hirado, and to lay the same even with the ground, so suddenly, that one would think they had been his greatest enemies, and this for no other reason, but because they were built of hewn stones, handsomer than the buildings of the country, and because the year of our blessed Savior's nativity was engraved in the front. . . . Not long after, and the very same year, the Court scrupled not to make them undergo a still severer trial, and to exact most convincing proofs, which of the two was the greater, their regard for the *shōgun*'s orders, or the love for their fellow Christians. The case was this: About 40,000 Christians, reduced to most desperate counsels by the many unparalleled cruelties and torments, which many thousands of their brethren had already suffered, rose up and retired into an old fortified place in the neighborhood of Shimabara, with a firm resolution to defend their lives to the utmost of their power. The Dutch, upon this, as friends and allies of the *shōgun*, were requested to assist the Japanese in the siege of this place, and the impending total destruction of the besieged Christians. Mr. Kockebecker, who was then the director of the Dutch trade and nation at Hirado, having received the *shōgun*'s order to this purpose, repaired thither without delay, on board a Dutch ship . . . and within a fortnight's time battered the town with 426 cannon balls, both from on board his ship, and from a battery which was raised on shore, and planted with their [the Dutch] own guns. This compliance of the Dutch, and their conduct during the siege, was entirely to the satisfaction of the Japanese. . . .

In the year 1641, soon after the total expulsion of the Portuguese, orders were sent up to quit our old factory at Hirado, to exchange the protection of a good and indulgent Prince, for the severe and strict government of Nagasaki, and under a very narrow inspection to confine ourselves within the small island, I should rather say, prison, which was built for the Portuguese. So great was the covetousness of the Dutch and so great the alluring power of the Japanese gold that, rather than to quit the prospect of a trade indeed most advantageous, they willingly underwent an almost perpetual imprisonment, for such in fact is our stay at Dejima . . . [they] chose to suffer many hardships in a foreign and heathen country, to be remiss in performing divine service on Sundays and solemn festivals, to leave off praying and singing of psalms in public, to avoid entirely the sign of the cross, the calling upon Christ in the presence of the natives and all the outward marks of Christianity, and lastly, patiently and submissively to bear the abusive and injurious behavior of these proud infidels towards us . . . nothing could be presented as more shocking to a generous and noble mind. . . .

No Japanese in general who seems to have any regard or friendship for the Dutch is looked upon as an honest man, and true lover of his country. This maxim is grounded upon the following principle, that it is absolutely contrary to the interest of the country, against the pleasure of their sovereign, nay, by virtue of the oath they have taken, even against the supreme will of the Gods and the dictates of their conscience, to show any favor to foreigners. Nay, they pursue this false reasoning still further, and pretend that a friend of foreigners must be of necessity an enemy to his country, and a rebel to his sovereign. For they say, if the country should happen to be attacked or invaded by these foreigners, the laws and ties of friendship would oblige him to stand by them, and consequently to become a traitor to his country and sovereign. . . .

The Dutch ships are expected in the harbor sometime in September, toward the latter end of the southwest monsoon, that being the only one proper for this navigation. As soon as the spy-guards with their glasses discover a ship steering towards the harbor, and send notice of her approach to the Governors of Nagasaki, three persons of our factory are sent with the usual attendants to meet her, about two miles without the harbor, and to deliver to our captain the necessary sealed instructions from the director of our trade, with regards to his behavior. The interpreter, and the deputies of the Governors, demand forthwith the list of the cargo and crew, as also the letters on board, which are carried to Nagasaki, where the Governors first examine, and then deliver them to our director. The ship follows as soon as possible, and after entering the harbor, salutes every imperial guard with all her guns, then casts anchor opposite the town about a musketshot from our island. If the wind be contrary, rowing boats (kept for this purpose by the common people of the town) are sent at our expense, but not at our desire, to tow her in by force. In still weather they send about ten of these boats; if it be stormy, and the wind contrary, they increase the number to fifty, and sometimes a hundred, so many as they think necessary, that is, at least twice the number there is occasion for. When the ship is entered in the harbor, two guard-boats with a good number of soldiers are put one on each side of her, and continued, being mounted with fresh troops every day, till she has left the harbor and has got to the main sea. As soon as the ship has dropped anchor, a great number of officers come on board, to demand all our guns, cutlasses, swords, and other arms, as also the gunpowder packed up in barrels, which are taken into their custody and kept in a store-house built for this purpose, till her departure. . . .

Of all the imported goods, raw silk is the best liked, though it yields the least profit of any. All sorts of stuff and cloth yield a considerable and sure profit, and should there be ever so much imported, the consumption in so populous a country would be still greater. Brazilwood, and hides, are also to be disposed of to very good advantage. The most profitable commodities are sugar, catechu, storax liquids (fragrant gum-resin or balsam of the tree *Liquid-ambar orientale*), patchouli, camphor of Borneo, looking-glasses, and several other things of this kind, but only when they have occasion for them and when the Chinese have imported them in small quantities: Corals and amber are two of the most valuable commodities in these Eastern parts of the world, but Japan has been so thoroughly provided by smugglers that at present there is scarcely fifty percent one may get from them, whereas formerly we could sell them ten, nay an hundred times dearer. The price of these things, and of all natural and artificial curiosities, varies very much according to the number and disposition of the buyers, who may be sure to get cent-per-cent clear profit by them, at whatsoever price they buy them. Formerly, when as yet we enjoyed full liberty in our trade and commerce, we seldom sent less than seven ships a year laden with the goods above mentioned. At present we never send above three, or four, one whereof goes first to Siam to make up part of her cargo with the commodities of that country. What remains unsold is laid up in our warehouses against the next year's sale. . . .

GROWTH OF COMMERCE

Money economy spread from urban areas to the countryside by the Genroku period (1688–1704) and the economic power of the merchants became entrenched. This trend was bitterly attacked by the noted neo-Confucian scholar Ogyū Sorai (1666–1728) when he responded to a request from Shōgun Yoshimune (r. 1716–1745) for his political views (Document 18).

Among the famous merchants of this age was one Mitsui Takahira Hachirōuemon (1655–1737) who created a "cash only" department store by the name of Echigoya in 1683, and laid the foundation for the later success of his family. He drew up the first formal household code for his family to follow and also provided his own recollections for his son to compile into a book entitled, Chōnin Kōken Roku *(Some Observations on Merchants). Document 19 is an excerpt from this work which exercised considerable influence over the practical business methods of later Tokugawa merchants.*

Behind the success of many great chōnin *enterprises was the great care that was taken to train their employees. Document 20 is taken from* Osaka Shōgyō Shūkanroku *(Records of Business Practices of Osaka) which was compiled by the Ministry of Agriculture and Commerce of the Meiji Government in 1882–1883 in an attempt to preserve for posterity the records of business practices of the Tokugawa period. Note the exacting training process, and the paternalistic control the master was able to exercise over all of his employees.*

As commerce grew, the volume of shipping between Edo and Osaka substantially increased. Initially marine transportation was handled by individual merchants and was a risky and costly affair. In 1694, under the leadership of one Ōsakaya Ibē of Edo, a shipper's association was formed which was called Tokumi Doiya.[22] *It divided owners of the cargos in ten groups (*tokumi*) which took turns administering the affairs of the association. The names of the merchants belonging to this association, given in Document 21, also show what commodities were imported to Edo from Osaka.*

---

[22]Or *tonya*, a wholesale merchant. The term *doiya* is a variation of *toiya*, with a phonetic change from "t" to "d" (voiced sound). *Toiya* is an older form of the word *tonya*.

*During the first decade of the nineteenth century, one of the member mer-
chants, Ōsakaya Mohē, reorganized the Higaki Shipping Association which also
divided the membership into ten groups (*tokumi*). It made forced contribution
(*myōgakin, literally thanks-offering) to the* bakufu *for the privilege of exclusive
association (Document 22). It was able to establish its own trading center, and
did a large amount of bridge repair work for the city of Edo. Its success was
most noted in 1808–1810. The irregularities in their practices, however, led to
various official sanctions and in the Tempō reforms of 1841, its association of
share-holders (*kabunakama*) was a target for immediate suspension.*

18 **Spread of Money Economy, 1716–1735**[23]   In olden days, the countryside had hardly any money and all the purchase was made with rice or barley
but not with money. This is what I [the author, Ogyū Sorai] experienced while
living in the countryside. However, I have heard that from the Genroku period
on, money economy has spread to the countryside, and they now use money to
purchase things. . . .

Nowadays [i.e., the Kyōhō period, 1716–1735], samurai are forced to live in
castle towns in discharge of their duties. Living away from home, in a manner
similar to travelers seeking lodging, requires cash for sustenance. They must sell
rice [the stipends that they receive from their lord] for cash, and purchase their
daily needs from merchants. In this way, merchants become masters while samurai are relegated to the position of customers, unable to determine prices fixed on
different commodities. In olden days when samurai lived on their own lands,
they had no need to sell their rice. Merchants came to buy rice, and under such
circumstances, samurai remained masters and the merchants their customers.
Prices of different commodities were dictated by the samurai class. This is the
law that was established by the ancient sage [i.e., Confucius] in his infinite
wisdom. It must remain inviolable through the ages. One recommendation I have
is to charge an exorbitantly high price for the rice and force the merchants to eat
grains other than rice.

19 **On Being a Good Merchant, 1726–1733**[24]   In Edo, some merchants
take on building for the government or other speculative ventures and make a
fortune at one mighty bound, but they only go to prove the common adage
that "he who lives by the river drowns in the river." It is like a gambler's

---

[23]Ogyū Sorai, *Seidan* (On Politics) as quoted in Kasahara Kazuo et al., *Seisen Nihonshi
Shiryōshū (Selected Documents on Japanese History)*, rev. ed., (Tokyo: Yamagawa
Shuppansha, 1970), p. 127.

[24]Adapted from E.S. Crawcour, "Some Observations on Merchants: A Translation of
Mitsui Takafusa's *Chōnin Kōken Roku*," in *TASJ*, 3rd Ser., Vol. 8 (1962), pp. 114–122.

money, which, as everyone knows, finally is lost in the way in which it was made.

. . . In business bargaining, you should concentrate on following the opportunities of the times, and in observing the times, you should consider how they might change. If you do not give some thought to your business from time to time . . . your shop's business finally will fall off, and you will lose a good patrimony. Never waste your attention on matters which have nothing to do with your work. Merchants who ape samurai or think that Shintō, Confucianism, or Buddhism will preserve their inner hearts will find that they will only ruin their houses if they become too deeply engrossed in them. . . . Remember that it is the family business which must not be neglected for a moment.

In this connection, there was a man in Edo called Fushimiya Shirōbei. His father was a timber merchant who made the most of his opportunities. When Shirōbei took over, he was very much the type who has to keep up with the neighbors and was extremely fond of ostentation. . . .

Later, Shirōbei sought permission for an exchange of goods at Nagasaki to the value of five thousand *kamme*.[25] His request was granted on payment of a contribution, and he proceeded down to Nagasaki for two years. He distributed large sums to the people of that place and to local temples and shrines. . . . However, just when he was astonishing everyone with his luxury, a petition was put in by Takagi Hikoemon, a town elder of Nagasaki, offering a bigger contribution than that paid by Fushimiya. As a result, Fushimiya had his license revoked, and Takagi got the concession. Shirōbei's position was therefore hopeless, and after twenty years he eventually ran out of food and died of starvation.

Now Takagi Hikoemon applied for permission to wear swords on the grounds that the above activity was on behalf of the government and took charge of government ships at Nagasaki, making a display of his authority. . . . With the little authority that he had, he despised local people, and as a result the servants who were his retainers learned from their superiors, as they say, and thus, through a brawl [with a low-ranking samurai of Lord X, a retainer of Lord Nabeshima] started in the action of a few attendants, Takagi's house perished.

Again, a merchant called Ishikawa Rokubei, of Obune-*chō*, Edo, who started off in the brokerage business, had a wife who was extraordinarily extravagant and went to the limit in finery. Retribution finally caught up with them. Along the route of the valiant Shōgun Tsunayoshi's first progress to Ueno, when this Rokubei's wife and her servants were watching in their ornamental dresses, the valiant *shōgun*, thinking that she was the wife of a *daimyō* or of some family of high rank, graciously had his aides make inquiries and was told that she was the wife of that fellow. After he had returned to the palace. Rokubei and his wife were summoned to the office of the town magistrate. It was considered that their extravagance was beyond their station and particularly their lack of respect for

---

[25]Of silver by weight. One *kamme* of silver weighed 10.05 pounds (troy) or 3.76 kilograms.

their superiors was outrageous. Their family property was forfeited, and, by the *shōgun*'s mercy, they got off with banishment from Edo. As they say, a curse always falls on the house where the hen does the crowing. . . .

Isoda, Iguchi, Ishiuchi, Horiuchi, Higuchi, the Fushimiya crowd, Kurata and Kinokuniya, merchants famous in Edo at that time, have all crashed or, if still carrying on, might as well not be. Merchants always have been in the position of having no fixed stipends, and so they grow rich through having a time of good fortune. However much wealth their children inherit, it is as though they were, thanks to their fathers' labors, holding in trust for a time money which is common currency. Thus, when the trustees fail to look after it properly, it immediately is dispersed.

In recent years, after their families die, young persons seclude themselves on the pretext of illness and behave as though in retirement. As they give themselves over to idleness, their behavior naturally deteriorates. Having no regard for reputation or appearances, they lose their sense of responsibility toward other people and carry on just as they please. By acting in this way, they start the decline of their families. They are not acting as human beings should. It is the law of nature that birds and beasts and in fact all things which dwell between heaven and earth—and, above all, human beings—should seek their sustenance by working at their callings. This being so, such behavior on the part of people far from being in their dotage displays ignorance of the will of heaven.

A Buddhist priest aims to spend his old age as head of a great temple and pass on his understanding of the Law to the congregation. *A fortiori*, anyone born a layman who prefers pleasures from an early age is doing nothing else but preferring hardships later. To make one's own house prosperous, to nurture one's family properly, to have a long life and to pass away with a clear conscience would be to be a living Buddha. On the other hand, to love pleasure when young, to have one's house decline in old age and not to be at ease at the end, is this not to go straight to eternal hell? . . . Everything changes in various ways, depending on where the heart is. Is it not true that things turn out as they do because people do not think highly of their calling or family?

A thing which is called good by people [need not be shared by the merchants]. When merchants become sages, their houses decline. In ruling the empire, there are the Way of the King and the Way of the Tyrant. Kings dislike fighting. They act not in their own interest but in the interests of the empire and the people. That is the Way of the King. Tyrants assume an outward appearance of benevolence but act in the interests of their families and themselves. That is the Way of the Tyrant. Realize that, from olden times, famous and clever generals have followed the Way of the Tyrant. To depart from benevolence for even a day is to be inhuman. On the other hand, however, to go too far in charity without counting the cost is stupid. You should understand this in a way which brings benefits in trade. It is, for example, the practice of benevolence for a commander to respect his officers and men. If in the future there should be further instances of the rise and fall of merchants, you should preserve them in these writings as instructive for later generations. . . .

20   Employees in a Commercial Establishment[26]   When a commercial establishment first hires a person, he is called a *detchi* (apprentice). . . . The large commercial establishments usually hire children from their branch houses (*bekke*), and call them *fudai kogai* (apprentices from branch families who are brought up in the master's house). If there are not enough children among the branch houses these establishments may hire from other families. They are also called *kogai* (apprentices brought up in the master's house). . . . When hiring children from branch houses, no surety certificate (*ukejō*) is required. However, when children are hired from other families, it is customary that the children's parents and relatives are required to submit surety certificates jointly signed by them. When hiring from other families, preference is given to those other than the first-born. This is so because the first-born will on attaining middle age assume responsibility for his own family's business, and he cannot be employed beyond that point. . . . People are hired when they are about ten years of age. Their tasks are almost exclusively to perform miscellaneous chores around the store. . . . As they become somewhat familiar with their tasks and grow a little older, they are sent out to run errands in the neighborhood. . . . As they reach the age of fifteen or sixteen, they are called one who has attained one-half manhood (*han-genbuku*), and are considered capable of assuming one-half of the responsibilities (*hannin-mae*) given to the clerks (*tedai*). They are allowed to shave their foreheads to give an angular look, and concurrently perform the tasks of handling cargos and money which are responsibilities of clerks (*tedai*), along with their normal tasks. . . .

Unless merchants rise up from the ranks of apprentices, their knowledge of the business cannot be enhanced. Therefore, those wealthy merchants who hire a large number of employees often choose to send their children to other families (establishments) to serve as apprentices. . . .

Those apprentices who are promoted from the position of assuming one-half of the responsibilities (*hannin-mae*) are called clerks (*tedai*). The clerks must be eighteen or nineteen years of age. However, during the three-year period immediately after their promotion, they are still asked to run the errands like their colleagues holding the position of *hannin-mae*. When apprentices are promoted to clerks, they must submit contracts countersigned jointly by their parents and relatives. The contract is required of everyone irrespective of his degree of intimacy with the master's house. Thereafter clerks must follow the manager's or

---

[26]Ōkubo, *op. cit.*, pp. 161–162.

head clerk's directions and engage in buying and selling commodities. They may also be permitted to make their own estimates in business transactions. If they fail, they may be reprimanded by the manager or head clerk, but they need not redeem the loss suffered as a result of their mistakes. . . . Some of them stay at the store front to engage in business transactions and meet customers. Others may do book-keeping, handle receipts and disbursements, or audit books. Still others may substitute for their master in his outside contacts, work diligently in public affairs, or engage in management of the kitchen. . . .

Anyone who is promoted from the rank of clerk is called manager (*shihainin*). He is the presiding officer of all business transactions of the store, and shoulders the gravest responsibility. The rise and fall of business fortunes of the master depend on his business acumen. . . . In the case of a large commercial establishment, there may be times when a branch house (*bekke*) is appointed above the manager to preside over all matters. Under such circumstances, the powers of a manager are greatly diminished, and are no different from those of the clerks. The term "branch house" was originally used to signify the final stage in the scale of promotion of employees who are permitted to commute to work from their own residences [instead of residing in the master's house]. Gradually the term became almost synonymous with a new position. Now, there are two kinds of branch families. One is the employee of a large commercial establishment. In this case, not only the person involved but also his heirs will continue to serve the master's house. While they serve their master's house, they will always follow the directions given by the master's house, including matters relating to their personal courses of action. . . . Another one refers to the employee of a medium-size business establishment. This type of employee, after going through the ladder of promotion as described earlier, is permitted to establish a branch house and receives the needed capital to start his own business. He does not again serve in his master's house. However, neither he nor his heirs will ever be allowed to forget the master-servant relations, and will continue to use the master's sign-curtain (*noren*) at their store front. These types of stores are called stores originating from one main store. In accordance with the regulations established by their association (*nakama*), some of the stores are allowed to engage in a similar type of business as that of the master and others are not. If a *bekke* opens a similar type of store as that of his master, he is enjoined from trading with his master's customers. He is often asked to join an association of his fellow traders. There are different regulations governing the act of joining an association. In general, a person must have served at least twenty years under his master, counting from the day he became an apprentice. He is then permitted to establish his branch house. And only after a proper recommendation is submitted by his master will he be able to engage in the same type of trade.

21 Organization of Tokumi Doiya, 1792[27]

From bygone times it was known as the Tokumi Doiya, and, according to the line of trade, names, or any changes of names, and seal and other alterations in the respective interests were reported to the town elders' office, which method is still practiced, and the membership runs up to a large number. The incentive to the organization of the guild was the nefarious actions of the seamen in taking advantage of any damage incurred and feigning to have met with accidents, so that unexpected losses were met by the merchants throughout the places served by the ships in question. Finally, during the Genroku era, these ships were chartered or built by the *toiya*, and when any consignments were made every means were taken toward safe transit in order to prevent loss. Members of the Tokumi Doiya who engaged in commerce on a large scale in the past have been summoned and ordered to tender a full list of names, but owing to the length of time which has elapsed since the last report was made, many changes have not been registered, so that the list will not serve today. In order to bring matters up-to-date, I hereby present the latest census of the Tokumi Doiya and its subsidiary associations:

Torimachi Toiya Guild,[23] 15 members. Silk piece goods, cotton goods, floss silk, ginned cotton, cutlery, lacquered wares, coarse wares, candles, foreign fancy goods.

Torimachi Subsidiary Guild (Shita-gumi).

Maruaikumi, 24 members. Coarse goods, fancy goods, lacquered wares, dye-stuffs, ironmongery, swords.

N.B.—These names have not as yet been reported.

Drug and Chemical Toiya, 25 members (of which 7 are inactive and 18 now in existence).

Omote-mise Toiya Guild, 12 members (of which 6 are inactive and 6 in existence). Tatami covers, green cloth, and mosquito netting.

Uchi-mise Toiya Guild, 10 members. Silk-piece goods, cotton goods, fancy goods, assorted ginned cotton, cutlery, candles.

Uchi-mise Guild's Subsidiary Association.

Kaya-chō Guild, 4 members. Dolls, toys, decoration swords, painted paper-lanterns, *bon*-festival lanterns.

Lacquer-ware Guild, 12 members. All kinds of lacquered wares.

Sake Guild, 45 members. Imported *sake*, vinegar, soy.

Nail and Ironmonger Guild, 14 members. Nails, iron, copper articles.

Paper Toiya, 9 members (of which 2 are inactive and 7 in existence). All kinds of paper, candles, parasols, dried bonito, vermicelli.

Ginned Cotton Toiya, 4 members.

---

[27]Takekoshi, *op. cit.*, pp. 512–513.
[28]The term "guild" stands for the Japanese word *kumi* or *gumi*, meaning an association.

N.B.—These suspended their trade a few years ago, but if taken up again, it must be so reported.

Kashi Toiya Guild, 22 members. Liquid oils.

Kashi Subsidiary Guild.

Cotton Dealers' Guild, 5 members. Ginned cotton.

Paper Dealers' Guild, Paper and candles.

Horidome Guild, 26 members (of which 15 are inactive and 11 in existence). Tatami covers, coarse goods.

Drug Stores, 33 members (of which 15 are inactive and 18 in existence). Drugs, chemicals, sugar, paints, incense, dyes.

Shimbori Guild, 12 members. Candles, paper, vermicelli, incense, dried bonito, edible seaweed, parasols, fern-rope, tatami covers, green cloth, hemp, taro, sail cloth, nets, locks.

Sumiyoshi Guild, 14 members (of which 4 are inactive and 10 in existence). Paper, coarse goods, candles.

Oil Dealers, 47 members (of which 3 are inactive and 44 in existence). Liquid oils.

Sanbam Guild, 4 members. Paper.

Rice-Bran Guild, 18 members (of which 4 are inactive and 14 in existence). Imported rice-bran.

Dried Articles Guild, 11 members. Dried articles.

Porcelain and Earthenware Guild, 32 members. Porcelain and earthenwares.

The above *toiya* are not new guilds lately organized, but have been in existence for some time, and their names have been registered at my office. . . .

Taru Yozaemon (Town Elder of Edo).

22   An Appeal to the Town Commissioners by Tokumi Doiya, 1803[29]

We meekly beg to submit our cause in writing. On behalf of the merchants and *toiya* of the Tokumi residing in your territory we beg to present our cause. That we have been treated with favor and benevolence since our immigration to these parts, being permitted to carry on our trade to this day, is true; this we respectfully acknowledge as a blessing, and for it we tender our humble gratitude. The aforementioned *toiya*, known as the Tokumi, the kinds of commodities handled and the numbers are as certified in the books herewith separately annexed.

The said members of the Tokumi engaged in the export of various commodities from the Kamigata Provinces (the Kyoto-Osaka region) loaded and discharged the same through the Higaki vessels from the beginning in order to ensure full supply on your domain. Previously those who were not members of the Tokumi Doiya were unable to import directly from the Kamigata area, but

---

[29]*Ibid.*, pp. 518–519.

lately parties not members of the Tokumi are able without any restraint to import directly from Kamigata just as well as the Tokumi Doiya, so that many are guilty of such violations of the regulations established by the Tokumi. And although we have deliberated on the matter, nothing could be done owing to the size of the territory, and the situation was left to take its own course to this day. As long as the non-*toiya* members traded in lines not handled by the Tokumi, matters ran smoothly, not necessitating any negotiations. However, the growing influence of these merchants and the increase in their number are of great concern to the Tokumi Doiya. If their activities are not checked, many members of the Tokumi may be forced to leave the guild. Although the members of the Tokumi Doiya have frequently discussed the proposition, it is impossible to regulate affairs when many of those engaged in direct import from Osaka do not become members of the guild. Moreover, even if inferior goods are imported there are not means of investigation or prohibiting the practice, to which we humbly call your Honors' attention. If the guild is to be dissolved, all goods imported thereafter will be of different grades, and supervision of importation cannot be made as heretofore; at the same time the random influx of goods will upset the market supply, which naturally will react upon the financial condition of the territory. The number of members of the Tokumi Doiya has in late years decreased, and no one will have any inclination to join if things are left as they are now. Moreover, when an organization in existence for years is allowed to fall, difficulties will naturally arise. . . . Therefore, since the case stands as explained, it is necessary to force the non-members to join the Tokumi Doiya to form a single organized unit. This would be, to our minds, the most convenient means of control. Further, those engaged in direct import, besides the Tokumi Doiya, should be included in one guild or another according to the line of business, and those in the suburbs engaged in direct import should be turned over to the traders in the city. These measures will insure continued existence of the Tokumi Doiya. . . . Although the nature of the Tokumi is one body and a unit, its field of activities covers a large variety of goods, and we endeavor to keep the markets of the city fully supplied. Therefore, if such transactions are also freely entered into by parties outside the organization, no order could be maintained, and, although we desire to attract such traders into the Tokumi, yet it is impossible within the limits of our powers. Such a state of affairs if left to its natural course will plainly dissolve the Tokumi Doiya, so that there is no way but to appeal for succor. We trust you will heed our pleas and lend your authority to restrict the transactions with the Kamigata to the Tokumi, which would be an act of deep benevolence and be greatly appreciated by the members of the Tokumi Doiya.

Third year of Kyowa [1803], fifth month, 17th day.

MANAGING THE ECONOMY

In 1757, devastated by floods and earthquakes, the Matsushiro han (located in the present-day Nagano prefecture) suffered its worst financial crisis. Its samu-

rai received only one half of their stipends, corruption was rampant, and tax payments were in serious arrears. Given full power by the daimyō *to restructure the* han *finance, Onda Moku (1717–1762) took the unprecedented step of consulting everyone whose lives would be affected by his reform measures. As seen in Documents 4 through 9, peasants were considered merely a means of obtaining tax revenue. They suffered the Ricardoian poverty, and their opinion mattered little to their rulers. The same documents show a tradition of arbitrariness, with officials disregarding almost totally the welfare of the people they governed. In contrast, Onda showed a refreshingly new approach. He instinctively knew that he needed the active cooperation of* han *officials and of the peasantry. In consulting with them and giving them something in return, he was engaged in* nemawashi *(touching base with those who are affected), one of the most cherished principles of Japanese management. Document 23 comes from his* Higurashi Suzuri, *a memoir in the style of occasional essays containing basic Confucian precepts.*

*Corporate philosophy, another pillar of modern Japanese management, is not a contemporary invention. One of its earliest examples can be found in the founder's precepts of the Sumitomo family completed around 1650 (Document 24). In a modified form, they still serve as the basic tenets for the Sumitomo group which is one of the largest Japanese corporate groupings (*keiretsu*) with enterprises in as diverse fields as coal and non-ferrous metal, mining and manufacture of iron and steel, machinery, electrical and communications equipment, chemical products, ceramics, real estate, finance and insurance and commerce. The common origin of this group is the medicine and book shop opened in Kyoto around 1630 by Masatomo (1585–1652), the first head of the Sumitomo family. Masatomo's precepts, written as admonitions, were given to members of his "household" which meant not just blood relatives but also employees. His precepts were later incorporated in the Sumitomo family code and in its "business principles." These principles, rewritten in 1928, remain the basic principles governing and binding all Sumitomo affiliates today. For the sake of comparison, they are concurrently reproduced below.*

23   **Restructuring Han Finance, 1757**[30]   Onda called all the clan officials together and said that although payments of stipends had been in arrears or had sometimes failed entirely he intended to see that they were paid accurately in the future. In return he instituted a system of sure rewards and certain penalties. He then ordered village headmen, rich farmers, and police officials to gather and to bring with them people who could speak their minds well and clearly. On the appointed day, Onda said as follows:

---

[30]From *Higurashi Suzuri* as translated in Isaiah Ben-Dasan, *The Japanese and the Jews* (New York and Tokyo: Weatherhill, 1972), translated by Richard L. Gage, pp. 78–85.

"I realize that because of the lord's financial predicament many of you have been caused a great deal of trouble. It may well be that in the future, as I attempt to fulfill my role as financial controller, you will be caused still further trouble, and for that I am sorry. But first of all I promise to propose nothing that is impossible; once I have made a statement I will not alter it. . . . Further, unless you and I discuss all matters openly with each other, it will be impossible to put the clan's financial situation in order. Since I cannot succeed by myself, I ask that all of you talk everything over with me freely. . . .

"Next, not only on auspicious occasions but also at all other times, I will allow no sending of gifts, no matter how inexpensive. I will not term such gifts bribes, since that would create difficulties for everyone. . . .

"In the future I intend to hear everyone's requests and pleas; therefore, there is no need to send bribes to anyone. This goes for all officials as well as for the farmers.

"The next point concerns tax collection. In the past one hundred from each one thousand available foot soldiers have been kept in the castle for various jobs. Each month the remaining nine hundred were sent to the villages to collect tribute rice. But from now on this practice will cease. . . .

"Although it is difficult to predict the distant future, I intend to fill this office for five years. During that time, I will levy no demands on you for regional construction or for various duties in the castle. . . .

[After discussing incidents of advances farmers were forced to pay on their taxes, loans forced on farmers and merchants by the *han*, and non-payment of taxes:]

"Be informed that all unpaid taxes to this point are forgiven. But anyone who fails to pay this year's tributes, though he be stark naked with poverty, will face a punishment worse than death. . . .

"Although we should like to return the advances and the advances on advances that some of you have paid, we lack the funds to do so. Furthermore, as you have heard, we intend to forgive all taxes in arrears to this point. Therefore, I request that all of you who have paid advances accept the loss. . . .

"I want you to return to your villages and tell the other farmers what I have said. All of you must deliberate on the question together before an answer. If you fail to agree, I must commit suicide (*seppuku*). Remember that the things I request are these: all advances paid to the present must be written off as losses in favor of the clan, and everyone must pay this year's tax rice without fail. There are some things to take into consideration, however, that make the picture brighter than you might think. . . . Do not forget that all bribes that were customarily paid in the past have been forbidden. This alone will save the villages about 100 *koku* of rice a year. The foot soldiers who formerly made monthly trips to collect taxes will no longer be lodged in your house. This means great savings in the housing and food that you provided. Furthermore, you will no longer be forced to supply people and funds for duties and services to officials. All the savings the elimination of these burdens bring to the farmers will amount to about seventy percent of this year's tax assessment. In addition, starting now I should like to put tribute taxes for the Yamashiro clan on a monthly installment basis.

"To those who lent money to the clan, we should like to return what we owe; but we do not have the funds at present. It may be that some of your children or grandchildren will find themselves in financial troubles or in hard times in the future. We should like to pay the money back to them when it becomes needed, but we will be unable to pay interest. All we can return is the principal. . . ."

He then said if any of them had been injured or harmed in any way during the past period of bad political administration they might unhesitatingly write down their complaints, which they might present after sealing them well. . . .

24 Sumitomo's Corporate Philosophy, c. 1630 and 1928[31]

(a) Founder's Precepts (c. 1630)

As in business, likewise in all other things, exercise prudence in all respects.

1. Do not purchase an article offered below the prevailing market price, whatever it is, without knowing its origin. Regard such an article as stolen.

2. Do not give even one night's lodging to anyone, or accept in custody a property of another, not even a (simple) braided hat.

3. Do not act as a guarantor for another.

4. Do not sell anything on credit.

5. Do not become angry and speak intemperately and harshly, whatever the other party says. Whatever the subject, speak patiently, over and over again.

(b) Sumitomo's Business Principles (1928)

1. Sumitomo shall achieve strength and prosperity by placing prime importance on integrity and sound management in the conduct of its business.

2. Sumitomo shall manage its activities with foresight and flexibility in order to cope effectively with the changing times. Under no circumstances, however, shall it pursue easy gains or act imprudently.

COMMERCE AS A CALLING

The prosperity experienced in the Tokugawa period was accompanied by the rise of the merchant class. Once placed at the bottom of the ladder in the four-class system, and scorned by the Confucianists as lesser men who were interested only in profit, the merchants acquired new self-confidence as their wealth and power grew. With it there were also attempts to redefine their role in society and justify the acquisition of profit.

---

[31]Courtesy of Mr. Sumitomo Yoshiteru and the Sumitomo Corporation.

Document 25 is taken from a Jodo Shinshū (True Pure Land Sect) tract which links commercial activities with Bodhisattva deeds. It was a clear departure from the traditional Buddhist view that termed greed as a cardinal sin and profit seeking as leading to a sure path of destruction. The Shin sect was most prevalent in the Ōmi region (the present-day Shiga prefecture). It was no accident that, along with the Ise region, Ōmi produced more successful merchants and entrepreneurs than the rest of the country in the early Tokugawa period, the same period when this tract was written.

Ishida Baigan (1685–1744) was born in a farm family, and as a young man served as an apprentice under a Kyoto merchant by the name of Kuroyanagi. His experience taught him the importance of frugality, honesty, and other basic values commonly associated with work ethic. He was convinced that merchants were also men, equal in standing in their ability to contribute to society as people from other walks of life. In 1722, he started a school in Kyoto to start propagating his views. This school was known as Sekimon Shingaku, or Shingaku for short. In his lifetime, the number of students did not exceed 400, but in the nineteenth century, it became one of the dominant schools of thought that had a significant impact on commercial practices. Many house codes written in the Tokugawa period show a distinct influence of Shingaku in their adherence to its ethical values. Document 26 is taken from Baigan's Tohimondo, *or Conversation between Town and Countryside (1739).*[32]

25   Just Profit and Bodhisattva Deeds[33]

In merchandising we receive remuneration for supplying the consumer with manufactured goods. The artisans receive their remuneration by producing the goods and supplying them to the consumer. What the world calls this remuneration is profit. But the basis of receiving this profit depends on profiting others. Thus both the business of merchants and of artisans is the profiting of others. By profiting others they receive the right to profit themselves. This is the virtue of the harmony of *jiri-rita* (profiting self while profiting others). The spirit of profiting others is the Bodhisattva spirit. Having a Bodhisattva spirit and saving all beings, this is called Bodhisattva deeds. Thus Bodhisattva deeds are just the deeds of mer-

---

[32]You may wish to compare Baigan's word *Shokubun* and Luther's word *Beruf.* Both of these words can be translated into English as "calling." See Robert Bellah, *Tokugawa Religion: The Values of Pre-Industrial Japan* (New York: Free Press, 1957), pp. 115, 123, 125, 164.

[33]From Naitō Kanji: *"Shūkyō to Keizai Rinri"* (Religion and the Economic Ethic, Jōdo Shinshū and the Ōmi Merchants). *Shakaigaku* (Sociology), Vol. 8, pp. 243–286, Tokyo 1941, as translated and cited in Bellah, *ibid.,* p. 120. Reprinted with the permission of the Free Press, a division of Simon & Schuster from TOKUGAWA RELIGION: The Values of Pre-industrial Japan by Robert Bellah. Copyright © 1957 by The Free Press. Copyright © by Robert N. Bellah 1984 Trust.

chants and artisans. In general the secret of merchants' and artisans' business lies in obtaining confidence through Bodhisattva deeds.

26   The Role of the Merchants, 1739[34]   If there were no trade, the buyer

would have nothing to buy and the seller could not sell. If it were thus, the merchants would have no livelihood and would become farmers and artisans. If the merchants all became farmers and artisans, there would be no one to circulate wealth and all the people would suffer. The samurai, farmers, artisans, and merchants are of assistance in governing the empire. If the four classes were lacking, there would be no assistance. The governing of the four classes is the role of the ruler. Assisting the ruler is the role of the four classes. The samurai is the retainer (*shin*) who has rank from old. The farmer is the retainer of the countryside. The merchant and artisan are retainers of the town. To assist the ruler, as retainers, is the Way of the retainer. The trade of the merchants assists the empire. The payment of the price is the stipend (*roku*) of the artisan. Giving the harvest to the farmer is like the stipend of the samurai. Without the output of all the classes of the empire, how could it stand? The profit of the merchant too is a stipend permitted by the empire. To call this, which is only the profit of your own trade, greedy and immoral is to hate the merchants and wish for their destruction. Why hate and despise only the merchants? As for your saying not to give a profit for trade, if one pays and deducts the profit it will destroy the laws of the empire. As business is ordered from above, profit is received. Thus the profit of the merchant is like a permitted stipend.

. . . As for the Way of the samurai also, if he does not receive a stipend, he is not fit for service. If one calls receiving a stipend from one's lord "greedy" and "immoral," then from Confucius and Mencius on down there is not a man who knows the Way. What sort of thing is it to say, leaving samurai, farmers, and artisans aside, that the merchants' receiving a stipend is "greed" and that they cannot know the Way?

---

[34]From *Tohimondō* as translated and cited in Bellah, *Ibid.*, p. 158.

CHAPTER IX

Intellectual Currents in Tokugawa Japan

Intellectually and institutionally, the Tokugawa period was the most vigorous of Japan's historical eras. It was deeply steeped in contrast and variation. On the one hand, there were Confucian scholars who did not hesitate to call themselves "eastern barbarians" and did not hide their adulation for the country of the "Sage," China. On the other hand, there were *kokugaku* (national learning) scholars who reveled in their ethnocentrism. Some avidly studied Western scientific methods, while others found inspiration in the textual criticism of Confucian or Japanese classics.

Neo-Confucianism as propagated by Zhu Xi (1130–1200, in Japanese, Shushi) of Song China became the most influential doctrine in shaping the thought and behavior of the Japanese people. This was in part due to the state sanction and encouragement given to its teachings. Tokugawa Ieyasu and his successors found its ideal of orderly submission to the authorities well suited to the *bakufu*'s desire to maintain a stable political and social order. Its ethical code gave jurisdiction to the theory of the four classes, and likened the samurai-administrators of Japan to the scholar-gentry class of China. In a sense, Tokugawa Japan was far closer to China in political outlook than any other period of Japanese history. In spite of its *han*-system, which was a formal feudal structure, the Tokugawa *bakufu* was far more centralized and exercised a larger degree of control over the entire country. Thus Confucianism, which flourished side by side with China's imperial system—which was highly centralized—could find fertile soil for growth in Tokugawa Japan.

However, official sanction alone cannot explain the strength exhibited by Neo-Confucianism. Its acceptance came also in part because of its rationalism, humanism and pragmatism. A favorite text of the Neo-Confucianists was "the investigation of things," taken from the *Great Learning (Daxue)*. The text taught the Japanese to look into the laws of human society and to take interest in natural phenomena. Zhu Xi's emphasis on basic human relationships, such as the Five Constant Virtues (see Document 1), gave the basis for formulating a secular society. And within this otherwise rigid legal and ethical structure, Confucianism also found a way to temper justice with mercy (see Document 7).

The Confucian orthodoxy in Tokugawa Japan was vigorously promoted by Hayashi Razan (1583–1657) who became an advisor to Ieyasu in 1608. In 1630 he established a private school in Ueno, Edo, which later became the official *bakufu* school by the name of Shōheikō. Initially only the *bakufu* samurai were admitted as its students, but later samurai from the *han* and commoners were also admitted. This example set by the *bakufu* to encourage learning was emulated by many *han* administrations in founding their own *han* schools in later years. Various *shōgun* and *daimyō* also became patrons of important Confucian scholars.

The establishment of the neo-Confucian orthodoxy of the Zhu Xi school did not deter the founding of other schools. There were among others, the Ōyōmei (Wang Yangming) school (Document 3) and the ancient learning (*kogaku*) school (Document 4), the latter resembling the Han learning school in Qing China. Even though there were proscriptions, the official attitude was altogether benign toward the heterodox schools. The rise of the *chōnin* class further spread the popularization of learning, which was represented by Ishida Baigan's (1685–1744) *shingaku* (study of the mind) and the education of the masses.

With the existence of the Zhu Xi, Wang Yangming and other schools, Tokugawa Japan resembled the neighboring Qing in the diversity of Confucian thought. However, unlike China, official Confucianism was not wedded to the civil service examination, and was thus relatively free from that stratifying influence. Confucian scholars advocated the use of men of talent, which was often implemented under the multi-*han* system, through the practice of delegation of power, and at times through the system of adoption.

The Confucian scholars were keenly aware of being Japanese, and there was a strong tendency to make the universalistic doctrine of Confucianism fit the particularistic needs of Japan. This trend was begun with Hayashi Razan, the first head of the University. In a similar vein Confucianism could give direction to the nationalistic tendencies, as witnessed in the compilation of the *Dainihonshi* (History of Great Japan), by the house of Mito.

The particularism and nationalism of these Confucian scholars were shared by the *kokugaku* scholars. In addition, they also shared the rationalistic approaches of the Confucianists in their study of Japanese classics. This was so in spite of their proclivity toward favoring the Shintō myths, and of their unnecessary glorification of Japan's past. The *kokugaku* scholars also provided a rallying point for the imperial restoration, by articulating the supremacy and legitimacy of the imperial line. Theirs could also become a voice of egalitarianism in that they suggested that under the emperor there was no distinction among the four classes (Documents 11 and 12).

Rationalism and the spirit of scientific investigation can be freely discerned in the examples set by the scholars of the Dutch studies (Document 10). Altogether, the Tokugawa era was a vibrant age, providing a springboard for Japan's modernization.

VARIETY OF TOKUGAWA CONFUCIANISM

Reproduced below are sample writings of Hayashi Razan (Documents 1 and 2), Nakae Tōju (Document 3) and Itō Jinsai (Document 4), representing the official Zhu Xi school, Ōyōmei (Wang Yangming) school, and ancient learning (kogaku) school, respectively. They attest both to the variety and vitality of Tokugawa thought.

Hayashi Razan was an advisor on education and foreign affairs to Tokugawa Ieyasu, and was responsible for drafting many of Ieyasu's laws and injunctions (Document 1, excerpted from several of his writings, shows the use of Confucian precepts to justify the authority of the Tokugawa bakufu *and the social order dictated by it). In his quest to make Confucianism the official doctrine, Razan sought Shintō as his natural ally against the more pervasive Buddhism. This is shown in Document 2. Incidentally, the work begun by Razan was continued by his heirs, and successive generations of the Hayashi family served the* bakufu *as* Daigakunokami *(Head of the University).*

Nakae Tōju (1608–1648) first studied Zhu Xi's teachings but at the age of thirty-seven turned to the teachings of Wang Yangming (1472–1529). Of special appeal to Nakae were Wang's notions of extending one's intuitive knowledge (ryōchi, or in Chinese, liang zhi) and of unity of knowledge and action.

Itō Jinsai (1627–1705) also studied Zhu Xi, but realized that Zhu Xi taught in Song China, hundreds of years apart from the time of Confucius. He thus started a school that advocated faithful study of the original texts of the Analects *and* Mencius.

1 **Natural Order and Social Order**[1] The Principle (*ri*, or in Chinese *li*) which existed constantly before and after heaven and earth came into being is called the Supreme Ultimate (*taikyoku*, Ch. *taiji*). When this Supreme Ultimate was in motion, it created the yang, and when it was quiescent, it created the

---

[1]As quoted in Hori Isao, *Hayashi Razan* (Tokyo: Yoshikawa Kōbunkan, 1964), pp. 249–251.

yin.[2] The *yin* and *yang* were originally of the same substance (*ki*, Ch. *qi*) but were divided into two complementary forces. They were further divided into the Five Elements (*go-gyō*, Ch. *wu xing*) which are wood, fire, earth, metal and water. When the Five Elements were further divided, they became all things under heaven. When these Five Elements were brought together to take shapes, people were also born.

All creatures existing between heaven and earth were shaped by the Five Elements. However, because of the difference in the Ether (*ki* Ch. *qi*), there emerged plants, animals and men. . . .

A concrete object comes into being because of the work of heaven and earth. All creatures, plants, animals and inanimate objects owe their existence to the will of heaven and earth. Thus not a single object lacks within it the principles of heaven. . . .

Therefore the Five Constant Virtues (*go-jō*, Ch. *wu chang*) of human-hearted-ness (*jin*, Ch. *ren*), righteousness (*gi*, Ch. *yi*), propriety (*rei*, Ch. *li*), wisdom (*chi*, Ch. *zhi*), and good faith (*shin*, Ch. *xin*) are given by heaven and exist on account of the principles of heaven. . . .

The five relationships governing the ruler and the subject, father and son, husband and wife, older brother and younger brother, and friend and friend have been in existence from olden days to the present time. There has been no change in these basic relations, and they are thus called the supreme way. In judging the worth of a person, one needs only to use these five relationships as the criteria, and teachings which try to implement the ideals of these five relationships are those of the sage and of the wise men. . . .

Heaven is above and earth is below. This is the order of heaven and earth. If we can understand the meaning of the order existing between heaven and earth, we can also perceive that in everything there is an order separating those who are above and those who are below. When we extend this understanding between heaven and earth, we cannot allow disorder in the relations between the ruler and the subject, and between those who are above and those who are below. The separation into four classes of samurai, farmers, artisans and merchants, like the five relationships, is part of the principles of heaven and is the Way which was taught by the Sage (Confucius). . . .

To know the way of heaven is to respect heaven and to secure humble submission from earth, for heaven is high above and earth is low below. There is a differentiation between the above and the below. Likewise among the people, rulers are to be respected and subjects are to submit humbly. Only

---

[2]The Chinese *yin-yang* theory conceives of the *yang* and *yin* as two opposite mutually complementary forces. The *yang* represents activity, masculinity, etc., while the *yin* represents passivity, femininity, etc. All natural phenomena result from the interplay of these two forces.

when this differentiation between those who are above and those who are below is made clear can there be law and propriety. In this way, people's minds can be satisfied. . . . The more the rulers are respected, and the more the subjects submit humbly, and the more the differentiation is made clear-cut, the easier it is to govern a country. Among the rulers, there are the Emperor, the *shōgun*, and the *daimyō*, and even among them there is also differentiation. . . .

2 **On the Unity of Shintō and Confucianism**[3] Our country is the country of gods. Shintō is the same as the Way of the King (*ōdō*). However, the rise of Buddhism made the people abandon the Way of the King and Shintō. Someone may ask how Shintō and Confucianism can be differentiated. I respond by saying that according to my observation the Principle (*ri*) is the same, but only its application differs. . . .

In comparing the books on the age of gods in the *Nihon Shoki* (Chronicles of Japan) with Master Zhou's (Zhou Dunyi, 1017–1073) *Taiji tushuo* (Diagram of the Supreme Ultimate Explained), I have yet to find any discrepancy in substantive matters. The Way of the King transforms itself into Shintō and Shintō transforms itself into the Way. What I mean by the term "Way" is the Way of Confucianism, and it is not the so-called alien doctrine. The alien doctrine is Buddhism.

3 **Nakae Tōju on Filial Piety**[4] Filial piety is the root of man. When it is extinguished from one's mind, his life becomes like a rootless plant, and only sheer luck prevents him from dying instantly. At that time our intuitive knowledge (*ryōchi*) provides a plateau of peace and security (*anshin ritsumei no chi*) [by commanding us to practice filial piety]. Once we depart from this plateau, we all suffer hardships, and our body and the world surrounding it become nothing but an empty dream. Anyone who dislikes this fate and tries to avoid the empty dream by seeking his solution elsewhere [other than filial piety], is very much confused. . . .

Filial piety represents the *summa bonum* and essence of the Way in the three realms of heaven, earth, and man. What gives birth to heaven, to earth, to human existence, and to all things, is nothing but this filial piety. Those who study need to study only this. Where is filial piety then? It is to be found in one's own person. Without one's own person, there is no filial piety, and without filial piety

---

[3]From *Hayashi Razan Bunshū* as reproduced in Ōkubo Toshiaki et al., eds., *Shiryō ni yoru Nihon no Ayumi (Japanese History through Documents), Kinseihen (Early Modern Period)* (Tokyo: Yoshikawa Kōbunkan, 1955), p. 191.
[4]From *Tōju Sensei Zenshū* as quoted in Ōkubo, *op. cit.*, pp. 194–195.

there is no person who is able to practice the Way to illumine the world [literally, four seas] and to become one with the divine. . . .

Filial piety is the very divine essence of the Great Void (*taikyo*, or in Chinese, *tai xu*),[5] and is the factor which enables the Sages to communicate to others of the miraculous work. It is like the handiwork of the august father who is placed together with heaven. Center means to place filial piety in the center. Sincerity means to make [the practice of] filial piety sincere. Teaching means to teach filial piety. Studying means to study filial piety. Unless filial piety is placed in the center of all these endeavors, some of them can become heresy or vulgar learning, and the people engaged in them consigned to an ignoble position. Take heed of these warnings.

4 **Itō Jinsai's Daily Observance**[6]   Confucius is my teacher. Anyone who claims to be a student must have the Sage as his guide. He must not hastily follow the footsteps of later Confucian scholars who engage in obsessive hair-splitting arguments for an appropriate means of obtaining the Way. In the end, he accomplishes nothing. Students cannot add or subtract a single letter from the sayings of the Sage. This is so because the two books of the *Analects of Confucius* and *Mencius* contain all the definitive teachings of the Way (*dōri*) past and present and all under heaven. They penetrate everything above and below. Confucian scholars of Song quote words of Buddha and Laozi to explain the precepts of the Sages. I am deeply aware of their falsehood.

. . . When I teach my students, I instruct them to read carefully the *Analects* and *Mencius* and to concentrate their thoughts on them. If the intent and the writing style of the Sages become evident to the mind's eye, the meaning and the basic thought pattern of the two books can be discerned. Thereafter, the meaning of individual terms can be clearly understood, and no grave mistake is likely to ensue. In scholarship, investigation of the meaning of individual terms in itself is not significant. However, once the meaning of an individual term is lost, mistakes may frequently occur. Therefore always attempt to find the correct meaning of individual terms by basing your interpretation of the *Analects* and *Mencius*, and compare the end result with the intent and writing style of the two books. Do not go blindly or in circles in your interpretation by mixing in your own private views.

---

[5]A concept advanced by the Sung philosopher Zhang zai (1020–1077). It is pure, all pervasive, and has no image, and is the very essence of the universe and of Ether (*chi*) which when condensed, forms the concrete objects of the physical universe.

[6]The first paragraph comes from Itō Jinsai's *Dōshi-mon (Children's Questions)* as reproduced in Ōkubo, *op. cit.*, p. 196. The second paragraph comes from *Gomō Jigi (Meaning of Terms in the Analects and Mencius)* as quoted in Ishida Ichirō, *Itō Jinsai* (Tokyo: Yoshikawa Kōbunkan, 1960), p. 128.

CONFUCIANISM AND POLITICAL ACTION

Unlike their counterparts in Qing China who were preoccupied with ethical introspection and textual criticism, Japanese Confucianists found their best expression in the pragmatic, mundane and political matters. The following two selections represent their sense of political service.

Kumazawa Banzan (1619–1691) became a retainer of Ikeda Mitsumasa, daimyō *of the Okayama-han at the age of sixteen. He interrupted his service at age twenty to study under Nakae Tōju, but returned to Okayama at the age of twenty-seven. In 1650, he was made a* bangashira *(group chief or elder), and given a stipend of 3,000* koku, *which was an unprecedented sum for scholars. Under Ikeda's benign protection and Kumazawa's leadership, Okayama became the major center of the Ōyōmei school, which brought the enmity of bakufu officials, and of Hayashi Razan in particular. In 1657, Kumazawa retired from active service, and concentrated on teaching. In 1697 he submitted an opinion to Shōgun Tsunayoshi, who ordered his arrest.*

The Daigaku Wakumon *(Document 5) was written toward the end of Kumazawa's life somewhere between 1686 and 1691. Like other Confucianists he looked for the emergence of a sage king who would bring about an ideal society. However, unlike those who were of Zhu Xi's persuasion, he taught not blind obedience, but insisted that the king ought to be worthy of his name by practicing* jinsei *(benevolent rule), among other things.*

In the economic sphere, he sought a return to the autarkic, agrarian society. This ideal was shared by Ogyū Sorai.

Ogyū Sorai (1666–1728) conveyed a sense of crisis for the samurai class. His was an age in which merchants prospered and rapid social changes took place. He advocated the return of the samurai class to their lands (see Chapter 8, Document 18), control of the population and actualization of a stable society that would bring back the balance between the four classes of samurai, farmers, artisans and merchants. If one were to preserve the stability of the regime, he reasoned that it required recruitment of men of talent in the bakufu *administration. That part of his treatise from* Seidan *(Political Proposals) is given in Document 6.*

5 The Heaven-Appointed Duty of Subjects[7]

Question: What is the Heaven-appointed duty of subjects?

Answer: The Heaven-appointed duty of the subject is to help his lord exercise benevolent government (*jinsei*) by obeying the judgment and commands of his lord, or making up for his shortcomings. He should impute goodness to his

---

[7]Galen M. Fisher, tr., "Dai Gaku Wakumon by Kumazawa Banzan," in *TASJ*, 2nd Ser., Vol. 16 (1938), pp. 271–273.

lord and take mistakes upon his own head. He should not assume authority for himself, but impute all authority to his lord. The way of the subject is symbolized by the earth: it should not rise above humble submission. Let him not be turned aside by thought of personal advantage. But if his lord should sin, let him shrink not from correcting the lord at any cost, for thus shall submission be saved from slavery. The Heavenly Way stoops to serve, the earthly way obeys superiors. The interchange of thought between superior and inferior is the law of ruler and subject. . . . Therefore, as has been said: "Let the ruler revere the counsel of his subjects and distrust his own wisdom. A sagacious ruler is calm, deep and judicial, and his subjects dwell in tranquility by willing submission. The Heavenly Way shows its glory by a magnanimous attitude towards all."

Question: Is there any means of foreseeing the approach of national calamities, misfortunes or crises?

Answer: History, both ancient and modern, Chinese and Japanese, proves that a country is well ruled when free course is given to public sentiment, and ill-governed when the channels of public speech are blocked. If the ruler of a country is stupid, public sentiment will have free course, while his cleverness will impede its open expression. There is a passage in the *Book of Changes* in which the cleverness of a ruler is condemned as tending to a fussiness quite irritative to the popular mind. . . . A too great confidence by the ruler in his own cleverness will make him unwilling to listen to damaging remarks by the general public, and to remonstrances made by his ministers. When a ruler murders a counsellor, his domain is sure to be overthrown. It has been said that outspoken words from a counsellor may not be becoming in a subject but, they are a blessing to the country. . . .

When the cleverness of a ruler makes him exacting and closely critical of the failures of his people, he will punish them too severely. This is contrary to the Heavenly Way, which guides the people by righteousness and mercy, rather than by threatening and punishment. When the government of a nation has gone astray, Heaven will chastise it through calamities. If storms and floods do not cause the government to mend its ways, Heaven will strike terror in the people's hearts by still greater disasters. Ruin will come at last if these two visitations are not sufficient to check the downward course. With gracious love toward the ruler, the Heavenly Way will make use of these means to prevent the final catastrophe. Rewards and punishments are negative in their nature, a form of necessary evil, while the principles of propriety and music are positive means of guiding the people. It is the Way of the King (ōdō) to praise the upright with magnanimity and let the perverse go unpunished, depending on their sense of shame to bring about amendment.

Question: If brilliance of mind forms the greatest virtue of a ruler, why is the cleverness resulting from it to be repressed?

Answer: Although a ruler may have a brilliant and virtuous mind, it may not enable him to discover the evildoings of his people, but it will enable him to conceal his own knowledge, to use the knowledge and welcome the remonstrances and warnings of his people. By such true wisdom will a ruler gain a happy, contented mind, establish peace in his realm, and leave a good name behind him. Hence the way of the ruler should be patterned after Heaven; that is, he should not be too severe or headstrong, nor dazzle with his dignity, nor be too harsh in punishing his subjects. Rather, he should be self-controlled and open in counsel, kindly in relations with his subjects, and tempering his knowledge with mercy.

6 **Proposal for Employing Men of Talent**[8] It is a general and lasting principle of the natural order that old things should pass away and new things be brought into existence. Everything between heaven and earth is subject to it, and no matter how much one may wish to preserve what is old, it is not within our power to do so. Trees fall into decay, crop succeeds crop every year, men grow old and die and young men take their places—all this happens in accordance with the principle of the natural order by which that which is below rises step by step to a superior position and, when it has reached its zenith, falls into decay and is in turn replaced from below.

Such are the principles of the *Changes*. But in the matter of government it is characteristic of human nature that the families of men who rendered services to the state in the past should be cherished and their succession assured as long as possible, and that within the family one should never entertain the idea of the early death of one's elders—one's great grandparents, grandparents, father or mother—but should pray that they may live forever. This means that there is a conflict between the principles of the natural order and the normal workings of human nature, for what is old must pass away, no matter how much we may wish to hold onto it. To conclude that it is best that all old things should be swept away at once is to carry wisdom to excess, and is not in accordance with the Way of the Sages. But merely to attempt to preserve what is old is to carry folly to excess and is also not in accordance with the Way of the Sages. The Way of the Sages treats human nature with respect and does not outrage men's feelings; its principles are consistent and clear, without any obscurities, and yet it does not consist in unthinking adherence to what is generally accepted—all these things are essential in ruling the people of a state.

Because of the principle in the natural order which I have mentioned, the descendants of Yao, Shun, Yü, T'ang and Wu have vanished without trace, and in Japan the descendants of Yoritomo and Takauji are now no more, while all the other famous families of that time have also become extinct. The ancestors of the present *daimyō* were men of insignificant social position who rose to power as a

[8]J. R. McEwan, *The Political Writings of Ogyū Sorai* (Cambridge: Cambridge University Press, 1962), pp. 77–83. Reprinted with the permission of Cambridge University Press.

result of their services in the field. Even so, *daimyō* living today who stand in the direct line of descent from these men are quite few. But if the men in high positions try to postpone the time when they should give place to others, and are so foolish as to attempt to keep things as they are by laying it down that the families which are in a superior position and those which are in an inferior position shall remain in that state forever, they will be acting against the principles of the natural order. As a result of this, persons of ability will disappear from among the upper class and in the course of time an age of disorder will come, in which men of ability will appear among the lower classes and overthrow the dynasty. The Sages were aware of this principle, and in order that their dynasties should last as long as possible they instituted a system of "rewards and punishments," encouraging and promoting to office men of ability from the lower classes, and removing men from the upper classes as the mind of Heaven willed it, either by their dying without direct descendants, or as a result of their committing some offense. When government is carried on in this way all men of ability are in positions of authority and those who have no ability are in positions of subordination, and because this is in accordance with the principles of the natural order the dynasty remains in power for a long time. It should be realized that if a ruler neglects this correspondence with the natural order, and is not conversant with the principles of governing the totality of Heaven, Earth and Man, his rule will not be in accordance with the mind of Heaven, and will not be true government.

Now the principle of the *Changes*, that things grow up from below, is no empty imagining. In the course of the year, spring and summer are the seasons in which the spirit of Heaven descends, the spirit of Earth rises, and the two combine harmoniously together so that all things grow. In autumn and winter the spirit of Heaven rises and the spirit of Earth descends, Heaven and Earth separate and cease to be in combination with the result that all things wither and die. A similar thing happens in the world of men.

When the members of the lower orders who possess ability are promoted, the will of those above is diffused throughout the lower classes in a way similar to the descent of the spirit of Heaven. But if good men among the lower orders are not promoted, the feelings of the lower orders are not made known to the upper class, as happens when the spirit of Earth does not rise. The upper and lower classes are then disunited and separated from one another as when Heaven and Earth are not united in harmonious combination, and the state declines in the same way in which all things wither and decay in autumn and winter.

The reason for the fact that after a long period of peace, good men are to be found among the lower orders while the members of the upper classes become more and more stupid, is that all human ability is produced by suffering difficulties and hardships. It is natural that a man's wits should be sharpened when he meets with difficulties and hardships and is knocked about in various ways. So we read in *Mencius* that when Heaven intends to confer a great office on a man it first makes him undergo all manner of hardships.[9] Such a man is particularly well-suited to government because he has acquired his intelligence in the course of being knocked about as a member of the lower orders, and is therefore well acquainted with the life of the common people. In the Way of the Sages, too, one is commanded to "raise up the worthy and talented," that is, to promote men from below. Again, the record of history shows that by far the greater number of men of worth and talent have come from the lower orders while they have been very rare among those who have enjoyed great emoluments for many generations. All the ancestors of those who for generations have received great emoluments and have occupied high offices acquired intelligence from the hardships which they suffered in the course of the life-and-death struggle of civil war. Hence they did great deeds and obtained great emoluments and high office. But their descendants have enjoyed great emoluments and high office by hereditary succession; they occupy their superior position by reason of their birth, and since they undergo no hardships at all they have no opportunity of developing intelligence. In their high positions they are separated from their social inferiors and are unable to understand their feelings. They are reared in the midst of the praise and adulation of their household retainers, so that they become conceited in a wisdom which they do not possess. They receive respect on account of their birth, and, believing that this is merely what is due them, are not disposed to be deeply grateful for the benefits which their superiors have conferred upon them, while in personal conduct they act in an arbitrary fashion and think of their social inferiors as so much vermin.

This is characteristic of human nature and it is only natural that this should come about, for these are faults which anyone in a superior social position can scarcely avoid even if he should be endowed with natural intelligence. Even the clever men who may happen to be among the upper classes are separated from the common people by such an unbridgeable gulf that they are unable to grasp their feelings. They are used to coming into contact with them only in the roles of superior and inferior and in formal situations. It is impossible for them to become really familiar with their inferiors in this way, for they get a very distant view of them by applying their faculties of intelligence and observation to intercourse of this kind. The result is that they become all the more convinced of their own superiority in intelligence. This characteristic of the human mind has existed unchanged throughout all history, and hence in the Way of the Sages the first thing spoken about is the promotion of talent from below, while "*seikan*," that is, the occupation of important offices by successive generations of the same family, is strongly deprecated. . . . Some think that if the present rulers are left as they are and good suggestions from the lower orders are put into effect, this fulfills the Sages' injunction to "raise up worthy and talented men." This is a useless quibble which slanders the doctrine of the Sages. If the members of the

---

[9]Mencius VI. 2, 15.

lower classes are simply made to voice their opinions and then these are put into effect, the manner in which the ideas of talented men in the lower classes are implemented will be very different from what they intended. What is more, if talented men are in the position of having to give their opinions in an inferior status they will be unable to speak freely. Again, even in the case of the same man, his ideas while he is in an inferior position will differ from those he will hold when he has been promoted to a position of authority because he will not have had the necessary experience. After he has been promoted and has had some experience of office his mind will work in a different way because of his change of position. Thus, when the Sages spoke of promoting the worthy and talented they did not refer to such sophistical nonsense as the opinion which I have mentioned. Further, acceptance of the principle of promoting men of worth and talent does not imply driving out all those who have held high positions in the past and reversing the position of rulers and ruled. If only two or three, or even only one or two, men of worth and talent are promoted from the lower classes, the hitherto unbroken precedent of hereditary succession will be destroyed and everyone will adopt a new attitude, each working with great diligence in imitation of the men who have been promoted, and thus by one stroke the entire country will be transformed into a better state.

CONFUCIAN JUSTICE

Between 1709 and 1716, Arai Hakuseki (1657–1725) was close to the seat of power, as the mentor and advisor to Shōgun Ienobu and Shōgun Ietsugu. His relationship to Shōgun Ienobu was exceptionally close, dating back to the day when the latter was lord of the Kōfu-han. In the nineteen years they knew each other, Hakuseki gave a cumulative total of 1299 lectures for Ienobu. Hakuseki's power and influence were recaptured in his autobiographical account, Oritakushiba no ki. *Document 7 is taken from that autobiography, which shows how in a Solomon-like fashion Hakuseki saved the life and reputation of a widow whose father and brother murdered her husband. There were differing legal concepts of the duties of a daughter toward her father, and toward her husband, and the two came into conflict in this case. The Confucian view of the position of women was also fully explicated.*

Aside from his autobiography, Hakuseki left the following works: The Koshitsū, *which treated ancient Japanese history;* Tokushi Yoron, *which gave his views on Japanese history to the time of the founding of the Tokugawa bakufu;* Hankanbu, *which gave genealogical records of the daimyō from the time of the battle of Sekigahara to the end of the reign of the fourth Shōgun Ietsuna; and* Seiyō Kibun *and* Sairan Igen, *which described the geography of the West and conditions of foreign countries. These two works were based on his interviews with a Sicilian missionary named Giovanni Sidotti, who broke the law to*

come to Japan in 1708, and on the information received from the Dutch in
Dejima. On account of this, some scholars credit Hakuseki with initiating a trend
toward Dutch studies.

7 **Tokugawa Justice under Confucian Precepts**[10]   In the year 1711,
eighth month, 17th day, after my lecture for the *shōgun* was over, I was shown a
very complex criminal case.

According to the document, there was a man from Matsushiro district in the
province of Shinano who came to Edo to engage in trade. His wife came from
the village of Kamabayashi in Kawagoe district in the province of Musashi. On
the 16th day of the seventh month, an elder brother of the wife came and lured
her husband to Kawagoe. On the 20th day of the same month, the brother again
came, and informed the younger sister: "Your husband went to his home on
business. It will not be long before he returns. Meanwhile why not come to the
father's house, and wait for his return?" On the 21st day, he took the wife to his
father's house. Many days passed and the husband was still absent. She inquired
of her father when the husband might return, and the father answered: "He said
he definitely would be home by the 28th." However, the first of the new month
came and there was still no sign of her husband. Worried about his safety, she
heard someone saying that there was a dead body of a man who obviously was
drowned in the river. With a foreboding she rushed to the river, but the body was
lying face down, and she could not identify it. She begged the father and brother
to let her see the face of the dead body, but was told not to worry about it. She
could not hold the suspense too much longer and the next day, she asked the
village head (*nanushi*) to retrieve the body, and it was indeed her husband's.

The village was in the territory held by Rōju Tajima no Kami Takatomo. The
officers, in the absence of Lord Takatomo, questioned her father and brother and
their servants, and finding some inconsistencies in their testimonies, searched
their house. The clothing and miscellaneous items belonging to the son-in-law
were discovered. They could not offer any word in their own defense and it
became clear that on the night of the 18th day of the seventh month, the father
and the brother had strangled the son-in-law and put his body in the water. There
was no question about the guilt of the two who had killed the son-in-law. However, there was a possibility that the wife was also culpable, since she was the
one to expose her father's crime. Thus Lord Takatomo sent his report to ask our
opinion.

---

[10]Arai Hakuseki, *Oritakushiba no ki (Records of Occasionally Burning Firewood)* in
Iwanami Shoten, *Nihon Koten Bunka Taikei (Major Compilation of Japanese Classics)*
Vol. 95 (Tokyo: Iwanami Shoten, 1969), pp. 336–343. An English translation (not com-
plete) can be found in G. W. Knox, "Autobiography of Arai Hakuseki" in *TASJ*, 1st Ser.,
Vol. 30 (1902), pp. 89–238.

I responded by saying: "This incident is at variance with the three basic principles [of Confucianism governing the relations between the ruler and the subject, father and son, and husband and wife], and cannot be dealt with in a normal manner. What I fear is that the incident not only touches on the relations between father and son, and husband and wife, but also has bearings on the important relations between the ruler and the subject."

The *shōgun* directed me to command the councillors (*hyōjōshū*) to search for precedents and report back to the *shōgun*. After I went home, I consulted privately with my friend Muro Kyūsō (1658–1734). Next morning he sent me a letter which stated that "a clear-cut decision can be reached on the basis of these sentences" and cited passages from a section on deep mourning, Chapter on Mourning Cloth in the *Book of Etiquette (Yi li)*. When I first discussed the case with Muro, I knew he and I were in agreement. I was grateful to him for providing me with this irrefutable reference.

On the 25th day, I was called into the presence of the *shōgun* and was given a copy of an opinion written by the Head of the University (*daigakunokami*) Hayashi Nobuatsu in response to the request made by the Council of Elders (*rōju*). The opinion cites the saying "Even though all men can become one's own husband, there is but one father." This saying was given by Lady Cai Zhong of Zheng in response to her daughter's inquiry about who was closer to her—her husband or her father. In that instance, it was the daughter's exposure which made the crimes of her father evident. The *Analects* states that "the son shall shield the crimes of his father." The Codes of Sui and Tang state that "anyone who exposes the crimes of his father and mother shall be put to death." However, if she reported on the crime without knowing that it was her father who killed her husband, then the judgment would be different. The Code of Yōrō in this country says that "anyone who informs on the wrongdoings of his father and mother shall be banished." The footnote to that specific code states that the applicable penalty is death by hanging.

The *shōgun* commented that "The words of Lady Cai Zhong need not be accepted in arriving at our judgment. . . . Confucius did not say that to conceal is the way of righteousness. . . ." He then asked for my opinion which was submitted to him on the 26th day. It was as follows.

". . . The officers who investigated the incident thought that there was a basic similarity in this case to that of the daughter committing the crime of informing on her father. The councillors after due deliberation stated that she ought to be banished and her property confiscated. The Head of the University submitted an opinion that she ought to be punished as one who committed the crime of informing on her father. . . . In my humble opinion, there are three factors to be considered:

"First, the case must be dealt with in accordance with the fundamental principles governing human relations. The so-called three fundamental principles are that the ruler is the lord over his subject, the father is the lord over his son, and the husband is the lord over his wife. The ruler, the father, and the husband must be respected equally, and served with the same diligence.

"Second, the etiquette concerning the wearing of mourning cloth can be used as a guide in the present case. According to the regulations established by the former kings in China, at the time of the father's death if a daughter is betrothed to be married but is still at home, or if she is separated from her husband and is living at her father's house, she is to wear hemp mourning cloth for three years. If she is married and is living with her husband, she is to wear mourning cloth irregularly for a period of one year only. This discrepancy . . . is explained in the Chapter on Mourning Cloth in the *Book of Etiquette*: 'There are three followings for women, which are applicable to every woman. Therefore when the girl is yet to be married, she follows her father. After her marriage, she follows her husband. After the death of her husband, she follows her son. The father is the heaven for the daughter, the husband is the heaven for the wife. A woman cannot wear her hemp cloth twice in deep mournings [for her father and husband]. This is likened to the fact that there are not two heavens. A woman cannot pay her respect to two persons.' This clearly tells us . . . that wife is to follow her husband and not her father.

"Third, flexibility must be our attitude in arriving at a decision. In everything there are constant elements and changing elements, and to bring about the way of heaven, we rely on both the principle (*kei*, in Chinese, *qing*) and its application (*ken*, in Ch. *chuan*). Scholars of old say that 'application is a means of fulfilling the principle.' When a daughter is still with her father, she follows him. When she marries she follows her husband. This is the application which takes into account the changing circumstances, and is consistent with the system established by the former kings. . . .

"There is no greater travesty of human relations than for one's father to kill one's husband. If she wishes to be true to her husband, she is unfilial to her father. No greater misfortune can befall an individual than this. . . .

"According to the system established by the former kings, a daughter who is married can no longer have her father as her heaven. Therefore, even if she has informed on the crime of her father in killing her husband, she cannot be dealt with in the same manner as those who inform on the crimes of their parents. Furthermore she did not knowingly inform on her father and brother in this case. The end of justice cannot be served by punishing her. Some say that at the time the crime of her father and brother was exposed, she should have committed suicide immediately. In this way she could maintain her chastity toward her husband and her filial and sisterly obedience toward her father and brother. . . . This is an argument advanced to blame others for their slightest imperfection. . . .

"According to the opinion of the councillors, the wife in this case is to be incarcerated for a period of one year, and thereafter she is to be condemned as a slave girl. According to the opinion of the Head of the University, 'If she knew that it was her father who killed her husband and informed on him, she must be put to death. If she did not know that it was her father who killed her husband and informed on her husband's death, she must still be condemned to become a slave girl.'

"If this woman can escape punishment as I am recommending, may I make another request of you. This poor widow has lost the man on whom she can depend. Being young there is no guarantee that she will be able to maintain her chastity. I am not only fearful of her inability to keep her chastity, but also of her breaking the law of the land. According to a well-established custom in our country, there are many who choose to become monks and nuns after the death of their fathers and husbands. We may subtly suggest to her that she become a nun for the sake of her father and husband, send her to a nunnery, shave off her hair, and let her enter a Buddhist order. The properties belonging to her father and husband are to be donated to the nunnery, which can in turn guarantee her livelihood for the rest of her life.[11] In this way not only the law of the land, but also her chastity can be preserved."

EDUCATION OF THE YOUNG

Tokugawa Japan was deeply committed to education. There was the Shōheikō, maintained by the bakufu, *and each of the* han *had a school for its retainers. There were hundreds of private schools available for both samurai and commoners, and temple schools (*terakoya*) also provided some rudiments of education.*

What curriculum was considered essential for these schools, especially as it pertained to the young? This question can find a ready answer in Kaibara Ekiken's little opus, Wazoku Dōshikun (Common Sense Teachings for Japanese Children) (Document 8).

Kaibara Ekiken (1630–1714) served under the Kuroda family, daimyō *of the Fukuoka-han, first as a medical doctor and then as a Confucian scholar in residence. A man of wide knowledge and a prolific writer, his works included* Yamato Honzō, *a book on Japanese plants and herbs;* Onna Daigaku *(Great Learning for Women), which was written probably in collaboration with his wife, Tōken; and* Ekiken Jikkun *(Ten Precepts of Ekiken), which popularized basic Confucian teachings.*

8   Education of Children[12]

(a) For the children in their sixth year.[13]

In January when children reach the age of six, teach them numbers one

---

[11]The crime of murder was punishable by decapitation, and the murderer's property as a rule was confiscated. Thus the arrangement suggested by Hakuseki represented a humane treatment for the wife.

[12]Matsuda Michio et al., eds., *Kaibara Ekiken* in Chūō Kōronsha, *Nihon no Meicho (Great Books of Japan)* Vol. 14 (Tokyo: Chūō Kōronsha, 1969), pp. 211–214.

[13]Meaning a child who is in his sixth calendar year. Thus a child who is born in December can be counted as two years old the following January.

through ten, and the names given to designate 100, 1,000, 10,000 and 100,000,000. Let them know the four directions, East, West, North and South. Assess their native intelligence and differentiate between quick and slow learners. Teach them the Japanese syllabary (*kana*) from the age of six or seven, and let them learn how to write. . . . From this time on, teach them to respect their elders, and let them know distinctions between the upper and lower classes and between the young and old. Let them learn to use the correct expressions.

(b) For the seventh year.

When the children reach the age of seven, do not let the boys and girls sit together, nor must you allow them to dine together. . . .

(c) For the eighth year.

This is the age when the ancients began studying the book *Little Learning*.[14] Beginning at this time, teach the youngsters etiquette befitting their age, and caution them not to commit an act of impoliteness. Among those which must be taught are: the daily deportment, the manners set for appearing before one's senior and withdrawing from his presence, how to speak or respond to one's senior or guest, how to place a serving tray (*skokuzen*) or replace it for one's senior, how to present a wine cup and pour *sake* and to serve side dishes to accompany it, and how to serve tea. Children must also learn how to behave while taking their meals. This includes how to accept *sake* and side dishes from one's senior, and how to greet prominent people at dinner parties. Teach them also how to conduct themselves at tea ceremonies.

Children must be taught by those who are close to them the virtues of filial piety and obedience. To serve the parents well is called filial piety (*kō*), and to serve one's seniors well is called obedience (*tei*). The one who lives close to the children and who is able to teach must instruct the children in the early years of their life that the first obligation of a human being is to revere the parents and serve them well. Then comes the next lesson which includes respect for one's seniors, listening to their commands and not holding them in contempt. One's seniors include elder brothers, elder sisters, uncles, aunts, and cousins who are older and worthy of respect. The way of a man is to observe the virtues of filial piety and obedience, and children must be taught that all goodness in life emanates from these two fundamental virtues. . . .

If the parents permit their children to hold other people in contempt, and take pleasure in their antics, the children will lose a sense of distinction between good and evil. They may view such antics lightheartedly, and cannot get out of their bad habits even after they become adults. They fail to become good children to the parents, or good younger brothers to the older brothers. They will be impo-

---

[14]*Xiao xue*, written by the Song scholar Liu Zucheng in 1187 under the direction of Zhu Xi. It contained the basic curriculum for young children including rules of etiquette and famous sayings and examples of good works excerpted from classics and other writings.

lite, unfilial and disobedient. These are caused by the foolishness of parents who encourage their children in evil-doing. As the children grow older, teach them to love their younger brothers and to be compassionate to the employees and servants. Teach them also the respect due their teachers and the behavior codes governing friends. The etiquette governing each movement toward important guests—such as standing, sitting, advancing forward, and retiring from their presence—and the language to be employed must be taught. Teach them how to pay respect to others according to the social positions held by them. Gradually the ways of filial piety and obedience, loyalty and trustworthiness, right deportment and decorum, and sense of shame must be inculcated in children's minds and they must know how to implement them. Caution them not to desire the possessions of others, or to stoop below one's dignity in consuming excessive amounts of food and drink. They must know at all times a sense of shame. . . .

Once reaching the age of eight, children must follow and never lead their elders when entering a gate, sitting, or eating and drinking. From this time on they must be taught how to become humble and yield to others. Do not permit the children to behave as they please. It is important to caution them against "doing their own things."

(d) From the spring of the eighth year.

On this spring, calligraphy lessons on the square-style (*kaisho*) and cursive-style (*sōsho*) writings must begin. . . . Teach them basic lessons in reading. Avoid the *Classics of Filial Piety, Little Learning*, and the Four Books which have long sentences. They are difficult to memorize and not interesting [to the children who may as a result] form an adverse opinion on learning. First of all, select short sentences, which are easy to read and comprehend. Then let the children learn them by rote memory.

(e) For the tenth year.

At the age of ten, let the children be placed under the guidance of a teacher, and tell them about the general meaning of five constant virtues and let them understand the way of the five human relationships.[15] Let them read books by the Sage and the wise men of old and cultivate a desire for learning. Select for them those books which are easily understood and which are suitable for moral instruction. The important passages must be clearly explicated for their benefit. Thereafter gradually expand their readings to include the *Little Learning*, and the Four Books and Five Classics. When not engaged in reading, teach them literary and military arts. Generally, the public starts instructing children in calligraphy at the age of eleven. I think it is too late. Unless children are taught from an early age, their hearts will become desolate, and their minds wild. They will dislike the teachings, and acquire a lazy habit. So teach the children early in life. . . .

---

[15]See Document 1.

(f) For the fifteenth year.

Fifteen is the age when the ancients began the study of the *Great Learning*.[16] From this time on, concentrate on the learning of a sense of justice and duty (*giri*). Students must also learn to cultivate their personalities and investigate the way of governing people. This is the way of the *Great Learning*. Those who are born in the high-ranking families have the heavy obligations (*shokubun*) of becoming leaders of the people, of having people entrusted to their care, and of governing them. Therefore, without fail, a teacher must be selected for them when they are still young. They must be taught how to read and be informed of the ways of old, of cultivating their personalities, and of the way of governing people. If they do not learn the way of governing people, they may injure the many people who are entrusted to their care by the Way of Heaven. That will be a serious disaster. Other people too, depending on their social status, have some work to do in the governing of the people. Therefore they must acquire knowledge concerning their work. Even though one may be born without a good mind, he can comprehend general outlines of the *Little Learning* and the Four Books. If he is intelligent, he must study widely and know many other things.

(g) At the twentieth year.

In olden days in China, when children reached the age of twenty, a capping ceremony was held to celebrate their coming of age (*genbuku*). The word *genbuku* means to put a cap on the head. In olden days, in Japan too, both the court nobles and samurai placed ceremonial caps (*koburi ebōshi*) on those who reached the age of twenty.... Once the *genbuku* ceremony is completed, the children become adults. From that moment on, they must discard their former childish way, follow the virtues of the adult society, reach out everywhere for knowledge, and act in an exemplifying manner....

DEATH AND A SAMURAI

*Bushidō, or the way of the samurai, was first articulated by Yamaga Sokō (1622–1685), the famed Confucian scholar and military strategist. In his view, the three classes of farmers, artisans, and merchants were engaged in economic activities, and thus could not act constantly in accordance with the Way of Confucianism. Thus it was left for the samurai to uphold and practice the Way, and to chastise the offenders. To become a good samurai, one ought to be conscious of his calling (*shokubun, or function*) as a samurai. In the final analysis, Sokō's approach was ethical and speculative in nature.*

In contrast, the precepts contained in Hagakure *or* Hidden Behind Leaves *were born of practical experiences of the samurai. If Sokō appealed to the intellect,* Hagakure *appealed to the heart. It taught how to face death in order to*

---

[16]*Da Xue*, one of the Four Books.

gain life and to serve one's own master. Death was welcomed even if it appeared
absurd in another's eyes. Hagakure was completed in 1716 by Yamamoto
Tsunetomo who chose the path of self-exile after the death of his master. The
book became the favorite of the samurai of the Saga-han, for use in training their
samurai spirit.

9 **From Hidden Behind Leaves**[17] The Way of the Warrior (*bushidō*) is to
find a way to die. If a choice is given between life and death, the samurai must
choose death. There is no more meaning beyond this. Make up your mind and
follow the predetermined course. Someone may say, "You die in vain, if you do
not accomplish what you set out to do." That represents an insincere approach of
the Kyoto people to the *bushidō*. When you are forced to choose between life
and death, no one knows what the outcome will be. Man always desires life and
rationalizes his choice for life. At that very moment, if he misses his objectives
and continues to live, as a samurai he must be regarded as a coward. It is difficult
to draw an exact line. If he misses his objectives and chooses death, some may
say he dies in vain and he is crazy to do so. But this must not be regarded as a
shameful act. It is of utmost importance for the *bushidō*. Day and night, if you
make a conscious effort to think of death and resolve to pursue it, and if you are
ready to discard life at a moment's notice, you and the *bushidō* will become one.
In this way throughout your life, you can perform your duties for your master
without fail. . . .

The twenty-one article precepts of Lord Nabeshima Naoshige (1538–1618)
which are posted on the wall contain an injunction saying, "On grave matters,
deliberations must be light." To this Ishida Kazue adds a commentary. "On
minor matters, deliberations must be heavy." There are not likely to be more than
two or three grave matters [occurring in one's lifetime]. You can carefully deliberate on these matters every day and understand their full meaning. Therefore
think ahead of time, and when an important event takes place, recall what you
have already deliberated and act accordingly. You can accomplish whatever is
necessary effortlessly. On the other hand, if you do not think of these grave
matters daily, and try to make a simple judgment on arriving at the scene, you
will meet failure and cannot take an appropriate action. I believe that when Lord
Naoshige said, "On grave matters, deliberations must be light," he wanted us to
be prepared day in and day out [for those rare grave occasions]. . . .

Someone went to Osaka and served there for several years and returned to
Saga recently. When he appeared in the Administrative Office to report to work,
he used the language of the Kyoto-Osaka region. It was an awkward experience
and everyone laughed at him. This reminds me of one basic principle, that is

---

[17]Yamamoto Tsunetomo, *Hagakure* in Chūō Kōronsha, *Nihon no Meicho, op. cit.*, Vol.
17, pp. 58, 76–78, 98–99.

when one goes to Edo or to the Kyoto-Osaka region for a length of time, speak daily our own local dialect. One can easily become contaminated by the way of life of Kyoto-Osaka or Edo, and look down on the customs in Saga as vulgar. If there is something good in Kyoto-Osaka or Edo, that same person may speak of it with envy. That is a senseless way and foolishness at its utmost. Our domain is great precisely because of its folkish style and simplicity. Frivolous imitation of the fashions of other domains does not produce constructive results.

When someone told the great monk Shungaku that "the Hokke sect is not good because it is too strong-willed," Shungaku replied, "It is because of this strong will, we became the Hokke sect. Otherwise there is no difference between us and other sects." To this I give my hearty agreement.

"The *bushidō* is nothing but one of desperate courage. If a samurai makes desperate efforts, even if he is alone, it is difficult to kill him with a force of several tens of samurai." So said Lord Naoshige. One cannot accomplish a great deed without losing his senses. Go out of your mind once, and work with all of your desperate courage. In the *bushidō*, do not contemplate any further. In the process of doing it, you will fall behind others. Think not even of loyalty (*chū*) or filial piety (*kō*). In the *bushidō* there is only one thing, that is desperate courage. All you must know is that in desperate courage one can naturally find both loyalty and filial piety. . . .

You may have heard of great masters and despair of the fact that you can never reach the state of their accomplishments. That is most lamentable. Great masters are men and so are you. If you set your mind never to take second place to anyone, and begin to work with that resolve, you will be on your way to a great attainment. "Confucius became a sage because at the age of fifteen he set his heart on learning. He did not become a sage because of his later works." That is what the scholar Ishida Kazue says. Buddhist scriptures say, "At the first awakening of the spirit, one has already obtained the true teachings of Buddha." It conveys the same message.

KNOWLEDGE OF THE WEST

At first only a trickle of the knowledge of the West filtered through the Dutch enclave of Dejima in secluded Japan. Then came the lifting of the ban on the importation of Western books except those that dealt with Christianity (under Shōgun Yoshimune in 1720), which gave a considerable impetus to the rise of scientific studies inspired by the West. During the time Tanuma Okitsugu served as rōju (Councillor or Elder, 1772–1787), Dutch studies extended to the economic fields. Near the end of the Tokugawa bakufu, Dutch studies provided the means for acquiring the knowledge of Western arms and military science.

Sugita Gempaku (1733–1817) was trained in traditional medicine and specialized in surgery. In 1771, he witnessed a dissection of a condemned criminal, and found that the human anatomy was exactly as described in a book, Tabulae Anatomicae, *which he acquired in Nagasaki. Thereafter he set out to translate the book against all odds, including his lack of knowledge of the Dutch. To him this was the beginning of Dutch studies in Japan, and in 1815 he wrote down a memoir of his experiences. An excerpt from his* Rangaku Kotohajime *(The Beginning of Dutch Studies) is given below.*

10 **The Beginning of Dutch Studies in Japan**[18]   Whenever I met Hiraga Gennai (1729–1779), we talked to each other on this matter: "As we have learned, the Dutch method of scholarly investigation through field work and surveys is truly amazing. If we can directly understand books written by them, we will benefit greatly. However, it is pitiful that there has been no one who has set his mind on working in this field. Can we somehow blaze this trail? It is impossible to do it in Edo. Perhaps it is best if we ask translators in Nagasaki to make some translations. If one book can be completely translated, there will be an immeasurable benefit to the country." Every time we spoke in this manner, we deplored the impossibility of implementing our desires. However, we did not vainly lament the matter for long.

Somehow, miraculously I obtained a book on anatomy written in that country. It may well be that Dutch studies in this country began when I thought of comparing the illustrations in the book with real things. It was a strange and even miraculous happening that I was able to obtain that book in that particular spring of 1771. Then at the night of the third day of the third month, I received a letter from a man by the name of Tokuno Bambei, who was in the service of the then Town Commissioner, Magaribuchi Kai-no-kami. Tokuno stated in his letter that "A post-mortem examination of the body of a condemned criminal by a resident physician will be held tomorrow at Senjukotsukahara. You are welcome to witness it if you so desire." At one time my colleague by the name of Kosugi Genteki had an occasion to witness a post-mortem dissection of a body when he studied under Dr. Yamawaki Tōyō of Kyoto. After seeing the dissection first-hand, Kosugi remarked that what was said by the people of old was false and simply could not be trusted. "The people of old spoke of nine internal organs, and nowadays, people divide them into five viscera and six internal organs. That [perpetuates] inaccuracy," Kosugi once said. Around that time (1759) Dr. Tōyō published a book entitled *Zōshi* (*On Internal Organs*). Having read that book, I had hoped that some day I could witness a dissection. When I also acquired a

---

[18]Sugita Gempaku, *Rantō Kotohajime (The Beginning of Dutch Studies in the East)* in Iwanami shoten, *Nihon Koten Bunka Taikei*, Vol. 95, *op. cit.*, pp. 487–493. The more popular title *Rangaku Kotohajime* was given by Fukuzawa Yukichi when he published the book in 1869, one year after the Meiji Restoration. See also a complete English translation by Matsumoto Ryozō, *Dawn of Western Science in Japan* (Tokyo: Hokuseidō Press, 1969).

Dutch book on anatomy, I wanted above all to compare the two to find out which one accurately described the truth. I rejoiced at this unusually fortunate circumstance, and my mind could not entertain any other thought. However, a thought occurred to me that I should not monopolize this good fortune, and decided to share it with those of my colleagues who were diligent in the pursuit of their medicine. . . . Among those I invited was one [Maeno] Ryōtaku (1723–1803). . . .

The next day, when we arrived at the location . . . Ryōtaku reached under his kimono to produce a Dutch book and showed it to us. "This is a Dutch book of anatomy called *Tabulae Anatomicae*. I bought this a few years ago when I went to Nagasaki, and kept it." As I examined it, it was the same book I had and was of the same edition. We held each other's hands and exclaimed: "What a coincidence!" Ryōtaku continued by saying: "When I went to Nagasaki, I learned and heard," and opened his book. "These are called *long* in Dutch, they are lungs," he taught us. "This is *hart*, or the heart. When it says *maag* it is the stomach, and when it says *milt* it is the spleen." However, they did not look like the heart given in the Chinese medical books, and none of us were sure until we could actually see the dissection.

Thereafter we went together to the place which was especially set for us to observe the dissection in Kotsukahara. . . . The regular man who performed the chore of dissection was ill, and his grandfather, who was ninety years of age, came in his place. He was a healthy old man. He had experienced many dissections since his youth, and boasted that he dissected a number of bodies. Those dissections were performed in those days by men of the *eta* class. . . . That day, the old butcher pointed to this and that organ. After the heart, liver, gall bladder, and stomach were identified, he pointed to other parts for which there were no names. "I don't know their names. But I have dissected quite a few bodies from my youthful days. Inside of everyone's abdomen there were these parts and those parts." Later, after consulting the anatomy chart, it became clear to me that I saw an arterial tube, a vein, and the suprarenal gland. The old butcher again said, "Every time I had a dissection, I pointed out to those physicians many of these parts, but not a single one of them questioned 'what was this?' or 'what was that?' " We compared the body as dissected against the charts both Ryōtaku and I had, and could not find a single variance from the charts. The Chinese *Book of Medicine* (*Yi jing*) says that the lungs are like the eight petals of the lotus flower, with three petals hanging in front, three in back, and two petals forming like two ears and that the liver has three petals to the left and four petals to the right. There were no such divisions, and the positions and shapes of intestines and gastric organs were all different from those taught by the old theories. The official physicians, Dr. Okada Yōsen and Dr. Fujimoto Rissen, have witnessed dissection seven or eight times. Whenever they witnessed the dissection, they found that the old theories contradicted reality. Each time they were perplexed and could not resolve their doubts. Every time they wrote down what they thought was strange. They wrote in their books, "The more we think of it, there must be fundamental differences in the bodies of Chinese and of the eastern barbarians [i.e., Japanese]." I could see why they wrote this way.

That day, after the dissection was over, we decided that we also should examine the shape of the skeletons left exposed on the execution ground. We collected the bones, and examined a number of them. Again, we were struck by the fact that they all differed from the old theories while conforming to the Dutch charts.

The three of us, Ryōtaku, [Nakagawa] Junan (1739–1786), and I went home together. On the way home we spoke to each other and felt the same way. "How marvelous was our actual experience today. It is a shame that we were ignorant of these things until now. As physicians who serve their masters through medicine, we performed our duties in complete ignorance of the true form of the human body. How disgraceful it is. Somehow, through this experience, let us investigate further the truth about the human body. If we practice medicine with this knowledge behind us, we can make contributions for people under heaven and on this earth." Ryōtaku spoke to us. "Indeed, I agree with you wholeheartedly." Then I spoke to my two companions. "Somehow if we can translate anew this book called *Tabulae Anatomicae*, we can get a clear notion of the human body inside out. It will have great benefit in the treatment of our patients. Let us do our best to read it and understand it without the help of translators." Ryōtaku responded: "I have been wanting to read Dutch books for some time, but there has been no friend who would share my ambitions. I have spent days lamenting it. If both of you wish, I have been in Nagasaki before and have retained some Dutch. Let us use it as a beginning to tackle the book together." After hearing it, I answered, "This is simply wonderful. If we are to join our efforts, I shall also resolve to do my very best." . . .

The next day, we assembled at the house of Ryōtaku and recalled the happenings of the previous day. When we faced that *Tabulae Anatomicae*, we felt as if we were setting sail on a great ocean in a ship without oars or a rudder. With the magnitude of the work before us, we were dumbfounded by our own ignorance. However, Ryōtaku had been thinking of this for some time, and he had been in Nagasaki. He knew some Dutch through studying and hearing, and knew some sentence patterns and words. He was also ten years older than I, and we decided to make him head of our group and our teacher. At that time I did not know the twenty-five letters of the Dutch alphabet. I decided to study the language with firm determination, but I had to acquaint myself with letters and words gradually.

NATIONAL LEARNING AND SHINTŌ REVIVAL

Even within the ranks of Confucian scholars, whatever their school might be, there was a strong current of nationalism and particularism. However, nowhere could that current be found stronger than in the school of national learning (kokugaku) *begun by Keichū (1640–1701) and Kada no Azumamaro (1669–*

1736), and transmitted to Kamo no Mabuchi (1697–1769), Motoori Norinaga (1730–1801) and Hirata Atsutane (1776–1843).

The kokugaku *scholars advocated a return to the pristine purity of Japan's past, unencumbered by the influence of Buddhism and Confucianism. They attempted to rediscover the "ancient way" not by means of later thought and approaches but by means of diligent study of Japanese classics and philology. They idealized the direct rule by the emperor under which there was no distinction between a samurai and a common man. They talked of the naturalness of the Japanese behavior as against the constraints imposed by the Confucian ethics. They spoke of reverence for the emperor and criticized the status quo under the* baku-han *system.*

Motoori Norinaga's Naobino Mitama *(The Spirit That Guideth Straight) is a general introduction to his massive* Kojikiden *(An Exposition of the Records of Ancient Matters) (Document 11). Here his* kokugaku *included elements of historiography, philology, literature and Shintō. With Hirata Atsutane, Shintō came into the forefront. His* Kodō Taii *(Outline of the Ancient Way) discusses Confucianism, Buddhism and Dutch studies, but contains a strong affirmation of the superiority of Shintō throughout the work (Document 12).*

11 Japan's Creation by Amaterasu[19]

Precious indeed is the country of Japan which was created by Amaterasu Ōmikami, the most awe-inspiring progenitor deity of the imperial family. The superiority of Japan over all other nations is nowhere better manifested than in this fact. There is no nation on earth which does not share in the beneficence of Amaterasu Ōmikami.

As Amaterasu Ōmikami held in her august hands the heavenly seals [i.e., the three imperial regalia held as a sign of succession to the imperial throne from generation to generation], and decreed that "this country shall be ruled by my august children forever and ever," all under heaven as far as the clouds could reach, and all the earth including the crevices that hid little toads became the country to be governed by the descendants of the Sun Goddess. Thus on earth, there is not a single deity who is unruly, nor is there a single person who does not pay obeisance to the emperor. For ages eternal, the emperor is to remain the ruler of the realm and to be worshipped as the descendant of Amaterasu Ōmikami. He partakes of the will of Amaterasu Ōmikami as his own will, and there can be no differentiation between the age of gods and today. He continues to govern the country peacefully in the manner set by the gods. And this is the reason why in

---

[19]Motoori Norinaga, *Naobino Mitama* in *Sekai Daishisō Zenshū (Complete Works of Great Thoughts of the World)*, Vol. 54 *Nihonshisō-hen (Japanese Thought)* (Tokyo: Shunjūsha, 1927), pp. 17–21. Here Norinaga's footnotes are selected and incorporated in the text which is translated.

the olden days the Japanese language lacked the term "the way" (*dao* in Chinese and *michi* in Japanese). When people spoke of the way they referred to the highway that was used for traveling. It is an alien manner to speak of the reasoning process or certain doctrines as this way or that way.

Those foreign countries are not created by Amaterasu Ōmikami, and as a result do not have preordained sovereigns. Evil-doing deities can freely act out their mischievous deeds. There is no kindness in people's hearts, and everything is given to confusion. If one gains control of a country, no matter how humble his origin may be, he can be proclaimed the sovereign. Thus those who are above are always watchful of their inferiors to guard against possible usurpations, and those who are below are constantly seeking an opportunity to do so. The two are hostile parties, and this is the reason why it has always been difficult to govern the country. In China, those who were called sages were those who had military power and knowledge who placated their own people to stage conquests of other countries and after having accomplished it, guarded against usurpation or conquest. For a while, they governed the country well and set examples for posterity. . . . Thus it is wrong to ascribe unusual virtues to those "sages" and liken them to gods. The rules which they arbitrarily established are called the way. This being the case, what the Chinese understand by the term "way" in the final analysis means only two things, namely a means of conquering another's country, and precautionary measures to prevent overthrow of one's own government. In planning to conquer another's country, it is necessary for the ruler to endeavor with all his mind, and in a self-effacing manner perform good deeds to his utmost to show his concern for his people. Thus the so-called "sage" can look like a good person, and the "way" he decrees can give an appearance of a faultlessly drafted beautiful code. However, the "sage" is actually a person who deviates from his own "way" to destroy his sovereign and usurp the throne. How can such a man be called good? Whatever he does is based on falsehood and he is a bad person beyond description. . . .

When one asks what constitutes the "way," the answer given is that it consists of human-heartedness and righteousness (*jingi*, in Chinese, *renyi*), propriety and yielding (*reijō*, in Ch., *lirang*), filial piety and brotherly obedience (*kōtei*, in Ch., *xiaoti*), and conscientiousness and trustworthiness (*chūshin*, in Ch., *zhongxin*). What skulduggery that is, trying to create minute regulations and teaching people in the strictest manner. Those Confucian scholars criticize the laws of later periods as contrary to the "way" of the earlier kings. Are they forgetting the fact that the so-called "way" of the earlier kings was nothing but the laws of old? They even concoct a theory of change as contained in the *Book of Changes* and feigning profundity, proclaim that they know all the mysteries surrounding heaven and earth. . . .

Altogether, the existence of heaven and earth is traceable to the work of gods. It is so miraculous and wondrous that man's finite knowledge cannot fully comprehend. Thus how can one say that he possesses the ultimate in knowledge?

However, there are many who consider the sayings of the "sage" as the ultimate in knowledge. How foolish can they be? In China too many of her people of later generations attempt to use their own reason in emulation of the "sage," and meet with failure. Those of us who are scholars of this great country must know these pitfalls and must not be misled by the theories advanced by the Chinese. They are fidgety and argumentative. As a result the hearts of the people become unruly, and everything is twisted to acquire the wrong meaning. In this manner, it becomes harder and harder to govern the country. Therefore the so-called "way" of the "sage," which is established to govern the country, can, on the contrary, become the root cause of misgovernment in the country.

. . . In the days of old, our country did not have that type of teaching. But the country was governed peacefully, and to the very bottom of the hierarchy there was no disturbance. The throne has been transmitted from generation to generation. If we call this fact in the manner of the Chinese, there can be no greater "way" than this. We do not have the word "way" in our vocabulary, precisely because we have always practiced the "way." Without having the word, we have always had the "way." . . . In China seldom has the "way" been practiced. This is the reason why they have so often made much of the teachings of the "way." Without knowing this truth, Confucian scholars in this country look down on our country by saying that we lack the "way." They admire only China and their offense can perhaps be forgiven. However, pitiful are the intellectuals of Japan who without comprehending this truth, enviously look upon China as the country which possesses the "way." They strain their arguments by saying that we also have the "way," referring to something which need not exist. This is no different from an argument between a monkey and a human being. The monkey may laugh at the human being by saying, "You have no fur." Then the man answers: "Oh yes, I have plenty of fur," and he proceeds to produce something he scantily possesses. That is the utterance a fool gives who does not know how much better off he is without the fur.

12 Excerpts from the Outline of the Ancient Way (Kodō Taii)[20] We call our scholastic tradition the "ancient learning" (kogaku) and our method of study the "ancient way" (kodō). This is so because our school is the one which honestly considers the facts relating to the beginning of heaven and earth and attempts to clarify the true way based on these facts. In doing so, it utilizes the ancient meanings and words in their pristine purity, in the form existing before the coming of Confucianism and Buddhism. Thus we call it the learning of the ancient way (kodōgaku). . . .

You may ask questions about the bases of my doctrine (michi, normally

---

[20]Hirata Atsutane, Kodō Taii in Sekai Daishisō Zenshū, op. cit., pp. 141, 147–149, 151–152, 155.

translated "way"). I do base my doctrine on the correct books in the imperial court which record and transmit to us the facts concerning the olden days. The true way (or doctrine, *michi*) is inherent in the facts [which are manifested to us]. However, most [Confucian] scholars claim that the way can only be attained through books which contain moral teachings. This is pure misapprehension. Moral teachings are lower than the facts in our hierarchical order. This is so because where there are facts, no moral teachings are needed. Moral teachings originate because there are no facts concerning the way. In China, the book of Laozi (*Daode jing*) succinctly remarks that "when the great way is on the wane, the doctrine of compassion and righteousness makes its appearance."

Moral teachings cannot penetrate the hearts of the people. For example, one does not encourage a samurai [in the art of bravery] by giving him a book which contains a teaching that when in the battle formation, he must charge ahead of his troops and must not get behind anyone else. It is better to show him books about battles which record how the brave men of old fought ahead of their troops and how they conducted themselves courageously to attain fame. . . . Or drawing on an example from a recent event, it is not sufficient to hear a teaching that one must avenge the wrong done to one's master. It is better to hear the true story of hardships the forty-seven samurai, headed by Ōishi Kuranosuke, had to suffer in order to avenge the wrong done to their master Asano Takumi-no-kami by killing Kira Kōzuke-no-suke. One can feel his hair standing on end and his eyes watering with tears as he hears this true story. It can stir one's emotion, and its import can be keenly felt and penetrated into one's heart. . . .

As I have just mentioned, the meaning of the true way cannot be perceived by moral teachings. Therefore it is necessary to have books which impart to us the facts essential to one's understanding of the true way of old. Of these books, the greatest is the *Kojiki* (*Records of Ancient Matters*). . . .

There are few people in our country who claim to be scholars of the way of gods, and respect only the *Nihon Shoki* (*Chronicles of Japan*). They combine the first two volumes of the *Nihon Shoki* and call them the books on the Age of Gods. Proclaiming without authority that they are scholars of Shintō, they publish the two books separately, and provide their own unnecessary and strained exposition in minute detail. They think that to know the facts concerning the beginning of the world, and about the gods, there is no other book, but this is a misconception. . . . When the *Nihon Shoki* was compiled, there was an attempt to make our national history similar to the history of China. Everything was recorded with this intent, and as a result it is clearly in the Chinese style, and lost much of the truth about the ancient times.

Inherently, intent (*kokoro*), facts (*waza*) and words (*kotoba*) explicative of the first two must correspond with one another. In the ancient times, there was a typical ancient style of intent, facts, and words. In the later ages, there was a typical later style of intent, facts, and words. In China, they have a peculiar Chinese style of intent, facts, and words. However, in the case of the *Nihon*

Shoki, it applied the intent of a later age to record the facts of the ancient age, and used the Chinese language to explicate the intent of our country. They did not fit together, and thus in many instances facts concerning the olden days were not perceived correctly. In the case of the *Kojiki*, not a single cute remark was added, and everything was transcribed exactly the way it was transmitted from the ancient times. Thus its intent, facts and words were all consistent with what happened in the ancient times. Its accuracy comes from the fact that it utilized mainly the language of the ancient times in its description. . . .

People of the world without fail point to our country and call it the country of gods. We also say that we are descendants of gods. . . . Our country was procreated by the gods by the special grace of the heavenly deities, and its difference from all other foreign countries is as wide as the distance between heaven and earth. Our country is so precious that it is beyond comparison. The fact of our country being a country of gods is not open to dispute, and even the lowest of men and women are unmistakably descendants of gods. However, pitiful indeed are those who do not know [our glorious] heritage.

Weights and Measures—
Metric and U.S. Equivalents

Linear Measure

1 *sun*	3.03 centimeters	1.193 inches
1 *shaku* (10 *sun*)	0.303 meter	0.995 foot
1 *ken* (6 *shaku*)	1.818 meters	1.987 yards
1 *jō* (10 *shaku*)	3.030 meters	3.316 yards
1 *chō* (60 *ken*)	109.1 meters	0.542 furlong
1 *ri* (36 *chō*)	3.927 kilometers	2.439 miles
1 traditional *ri* (6 *chō*)	654.6 meters	3.252 furlongs

Square Measure

1 *gō*	0.330 square meter	1.083 square feet
1 *bu* (or *tsubo*, 10 *gō*)	3.306 square meters	3.615 square yards
1 *se* (30 *bu* or *tsubo*)	99.17 square meters	19,726 square rods
1 *tan* (10 *se* or 300 *bu*)	9.92 ares	0.245 acre
1 *chō* (10 *tan*)	99.17 ares	2.45 acres

Prior to Hideyoshi's decree of 1598

1 *tan* (360 *bu*)	11.904 ares	0.294 acre
1 *chō* (10 *tan*)	119.04 ares	2.94 acres

Weights

1 *momme*	3.750 grams	2.115 drams
1 *kin* (160 *momme*)	0.600 kilogram	1.322 pounds
1 *kan* (1,000 *momme*)	3.750 kilograms	8.26 pounds

Liquid and Dry Measures

1 *gō*	0.180 liter	1.525 gills	0.328 pint
1 *shō* (10 *gō*)	1.804 liters	3.81 pints	1.638 quarts
1 *to* (10 *shō*)	18.04 liters	19.06 quarts	2.048 pecks
1 *koku* (10 *to*)	180.4 liters	47.6 gallons	5.12 bushels
1 *koku* of brown rice	150 kilograms		5.01 bushels

Note: the term *masu* may at times be used in place of the term *shō* (1.805 liters). Rice and other grains are often measured by *hyō*, which means a bag or bale. One *hyō* normally contains four *to* (1 *to* equals 2.048 pecks) of rice. The term *ryō* represents a unit of gold currency and must not be confused with terms of weights and measures.

Glossary of Japanese Terms

ando no kudashibumi: A writ of assurance given to military households, temples, and shrines by the Kamakura and Muromachi *bakufu,* confirming their rights to hold lands in fief (*chigyō-chi*).

bakufu: Headquarters of the *shōgun:* or the shogunate.

baku-han: A term describing the Tokugawa system of government in which the *bakufu* exercised authority over *han.*

bodhisattva: (Buddhism) One who has attained enlightenment, but postpones entering Nirvana in order to help others attain enlightenment.

bugyō: An official of the *bakufu* charged with specific administrative functions: commissioner.

bummei kaika: "Civilization and enlightenment," a primary slogan of Meiji intellectuals promoting Westernization.

bunkoku: (1) In the Heian period, the term referred to provinces over which court nobles were given the functions of governor; (2) in the Sengoku period, territories held by *sengoku daimyō.*

buke shohatto: "Laws for military households," first issued in 1615.

chigyō: To have right over land and hold it in fief; in the Tokugawa period, the term also referred to land granted by the *bakufu* or *han* as stipend.

chokkatsuryō: See *tenryō.*

chokunin: Under the system established by the Meiji constitution, those civil servants of first and second ranks were technically appointed to their posts by an imperial command (*chokunin*), and were so called.

chōnin: Townspeople, urban dwellers who were not samurai; merchants and artisans.

chū: Loyalty.

daijōkan: (1) The Council of State under the *ritsu-ryō* system. It supervised eight ministries under it; (2) the highest organ of state in the Meiji government from 1868 to 1885.

daikan: (1) One who performs on behalf of his master, deputy; (2) an official of a *daimyō* in charge of collecting taxes; (3) a *bakufu* official responsible for collecting taxes and civil administration in *tenryō*.

daimyō: (1) During the Tokugawa period, those fief holders who had territories producing 10,000 *koku* or more of rice; (2) in the later Heian period and the Kamakura period, holders of large *myōden*. See also *shugo daimyō* and *sengoku daimyō*.

dangō: Consultation among participants before making bids for large construction projects.

detchi: An apprentice in a commercial establishment.

dōmin: (1) People who were native to certain localities; (2) also used as a pejorative term for farmers.

dōri: Propriety or practical reason; the correct way in which man must act; the way consistent with the nature of things.

fudai: "Hereditary" *daimyō,* comprising the descendants of those men who, almost without exception, recognized Ieyasu as their overlord on or before 1600.

fukoku kyōhei: "Rich nation, strong army," one of the primary slogans of Meiji leaders to strengthen the nation.

genrō: Elder statesmen, men who served collectively and individually as the Emperor's closest advisers from the 1890s through the 1930s. Only nine men received the designation to this extraconstitutional but extremely powerful position.

genrōin: Council of Elders, or Senate: an early Meiji legislative organ established in 1875, which was disbanded in 1890 prior to the convening of the Diet under the Meiji constitution.

gō: An administrative unit under the *ritsu-ryō* system, normally comprising several villages (*ri*); county.

gokenin: "Men of the household," direct or close vassals of the *shōgun.*

goningumi: A group of five who shared collective responsibility.

gun: District, (1) a subdivision of a province, also rendered *kōri* in traditional Japan; (2) from 1879 to 1921, the *gun* was an administrative subdivision of a prefecture.

haihan chiken: Replacing the *han* with prefectures.

hakkō ichiu: Literally, "all under heaven under one roof," hence to spread the benevolent rule of the emperor throughout the world, a slogan used by the militarists in the 1930s.

han: A domain belonging to a *daimyō,* with its own administrative structure.

hanseki hōkan: Return of feudal domains and census registers.

hatamoto: "Bannermen," enfeoffed vassals of the Tokugawa *shōgun* with stipends ranging from 500 *koku* to 10,000 *koku* with the privilege of audience with the *shōgun.*

honke: "Main family," patron of *shōen*; main family as against branch families (*bunke*).

hyakusho: Farmers; also collectively common people.

ichi: Market, or marketplace.

ikki: Uprising.

ishin: Restoration, also used specifically to refer to the Meiji Restoration.

jinsei: Benevolent rule, found in Confucian writings.

jiriki: (Buddhism) Dependence on one's own power to attain enlightenment.

JIT: Just-in-time method of manufacturing.

jitō: Stewards; (1) in the Heian period, officials appointed by the *ryōshu* to facilitate *shōen* administration; (2) in the Kamakura and Muromachi periods, the term stood for "military land stewards," who were placed in *shōen* and territories directly held by the *bakufu.* (3) In the Tokugawa period, those *hatamoto* who had their own *chigyō* or those retainers of *daimyō* who had the right to collect their own land revenue were also called *jitō.*

jitō-uke: An arrangement under which the *jitō* pledged to pay a set amount of annual rent to the *ryōshu* in return for the right to manage or control the *shōen.* Practiced in the Kamakura period.

jōi: Expelling barbarians (foreigners).

kaikoku: "Opening the country" to end the seclusion policy.

kalpa: (Buddhism) A general term for a long period that cannot be defined by months or years.

karma: (Buddhism) Action bringing upon oneself the inevitable results either in this life or in reincarnation; the law of cause and effect.

karō: "House elders," important retainers of a *daimyō* who exercised administrative control over other retainers on his behalf.

kashindan: Corps of retainers of a *daimyō*.

kebiishi: Police officers, constables.

keichō: Tax register.

Keidanren: Federation of Economic Organizations

keiretsu: Enterprise groups; Each group of affiliated business enterprises is normally centered around a major city bank. A trading company in the group may also serve a coordinating function.

Keizai Dōyūkai: Japan Association of Corporate Executives

ken: Prefecture, an administrative division established in 1871 signifying the implementation of direct rule by the central government.

kirishitan: Japanese rendition for "Christian."

ko: Households.

kō: Filial piety.

kōan: (Buddhism) Public themes devised for Zen meditation.

kōgi: Deliberation openly arrived, or "public opinion."

kōri: District, see *gun* above.

kōron: Public matters openly discussed, consensus reached.

koseki: Population register.

ku: (1) In the early Meiji period, it referred to an administrative subdivision that replaced previous townships and villages; (2) currently, the term refers to a ward, which is an administrative subdivision of major cities.

kubunden: Allotment land.

kuge: Court noble.

kuji: Lawsuits.

kuni: Province.

kuni no miyatsuko: Title of territorial aristocracy prior to the Taika reform of 645.

kuni no tsukasa: Provincial governor.

kyūnin: Samurai receiving stipends from a *daimyō.*

machi-bugyō: Town commissioner.

machi-doshiyori: Town elders.

mappō: (Buddhism) The latter degenerate days.

metsuke: A public censor or spy.

meyasu: Legal briefs, petitions, or written complaints.

minbu: Ministry of Popular Affairs.

myōshu: Holders of rights to *myōden.*

myōden: First accepted by provincial governors as basic taxable units within their domains, and later by the *ryōshu* as basic rent-paying units in their *shōen.*

nanushi: In the Tokugawa period, (1) a *hyakushō* appointed to become village head to engage in civil administration of a village; (2) or a *chōnin* who engaged in civil administration under the supervision of *machi-doshiyori.*

nemawashi: Prior consultation; touching base with interested parties before decisions are made to avoid conflict.

nembutsu: (Buddhism) To recite the name of Amida Buddha in the formula, *Namu Ami Dabutsu.*

nengu: Annual rent or tax. The term rent is used when the *nengu* was collected by *shōen* or other private and semiprivate authorities, and tax is used when the *nengu* was collected by *bakufu* or *han* or other duly constituted public authorities.

Nikkeiren: Japan Federation of Employers' Associations

ōdō: Kingly way, found in Confucian writings.

ōjō: (Buddhism) To go to the other shore to live, hence to attain enlightenment or Nirvana.

onchi: Land given to samurai for meritorious service.

QC: Quality control.

rakuichi: Free market.

rakuza: Abolition of the *za.*

ri: The smallest administrative unit under the *ritsu-ryō* system; village.

ri: Principle(s), found in Confucian writings.

ritsu-ryō: Penal and administrative codes; and when used in conjunction with the term "*kokka*" (state or nation), it refers to a country governed by *ritsu* and *ryō,* as under the Taihō-Yōrō codes.

rōjū "Elders," or senior counsellors in the Tokugawa *bakufu* administration.

ryōshu: Lord of *shōen.*

sakoku: Closing the country to foreign commerce and intercourse.

sankin-kōtai: Alternate attendance.

satori: (Buddhism) Sudden enlightenment in Zen Buddhism.

seikanron: An opinion expressed by Saigō Takamori and his followers in the early 1870s advocating the dispatch of expeditionary forces to Korea.

sengoku daimyō: Daimyō who replaced *shugo daimyō* in the Sengoku period, each having his own domain, the first true *daimyō.*

seirei toshi: Administratively designated cities. Large cities which are given some of the legislative and administrative powers normally reserved for prefectural government. As of the fall of 1996, the following cities were so designated: Yokohama, Osaka, Nagoya, Sapporo, Kobe, Kyoto, Fukuoka, Kawasaki, Hiroshima, Kita Kyushu, Sendai, and Chiba.

shiki: Rights to recompense for performing certain functions under the *shōen* system.

shikimoku: Formulary; written codes in the medieval period.

shikken: The position held by the Hōjō family during the Kamakura period as *shōgun's* regent.

shimbun: Newspaper.

shimpan: Daimyō who were collaterally related to the main Tokugawa *shōgun* family.

shō: A short form for *shōen.*

Shinkansen: New trunk line, the high-speed lines using "bullet trains."

shōen: Private estate that was exempted from central government control; see introduction to Chapter IV.

shōgun: A short form for *Sei-i tai shōgun,* or barbarian-subduing generalissimo. From 1192 to 1867, this title was assumed by the head of a *bakufu* who exercised both military and civil authorities.

shokubun: Obligations, functions, or callings, found in Confucian writings.

shokusan kōgyō: Encouragement of industries, a policy adopted by the early Meiji government.

shōmyō: In the medieval period, those who held relatively small *myōden*; during the Tokugawa period, those fief holders who had smaller territories than *daimyō.*

shōya: A *hyakushō* appointed to become village head to engage in civil administration of a village. This term was used in the Kansai region, whereas the term *nanushi* was used mainly in the Kantō region.

shugo: "Protector," a post created in 1185 by Minamoto no Yoritomo, which at first had limited functions. However, it extended its functions to include those normally exercised by provincial governors through the Muromachi period.

shugo daimyō: A term describing those *shugo* who, during the Muromachi period, converted territories under their jurisdiction as their own domains.

shugo-uke: The practice of permitting the *shugo* to submit only a set amount of annual rent in return for the actual control of the *shōen.*

sō: A village organization, which during the period of *shōen*'s disintegration, attempted to express the will of the village community or to take joint action.

sōnin: Under the system established by the Meiji constitution, those civil servants of third rank or lower were technically recommended for appointment by the prime minister (*sōnin*) and were thus so called.

sōryō: The heir, later also used to signify oldest son or daughter.

sukiya: A building in which tea ceremony is performed.

tahata: Fields and gardens; paddy fields and dry fields.

tariki: (Buddhism) Dependence on the original vow of Amida Buddha to attain rebirth in the Western paradise.

tatemae: A "principle" or stated reason which may differ from the real intention (*honne).*

tato: Farmers who exercised some of the rights of landlords in the *shōen* system during the Heian period.

tedai: (1) Minor officials in the Tokugawa period engaged in tax collection and other duties; (2) clerks in a commercial establishment.

tenryō: The territory directly held by the Tokugawa *bakufu.*

toiya or *tonya:* A wholesale merchant.

tokusei: Act of grace, hence forgiveness of debts.

tozama: "Outer" *daimyō,* comprising the descendants of those men who pledged allegiance to Ieyasu on or after 1600.

wabi: Enjoyment of an austere type of beauty, and finding fulfillment in poverty. A state of mind as well a moral principle.

yin-yang: In Chinese naturalist philosophy, *yin* is female, dark and negative, and *yang* is male, light and positive. The two principles complement and balance each other.

za: Medieval Japanese trade or craft guilds that attempted to establish local monopoly rights.

zaibatsu: The "financial clique" or the great conglomerates, such as Mitsui and Mitsubishi, which exercised profound influence over the Japanese economy from late Meiji to early 1940s.

zaikai: the financial world, financial circles.

zasshō: Officials of governmental bureaus, *shōen,* or *bakufu,* who engaged in miscellaneous functions.

zazen: (Buddhism) To sit in Zen meditation.

zukuri: the style of architecture that comprises a small space, uses natural wood, with little or no ornamentation.

Chronology of Japanese History

Pre- and Proto-Historical Eras

Before 30,000 B.C.	Paleolithic culture
ca. 10,000 B.C.–250 B.C.	Jōmon culture
ca. 300 B.C.–A.D. 250	Yayoi culture
ca. 100 B.C.	Beginning of rice cultivation in wet fields
A.D. 57	Japanese kingdom of Nu offers tribute to the Later Han court
A.D. 239	Pimiko (Himiko) sends an envoy to Chinese kingdom of Wei
ca. A.D. 300–710	Tomb (*kofun*) culture

Asuka (or Kofun) Period

552 (or 538)	Introduction of Buddhism from Paikche
593–622	Prince Shōtoku's regency
600	First embassy to Sui dynasty
604	The seventeen-article constitution
607	Horyūji temple completed
·645–46	The Taika reforms
672	Prince Ōama (later Emperor Temmu) usurps the throne
694	Capital city, Fujiwarakyō established
701	The Taihō code

Nara Period (710–84)

710	Nara becomes the first "permanent" capital
712	Compilation of the *Kojiki* completed

720	Compilation of the *Nihon Shoki* completed
723	Private ownership of reclaimed lands permitted
743	Permanent privatization of reclaimed lands permitted; emergence of *Shōen*
751	The *Kaifūsō*, a collection of Chinese poetry, compiled
752	Dedication of the Great Buddha of Tōdaiji
756	Establishment of the imperial treasure house, Shōsōin
759	Compilation of the *Manyōsūu* is completed around this time
784	The capital is moved to Nagaoka
788	Saichō establishes the temple Enryakuji in Mt. Hiei

Heian Period (794–1185)

794	The capital is moved to Kyoto (Heiankyō)
792	The *kondei* system replaces "military conscription"
823	Kūkai appointed abbot of Tōji
858	Fujiwara Yoshifusa assumes the position of *sesshō*
894	Sending envoy to Tang China suspended
905	Completion of the *Kokinshū,* the first imperial anthology of *waka*
985	Genshin completes the *Ōjōyōshū*
995	Fujiwara no Michinaga becomes head of the Fujiwara family; its golden age begins
996	Lady Sei Shōnagon's *Pillow Book* is completed
1008	The *Tale of Genji* by Lady Murasaki is completed around this time
1017	Michinaga becomes *sesshō,* zenith of the Fujiwara power
1086	Cloistered government (*insei*) is established by retired Emperor Shirakawa
1156	The Hōgen war
1159	The Heiji war
1167	Taira no Kiyomori becomes *dajō daijin*
1175	Hōnen establishes the Jōdo sect
1185	Fall of the Taira family

Kamakura Period (1185–1333)

1185	The battle of Dannoura, the Taira army is annihilated
1192	Minamoto no Yoritomo is appointed *shōgun*

1199	Death of Yoritomo; the Hōjō family assumes control of the *Bakufu*
1205	Hōjō Yoshitoki assumes the office of regent (*shikken*) to the *shōgun*
	The *Shin Kokinshū* is completed
1218	The early versions of *The Tale of Heike* in existence around this time
1221	The Jokyū war
1224	The True Pure Land sect is founded by Shinran
1227	Dōgen establishes the Sōtō sect of Zen Buddhism
1232	The *Jōei Shikimoku* is promulgated
1253	The Nichiren sect is founded by Nichiren
1274	The first Mongol invasion
1281	The second Mongol invasion
1297	*Tokusei* decree issued by the Kamakura *Bakufu*
1330	Yoshida Kenkō completes his collection of essays, *Tsurezuregusa*
1333	Collapse of the Kamakura Bakufu

Muromachi Period (1338–1573)

1333	Emperor Godaigo's Kemmu Restoration
1335	Revolt of Ashikaga Takauji
1337	Godaigo flees to Yoshino and establishes the Southern Court.
1338	Ashikaga Takauji is appointed *shōgun* by the Northern Court
1392	Unification of the Northern and Southern Courts
1397	Construction of the Golden Pavilion begins
1401	The third shōgun, Yoshimitsu, sends an embassy to Ming China
1428	Peasant uprisings (*tsuchi ikki*) in Kyoto and surrounding provinces
1467–77	The Ōnin War
1483	Retired shōgun Yoshimasa settles in the Silver Pavilion
1543	A Portuguese ship arrives at Tanegashima, first musket in Japan.
1549	St. Francis Xavier arrives in Japan, establishes first mission in Kagoshima

Azuchi Momoyama—Period of Unification (1568–1600)

1568	Oda Nobunaga enters Kyoto, beginning of national unification
1571	First Portuguese merchant ship arrives at Nagasaki
	Nobunaga attacks Mt. Hiei, burns the temple Enryakuji
1576	Nobunaga begins construction of Azuchi castle
1579	Alessandro Valignano, supervisor of the Jesuit missions in Asia, arrives in Japan
1580	Burning of Ishiyama Honganji, headquarters of the Ikkō sect
1582	Toyotomi Hideyoshi assumes power
	Beginning of the nationwide cadastral survey
1583	Hideyoishi begins construction of Osaka castle
1587	Partial proscription of Christianity by Hideyoshi
1588	Confiscation of swords from peasants
1590	Hideyoshi's Odawara campaign, completion of unification
1592	Hideyoshi invades Korea
1597	Second invasion of Korea
1598	Death of Hideyoshi
1600	Tokugawa Ieyasu triumphs in the battle of Sekigahara

Tokugawa Period (1600–1867)

1603	Ieyasu is appointed *shōgun*
1614	Ban on Christianity extended nationwide
1615	Second and final siege of Osaka castle
	Promulgation of the *Buke Shohatto*
1620	Building of the Katsura detached palace is begun (completed around 1662)
1635	The system of alternate attendance (*sankin kōtai*) is introduced
1636	Completion of the artificial island of Dejima
	Nikkō Tōshōgū is erected
1637–38	The Shimabara rebellion
1639	Closing of the country; expulsion of Portuguese merchants from Dejima
1641	Dutch factory removed from Hirado to Dejima
1643	Sale of land in perpetuity forbidden

1657	Meireki fire ravages Edo, death toll reaches 100,000
	Compilation of the national history *Dai Nihon Shi* begins
1673	Parcelization of land forbidden
1688–1704	The Genroku period, blossoming of the *chōnin* culture
1703	Akaho's forty-seven *rōnin* avenge their master's death
1709	Arai Hakuseki becomes a key adviser to Shōgun Ienobu
1720	The ban on Western books relaxed
1732	The Kyōhō famine in southwestern Japan
1774	*Kaitai Shinsho,* a translation of *Tabulae Anatomicae,* is published
1782–87	The Temmei famine
1787	Rōju Matsudaira Sadanobu's Kansei reforms
1790	Utamaro begins producing his *Ukiyo-e*
1804	Russian envoy Rezanov reaches Nagasaki
1808	British frigate *Pheton* successfully enters Nagasaki Harbor
1809	Mamiya Rinzō's exploration proves that Sakhalin is an island
1823	von Siebold arrives in Japan as physician to the Dutch factory
1825	An edict to drive off foreign vessels is issued
1833–37	The Tempō famine
1837	Insurrection of Ōshio Heihachirō
1841	Rōju Mizuno Tadakuni's Tempō reforms
1853	Arrival of Commodore Perry in Uraga
1854	The Treaty of Kanagawa signed with the United States
1858	Ii Naosuke becomes *tairō.* Signing of a commercial treaty with United States
1859	The Ansei purge
1860	First Japanese mission to the United States
	Assassination of Ii Naosuke
	Kōbu gattai, as symbolized in Kazunomiya's marriage to shōgun Iemochi
1866	Satsuma-Chōshū alliance
1867	Keiki restores political power to the Imperial Court

Appendix 4

Administrative Map of Japan

Legends for Administrative Map of Japan

The boundaries shown in the map are boundaries of the present-day prefectures. Each prefecture is given a number which corresponds to the name given below. These numbers may also be used to identify traditional names of areas occupied by these prefectures. A present-day prefecture may contain a number of traditional administrative divisions. When that occurs, these place names are given sequentially from north to south, and east to west.

Macron signs to indicate long vowels are utilized in this section, even though such signs are normally omitted from place names.

Prefectures in Present-Day Japan	*Traditional Names in Use Prior to 1868*
Hokkaidō Region	
1. Hokkaidō	1. Ezo
Tōhoku Region	
2. Aomori	2. Mutsu
3. Akita	3. Dewa (Ugo)[1]
4. Iwate	4. Mutsu (Rikuchū)
5. Yamagata	5. Dewa (Uzen)
6. Miyagi	6. Mutsu (Rikuzen)
7. Fukushima	7. Mutsu (Iwashiro, Iwaki)
Kantō Region	
8. Tōkyō	8. Edo, Musashi
9. Gumma	9. Kōzuke
10. Tochigi	10. Shimotsuke
11. Ibaraki	11. Hitachi, Shimousa
12. Saitama	12. Musashi
13. Chiba	13. Shimousa, Kazusa, Awa
14. Kanagawa	14. Musashi, Sagami
Chūbu Region	
15. Niigata	15. Echigo, Sado
16. Nagano	16. Shinano
17. Yamanashi	17. Kai

---

[1]The Tōhoku region traditionally consisted of two provinces of Mutsu and Dewa. In 1869, the Meiji government divided these two provinces into seven separate administrative entities. Their names are shown in parentheses from 3 through 7. The present-day Aomori prefecture inherited the name Mutsu under this plan.

18. Shizuoka	18. Izu, Suruga, Tōtōmi
19. Toyama	19. Ecchū
20. Gifu	20. Hida, Mino
21. Aichi	21. Mikawa, Owari
22. Ishikawa	22. Noto, Kaga
23. Fukui	23. Echizen, Wakasa

Kinki Region

24. Shiga	24. Ōmi
25. Mie	25. Ise, Iga, Shima, Kii
26. Kyōto	26. Yamashiro, Tango, Tanba
27. Nara	27. Yamato
28. Ōsaka	28. Kawachi, Settsu, Izumi
29. Wakayama	29. Kii
30. Hyōgo	30. Tanba, Settsu, Tajima, Harima

Chūgoku Region

31. Tottori	31. Inaba, Hōki
32. Okayama	32. Mimasaka, Bizen, Bicchū
33. Shimane	33. Izumo, Iwami
34. Hiroshima	34. Bingo, Aki
35. Yamaguchi	35. Suō, Nagato (Chōshū)

Shikoku Region

36. Kagawa	36. Sanuki
37. Tokushima	37. Awa
38. Kōchi	38. Tosa
39. Ehime	39. Iyo

Kyushu Region

40. Ōita	40. Bungo, Buzen
41. Miyazaki	41. Hyūga
42. Fukuoka	42. Buzen, Chikuzen, Chikugo
43. Kumamoto	43. Higo
44. Kagoshima	44. Ōsumi, Satsuma
45. Saga	45. Hizen
46. Nagasaki	46. Hizen, Iki, Tsushima

Okinawa Region

47. Okinawa[2]	47. Ryūkyū

[2]Officially became part of Japan in 1872.

Index to Present-Day Place Names

Prefectures and their capital cities often share same names. Those names appearing in *italics* represent cities which are not administrative capitals of their respective prefectures.

Index to Traditional Place Names

Index

David J. Lu is professor emeritus of history and Japanese studies at Bucknell University. He has maintained close contact with Japanese political and business leaders and the scholarly community through his frequent visits to Japan, including a year as a Fulbright scholar and a year as resident director of the Associated Kyoto Program at Doshisha University. His works reflect his desire to be a bridge builder. He writes in English about Japanese history and business practices, and in Japanese about American history and society. The latter includes writing regularly for the *Sekai to Nippon* (The World and Japan), a Japanese weekly journal of opinion.

This book is compiled to share with the readers his wide-ranging interest in Japan developed over his thirty-five-year teaching career and his lifelong contact with Japan. It combines the perspectives of an insider with those of an outsider. He is an insider because of his birth in Taiwan which was then a Japanese colony, of his Japanese education through Higher School (*kotō gakkō*), and of his position as a respected columnist in Japan. Yet he is an outsider because of his American graduate education, long academic career, and citizenship. This combination has earned praise from Japanese readers for his earlier works: "Professor Lu is one of the very few Americans who can see the reality beneath the obvious surface," commented a former Minister of Justice. "He does not hesitate to criticize Japan, but does it without malice. His books can be respected and trusted." That even-handed approach is also evident in this work.

David Lu lives in Milton, Pennsylvania, the birthplace of Dr. J.C. Hepburn, the first American Protestant missionary to Japan, and creator of the Hepburn system of Romanization. With his wife, Annabelle, he does some gardening, but is also busily at work on a three-volume history of Japan.

Books by David Lu

From the Marco Polo Bridge to Pearl Harbor (1961), Japanese edition (1967)
Sources of Japanese History, two volumes (1974)
Perspectives on Japan's External Affairs: Views from America (1982)
Inside Corporate Japan: The Art of Fumble-Free Management (1987)

Published in Japanese in Japan

*The Great Society That the Pioneers Built: A Bicentennial History of the
   United States* (1976)
The Life and Time⌐ of Foreign Minister Matsuoka Yōsuke, 1880–1946 (1981).

Translated works

Usui Katsumi and Hata Ikuhiko, *The China Quagmire: Japan's Expansion on
   the Asian Continent, 1933–1941* (1983)
Ishikawa Kaoru, *What Is Total Quality Control? The Japanese Way* (1985)
Japan Management Association, *Kanban and Just-In-Time at Toyota* (1986)
Nemoto Masao, *Total Quality Control for Management* (1987)
Karatsu Hajime, *TQC: Wisdom of Japan* (1988)